Page

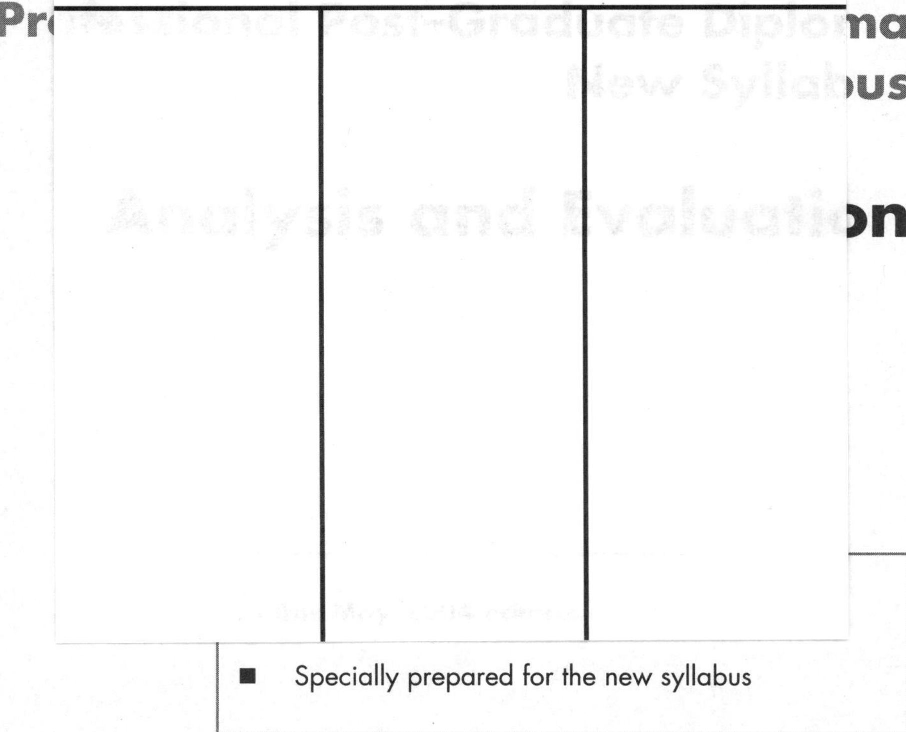

- Specially prepared for the new syllabus

BPP Professional Education

**May 2004**

**First edition May 2004**

*ISBN 0 7517 1113 6*

***British Library Cataloguing-in-Publication Data***
*A catalogue record for this book*
*is available from the British Library*

*Published by*

*BPP Professional Education*
*Aldine House, Aldine Place*
*London W12 8AW*

*www.bpp.com*

*Printed in Great Britain by W M Print*
*45-47 Frederick Street*
*Walsall*
*West Midlands*
*WS2 9NE*



*We are grateful to the Chartered Institute of Marketing for permission to reproduce in this text the syllabus, tutor's guidance notes and past examination questions.*

# How to use this Study Text

## Aims of this Study Text

**To provide you with the knowledge and understanding, skills and applied techniques required for passing the exam**

The Study Text has been written around the CIM Syllabus, which is reproduced below.

- It is **comprehensive**. We do not omit sections of the syllabus as the examiner is liable to examine any angle of any part of the syllabus – and you do not want to be left high and dry.
- It is **on-target** – we do not include any material which is not examinable. You can therefore rely on the BPP Study Text as the stand-alone source of all your information for the exam.

**To allow you to study in the way that best suits your learning style and the time you have available, by following your personal Study Plan (see below)**

You may be studying at home on your own until the date of the exam, or you may be attending a full-time course. You may like to (and have time to) read every word, or you may prefer to (or only have time to) skim-read and devote the remainder of your time to question practice. Wherever you fall in the spectrum, you will find the BPP Study Text meets your needs in designing and following your personal Study Plan.

**To tie in with the other components of the BPP Effective Study Package to ensure you have the best possible chance of passing the exam**

| Recommended period of use | Elements of BPP Effective Study Package |
| --- | --- |
| 3–12 months before exam | **Study Text**<br>Acquisition of knowledge, understanding, skills and applied techniques. |
| 1–6 months before exam | **Practice & Revision Kit (9/2004)**<br>Tutorial questions and helpful checklists of the key points lead you into each area. There are then numerous Examination questions to try, graded by topic area, along with realistic suggested solutions prepared by marketing professionals in the light of the Examiner's Reports. The September 2004 edition will include the Specimen Paper. |

## Settling down to study

By this stage in your career you may be a very experienced learner and taker of exams. But have you ever thought about *how* you learn? Let's have a quick look at the key elements required for effective learning. You can then identify your learning style and go on to design your own approach to how you are going to study this text – your personal Study Plan.

| Key element of learning | Using the BPP Study Text |
|---|---|
| Motivation | You can rely on the comprehensiveness and technical quality of BPP. You've chosen the right Study Text – so you're in pole position to pass your exam! |
| Clear objectives and standards | Do you want to be a prizewinner or simply achieve a moderate pass? Decide. |
| Feedback | Follow through the examples in this text and do the Action Programme and the Quick Quizzes. Evaluate your efforts critically – how are you doing? |
| Study Plan | You need to be honest about your progress to yourself – don't be over-confident, but don't be negative either. Make your Study Plan (see below) and try to stick to it. Focus on the short-term objectives – completing two chapters a night, say – but beware of losing sight of your study objectives. |
| Practice | Use the Quick Quizzes and Chapter Roundups to refresh your memory regularly after you have completed your initial study of each chapter. |

These introductory pages let you see exactly what you are up against. However you study, you should:

- **Read through the syllabus** – this will help you to identify areas you have already covered, perhaps at a lower level of detail, and areas that are totally new to you
- **Study the examination paper section**, where we show you the format of the exam (how many and what kind of questions and so on)

## Key study steps

The following steps are, in our experience, the ideal way to study for professional exams. You can of course adapt it for your particular learning style (see below).

Tackle the chapters in the order you find them in the Study Text. Taking into account your individual learning style, follow these key study steps for each chapter.

| Key study steps | Activity |
|---|---|
| Step 1<br>*Chapter topic list* | Study the list. Each numbered topic denotes a **numbered section** in the chapter. |
| Step 2<br>*Setting the Scene* | Read it through. It is designed to show you **why the topics in the chapter need to be studied** – how they lead on from previous topics, and how they lead into subsequent ones. |
| Step 3<br>*Explanations* | Proceed **methodically** through the chapter, reading each section thoroughly and making sure you understand. |
| Step 4<br>*Key Concepts* | **Key concepts** can often earn you **easy marks** if you state them clearly and correctly in an appropriate exam. |
| Step 5<br>*Exam Tips* | These give you a good idea of how the examiner tends to examine certain topics – pinpointing **easy marks** and highlighting **pitfalls**. |
| Step 6<br>*Note taking* | Take **brief notes** if you wish, avoiding the temptation to copy out too much. |
| Step 7<br>*Marketing at Work* | Study each one, and try if you can to add flesh to them from your **own experience** – they are designed to show how the topics you are studying come alive (and often come unstuck) in the **real world**. You can also update yourself on these companies by going on to the World Wide Web. |
| Step 8<br>*Action Programme* | Make a very good attempt at each one in each chapter. These are designed to put your **knowledge into practice** in much the same way as you will be required to do in the exam. Check the answer at the end of the chapter in the **Action Programme review**, and make sure you understand the reasons why yours may be different. |
| Step 9<br>*Chapter Roundup* | Check through it very carefully, to make sure you have grasped the **major points** it is highlighting |
| Step 10<br>*Quick Quiz* | When you are happy that you have covered the chapter, use the **Quick Quiz** to check your recall of the topics covered. The answers are in the paragraphs in the chapter that we refer you to. |
| Step 11<br>*Illustrative question(s)* | Either at this point, or later when you are thinking about revising, make a full attempt at the **illustrative questions**. You can find these at the end of the Study Text, along with the **Answers** so you can see how you did. |

## Developing your personal Study Plan

Preparing a Study Plan (and sticking closely to it) is one of the key elements in learning success.

First you need to be aware of your style of learning. There are four typical learning styles. Consider yourself in the light of the following descriptions. and work out which you fit most closely. You can then plan to follow the key study steps in the sequence suggested.

| Learning styles | Characteristics | Sequence of key study steps in the BPP Study Text |
|---|---|---|
| Theorist | Seeks to understand principles before applying them in practice | 1, 2, 3, 7, 4, 5, 8, 9, 10, 11 (6 continuous) |
| Reflector | Seeks to observe phenomena, thinks about them and then chooses to act | |
| Activist | Prefers to deal with practical, active problems; does not have much patience with theory | 1, 2, 8 (read through), 7, 4, 5, 9, 3, 8 (full attempt), 10, 11 (6 continuous) |
| Pragmatist | Prefers to study only if a direct link to practical problems can be seen; not interested in theory for its own sake | 8 (read through), 2, 4, 5, 7, 9, 1, 3, 8 (full attempt), 10, 11 (6 continuous) |

Next you should complete the following checklist.

Am I motivated? (a) ☐

Do I have an objective and a standard that I want to achieve? (b) ☐

Am I a theorist, a reflector, an activist or a pragmatist? (c) ☐

How much time do I have available per week, given: (d) ☐

- The standard I have set myself
- The time I need to set aside later for work on the Practice and Revision Kit
- The other exam(s) I am sitting, and (of course)
- Practical matters such as work, travel, exercise, sleep and social life?

**Now:**

- Take the time you have available per week for this Study Text (d), and multiply it by the number of weeks available to give (e) (e) ☐
- Divide (e) by the number of chapters to give (f) (f) ☐
- Set about studying each chapter in the time represented by (f), following the key study steps in the order suggested by your particular learning style

This is your personal **Study Plan**.

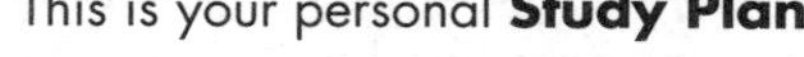

## Short of time?

Whatever your objectives, standards or style, you may find you simply do not have the time available to follow all the key study steps for each chapter, however you adapt them for your particular learning style. If this is the case, follow the Skim Study technique below (the icons in the Study Text will help you to do this).

### *Skim Study technique*

Study the chapters in the order you find them in the Study Text. For each chapter, follow the key study steps 1–2, and then skim-read through step 3. Jump to step 9, and then go back to steps 4–5. Follow through step 7, and prepare outline Answers to the Action Programme (step 8). Try the Quick Quiz (step 10), following up any items you can't answer, then do a plan for the illustrative question (step 11), comparing it against our answers. You should probably still follow step 6 (note-taking).

## Moving on...

However you study, when you are ready to embark on the practice and revision phase of the BPP Effective Study Package, you should still refer back to this Study Text:

- As a source of **reference** (you should find the list of key concepts and the index particularly helpful for this)
- As a **refresher** (the Chapter Roundups and Quick Quizzes help you here)

## A note on pronouns

On occasions in this Study Text, 'he' is used for 'he or she', 'him' for 'him or her' and so forth. Whilst we try to avoid this practice it is sometimes necessary for reasons of style. No prejudice or stereotyping accounting to sex is intended or assumed.

# Syllabus

## Aims and objectives

The *Analysis and Evaluation* module covers the first part of strategic marketing in a strategic and global context. It aims to provide participants with the knowledge and skills required to undertake strategic analysis and evaluation of the organisation's current situation as a foundation for making strategic marketing decisions. It sets strategic marketing in context as a key creator of stakeholder value and deals with strategic insights into the organisation, its customers and the challenges it faces.

## Related statements of practice

4d.1 Define intelligence requirements and lead the intelligence gathering process.

4d.2 Develop a detailed understanding of the organisation and its environment.

## Learning outcomes

Participants will be able to:

- Explain the concept of business orientation and critically appraise the different orientations in management and planning and the roles of marketing used by organisations.
- Identify the business intelligence required to inform the organisation's strategy-making activities in domestic and international markets.
- Assess the impact of the major trends in the strategic and global context on the strategy making process.
- Conduct and synthesise a detailed strategic audit of the organisation's internal and external environments, including an evaluation of business performance, using appropriate tools and models and analysis of numerical data and management information to support decisions on key strategic issues.
- Appraise the nature of culture in organisations and the importance of its 'fit' with strategy and operations across different cultures.
- Synthesise a coherent and concise assessment of the situation facing an organisation and develop alternative scenarios.

## Knowledge and skill requirements

| Element 1: Strategic management and the role of marketing (10%) | |
|---|---|
| 1.1 | Demonstrate an understanding of the role of marketing in creating exceptional value for customers and shareholders. |
| 1.2 | Demonstrate an understanding of the role of marketing in organisations that are driven by performance measures other than shareholder value, eg not-for-profit organisations. |
| 1.3 | Critically evaluate the characteristics of the marketing models and criteria for success used in organisations with a strong market orientation. |
| 1.4 | Critically evaluate the characteristics of marketing models used by, and the challenges facing marketing in, organisations with a weak market orientation. |
| 1.5 | Give examples of the strategic planning process used in organisations and evaluate marketing's role within it. |

| Element 2: Evaluation of business and marketing performance (30%) | |
|---|---|
| 2.1 | Critically evaluate and use quantitative techniques for evaluating business and marketing performance over current and historic business cycles. Techniques to be covered should include:<br>– Balanced scorecard, with an emphasis on customer and innovation measures<br>– Evaluation of marketing performance including the audit of marketing activities and valuation of marketing assets, such as brands<br>– Financial techniques such as shareholder value analysis (using total shareholder return and economic profit), financial ratio analysis, benchmarking, and evaluation of historical financial decisions. |

| Element 3: Analysis of the internal environment (20%) | |
|---|---|
| 3.1 | Use and appraise the available techniques and processes for the objective assessment of the internal environment of an organisation, including portfolio analysis, value chain, innovation audit and cultural web. |
| 3.2 | Critically evaluate the resource-based and asset-based views of the organisation. |
| 3.3 | Demonstrate the ability to use appropriate information and tools to evaluate the core competencies, assets, culture and weaknesses of an organisation. |
| 3.4 | Assess the 'fit' between an organisation's culture and its current strategy. |
| 3.5 | Summarise the salient factors and insights emerging from the internal analysis. |

| Element 4: Analysis of the external environment (20%) | |
|---|---|
| 4.1 | Use and appraise the available techniques and processes for the objective assessment of the external environment covering the macro-environment, competitive environment, customers, channels and evaluation of the organisation's offers against customer needs. |
| 4.2 | Define the organisation's intelligence needs, research needs and resources required to support an analysis of the external environment. |
| 4.3 | Acquire and use appropriate information and tools to evaluate the organisation's current competitive position, position within the value chain and sources of competitive advantage. |
| 4.4 | Develop customer insights by analysing potential and current customer bases and developing an understanding of their needs, preferences and buying behaviours (as prelude to segmentation). |
| 4.5 | Use relevant techniques such as forecasting to quantify the opportunities available to an organisation and any threats to its position. |
| 4.6 | Summarise the salient factors and insights emerging from the external analysis. |
| 4.7 | Consolidate, synthesise and distil the analysis of the internal and external environments to provide an insightful summary of the organisation's marketing position and performance. |
| 4.8 | Identify the implication for the organisation's future and strategic decisions to be made using conclusions drawn from the internal and external analysis. |

| Element 5: Characteristics of the global and international marketplace (20%) | |
|---|---|
| 5.1 | Assess the variances in key factors influencing customer buying behaviours and competition in global and international markets. |
| 5.2 | Identify the specific challenges in collecting and interpreting information to develop a detailed understanding of customers and markets in a foreign market and explain how they may be overcome. |
| 5.3 | Identify and assess the processes, techniques and factors to be used in assessing the attractiveness of international markets (eg assessing rate of development of economic development, cultures, consumer profiles etc). |
| 5.4 | Assess the position of an organisation working in an international or global marketplace. |
| 5.5 | Critically assess the capability of an organisation to expand in international markets taking into account factors such as its cultural expertise, organisational structure issues, current strategic objectives (defending home market from attack, operating in foreign market, etc), etc. |
| 5.6 | Critically evaluate the effectiveness and value of ICT in cross-border marketing. |

# Assessment

CIM will offer a single form of assessment based on the learning outcomes for this module. It will take the form of an invigilated, time-constrained assessment throughout the delivery network. Candidates' assessments will be marked centrally by CIM.

# Overview and rationale

## *Approach*

This module has been developed to provide the knowledge and skills for analysis and evaluation of performance required by strategic marketers. It is based on the statements of marketing practice to ensure that it prepares participants for practice at a strategic marketing level. Participants and tutors will note that the module is integrated both horizontally and vertically across the range of CIM syllabus modules.

Participants with appropriate experience should find that they are able to apply the knowledge learned immediately within their organisation and therefore add value quickly to themselves and their employer.

## *Syllabus content*

The balance of weighting allocated to each of the five elements reflects the importance of the area to the achievement of learning and performance outcomes, and the depth and breadth of the material to be covered. Although each area may be regarded as a discrete element, there are clear progressions and overlaps in the knowledge and skills requirements have important implications for the delivery of the module.

**Element 1: Strategic management and the role of marketing (10%)**

This element focuses on the role of marketing within organisations, and in particular the difference in its role on organisations with varying degrees of market orientation and contexts. It is important that participants understand how marketing creates value for customers, shareholders and other stakeholders and how the role can alter in different contexts. Within this, the different criteria used to define and assess success should be explored.

**Element 2: Evaluation of business performance (30%)**

Organisations need to evaluate their past and current performance to make informed decisions about future activity. This element looks at the processes and techniques available to do this, acknowledging their strengths and limitations. In particular participants should be aware of the measures and quantitative techniques used, both financial and marketing-based. Emphasis is placed on sources of data and potential bias.

**Element 3: Analysis of the internal environment (20%)**

The first stage in objectively analysing an organisation's position is to review its internal capabilities and environment. This element examines the available techniques and processes, emphasising the need for objectivity. Participants should understand corporate capabilities, identify core competencies, and itemise and evaluate marketing assets. The relationship between culture and strategy is also important, particularly the degree of market orientation. There is a clear expectation that participants will be able to demonstrate effective use of a variety of techniques for analysis and evaluation such as Porter's value chain and portfolio analysis.

**Element 4: Analysis of the external environment (20%)**

This element builds on the internal environmental analysis, turning to the organisation's position in the external environment. Again the available techniques and processes are examined. Participants should be familiar with and able to conduct an analysis of and draw conclusions from both the macro level and the micro level, paying particular attention to the quantification of trends. Participants are expected to demonstrate knowledge of and ability to use the relevant frameworks and models such as PEST/SLEPT and Porter's Five Forces. At the end of this element, participants should be able to draw together the results from their internal and external analyses to provide an objective summary of an organisation's competitive position and performance. In addition they should be able to review the implication for the organisation's future.

**Element 5: Characteristics of the global marketplace (20%)**

As organisations increasingly operate in a global marketplace, there is a need to appreciate the difference in approaching foreign markets and dealing with foreign competitors. Participants should be aware of and be able to evaluate the available frameworks and their appropriateness. This module covers entry evaluation procedures for candidate countries as well as the role of the internet in developing the global village.

## *Delivery approach*

Although it is expected that the learning outcomes should be achieved as discrete goals of attainment, it is assumed that tutors will also recognise and impart an understanding of the integrated nature of the syllabus content. Practical exercises, such as data gathering and the application of models and frameworks are critical to the development of skills required in this module. Particular emphasis should be placed on the critical and objective evaluation of data, being aware of potential bias. It is important that the projects or case studies illustrate the integration of analysis and evaluation within the process of strategy formulation.

# The Exam Paper

## Assessment methods and format of the paper

| | | *Number of marks* |
|---|---|---|
| Part A: | one compulsory question based on an industry scenario or a company mini-case study: this question will be broken down into parts, typically three | 50 |
| Part B: | choice of two questions from four | 50 |
| | | 100 |

The examination will be based on the stated learning outcomes and every examination will cover at least 80% of the syllabus content.

Time allowed: 3 hours

**Note**. Earlier drafts of the assessment methodology for this paper spoke in terms of Parts A, B and C, with one question from a choice of two being answered in each of Parts B and C. This proposal has been superseded by the format described above.

# About this BPP Study Text

## The CIM qualification scheme

The CIM Professional Post-Graduate Diploma (PPGD) is very different from its predecessor. Like the Professional Certificate and the Professional Diploma, it is the result of an extensive research, consultation and course design project. As a result of this work, the three levels of qualification are embedded in a supporting **conceptual framework**.

## Statements of Marketing Practice

Statements of Marketing Practice (SOMPs) define what marketers actually do at various levels in organisations. They are based on research and provide the foundation for the examination syllabuses. You will find a section headed 'Related Statements of Practice' preceding the syllabus in each BPP Study Text. These are the SOMPs that that unit of study is intended to support. The knowledge and skill requirements given in the syllabus for each unit underpin the SOMPs.

## Strategic marketing and the PPGD

The PPGD is intended for the **aspiring strategic marketer**, that is, for the person who is moving or will shortly move into a role with influence at the strategic level. The primary role of strategic marketing is to identify and create value for the business through strongly differentiated positioning. It does this by influencing the strategy and culture of the organisation towards a strong customer focus.

## The PPGD

The PPGD is organised into four units: Analysis and Evaluation, Strategic Marketing Decisions, Managing Marketing Performance and Strategic Marketing in Practice. Just as at the lower levels of the CIM qualification, the fourth unit, Strategic Marketing in Practice, is an integrative unit that draws together the threads of the other three units. However, perhaps more than is the case at the lower levels, the first three units **are themselves highly integrated**. They proceed in a logical sequence, which is based on the well-known rational model of strategy. This is split into three consecutive parts that are accurately reflected in their titles. Between them, they cover the whole field of strategic marketing, but they are not separate from each other, because business strategy itself is not compartmentalised. The split is merely one of convenience. It is important that you understand this, because you must make appropriate connections in your understanding and not regard the units as hermetically sealed off, one from another.

There is, in fact a great deal of commonality of subject matter in the first three units; the distinction between them lies in the way the ideas and techniques are used and the purposes they serve. This is reflected in the syllabuses for the three units. Let us take an important example that appears in all three: the idea of **shareholder value**.

Creating, safeguarding and enhancing the wealth of shareholders are what business is about. For marketing to play its proper role it must be able to demonstrate that it generates a return on the assets it uses and that in specifically financial terms it is worthwhile. The only satisfactory way to do this is by using the techniques of financial appraisal, such as ratio analysis and discounted cash flow. Now the idea of shareholder value is important at all stages of strategic management. At the analysis stage it is used to measure the current and past success of the company and its competitors. At the stage of strategic choice, it is the yardstick by which competing future strategies are measured. And at the implementation stage it is the basis of the strategic control system, setting the desired standard for performance.

## Study Text coverage

As always, we have aimed to provide you with comprehensive coverage of your exam syllabus and the three Study Texts covering the first three units have been prepared with this aim in mind. This means that there is considerable repetition of material in these three Study Texts, reflecting as they do, the repetition in the syllabuses. This has the advantage that each Study Text is complete in its coverage. On the other hand, it also means that each one is perhaps rather larger than it otherwise might be. Nevertheless, we feel that completeness of coverage is more important than mere handiness.

# Part A

# Strategic management and the role of marketing

# The Roles of Marketing

1

| Chapter Topic List | |
|---|---|
| 1 | Setting the scene |
| 2 | The roles of marketing |
| 3 | What is strategy? |
| 4 | Role of marketing in market-led strategic management |
| 5 | Synergistic planning |
| 6 | The strategic planning process |
| 7 | Other models for setting direction |
| 8 | Tactical and resource planning |
| 9 | Corporate strategy and marketing strategy |

## Syllabus Content

- The role of marketing in creating exceptional value for customers and shareholders
- Marketing models
- The strategic planning process

## Key Concepts Introduced

- Marketing
- Market orientation
- Strategy
- Key tasks
- Tactics
- Policy
- Strategic management
- Priorities
- Corporate strategy
- Business strategy
- Synergystic planning
- Critical success factors

# 1 Setting the scene

**1.1** The syllabus for this first paper in CIM's Professional Post-graduate Diploma deals with two main matters.

(a) First, it introduces the wide subject of **corporate strategy**, which essentially forms the material basis of the whole Diploma. An important aspect of this introduction is an explanation of the way that 'strategy' and 'marketing' relate to one another.

(b) Second, it covers the **strategic analysis** phase of the classic system of corporate planning. Subsequent phases are dealt with in later papers.

**1.2** This chapter aims to provide the introductory material required to fulfil the purpose outlined in Paragraph 1.1(a) above. It thus constitutes an introduction to the whole of the Diploma.

**1.3** It is important to be aware that the terminology commonly used in this area of study is rather imprecise: 'strategy', 'corporate strategy', 'business strategy', 'marketing' and 'marketing strategy' are terms that are often used as if they were interchangeable. We attempt in this chapter to use them rather more precisely and consistently and you should aim to do the same.

# 2 The roles of marketing

**Key Concept**

**Marketing** is the management process responsible for identifying, anticipating and satisfying customer requirements profitably. (CIM)

**2.1** You are probably very familiar with the CIM's own definition of marketing, which we reproduce in the Key Concept box above, and, indeed, may have thought it worth committing to memory. While useful in its way, this definition is not the only one we might consider; in fact there are many. Here is what *Dibb, Simkin, Pride and Ferrel* have to say:

> Marketing consists of individual and organisational activities that facilitate and expedite satisfying exchange relationships in a dynamic environment through the creation, distribution, promotion and pricing of goods, services and ideas.

This is a more detailed definition and has the advantage of being very specific about the activities it includes under the umbrella term 'marketing'.

**2.2** There is one important problem with both of these approaches to marketing and that is their tendency towards **over-inclusiveness**. We see this most clearly when we think about the activity we know as **production**. Taking the CIM definition first, if we ask 'Does the production function have anything to do with satisfying customer requirements profitably?' we must, if we are fair, answer 'Yes, it does.' If production is to the wrong standard, or at too great a cost, or late, customer satisfaction will be reduced. A very similar question could be asked about the phrase 'creation ... of goods...' in the definition of Dibb *et al*, and it would have to be answered in the same way. Now, it is clear that it would be going too far to suggest that production is a core marketing activity and should be controlled by the Marketing Director.

**2.3** While it is not so obvious in the case of functions such as finance and human resource management, the same argument applies to them. We are driven to the conclusion that neither definition we have looked at is much good at explaining the relationship between marketing and the other functions to be found in any given organisation.

**2.4** The related term 'marketing concept' is worth looking at if we wish to understand more deeply. *Philip Kotler*, one of the best known of writers on marketing subjects says this:

> The marketing concept holds that the key to achieving organisational goals lies in determining the needs and wants of target markets and delivering the desired satisfactions more efficiently and effectively than the competition.

**2.5** In Kotler's statement we see a clue to resolving the problem we have identified. It is necessary for us to strike a clear distinction between marketing as an **activity** and marketing as a **concept** of how an organisation should go about its business. This will enable us to approach other parts of the organisation in a rational and practical manner, acknowledging their contribution rather than seeking pre-eminence. If we do this, we will be in a position to promote the marketing concept as a thing separate from our own professional specialisations.

The HR function is particularly important because of the increasing need for high quality people to deliver high quality goods and service. This is especially true in those roles that have direct contact with the customer.

## Models of marketing

**2.6** The material below is taken from the introduction to the syllabus for Stage 3 of the CIM qualification. It therefore represents an authoritative view of just what marketing is.

**2.7** The type, or model , of marketing practised in any organisation depends on a number of factors, not least of which are the nature of the business context and the organisation's dominant orientation. Marketing activities in organisations can be grouped broadly into four models:

(a) **Sales support** – The emphasis in this model is essentially reactive: marketing supports the direct sales force. It may include activities such as telesales or telemarketing, responding to inquiries, coordinating diaries, customer database management, organising exhibitions or other sales promotions, and administering agents. These activities usually come under a sales and marketing director or manager. This form of marketing is common in SMEs and some organisations operating in a B2B context.

(b) **Marketing communications** – The emphasis in this model is more proactive: marketing promotes the organisation and its product/service at a tactical level, either to customers (pull) or to channel members (push). It typically includes activities such as providing brochures and catalogues to support the sales force. Some B2C organisations may use marketing to perform the 'selling' role using direct marketing techniques and to manage campaigns based on a mix of media to raise awareness, generate leads and even take orders. In B2B markets, larger organisations may have marketing communications departments and specialists to make efficient use of marketing expenditures and to coordinate communications between business units.

(c) **Operational marketing** – The emphasis in this model is for marketing to support the organisation with a coordinated range of marketing activities including market research, brand management, product development and management, corporate and marketing communications, and customer relationship management. Given this breadth of activities, planning is also a function usually performed in this role but at an operational or functional level. Typically part of FMCG or B2C organisations, the operational marketing role is increasingly used in B2B organisations.

(d) **Strategic marketing** – The emphasis in this model is for marketing to contribute to the creation of value and competitive customer strategy. As such, it is practised in customer-focused and larger organisations. In a large or diversified organisation, it may also be responsible for the coordination of marketing departments or activities in separate business units. Strategic marketing decisions, when not made by professional marketers, are taken by business leaders.

Professional marketers are likely to be responsible for strategic marketing only in those organisations with a strong market (note, not necessarily *marketing*), or customer, orientation or with separate marketing departments in business units that require coordination. In organisations with a weak customer orientation (typically those with a production, sales, product or technology orientation), the role of marketing is likely to be limited to one of sales support or marketing communications.

## Marketing contexts

**2.8** Organisations operating in a variety of contexts use different marketing activities. There is no 'one size fits all' approach. Organisations and their marketers have to select and use techniques appropriate to their specific context. Typically marketing contexts are summarised as:

| Context | Characteristics |
|---|---|
| FMCG | Used in organisations with a strong market orientation, the 'standard' model of marketing is based on identification of customers' needs and techniques of segmentation, targeting and positioning supported by branding and customer communications. |
| B2B | The model of marketing adopted depends on factors such as the importance of face-to-face selling, the dominant orientation and power of buyers. Markets are often less information-rich than FMCG markets, which constrains marketing decisions. |
| Capital projects | A variant of the B2B model where opportunities for positioning are few and the value of any single order constitutes a significant proportion of turnover in a period. |
| Not-for-profit | The organisation is not driven by shareholder value and competition may not be a significant factor in strategy. |
| SMEs | Operating in any of the above sectors, SMEs are characterised by their limited marketing resources and the limited use of marketing techniques. |

**2.9** Not-for-profit organisations are driven not by shareholders but by other stakeholders, such as government (public sector), beneficiaries (charities) and volunteers (voluntary sector). The concept of shareholder value may not be relevant in these organisations where instead concepts such as 'best value' (public sector) and the level of disbursements to beneficiaries operate. The element of competition may not be explicit in the strategy of these organisations, whose strategies may be more collaborative. Such organisations may use a narrower a more tactical repertoire of marketing techniques than larger commercial organisations with a strong market orientation and driven by shareholder value.

## Strategic marketing activities

**2.10** The full spectrum of strategic marketing activities is illustrated in the statements of marketing practice on which this syllabus is based. They include:

- Research and analysis
- Strategy making and planning
- Brand management
- Implementing marketing programmes
- Measuring effectiveness
- Managing marketing teams

**2.11** It goes without saying that strategic marketing operates in a global context. This is not to say that the syllabus has nothing to offer the organisation pursuing a domestic strategy or entering its first foreign market. Even if an organisation is not operating across borders, it is likely to be working in a market in which competitors based in other countries are operating – in other words, a global context. Throughout this syllabus the term 'global context' embraces domestic and international activities as well as true global activities of the largest organisations.

## Plans and planning processes

**2.12** The planning processes used in organisations are typically geared to the annual operating and financial reporting cycle. In those organisations in which annual or longer term plans are produced, these plans are usually at three levels.

- Corporate level
- Business level
- Functional level

**2.13** Marketing contributes to corporate and business plans and develops its own functional plan at an operational level. In organisations with strong strategic management practices (often those with a strong customer orientation), plans are likely to contain the strategies of the organisation or business. In organisations where plans are effectively 'budgets', strategy is unlikely to be explicit. It is therefore important to recognise that:

- The terms 'strategy' and 'plan' may not be the same
- Strategy making and planning may be different processes in organisations
- Organisations approach strategy formulation in a range of formal and informal ways

**2.14** What is sometimes referred to as the 'strategic marketing plan' can take different forms in different organisations. For example:

- It may be the name given to the plans that coordinate the marketing activities of the different businesses or units throughout an organisation.

- It may be synonymous with the term 'business plan' or 'corporate plan' in an organisation with a strong customer focus or responsibility only for marketing products made elsewhere and bought in.

- It may simply be the name given to the marketing plan, which specifies the objectives or targets, activities, resources and budgets of the marketing function.

However, it should be recognised that the majority of organisations do not produced a strategic marketing plan. The major plans that specify and control the organisation's strategy are corporate or business plans, into which strategic marketing should have input.

## The role of strategic marketing

**2.15** In organisation where strategic marketing does not exist as a function, the process or decisions are still undertaken by senior managers or business leaders. Where it is an explicit function, the strategic marketing role will usually be performed by a marketing function in a business unit and by a corporate level marketing function, which may also have a responsibility for coordinating the activities of marketing departments in business units.

**2.16** The primary role of strategic marketing is to identify and create value for the business through strongly differentiated positioning. It achieves this by influencing the strategy and culture of the organisation in order to ensure that both have a strong customer focus. When this role is carried out by a marketing specialist, it is called 'marketing director' or 'strategic marketing manager', sometimes based in a department called 'marketing' rather than 'strategic marketing'. Strategic marketers should champion the customer experience and exert a strong influence on the organisation to adopt a customer orientation, contribute along with other directors and senior managers to its competitive strategy, align the organisation's activities to the customer, and manage the organisation's marketing activities.

**2.17** During strategy formulation, strategic marketing is about choices that customer-focused organisations make on where and how to compete and with what assets. It is also about developing a specific competitive position using tools from the marketing armoury including brands, innovation, customer relationships and service, alliance, channels and communications, and increasingly, price. Strategic marketing does not own the business strategy but, like other departments and functions, should contribute to it and control the operational levers that make a strategy effective. However, marketing has an exceptional contribution to make in identifying opportunities and determining ways to create value for customers and shareholders.

**2.18** During implementation, strategic marketing is the 'glue' that connects many aspects of the business. It will often manage one or a portfolio of brands. Increasingly, it works with HR to ensure that the culture and values in the organisation are consistent with the brand and to ensure that marketing competencies are part of the overall framework for staff development across the business. Strategic marketing also has responsibility for directing the implementation of marketing activities needed to execute the organisation's strategy. Other key tasks of strategic marketing in today's organisations are:

(a) Contributing to strategic initiatives being undertaken by the organisation, for example marketing input to a 'due diligence' evaluation of a prospective merger or acquisition. In some cases, strategic marketers will be managing multi-disciplinary teams.

(b) Co-ordinating and managing customer information across the organisation within the data protection and privacy legislation. This involves close relationships with the IT function.

(c) Developing and driving the business case for investment in brands, new products and services

(d) Championing and developing innovation and entrepreneurship within the organisation

(e) Ensuring that the marketing function is appropriately skilled and resourced

(f) Providing input with finance on the valuation of brands for reporting and disclosure

**2.19** This concept of strategic marketing draws heavily on theory and practice of strategic management, not just of marketing. This is an important distinction since strategic marketing is as much a part of directing how the organisation competes as it is a part of marketing itself. Professional marketers engage in relationships with most functions within the organisation and are 'business people' rather than 'technical marketers'. This is particularly so at the strategic level. It requires participants at this level to embrace a wider range of management theory and practice than has been the case in the past. In addition to traditional marketing theory, strategic marketing also embraces:

- Business and corporate strategy
- Investment decisions
- Culture and change management
- Quality management
- Programme and project management

**2.20** Marketers still have an essential role to play in contributing their specialist marketing skills to the formulation, implementation and control of strategy. While this syllabus does embrace the wider business skills also expected of the strategic marketer, it still places a high priority on these specialist marketing skills.

## Marketing and other functions

**2.21** Within any organisation, the marketing function must work closely with other departments in order to implement the marketing concept. However, marketers must accept that other functions have their legitimate concerns and their own routes towards the ultimate goal of customer satisfaction. Indeed, the achievement of that goal is just as much dependant on functions other than marketing as it is on marketing itself. Here are some examples.

(a) The **finance department** is responsible for raising the working capital that permits the granting of favourable credit terms to customers.

(b) The **HR department** is responsible for recruiting and training the customer service agents, delivery staff and service engineers whose daily interaction with customers forms the cutting edge of the organisation's image and reputation.

(c) **Purchasing managers** control much of the process by which a given level of quality and reliability is incorporated into products.

### Action Programme 1

Suggest another role for each of the departments above that supports the marketing concept.

## Marketing activities

**2.22** As you might expect, the basic marketing mix offers us a good framework to discuss how marketing activities relate to other organisational functions.

**2.23 Product.**

(a) **Product development and enhancement** of physical products is carried out in co-operation with R&D and production. These functions will tend to be represented by engineers, whose approach is likely to be very different from that of a marketer. Where the product partakes extensively of the character of a service or when it is a pure service, technical expertise will still be required. For example, if a firm of solicitors wished to provide independent financial advice, the very demanding regulatory regime governing such services would have a major impact on the marketing of the new service.

(b) **Packaging** is a specialist activity requiring major creative input. However, it is also the subject of major technical innovation in materials, which makes its own input into the appearance of packaged products.

**2.24 Place**. A great deal of the work of distribution is a marketing speciality, including such matters as dealer relations, outlet planning and channel design. However, professional logisticians provide indispensable input in areas such as stockholding and control, transport operations and delivery tracking. Export operations are particularly demanding of specialised shipping and forwarding expertise.

**2.25 Promotion**. Promotion is, of course, the focus of a great deal of marketing attention and might, with justification, be regarded as the marketing specialist's home turf. Nevertheless, it does not take place in a vacuum. It must not promise what cannot be delivered; it must work within budget (particularly where sales promotion is concerned); and individual aspects of promotion must not undermine the overall corporate image.

**2.26 Price**. Cost is a major consideration in price-setting and here the marketer must utilise the expertise of the cost accountant. We will consider some important aspects of cost accountancy in Chapter 7. Also associated with this aspect of the mix is the whole topic of terms of sale: expert advice is necessary if maximum protection is to be obtained against the problem of the customer who does not or cannot pay.

## Marketing-led and market-led orientation

**2.27** Given that marketing is a process, an organisational function, and an academic discipline, it is worth going back to first principles. A **market** is a customer or a group of customers.

**Key Concept**

**Market orientation** is 'an organisational culture where beating the competition through the creation of superior customer value is the paramount objective throughout the business'. (Piercy, *Market Led Strategic Change*, 2001)

**2.28** A **marketing-led organisation is led by the marketing department**. Marketing orientation might just refer to increased power for marketing personnel. The customer, however, is not necessarily at the heart of **everyone's** thinking.

**2.29** In a company with a market orientation, the aim of **providing superior customer value** dominates all thinking.

- What the business is
- Which markets to service
- Investments and acquisitions
- Which people to employ and how to promote them

**2.30** In **market-led** organisations, the marketing department is not in a world of its own. Customer value is designed and created by **multi-function** product teams supporting **all the business functions**.

**2.31** Focusing on customers and their needs is something which should be your meat and drink. Hooley *et al* (*Marketing Strategy and Competitive Positioning)* identify the following components of a market orientation.

- **Customers**: know them well enough to give superior value.
- **Competition**: what are their short- and long-term capabilities?
- **Inter-functional**: mobilise the entire company to create superior customer value.
- **Culture**: employee behaviour should be managed to ensure customer satisfaction.
- **Long term profit focus**: have a strategic but realistic vision.

**2.32** These issues will be discussed in later chapters.

## Marketing at Work

***Tata Motors***

*Tata* is a major Indian industrial conglomerate. *Tata Motors* was until recently a lorry-manufacturing company. When the company decided to enter the car market, it developed the *Indica* from nothing in three years and at a cost only one third as great as a European or US equivalent project. However, when the product was launched there were immediate problems with the suspension and air conditioning and most of all with after-sales service. The initial, corporate-culture conditioned response was 'we haven't done anything wrong'. However, the CEO insisted that the customer had to be put first. Five hundred engineers were sent out into the market place to talk to buyers. Customers were invited into the factory to describe their experiences.

The next generation Indica was ready three years later and quickly became a big seller in the small car segment.

# 3 What is strategy?

**3.1** This section is about corporate strategy and how marketing relates to it. We have already discussed some ideas about this relationship and will return to it later. In this section we will look a little more deeply into the fundamental idea of strategy in business and what it involves.

## Marketing at Work

**Hong Kong Telecom**

*Hongkong Telecom* is a subsidiary of Cable & Wireless. The Chinese telecoms market is conservatively estimated to be worth more than £368 billion: only one in six Chinese households currently possesses a land-based phone line. The company has seen double-digit growth over the past three years in a highly competitive market, and is, according to chief executive Linus Chiang, 'poised on the cusp of a reincarnation'.

*Competition*

The company lost its domestic monopoly in 1995. 'We were printing money,' Cheung says. 'Suddenly we were faced with competition and huge technological advances. We were good technically and technologically, but not in terms of service and efficiency.'

'Rather than trying to fight off the competition by legalities and by making life more difficult for customers by forcing different dialling codes and so forth onto them, we have embraced competition and taken advantage of it. In the short term that approach is not helpful. But we are taking a long-term view and using competition as a driving force, an agent for change.'

*Culture and human resources*

The key to success, he asserts, is attitude, a performance culture and a service culture. Hongkong Telecom employees are judged against three key criteria: 'One, are you bold and decisive? Two, are you results-rather than activity-oriented? Three, are you effective – in other words, do you make things simple for internal and external audiences?'. There have been 2,500 voluntary redundancies over the past three years, and they are increasingly demanding on remaining managers. 'We are de-layering and fast-tracking and weeding out incompetence,' says Cheung.

Cheung introduced Operation Excel, a programme that focuses on revenue enhancement and cost control, and rewards initiative, performance, teamwork and results, as an antidote to the complacency bred by monopoly. The programme has helped effect transition to a dynamic performance culture.

There have been some novel initiatives. Cheung jokes that he is the Postmaster General as well as the CEO. 'I looked at the way we were distributing our four million telephone bills each month, and my boyhood newspaper delivery experience came in handy. I found we could achieve significant savings by utilising our employees to deliver some of our bills. Staff are able to make additional income too.' What's more, he has galvanised the entire workforce to sell mobile phones. And he leads by example, travelling business rather than first class on his frequent trips abroad.

*Product/service innovation*

Most significantly, the company has switched its focus from international direct dialling to other areas, including fixed line, mobile, and interactive services. They won the licence for video-on-demand and home shopping in November, and it is a world first, using complex technology to deliver laser disk quality movies, karaoke, gambling, computer games, TV shopping, etc. Accessible by anyone with a telephone and a TV set using a single controller, the service has the potential to reach Hong Kong's 1.5 million households over the next five years. Another innovation is Netvigator, an Internet access service launched into a marketplace of 80 competitors. To differentiate their offering, they focused on the customer interface, delivering useful, immediate information.

*Competitive strategy*

Hongkong Telecom's competitive differentiator is to respond to customer needs. Finance director David Prince explains: 'In telecoms, competitors tend to start from price, because what we have are effectively commodity products. We are trying to bring more creativity in marketing and customer service to telecoms. We differentiate ourselves from the competition on quality rather than price, by providing a total package to suit individuals' lifestyles.' When it lost its lead to Hutchison in the mobile phone market, Hongkong Telecom held its prices but improved its technology so that, for example, mobiles work in tunnels and underground trains.

## Key Concepts

**Strategy**: a course of action including the specification of resources required to meet a specific objective.

**Tactics**: the deployment of resources to execute an agreed strategy.

**Policy**: a general statement providing guidelines for management of decision making.

3.2 The terminology of strategic management is not universally defined. There is a number of words that are used almost interchangeably in daily life: strategy, tactics, mission, object, aim, target, goal, policy. We will develop our definitions as we progress through the subject matter of this Study Text. There are several points to note about the Hongkong Telecom case example.

- The **objective** is survival and growth.
- The **strategy** is a changed approach to products and markets. (Other strategies could have been chosen to meet this objective.)
- A **policy** is that senior managers travel business class rather than first class.
- The **resources** include the technological infrastructure and getting better performance out of existing personnel.

## Marketing at Work

A government's *objective* of reducing road traffic accidents might be achieved in a number of ways, for example: stricter policing; traffic calming; lower speed limits; tougher driving tests and so on.

## Key Concept

**Strategic management**: the development, implementation and control of agreed strategies. There is more to strategy than merely **deciding** what you want to achieve and how you are to achieve it.

**3.3** Strategic management involves:

| Phase | Application in Hong Kong telecom case example |
|---|---|
| Analysis | Discerning trends in the environment, looking at competitors |
| Choice | Embrace change rather than resisting it |
| Implementation | The *process* of changing the culture and organisation, and bringing the new products and services on-stream |
| Control | After the strategies have been implemented, how successful have they been? |

**3.4** **Strategy** is defined by *Johnson and Scholes* in this way.

> 'the direction and scope of an organisation over the long term which achieves advantage for the organisation through its configuration of resources within a changing environment to meet the needs of markets and to fulfil stakeholder expectations.'

## Levels of strategy in an organisation

**3.5** Any level of the organisation can have objectives and devise strategies to achieve them. The strategic management process is multi-layered.

**3.6** *Hofer and Schendel* refer to three levels of strategy: corporate, business and functional/operational. The distinction between corporate and business strategy arises because of the development of the **divisionalised** business organisation, which typically has a corporate centre and a number of strategic business units (SBUs). *Chandler* described how four large US corporations found that the best way to divide strategic responsibility was to have the corporate HQ allocate resources and exercise overall financial control while the SBUs were each responsible for their own product-market strategies. Functional operational strategies are then developed for component parts of SBUs.

## Corporate strategies

### Key Concept

**Corporate strategy** is concerned with what types of business the organisation is in. It 'denotes the most general level of strategy in an organisation' (Johnson and Scholes).

*Levels of strategy*

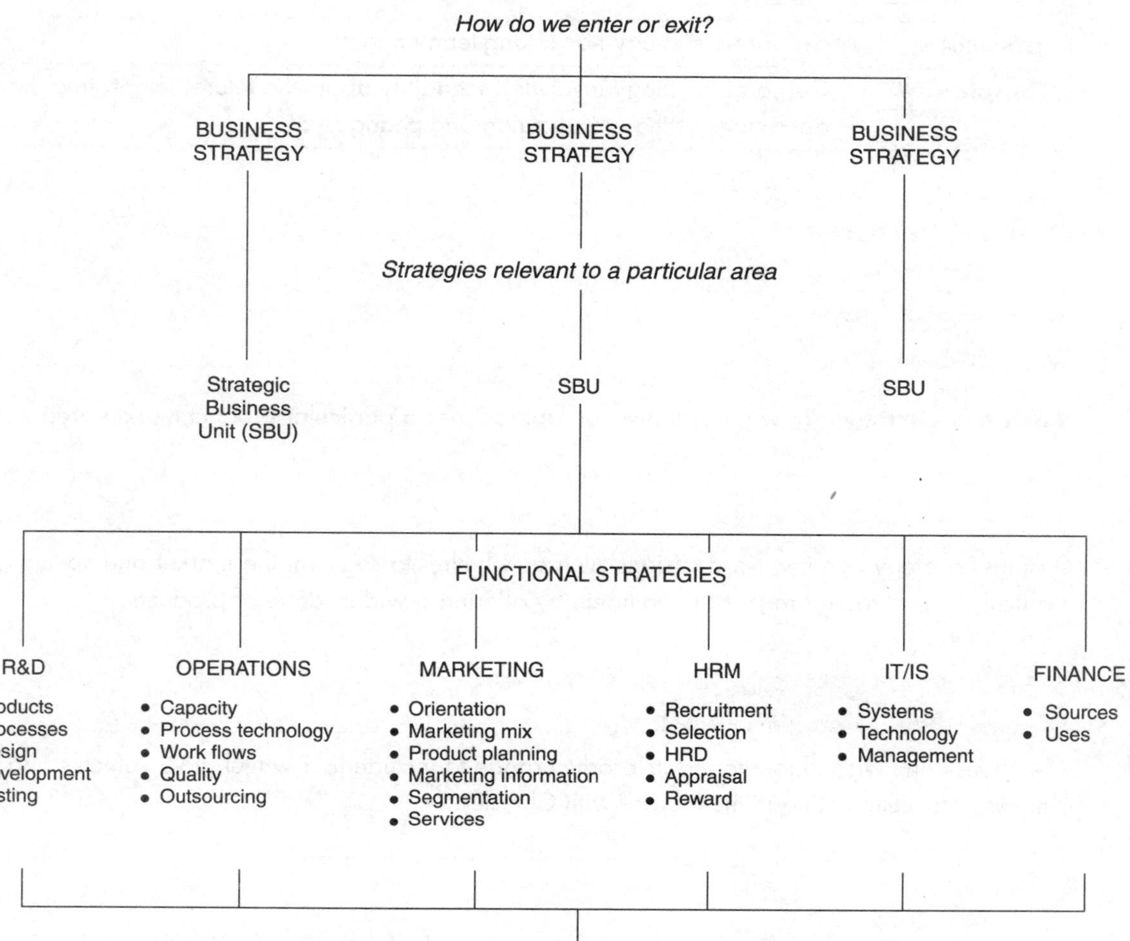


**3.7** It is important for us as marketers and students of marketing to understand the principle discussed in Section 2 of this chapter and illustrated above: while the wider concepts of marketing are closely allied to the concept of overall strategy, the **specific marketing activities** we are familiar with, such as product planning, advertising and channel management make up just **one function among many**. We must be careful not to claim pre-eminence for this **functional** aspect of marketing.

## 3.8 Defining aspects of corporate strategy

| Characteristic | Comment |
|---|---|
| **Scope of activities** | Strategy and strategic management impact upon the whole organisation: all parts of the business operation should support and further the strategic plan. |
| **Environment** | The organisation counters threats and exploits opportunities in the environment (customers, clients, competitors). |
| **Resources** | Strategy involves choices about allocating or obtaining corporate resources now and in future. |

| Characteristic | Comment |
|---|---|
| **Values** | The value systems of people with power in the organisation influence its strategy. |
| **Timescale** | Corporate strategy has a long-term impact. |
| **Complexity** | Corporate strategy involves uncertainty about the future, integrating the operations of the organisation and change. |

## Business strategy

### Key Concept

**Business strategy**: how an organisation approaches a particular product market area.

**3.9** Business strategy can involve decisions such as whether to segment the market and specialise in particularly profitable areas, or to compete by offering a wider range of products.

### Marketing at Work

Mercedes-Benz wished to expand its product range to include four wheel drive vehicles and smaller cars, culminating in the merger with Chrysler.

**3.10** Some large, diversified firms have separate **strategic business units** (SBUs) dealing with particular areas. Business strategy for such large organisations is strategy at the SBU level.

## Functional/operational strategies

**3.11** Functional/operational strategies deal with specialised areas of activity.

| Functional area | Comment |
|---|---|
| **Marketing** | Devising products and services, pricing, promoting and distributing them, in order to satisfy customer needs at a profit. Marketing and corporate strategies are interrelated. |
| **Production** | Factory location, manufacturing techniques, outsourcing and so on |
| **Finance** | Ensuring that the firm has enough financial resources to fund its other strategies by identifying sources of finance and using them effectively |
| **Human resources management** | Secure personnel of the right skills in the right quantity at the right time, and to ensure that they have the right skills and values to promote the firm's overall goals |

| Functional area | Comment |
|---|---|
| **Information systems** | A firm's information systems are becoming increasingly important, as an item of expenditure, as administrative support and as a tool for competitive strength. Not all information technology applications are strategic, and the strategic value of IT will vary from case to case. |
| **R&D** | New products and techniques |

# 4 Role of marketing in market-led strategic management

**4.1** Marketing expertise and personnel are important drivers in taking a firm to the customer, as the example below suggests.

## Marketing at Work

***Waterford Wedgwood/Royal Doulton***

From *Financial Times 1 May 2001*

Royal Doulton, one of the great names in British ceramics, is shrinking to survive. A philosophy of winning sales at all cost triggered a series of losses and a management shake-up under Hamish Grossart, the company director appointed in 1998. The contraction of Royal Doulton, which is based in Stoke-on-Trent, mirrors a decline in the whole Staffordshire ceramics industry.

Wedgwood, Royal Doulton's main rival, seems curiously insulated from the pain. At its pretty campus-style site just outside Stoke-on-Trent, robot delivery trucks glide quietly between the workbenches where craftspeople assemble items for its classic Jasperware range.

The business, a division of Waterford Wedgwood, the Irish luxury goods group chaired by Sir Anthony O'Reilly, made operating profits last year of €18.7m (£11.6m). This compared with a loss of £9.6m at Royal Doulton. Wedgwood's sales were a third higher than its rival, while its workforce was two-thirds smaller.

At Royal Doulton, Mr Nutbeen (CEO) is resigned to indifference from the City.

Redmond O'Donoghue, Waterford Wedgwood's genial president, frets that its shares trade on a prospective p/e of about 12 compared to multiples of some more than 20 for luxury goods business such as *Bulgari, Tiffany* and *LVMH*. That Mr O'Donoghue can afford such aspirational worries is partly the result of Waterford Wedgwood's revamp of its ceramics division in the late 1990s. At the time, it was sharply criticised by some analysts for investing about £30m in automating what many saw as a dying business.

But the move was justified by revival in sales, triggered by the reinvention of the previously fusty Wedgwood brand using experience and knowledge gained in the Waterford glassware business. Independent designers, such as Paul Costellow, brought their own followings to the brand, as well as fresh design thinking.

Marketing, not production, now drives the business. The Duchess of York, retained expensively for a few day's work a year, has proved an improbably potent ambassador for the brand in the US.

Waterford Wedgwood's glossy magazine includes interviews with Washington socialites and features on vacations in the Hamptons.

The next fundamental shift, says Mr O'Donoghue, is for Wedgwood to crank up its sales in giftware, as Waterford has already done.

Royal Doulton also likes to think of itself as a luxury giftware group. If Mr Nutbeen is serious about this, lines such as resin *Mr Men* figurines, at £8 each, seem unlikely to survive a cull this summer. Royal Doulton executives resent suggestions they are copying Wedgwood's ideas. But whatever the inspiration, the losses are falling. Mr Nutbeen says they will eventually be replaced by double-digit returns.

Both businesses would be envious of the 10 percent profit margin achieved by Portmeirion, a much smaller Stoke-on-Trent ceramics company.

*Website addresses*

www.wedgwood.co.uk www.royal-doulton.com

---

## Market-led strategic change

**4.2** Market-led strategic change rests on the following assumptions (Piercy, 2001).

| Assumptions | Application in Wedgwood and Royal Doulton |
|---|---|
| All organisations must follow the dictates of the market to survive. | Risk of relying on current tableware market. Company had to find new customers. |
| Organisational effectiveness can be pursued by being market-led, focusing on the customer. | Winning sales at all costs. The firm needed **marketing** knowledge and implementation skills, by reinventing Wedgwood Brand. |
| Barriers to being market-led come, not from ignorance of customer characteristics, but from the way organisations are run. | Experience in one part of the business was applied elsewhere. There must have been good communications to ensure knowledge transfer. |
| Becoming market-led often needs an upheaval. | New designers, and more resources focused on the customer communications. |
| Deep seated strategic change, not just hiring a marketing executive. | Change from providing tableware to offering giftware. |

**4.3** In short the pursuit of **customer satisfaction** is at the heart of the market-led company. Piercy makes a distinction between **marketing** and **going to market**. Markets are more important than marketing, *per se*, and markets and customers are important for everyone in a company (not just the marketing department). '**Going to market** is a process owned by everyone in the organisation ... the context for marketing should be the **process** of going to market, not the marketing department.'

**4.4** According to Piercy, the process of going to market needs to be **managed**.

(a) **Strategies** are based on customers and markets.

(b) **Internal programmes** and **external actions** are driven by such strategies.

(c) The company must **deliver its strategy** into the market. This involves more than the marketing department.

(d) **Cross-functional teams** cross organisational boundaries to get the job done.

(e) New types of **relationships** are created.

(f) New ways of doing business are supported by a new **information technology** infrastructure.

## Challenges for the market-led organisation

**4.5** Four broad issues arise for the market-led organisation (Piercy, 2001).

| Issue | Comment |
|---|---|
| **New customers** | ■ **Rising expectations**: customers exposed to world class service will expect it everywhere<br>■ **Sophistication**: customers can see through marketing-speak, and want transparency<br>■ Increased **cynicism** about marketing |
| **New competitors** | ■ From **overseas**<br>■ **Reinventing** the business (eg Direct Line Insurance) |
| **New type of organisation** | ■ **Outsourcing** arrangements<br>■ **Collaboration** arrangements<br>■ **Alliances** (eg airlines)<br>■ **Stakeholder** influences |
| **New ways of doing business** | ■ **Customer-specific** marketing<br>■ **Databases** are used to develop profiles of individual customers to entice them into a **relationship**<br>■ **Internet marketing**: buyers and sellers can conduct a dialogue as the Internet is interactive<br>■ **Customer co-operatives**: Internet newsgroups and chatrooms enable customers to get together perhaps to negotiate discounts or to share experience of a brand |

## Role of marketing in market-led firms

**4.6** What might be the role of marketing and marketing management in this particular context? Kashani (*Financial Times*, Mastering Management series) argues that the role of marketing has changed significantly but has also become much more important to the activities of many firms. The changes he notes are these.

(a) **From staff to line**. Marketing thinking and action are better integrated into the day-to-day decisions of managers running important parts of the business. In other words, instead of a separate, staff marketing department going its own way and putting a promotional gloss on what the organisation does, marketing is more involved in line decisions, such as segment or product management.

(b) **From specialist to strategic**. 'Marketing in the organisation has evolved beyond its traditional specialist focus. Tasks once exclusively associated with marketing, such as market and competitive assessment or end-user communication, are now only a part of a far more integrated marketing process that may include other functions such as upstream product development or downstream management of distribution.'

(c) **From isolated to widespread**. Marketing has become more diffused within the organisation, and is no longer the concern of the few. In short, Kashani argues, the market orientation is spreading.

(i) 'Companies are inculcating their managers in various back office functions with market and customer-mindedness – the very attributes that were the exclusive domain of marketing people.

(ii) A widespread appreciation of market forces and customer needs and how parts of an organisation may contribute to creating a superior customer value is a necessity if the entire organisation is to become market responsive.'

## Marketing at Work

*Marketing Business* described change in the financial services sector. In a service business such as the Halifax, group marketing staff report to a main board director who is head of personnel. This is because service businesses are people businesses, and 'in a corporate brand, the brand is everybody and the brand strategy is the corporate strategy'.

*Website address*: www.halifax.co.uk

## Exam Tip

It is worth emphasising that this paper is about strategy rather than the design of tactical marketing programmes. The list below, Piercy (2001), covers some of the issues.

- Customers: does the firm take customers seriously and work for customer satisfaction? How do you create a customer-focused organisation?
- How are markets defined and segmented around issues that matter to customers?
- How do we create a value proposition based on our mission and our ability to differentiate from competitors?

## Action Programme 2

An IMD survey put 'knowledge of other [business] functions beyond marketing' as fairly low on the list (4th from bottom). Given that this survey covered only marketing managers, how significant do you think it is that they seem relatively unconcerned with understanding other business functions such as the production department and the finance department? Do they know enough already, or do you think a failure to understand how the rest of the organisation works could be a weakness, especially given that a market-led company embodies everybody?

## Thinking about the future

**4.7** It is worth having a look at the way things are developing. Introducing the *Financial Times Mastering Marketing* series, Kotler made the following predictions.

| Trend | Comment |
|---|---|
| **Disintermediation** | All products can be bought off in the Internet, meaning that there is less need for intermediaries |
| **Retailers** | Simple shopping is out, as people can buy supplies over the Internet. Shops become entertainment venues (eg bookshops with coffee shops) |
| **Mass customisation** | Customers can order bespoke products but these can be produced with the efficiency of mass production |
| **Data mining** | Firms get more information about customers and use it for cross selling |
| **Management information** | Real information about customer profitability can be obtained |
| **Long-term supplies** | Customers will be offered life-time supplies |
| **Outsourcing** | This will be the norm |
| **Franchising** | Most field sales people will become franchisees |
| **End of mass TV** | TV advertising takes on the characteristics of magazine advertising, with a proliferation of TV and Internet channels made possible with digital TV |
| **Sustainable competitive advantages** | Benchmarking, reverse engineering and technological leapfrogging |

### *Marketing in non-profit-making organisations*

**4.8** **Governments** and **non-profit-making organisations** might adopt a marketing orientation to achieve their objectives more effectively. The marketer's skills are relevant but the 'profit' aspect of marketing is absent.

(a) Governments wish to promote or discourage certain activities or attitudes.

(b) The main purpose of a non-profit-making organisation will be to satisfy the needs and wants of a group or section of a community.

### Action Programme 3

What would be the effects of introducing a marketing approach to a charity?

**4.9** Non-profit marketing differs from marketing for profit.

(a) Whereas marketers in a profit-making organisation can focus mainly on customers, many non-profit-making organisations have two major publics that they must satisfy.

- **Donors** (who provide the funds, the **customers**)
- **Beneficiaries** (the **consumers**)

(b) Whereas profit-making organisations can work primarily towards a profit objective, non-profit-making organisations are likely to have **complex multiple objectives**, which are hard to measure.

(c) Non-profit-making organisations often come under more **public scrutiny** than profit-making organisations.

**Exam Tip**

*An old syllabus exam featured a question on the marketing issues faced by a wildlife conservation charity. The examiner noted that weaker candidates paid little attention to the nature of the organisation and its complex set of stakeholders and influences, both internal and external.*

**Marketing at Work**

Corporate culture, as a dimension of management theory, has only attracted attention since the 1970s. In companies such as *Body Shop* the culture is obvious and is used as a marketing platform. It is sustained through the selection of new franchisees with similar cultural values and ideals.

*Website address*: www.the-body-shop.com

# 5 Synergistic planning

**Key Concept**

**Synergistic planning** is a rational process of determining future action based on realistic consideration of the current situation and the desired outcome.

**5.1** The Stage 2 syllabus introduces the concept of the **synergistic planning process**. Since we are going to be discussing planning in some detail, it is worth revising this topic.

**5.2** Synergistic planning has been described in several ways. We will discuss it under four main headings.

(a) Determining the desired outcome
(b) Analysing the current situation
(c) Designing possible routes from (b) to (a)
(d) Deciding what to do and how to do it

## The synergistic planning process

5.3 **The desired outcome**. Any process of planning must start with a clear definition of **what is to be achieved**. This process of objective setting is frequently undertaken in a very superficial manner in the real world and sometimes hardly performed at all. There may be an assumption that 'everybody knows what we are trying to achieve' or reference back to long-established objectives that have lost some or all of their relevance under current circumstances. Only when objectives are clearly defined can possible courses of action be assessed and eventual success or failure be measured. The process of definition is not complete until everyone concerned has agreed on a **single clear statement** of what is to be attained. **Vagueness** and **ambiguity** of language are to be avoided, but appear all too often for political purposes, since they allow different interpretations to be used by parties pursuing different agendas. Vagueness and ambiguity hamper affective action.

5.4 **The current situation**. Any plan must take into account circumstances that will affect attainment of the objective. The first step is to establish just where the individual or organisation stands to begin with. Current circumstances will include a vast array of factors, some of far more immediate importance than others. An important aspect of the current situation is the **potential** that exists for future developments that may affect possible future action. You should be familiar with the idea of SWOT – strengths, weaknesses, opportunities and threats. Strengths and weaknesses exist now; opportunities and threats have potential for the future. SWOT is a very common model for analysing the existing situation and widely used in marketing.

5.5 **Possible routes from (b) to (a)**. Simple problems, when analysed, often suggest a single, fairly obvious route to a satisfactory solution. If you come home from a skiing holiday and find that a cold snap has left you with a burst pipe, you have little alternative to turning off the water at the main and trying to find a plumber (unless you are a plumber yourself, of course). The analysis of more complex problems will tend to suggest a **range of possible courses of action**. There is a requirement for both experience and imagination here. Experience will suggest routes that have proved satisfactory in similar circumstances in the past. Imagination suggest both modifications to such plans and completely new ones.

5.6 **Deciding what to do and how to do it**. When a range of possible plans has been outlined, it then becomes necessary to go through a **process of selection**, normally by considering such matters as those below.

(a) Probability of success
(b) Resources required
(c) Acceptability of the proposed action and its implications
(d) Potential obstacles

The process of planning is not complete when a course of action has been chosen. It is then necessary to prepare **detailed plans** for all the groups and individuals involved. These must be **integrated** in such a way that all action undertaken supports the attainment of the overall objective. **Performance measures** and **control mechanisms** must also be established so that effort is not wasted and obstacles can be overcome.

## Synergistic planning and marketing

5.7 Our description of synergistic planning above was deliberately couched in very general terms in order to emphasis its wide applicability. It is not just a marketing technique. However, you should be able to relate its features to what you already know about the processes of marketing planning. We will also be applying these ideas in the wider context of strategic planning.

# 6 The strategic planning process

## Marketing at Work

The European defence industry faces lower government spending, a changed strategic environment, and greater competition as contracts are put out to open tender. There is greater competition in export markets.

*Planning*

A number of assumptions can be made about the environment and customer demands.

- Military needs are for mobile and flexible forces, with fewer tanks, and more flexible 'high-tech' weaponry.
- For economic reasons, reliability and maintainability are desired.
- There should be military applications of civilian technology.
- The Ministry of Defence has also tightened up on procurement, replacing cost-plus contracts with competitive tenders.
- Defence is big business. Most European firms have been hampered by their small size in comparison with US firms. Mergers are in progress.
- The strategic environment is changing with 'rogue states' and so on, the target of US concern.

Defence firms are undertaking strategic management. All firms are concerned with cash flow and productivity. Strategic planning departments have been set up to provide necessary inputs and analyses.

*Website address*: www.defence-data.com

## Levels of strategy

**6.1** As discussed in Section 3, we may identify three levels of strategy in a large organisation.

- Corporate strategies
- Business strategies
- Operational and functional strategies

**6.2** **Corporate strategy** might involve diversifying into a new line of business or closing a business down. It might mean global expansion or contraction.

**6.3** **Business strategy** might involve decisions as to whether, in principle, a company should:

- Segment the market and specialise in particularly profitable areas
- Compete by offering a wider range of products
- Offer a differentiated product

**6.4** Some large, diversified firms have separate **strategic business units** dealing with particular areas.

**6.5** **Functional/operational strategies** deal with specialised areas of activity.

## Marketing at Work

***BT, Vodafone and J-phone***

BT had hoped to build up a mobile phone presence in Japan, but high levels of debt led it to announce the sale of its Japanese interests in J-phone to Vodafone for £3bn. Vodafone now has full control of J-phone. J-phone has been growing but apparently Vodafone wants it to compete more aggressively with *NTT DoCoMo*, Japan's largest mobile phone company, but behind Vodafone globally. J-phone has cutting edge technology, is innovative and highly profitable, but has 16% of the market compared to NTT CoCoMo's 60%.

*Website addresses*

www.vodafone.com
www.nttdocomo.com
www.bt.co.uk

*Financial Times,* 1 May 2001

## A corporate strategic planning model

**6.6** On the next page is one model of the corporate strategic planning process. We have identified **three** stages. These are described briefly in the paragraphs below.

### *Strategic analysis*

**6.7** Strategic analysis is concerned with understanding the strategic position of the organisation.

(a) **Environmental analysis** (external appraisal) is the scanning of the business's environment for factors relevant to the organisation's current and future activities.

(b) **Position or situation audit**. The current state of the business in respect of resources, brands, markets etc.

(c) **Mission**

(i) The firm's long-term approach to business
(ii) The organisation's value system

(d) **Goals** interpret the mission to the needs of different stakeholders (eg customers, employees, shareholders).

(e) **Objectives** should embody mission and goals. Generally, they are **quantitative** measures, against which actual performance can be assessed.

(f) **Corporate appraisal**. A critical assessment of the Strengths, Weaknesses, Opportunities and Threats (SWOT) in relation to the internal and environmental factors affecting an organisation.

(g) **Gap analysis**. A projection of current activities into the future to identify if there is a difference between the firm's objectives and the results from the continuation of current activities.

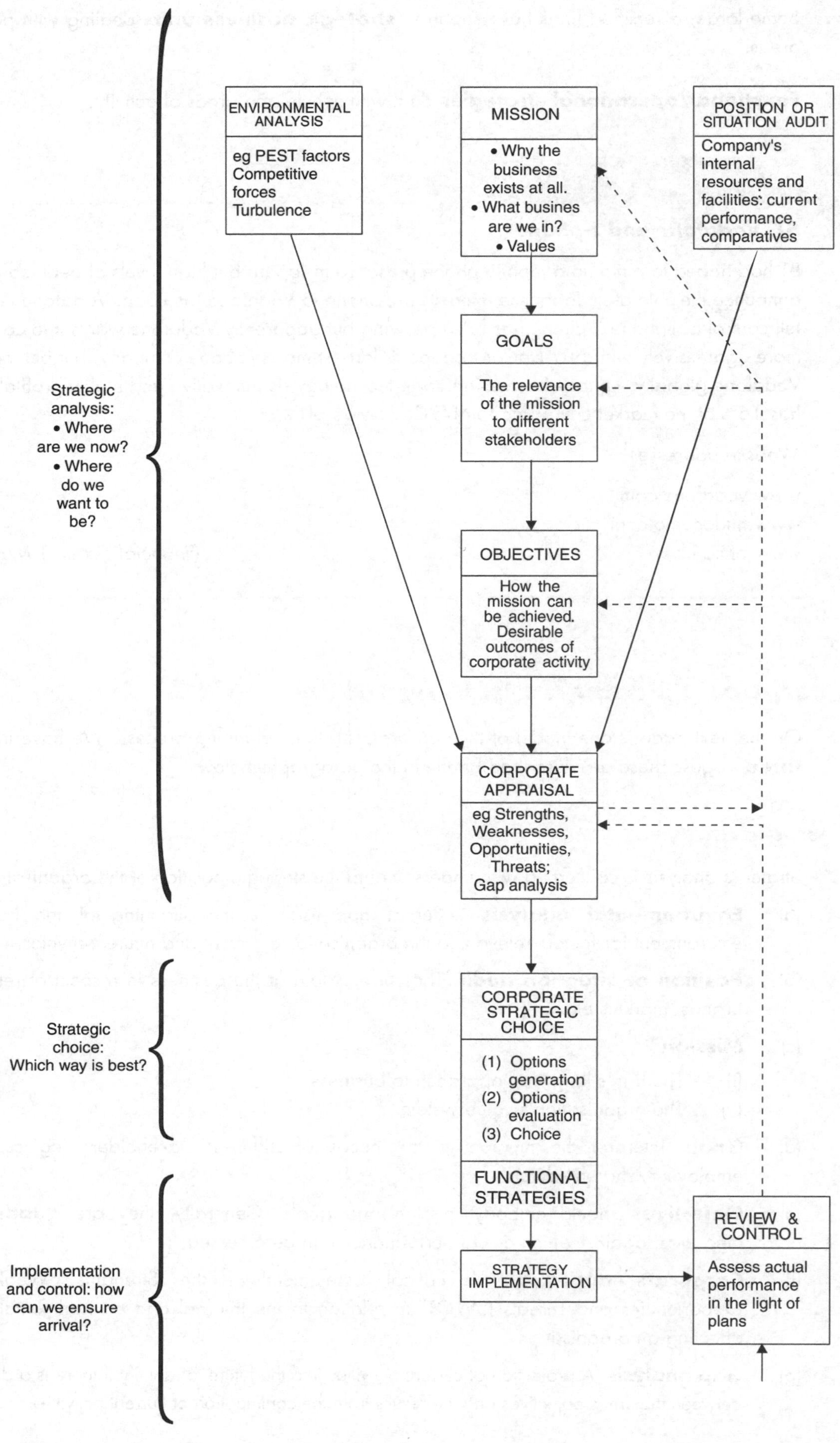
ENVIRONMENTAL ANALYSIS
eg PEST factors
Competitive forces
Turbulence
MISSION
• Why the business exists at all.
• What busines are we in?
• Values
POSITION OR SITUATION AUDIT
Company's internal resources and facilities: current performance, comparatives
GOALS
The relevance of the mission to different stakeholders
Strategic analysis:
• Where are we now?
• Where do we want to be?
OBJECTIVES
How the mission can be achieved. Desirable outcomes of corporate activity
CORPORATE APPRAISAL
eg Strengths, Weaknesses, Opportunities, Threats; Gap analysis
CORPORATE STRATEGIC CHOICE
(1) Options generation
(2) Options evaluation
(3) Choice
Strategic choice: Which way is best?
FUNCTIONAL STRATEGIES
STRATEGY IMPLEMENTATION
REVIEW & CONTROL
Assess actual performance in the light of plans
Implementation and control: how can we ensure arrival?

**6.8** Note that you might decide the mission after assessing the needs of the organisation and its environmental situation.

**Exam Tip**

*You may have to suggest a new mission, sometimes for the organisation as a whole and sometimes for the marketing function.*

### *Strategic choice*

**6.9** **Strategic choice** is based on strategic analysis.

(a) **Strategic options generation**. Here are some examples.

- Increase market share
- International growth
- Concentration on core competences
- Acquisition

(b) **Strategic options evaluation**. Alternative strategies are developed and each is then examined on its merits.

- Acceptability to the organisation's stakeholders
- Suitability
- Feasibility

(c) **Strategy selection**

- **Competitive strategy** is the generic strategy determining **how you compete**.
- **Product-market strategy** determines **where you compete**.
- Institutional strategies determine the **method of growth**.

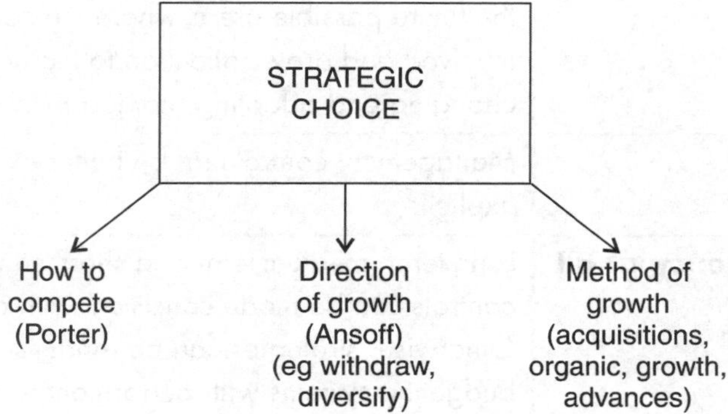


### *Implementation*

**6.10** The implementation of the strategy has to be planned. This is the conversion of the strategy into detailed **plans or objectives for operating units**.

(a) Some plans go into detailed **specifications** as to how the activities should be carried out.

(b) Others will specify **targets** which managers are expected to reach on their own initiative.

(c) The planning of implementation has several aspects.

(i) **Resource planning** (ie finance, personnel). This involves assessing the key tasks, and the resources to be allocated to them.

(ii) **Systems**. Systems are necessary to provide the necessary strategic information, as well as essential operational procedures. Control systems are used to assess performance.

(iii) **Organisation structure**

## Action Programme 4

Ganymede Ltd is a company selling widgets. The finance director says 'We plan to issue more shares to raise money for new plant capacity – which will enable us to enter the vital and growing widget markets of Latin America. After all, we've promised the shareholders 5% profit growth this year, and trading is tough'.

Identify the corporate, business and functional strategies in the above statement.

# Is strategic planning necessary?

### 6.11 Advantages of a formal system of strategic planning

| Advantages | Comment |
|---|---|
| **Identifies risks** | Strategic planning helps in managing risks. |
| **Forces managers to think** | Strategic planning can encourage creativity and initiative by tapping the ideas of the management team. |
| **Forces decision-making** | Companies cannot remain static – they have to cope with changes in the environment. A strategic plan helps to chart the future possible areas where the company may be involved and draws attention to the need to keep on changing and adapting, not just to 'stand still' and survive. |
| **Better control** | Management control can be better exercised if targets are explicit. |
| **Enforces consistency at all levels** | Long-term, medium-term and short-term objectives, plans and controls can be made consistent with one another. Otherwise, strategies can be rendered ineffective by budgeting systems with performance measures which have no strategic content. |
| **Public knowledge** | An entrepreneur who builds a long-lasting business has 'a theory of the business' which informs his or her business decisions. In large organisations that theory of the business has to become public knowledge, as decisions cannot be taken only by one person. |
| **Time horizon** | Some plans are needed for the long term. |

| Advantages | Comment |
|---|---|
| **Co-ordinates** | Activities of different business functions need to be directed towards a common goal. |
| **Clarifies objectives** | Managers are forced to define what they want to achieve. |
| **Allocates responsibility** | A plan shows people where they fit in. |

**6.12** The problem is that the further ahead you look the more imprecise planning becomes.

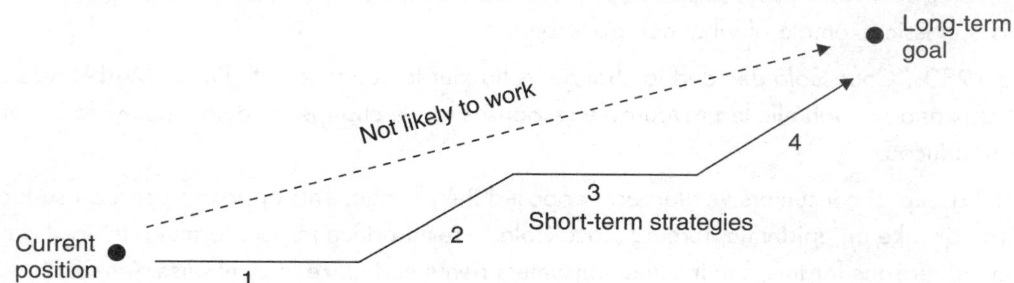


Forecasting becomes more uncertain with each key variable, such as interest rates and employment levels, becoming more and more difficult to predict. Long-term plans therefore have to be 'broad brush' pictures of the organisation's future. Modification will be necessary as more information becomes available and managers need to be clear that long-term goals are most likely to be achieved by a series of short-term strategies which may not follow a direct path.

**6.13** **Long-term thinking**, even beyond the **planning horizon** (the furthest time ahead for which plans can be usefully quantified) is still a useful activity as it provides managers with a picture of how the organisation should be developing a **vision** for the future.

## Exam Tip

*One of the mistakes often made by CIM students is to develop plans which are unrealistic. A frequent factor in this is the failure to consider the time frame of plans. Here is an example.*

(a) *Objective: to double sales over the next twelve months.*

(b) *Student's proposed strategy: to double the sales force.*

(c) *Reality. Such a decision taken and implemented today might increase sales by perhaps 50%, but not the required 100%. This is because the plan fails to consider the time lags and practical issues involved in implementing the strategy. Recruitment, selection and training of the additional sales team is likely to take at least six months to complete. The additional sales team will therefore only be effective for about half a year.*

# 7 Other models for setting direction

**7.1** The case example below is an example of planning and control which went horribly wrong. You might yawn when you see Coca-Cola, yet again, in a marketing text – however, as Coca-Cola is one of the world's most successful consumer marketing companies, it seems perverse to exclude it.

## Marketing at Work

This is a classic example of what can go wrong.

In the 1980s, *Coca-Cola* decided to change its flavour to compete with Pepsi. Market research, taste tests and so forth elicited favourable responses to the change, and so the new formulation was introduced.

A small group of consumers vociferously opposed the change. This opposition spread suddenly and rapidly like an epidemic, forcing Coca-Cola to re-introduce the old formula. It was hard to detect the reasons for this, but if some consumers perceived Coke to symbolise 'American values', then changing the formula appeared to be an assault on them.

This case exemplifies four issues.

1. The limitations of planning and research. Clearly the emotional impact of the brand change had not been considered.
2. The environment is not predictable (as it rapidly became fashionable not to drink the new formula).
3. Small causes (a few disaffected Coke-drinkers) can generate major consequences.
4. The limitations to organisational gathering of information.
5. Consumers, who had initially favoured the product, turned against it, for reasons that could not be predicted by market researchers.

*Website address*: www.coca-cola.co.uk (or local equivalent)

**7.2** Criticisms of the strategic planning model concern how it has worked in **practice** and more fundamental problems of **theory**.

### 7.3 Criticisms of strategic planning in practice

| Problem | Comment |
|---|---|
| **Practical failure** | Empirical studies have not proved that formal planning processes (the delineation of steps, the application of checklists and techniques) contribute to success. |
| **Routine and regular** | Strategic planning occurs often in an annual cycle. But a firm cannot allow itself to wait every year for the appointed month to address its problems. |
| **Reduces creative initiative** | Formal planning discourages strategic thinking. Once a plan is locked in place, people are unwilling to question it. |
| **Internal politics** | The assumption of objectivity in evaluation ignores political battles between different managers and departments. |
| **Exaggerates power** | Managers are not all-knowing, and there are limits to the extent to which they can control the behaviour of the organisation. |

### 7.4 Criticism of the rational model in theory

| Criticism | Comment |
|---|---|
| **Formalisation** | We have no evidence that any of the strategic planning systems – no matter how elaborate – succeed in capturing (let alone improving on) the messy informal processes by which strategies really do get developed. |
| **Detachment: divorcing planning from operations** | Managers manage by remote control. Senior managers at the top 'think great thoughts' while others scurry beneath them. This implies that managers do not really need day-to-day knowledge of the product or market. |
| **Formulation precedes implementation** | A strategy is planned – then it is implemented. But defining strengths and weaknesses is actually very difficult in advance of testing them. |
| **Predetermination** | Planning assumes that the environment can be forecast, and that its future behaviours can be controlled, by a strategy planned in advanced and delivered on schedule. This is only true of stable environments. |

e.g.

## Marketing at Work

This is a classic example of what can go unexpectedly right.

*Honda* is now one of the leading manufacturers of motorbikes. The company is credited with identifying and targeting an untapped market for small 50cc bikes in the US, which enabled it to expand, trounce European competition and severely damage indigenous US bike manufacturers. By 1965, Honda had 63% of the US market. But this occurred by accident.

On entering the US market, Honda had wanted to compete with the larger European and US bikes of 250ccs and over. These bikes had a defined market, and were sold through dedicated motorbike dealerships. Disaster struck when Honda's larger machines developed faults – they had not been designed for the hard wear and tear imposed by US motorcyclists. Honda had to recall the larger machines.

Honda had made little effort to sell its small 50cc motorbikes – its staff rode them on errands around Los Angeles. Sports goods shops, ordinary bicycle and department stores had expressed an interest, but Honda did not want to confuse its image in its 'target' market of men who bought the larger bikes.

The faults in Honda's larger machines meant that reluctantly, Honda had to sell the small 50cc bikes just to raise money. They proved very popular with people who would never have bought motorbikes before. Eventually the company adopted this new market with enthusiasm with the slogan: 'You meet the nicest people on a Honda'. The strategy had emerged, against managers' conscious intentions, but they eventually responded to the new situation.

*Website address*: www.honda.co.uk

# Alternatives to planning

## *No strategic planning: 'freewheeling opportunism'*

**7.5** The **freewheeling opportunism approach** suggests firms should not bother with strategic plans and should **exploit opportunities** as they arise, judged on their individual merits and not within the rigid structure of an overall corporate strategy.

(a) **Advantages**

(i) Opportunities can be seized when they arise, whereas a rigid planning framework might impose restrictions so that the opportunities are lost.

(ii) It might encourage a more flexible, creative attitude among lower-level managers.

(b) **Disadvantages**

(i) **No co-ordinating framework** for the organisation as a whole.

(ii) The firm ends up **reacting** all the time rather than acting purposively.

## *No strategic planning: incrementalism*

**7.6** *Herbert Simon* suggested that managers do **not optimise (ie get the best possible solution), but instead they satisfice**. Managers are limited **by time**, by the **information** they have and by their own **skills**, habits and reflexes. They do not in practice evaluate **all** the possible options open to them in a given situation, but choose between relatively **few alternatives**. This is called **bounded rationality**.

(a) Strategy making tends to involve **small scale extensions of past policy** – **incrementalism** – rather than radical shifts following a comprehensive rational 'search' and evaluation of the alternatives.

(b) In marketing terms, **small scale adjustments of current marketing programmes may not be enough either to:**

- **Move** with existing customers and their needs
- **Identify** new markets or sets of customers

## *No strategic planning: crafting emergent strategies*

**7.7** Some strategies do not arise out of **conscious** strategic planning, but result from a number of ***ad hoc* choices**, perhaps made lower down the hierarchy, which may not be recognised at the time as being of strategic importance. These are called **emergent** strategies. They develop out of **patterns of behaviour**, in contrast to planned strategies which are imposed from above.

## Action Programme 5

Aldebaran Ltd is a public relations agency founded by an entrepreneur, Estella Grande, who has employed various talented individuals from other agencies to set up in business. Estella Grande wants Aldebaran Ltd to become the largest public relations agency in North London. Management consultants, in a planning document, have suggested 'growth by acquisition'. In other words, Aldebaran should buy up the other public relations agencies in the area. These would be retained as semi-independent business units, as the Aldebaran Ltd group could benefit from the goodwill of the newly acquired agencies. When Estella presents these ideas to the Board there is general consensus with one significant exception. Livia Strange, the marketing director, is horrified. 'How am I going to sell this to my staff? Ever since we've been in business, we've won business by undercutting and slagging off the competition. My team have a whole culture based on it. I give them champagne if they pinch a high value client. Why acquire these new businesses – why not stick to pinching their clients instead?'

What is the source of the conflict?

---

**7.8** *Mintzberg* uses the metaphor of **crafting strategy** to help understand the idea. Emergent strategies can be shaped by managers.

**Exam Tip**

*The assumption in many mini-cases is that planning is a 'good thing' – but you need to be aware of the potential limitations of plans, if only to understand what might go wrong or to suggest alternative ways of developing strategy. Where there is high uncertainty, your plans will, inevitably, be tentative, and you may need to develop contingency plans – or at least identify the need to develop them – in your answer.*

---

# 8 Tactical and resource planning

**8.1** Tactics involves the deployment of **resources in an agreed strategy**. In implementing a corporate plan, departments and functions in the organisation will be carrying out specific tasks within their areas of expertise.

**8.2** It helps to envisage a hierarchy of objectives to show how corporate objectives are communicated to different levels of the organisation. The **hierarchy of objectives** which emerges is as follows.

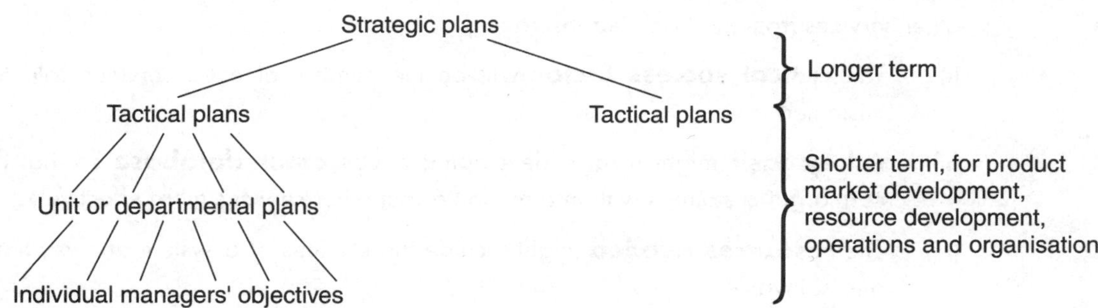


**8.3** With this in mind, we can translate corporate strategy into tactical demands, by use of **critical success factors**.

## Resources, tactics and CSFs

### Key Concepts

(a) **Critical success factors (CSFs)** 'are those factors on which the strategy is fundamentally dependent on its success'.

(b) **Key tasks** are what must be done to ensure each critical success factor is achieved.

(c) **Priorities** indicate the order in which tasks are achieved.

For example, The critical success factor to run a successful mail order business is speedy delivery. Some CSFs are generic to the whole industry, others to a particular firm: a CSF of a parcel delivery service is that it must be quicker than the normal post.

### Action Programme 6

Draw up a list of four critical success factors for the strategy of the organisation for which you work.

**8.4 EXAMPLE**

CSFs can be used to translate strategic objectives into performance targets and tactical plans. Dogger Bank wants to increase profits.

(a) **Business objective**: grow profits.

(b) **Strategy**: increase revenue per customer.

(c) **Tactics**: Increasing revenue per customer might not be possible unless customers buy other services from the bank (eg insurance).

  (i) The **critical success factor** will be the number of extra services sold to each customer.

  (ii) A **key task** might involve developing a **customer database** so that the firm can target customers with information about other services more effectively.

  (iii) The **resources needed** might include the services of a system analyst, hardware and software.

## Clarifying the level

**8.5** Bear in mind that strategy and tactics are a means to an end, and do not get too worried about definitions and logic chopping.

**8.6** In the last section we described the overall corporate planning process. Yet, from the office junior to the managing director, **everyone plans their work and decides how best to allocate their resources** (possibly only time) to **achieve the objectives** which have been set. As a result people **at all levels** of the organisation will talk about their objectives, strategy and tactics. To avoid confusion it is necessary to clarify the level in the organisation at which the individual is working.

**8.7** Imagine that you are on a flight of stairs. As you step down from one level to another, the tactics of the higher level becomes the strategy of the lower one.

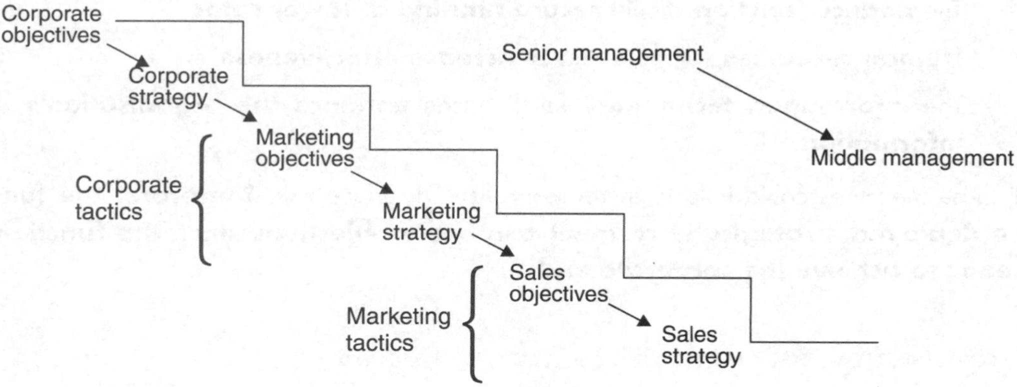


**8.8** **At what management level are you positioned**? This is the first question you need to ask yourself when presented with a new planning project or scenario in the exam.

(a) The **process and framework** of planning is the same whether you are the managing director, marketing manager or sales manager.

(b) The **focus does differ** and it is essential that you keep a clear picture of who you are and what your area of authority is.

**Exam Tip**

*It is easy for a marketing student when questioned on corporate planning to write extensively on strategy for the marketing mix and give scant attention to operations, finance and organisational considerations.*

*On the other hand, you may be asked to restrict yourself to marketing issues. The marketing strategy should include decisions about the positioning of the product range. You would not recommend changing the reward structure, increasing the dividend, or cutting the production workforce.*

## *Corporate objectives: growth in profit, survival, risk*

**8.9** At **corporate level** the focus is on the **organisation as a whole**.

(a) Corporate objectives will be **expressed in financial terms**, for example return on investment or profit. Corporate objectives are often concerned with achieving **growth consistent with limiting risk**. The **stakeholders** in an organisation (ie all those, not only shareholders, who have an interest in what the organisation does) would not normally support high growth objectives which demanded the taking of very high risks.

(b) **Corporate strategy** directs the functional areas of the business (eg finance, operations and marketing).

**8.10** In seeking to grow profitably and reduce risk, **corporate planning will deploy the functional activities of the business to these ends. The functional activities are the resources of the business**.

- **Marketing** activities can be deployed **to increase (profitable) sales**.
- The **production** function can be asked to **reduce unit costs**.
- The **finance function** should **secure funding at lower rates**.
- **Human resources** will be asked to **increase effectiveness**.
- The **information technology** function can **enhance the organisation's use of information**.

All these measures could help to increase profit and reduce risk. **Therefore, the functions are deployed strategically to meet corporate objectives since the functions are means to achieve the corporate ends**.

### *Corporate tactics become marketing strategies*

**8.11** Once you understand this, we can move on to the next level.

(a) For a **marketing director,** growth in profitable sales becomes the **marketing objective**. It derives from, and is consistent with but not separate from, the corporate objectives.

(b) The **marketing strategy** is the way in which the marketing function organises its activities to achieve a profitable growth in sales.

(i) It could for example seek to do this by introducing new products/services (Ansoff's growth strategy of product development) or by seeking new customers (Ansoff's marketing development).

(ii) At a **marketing mix level**, sales might be increased profitably by a variety of methods such as increasing or decreasing prices, expanding the sales force, investing more money in advertising and so on.

**8.12** Both **strategy and tactics are means to ends**, in other words, ways of achieving objectives. The difference between **strategy and tactics is simply one of detail** and depends on the level from which you are looking.

(a) To a marketing director, the cleanliness of a room will be a mere detail.

(b) To the office cleaner it will however be an objective and entail a plan.

- Audit (take stock, decide what state of cleanliness the room is currently in)
- Decide objectives (what state the room needs to be in by a given time)
- Decide broad strategies (vacuuming, tidying, dusting)
- Decide tactics (where to start, what to use)
- Schedule the order of actions

**Exam Tip**

*Once you realise that the difference between strategy and tactics is a movable line you should feel a great deal more comfortable when drawing up your marketing plans. You do not really need to be precise in your categorisation. The word 'tactics' does not really*

*need to be employed at all. You could move from objectives to strategies (using the Ansoff growth matrix) to the marketing mix. In drawing up your plans for the marketing mix you should move from the general to the particular. For example, a marketing communications manager will decide the balance between pull and push strategies, before getting down to the detail of which particular exhibitions to show the firm's wares in.*

---

**8.13** It is very important to get your thinking clear about this, otherwise your marketing plan and its relationship to the corporate plan will appear confused and your proposals will lose their credibility. To help you further in your thinking please examine and reflect upon the following table.

Eight ways to distinguish between strategic and tactical decisions

1 **Importance:** Strategic decisions are significantly more important.

2 **Level at which conducted:** Strategic decisions usually by more senior management.

3 **Time horizon:** Strategies = longer term. Tactics = shorter term.

4 **Regularity:** Strategy formulation is continuous whereas tactics are periodic.

5 **Nature of problem:** Strategic problems are unstructured and often unique, involving risk and uncertainty. Tactical problems are more structured and repetitive with risks easier to assess.

6 **Information needed:** Strategies require more external information. Tactics depend more on internally generated information.

7 **Detail:** Strategy is broad. Tactics are narrower.

8 **Ease of evaluation:** Strategic decisions are more difficult to make and evaluate.

Source: adapted from *Strategic Marketing,* Weitz and Wensley, 1993

**8.14** To conclude, at **marketing department** level the focus is on the marketing activity.

(a) **Objectives** are developed in line with the corporate objectives and strategy and they are expressed in marketing terms (for example, market share or sales volume).

(b) **Marketing strategy indicates how the marketing mix** will be set to achieve these objectives and the marketing tactics include details of their implementation. In turn these details are expressed in terms of distribution, research, advertising and sales objectives and strategies.

# 9 Corporate strategy and marketing strategy

## How marketing can contribute to the corporate plan

**9.1** Marketing makes a particularly important input to the corporate planning decisions. Information inputs from marketing to the **corporate** planning decisions perform a double duty in that they also provide the bases for deciding marketing objectives and strategies. **Marketing research**

is vital to **all stages** of the marketing plan hence the need for an effective marketing information system.

| Aspect | Comment |
|---|---|
| **The environmental audit** | Reviews the organisation's position in relation to changes in the external environment (social/cultural, legal, economic, political and technological) and provides information which directly affects the setting of corporate objectives. The market place is, by definition, part of the 'environment'. |
| **Competitor analysis** | Provides competitor intelligence, competitor response models and so on which again influence corporate objectives, strategy and contingency planning. |
| **The customer audit** | Assesses the existing and potential customer bases to provide information as to whether to develop new markets. |
| **Product portfolio analysis** | Provides input for decisions as to whether to drop particular products and/or add new ones. |
| **The sales forecast** | Provides the basis for all other functional activities as well as marketing. |

## Exam Tip

Students often find it difficult to relate marketing objectives clearly to corporate objectives and even more difficult to distinguish clearly marketing objectives from corporate objectives. There can be no corporate plan which does not involve products/services and customers. The following diagram from Kotler clearly expresses the interactive two-way relationship between marketing plans and strategic business planning.

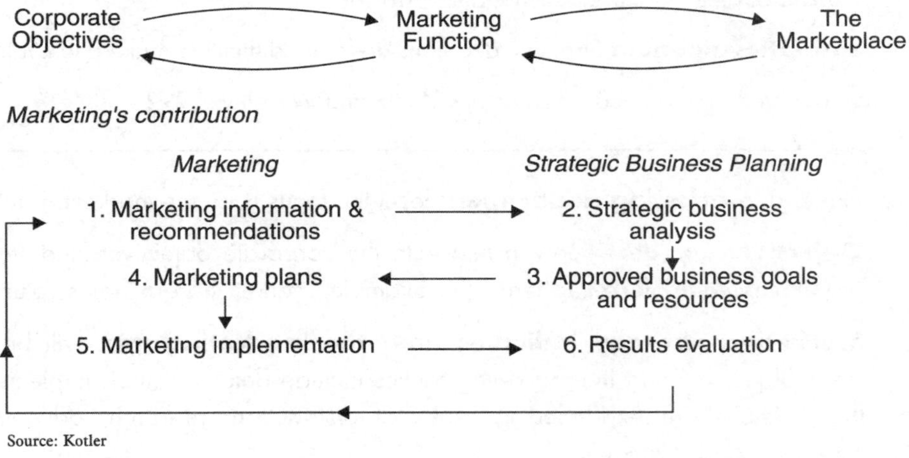


Source: Kotler

**9.2** The **marketing plan** uniquely is concerned with **products** and **markets**.

(a) These are typically stated in terms of market share, sales volume, levels of distribution and profitability.

(b) Decisions might be taken as to the type of products sold to particular customer groups.

**9.3** The marketing manager's plans are often frustrated by other people in the organisation. These 'blockers' can be people in the marketing department but are more likely to be people in other departments. The less an organisation is truly market orientated, the more likely it is that marketing plans are ineffective. Each functional area has its own particular concerns and constraints and, at strategic level, marketers have to take these into account if they want to achieve anything.

## Chapter Roundup

- Take to heart Kotler's distinction between **marketing activity** (the functions performed by the marketing department) and the **marketing concept** (satisfying customer needs to attain organisational goals).
- Within any organisation the marketing function must work with other departments (especially HR) to implement the marketing concept.
- A **market-led firm** is a company in which everyone puts the customer at the centre of decision-making. The customer is not owned by the marketing department.
- Elements of a **market-orientation** include culture, capabilities, organisation, and strategic thinking.
- **Marketing personnel are catalysts** in generating a market-orientation and promoting market-led strategic change.
- **Barriers** to being market-led mainly rest in the way the business is run.
- The role of marketing has changed from being an isolated, specialist staff department to being **integrated** with line management, **widespread** in the organisation and involved in strategic decision making.
- **Strategy** exists on three levels: corporate, business and functional/operational. The marketing concept informs strategy: a defined course of action to achieve specific objectives.
- **Strategic management** is the development, implementation and control of these strategies.
- **Synergistic planning** is a rational process of determining further action based on realistic consideration of the current situation and desired outcome.
- In addition to their focus on **customers**, marketers who want to have a strategic role must consider **competitors** and the organisation's **other stakeholders**.
- **Planning's function** is to co-ordinate resources to increase the chances of achieving objectives. Planning involves making decisions about what has to be done, how and when it should be done and who should do it. An integral part of the planning process is **control**. If plans are to be successful then systems must be established for their modification in the light of outcomes.
- It is important to recognise the **hierarchical** level of planning and control decisions, because decision makers can only make plans or take control action within the sphere of the **authority** that has been **delegated** to them.
- **Corporate decisions** relate to the scope of a firm's activities, the long-term direction of the organisation, and allocation of resources. The '**planning**' **model of strategy formation** suggest a logical sequence which involves **analysing** the current situation, **generating** choices (relating to competitors, products and markets) and **implementing** the chosen strategies.
- There are problems with the 'planning' model. Other models of strategy formation include **incrementalism** and **crafting emergent strategies**.
- There is a **hierarchy of objectives**. Corporate objectives are often expressed in financial terms. Corporate strategies deploy the functions of the business. Corporate strategies set marketing objectives.

## Chapter Roundup (cont'd)

- Marketing contributes significantly to **corporate planning** and formulating **corporate objectives,** as markets and customers are a key part of the corporate environment and are key to the firm's survival.
- Marketing therefore has a lead role in other business functions. Anticipated sales, for example, determine the **volume** produced by the production function. However, available **production capacity** can lead to constraints on what is produced, and **financial limitations** offer a limit to the resources available.

## Quick Quiz

1 What is marketing?

2 What is sales support?

3 What distinguishes a market-led from a marketing-led organisation?

4 What are the underlying assumptions of market-led strategic change?

5 Identify some key issues for market-led companies.

6 What changes might occur in the role of marketing expertise and personnel in a market-led organisation?

7 How would you distinguish between the long- and short-term?

8 What is the purpose of tactical planning?

9 How can critical success factors be used in operations planning?

10 What is the focus of a plan at corporate level? and marketing department level?

11 Give five information inputs which marketing makes to corporate planning.

## Answers to Quick Quiz

1 As a strategic **concept**, marketing promotes the overriding need to achieve customer satisfaction profitably. As a **function**, marketing is concerned with the management of the marketing mix, usually in collaboration with other functions.

2 An essentially reactive model of marketing that supports the sales force with such activities as telemarketing, organising exhibitions and responding to enquiries.

3 A **market-led** organisation focuses on the customer; a **marketing-led** organisation focuses on the marketing department.

4 Organisations must focus on the customer to survive and to be efficient; difficulty in doing this is most likely to raise from internal practices that require significant change to overcome.

5 New customers, new competitors, new organisational types and new ways of doing business.

6 From staff to line; from specialist to strategic; from isolated to widespread.

7 The long-term lies beyond the time horizon of plans that can be usefully quantified.

8 To implement overall or strategic plans by specifying the detail of what is to be done.

9 Since the strategy is dependent on CSFs for its success, CSFs may be used to design an effective structure of tasks to implement the strategy.

10 At corporate level, the focus is on overall success for the whole organisation. The marketing department focuses on its own marketing mix activities with the intention of increasing profitable sales.

11 Environmental audit, competitor analysis; customer audit; product portfolio analysis; sales forecast.

## Action Programme Review

1 (a) **Finance** is all-pervasive. Forecasts for sales revenues affect profit; marketing activities require resources which cost money. Finance is a resource in itself, but also it is the 'language' by which the organisation's performance is reported and controlled.

(b) **Human resources** are the 'people' element of the marketing mix for services. Human resources management specialists are involved in recruiting and training marketing personnel and ensuring that staff pursue organisational objectives.

(c) **Purchasing** – affects product quality, reliability and availability thus playing a significant role in the consumer's image of the product in the marketplace.

2 If market-led strategy is necessary throughout the company, then understanding how other functions in the company work would seem significant – otherwise marketing will be conducted in a vacuum.

3 (a) The reasons for the organisation's existence should be expressed in terms of the consumer or client.

(b) Marketing research should be used to find out:

(i) Who needs help, and in what ways, and how satisfactory is the current help provided

(ii) Where funds should be raised, and what the best approaches should be

(iii) Which political figures are susceptible to lobbying and how such lobbying should best be conducted

(c) Target markets would be identified for charitable acts, fund-raising and influencing.

(d) The charity might also wish to promote an image to the public, perhaps by means of public relations work.

(e) The management of the charity will be aware that they are in competition for funds with other charities, and in competition with other ways of spending money in trying to obtain funds from the public. It should organise its 'sales and marketing' systems to raise funds in the most effective way.

(i) Many charities now engage in telemarketing.

(ii) Many charities have acquired logos – even NHS hospitals have acquired them.

4 The corporate objective is profit growth. The corporate strategy is the decision that this will be achieved by entering new markets, rather than producing new products. The business strategy suggests that those markets include Latin America. The functional strategy involves the decision

to invest in new plant (the production function) which is to be financed by shares rather than loans (the finance function).

**5** Livia Strange's department has generated its own pattern of competitive behaviour. It is an emergent strategy. It conflicts directly with the planned strategy proposed by the consultants. This little case history also makes the additional point that strategies are not only about numbers, targets and grand plans, but about the organisational cultures influencing a people's behaviour.

**6** What would drive your organisation out of business?

## Now try Question 1 at the end of the Study Text

# Part B

## Performance evaluation

# Basic Numerical Analysis

2

| Chapter Topic List | |
|---|---|
| 1 | Setting the scene |
| 2 | The role of finance in marketing |
| 3 | The balance sheet |
| 4 | Profit or cash? |
| 5 | The profit and loss account |
| 6 | Ratio analysis |
| 7 | Segmental analysis and customer profitability |
| 8 | Productivity |
| 9 | The components of time series |
| 10 | Finding the trend |
| 11 | Finding the seasonal variations |
| 12 | Forecasting and time series analysis |

## Syllabus content

- Critical, quantitative evaluation of business and marketing performance over current and historic business cycles

## Key Concepts Introduced

- Assets
- Liability
- Capital
- Liquidity
- Profitability
- Customer/segment profitability
- Productivity
- Time series
- Trend
- Seasonal variations

# 1 Setting the scene

1.1 Element 2 of your syllabus requires you to be familiar with a range of techniques that could be used for measuring performance. This chapter covers the basic processes involved in these techniques. They are all numerical and largely relate to financial data. However, note that we reserve discussion of the financial arithmetic needed for shareholder value analysis to the next chapter.

1.2 Finance is a common language of business, enabling the costs and benefits of different courses of action to be quantified and compared. You may be expected to demonstrate your understanding of the financial implications of the marketing strategies which you propose. In this chapter we discuss some fundamental techniques of analysis.

1.3 Some of the material in this chapter may strike you as rather technical. We think it unlikely that your examination will require you to perform complex calculations but we believe that you will have to demonstrate an appreciation of what these techniques can and cannot do and an understanding of the implications of their results. Note that some *simple* computation *is* likely to be required in your paper.

# 2 The role of finance in marketing

2.1 Those developing marketing strategy should:

(a) **Understand the impact of their decisions on the finances** of the business

(b) Be able to **work effectively with the finance professionals** in the business

(c) Be **competent in the use of financial techniques** necessary in day-to-day management and planning for their own departments

2.2 **Financial comparisons can aid decision-making**

(a) **Past comparisons and trends**. Looking back at the organisation's financial history and records can identify similar situations and help draw conclusions and trends from the information.

(b) **Competitor analysis**. Examining published information of other organisations, such as competitors, for financial indicators may aid decision-making.

(c) **Forecasting** the future is based in part on financial assumptions.

(d) **Modelling**. Financial data may be used to model the effect of decisions.

## The finance department and marketing

2.3 The finance department has three important accounting roles, and produces three different forms of output, all of which are relevant to the marketing department.

(a) **Financial accounting**. For all limited companies, the financial statements are published in a document called the **annual report and accounts**. This is a legal requirement, to let shareholders know how their business is doing.

(i) It will include a **balance sheet**, a **profit and loss account** and a **cash flow statement**. These must follow certain rules laid down by law and by Financial Reporting Standards.

(ii) The annual report also includes a **directors' report** and a **chairman's report** which talk about the past and future of the company in general terms.

(iii) Financial accounting is **important to marketing activities** because the financial effects of marketing activities must be recorded properly and accurately.

(iv) The financial statements are an important communication to outsiders, and thus have a **PR impact**.

(b) **Management accounting**. Management accounts will be produced, usually on a monthly or quarterly basis. These accounts are intended to help the decision-making process within the company.

(c) **Corporate finance** is concerned with ensuring that sufficient **funds** are available to the business in order for it to pursue its objectives. For example, a £25m advertising campaign requires the organisation to have these funds to spend.

## Action Programme 1

Obtain some company reports which contain published accounts. These can be obtained from a variety of sources, including via the *Financial Times* annual report service. Examine the content of the accounts.

## Marketing at Work

The history of the *dot.coms* in 2000 is a salutary lesson of failure to observe financial fundamentals.

Investors piled in huge amounts of money, and dot.coms were rewarded by high share prices, enabling them to raise more money.

A number of different valuation models were adopted, and investors (and stock brokers) abandoned boring performance indicators such as profitability. Internet start-ups raised large capital sums from investors and their corporate performance was assessed on the basis of:

- Market share (bought at whatever expense) or number of subscribers. In January 2001, *amazon.com* announced it was to lay off staff in a bid to return to operating profitability.
- 'Cash burn' – effectively, the rate of cash outflows. Obviously a lower burn rate was 'healthier'. Companies like boo.com invested heavily in the website and promotion but did not have enough cash. It was noted that they failed to appoint a finance director until too late.

Few business-to-consumer dot.coms survived. On a more positive note, the *Financial Times* reported on 1 May 2001 about *Ebookers*:

'Shares in *Ebookers.com* rose 19 percent yesterday after the online travel company said it was on track to achieve positive cash flows by the fourth quarter of this year or first quarter of 2002 at the latest.

'The company said its cash burn would fall from \$3m (£2m) to less than \$1.5m a month in the second half, helping its transition to positive cash flows.

'Ebookers also reported sales in the first quarter to March 31 above analysts' expectations. Pre-tax losses were \$12m (\$22m).

' 'Our focus right now is on cash flow profitability,' said Navneet Bali, finance director. 'Real profitability should follow through soon thereafter because we don't have many fixed assets.'

'Ebookers.com operates in one of the few areas where business-to-consumer e-commerce is still regarded as a promising market.

'Ebookers is already present in 11 European countries and has built strong relationships with airlines over nearly 20 years through its offline subsidiary Flightbookers. Analysts are predicting a \$31.7m loss this year. But after next year's transition to profits of \$2.3m, the company is expected to generate profits of \$20m and earnings per share of 78 cents in 2003. Hence the significance of yesterday's reiteration of the company's cash flow goals and subsequent share price rise. Nevertheless, investors should be packed for a long haul.'

---

# 3 The balance sheet

## The accounting equation

**Key Concepts**

The **assets** of a business are the things it owns which offer an economic benefit.

A **liability** is money owed by a business, for whatever reason. For example, at anyone time, it might owe money to suppliers for goods it has purchased but not yet paid for (trade creditors). It might owe tax.

The **capital** is the amount invested by the owners in the business. Arguably the business 'owes' it to the owners (in a similar way to owing money to creditors).

**3.1** We can put assets together and this gives us the **accounting equation**:

Capital + Liabilities = Assets

This could equally well be written:

Capital = Assets – Liabilities

Since the second part of this equation is what we call **net assets**, we can write, even more simply:

Capital = Net assets

## The balance sheet

**3.2** The accounting equation explains why the 'net assets' and the total of 'capital and reserves' are both equal to £16,100,000 in 20X1 in the balance sheet shown below.

ARC LIMITED
BALANCE SHEETS AT 31 DECEMBER 20X1

| | *20X0* | | *20X1* | |
|---|---|---|---|---|
| *Fixed assets* | £'000 | £'000 | £'000 | £'000 |
| Intangible assets | 100 | | 100 | |
| Tangible assets | 7,900 | | 12,950 | |
| Investments | 100 | | 100 | |
| | | 8,100 | | 13,150 |
| *Current assets* | | | | |
| Stocks | 5,000 | | 15,000 | |
| Debtors | 8,900 | | 27,100 | |
| Cash at bank and in hand | 600 | | - | |
| | 14,500 | | 42,100 | |
| *Creditors: amounts falling due within one year* | | | | |
| Bank loans and overdrafts | - | | 16,200 | |
| Trade creditors | 6,000 | | 10,000 | |
| Accruals and deferred income | 800 | | 1,000 | |
| Other creditors including taxation | 6,200 | | 11,200 | |
| | 13,000 | | 38,400 | |
| *Net current assets* | | 1,500 | | 3,700 |
| *Creditors: amounts falling due after more than one year* | | | | |
| 15% debenture stock | | 600 | | 750 |
| *Net assets* | | 9,000 | | 16,100 |

| | *20X0* | | *20X1* | |
|---|---|---|---|---|
| | £'000 | £'000 | £'000 | £'000 |
| *Capital and reserves* | | | | |
| Called up share capital | | | | |
| Ordinary shares of £1 each | | 6,000 | | 6,000 |
| Profit and loss account reserve | | 3,000 | | 10,100 |
| | | 9,000 | | 16,100 |

**3.3** Particular aspects to note about the balance sheets shown above are as follows.

(a) **Date**. The balance sheet is headed up 'as at 31 December 20X1'. This is telling the user that it is a picture of the affairs of the company **at a point in time**. Over time this picture will change.

(b) **Comparative figures** (figures for the previous period) are always given to indicate movement. They should be prepared on a consistent basis and usually refer to the balance sheet one year ago.

(c) **Equation balances. In the example, capital and reserves (or shareholders' funds) equal net assets.**

**3.4** We will now briefly discuss each heading.

## Fixed assets

**3.5** A **fixed asset** is any asset, tangible or intangible, acquired for retention by a **business** to give continuing economic benefits (ie it must be in use for over one year) by **the business**, and not held for resale in the normal course of trading.

(a) A **tangible** fixed asset is a physical asset. A salesman's car is a tangible fixed asset.

(b) An **intangible** fixed asset does not have a physical existence. The expense of acquiring **patent rights** and some NPD costs on occasions would be classified as an intangible fixed asset. The value of a **brand name** also comes under this category although this is a matter of considerable dispute. (We deal with this later in this section.)

(c) **Investments** held for the long term would be classified as fixed assets.

**3.6** Fixed assets, except freehold land, **wear out or lose their usefulness in the course of time**. The accounts of a business try to recognise this by gradually writing off the asset's cost in the **profit and loss account** over several accounting periods to reflect the loss in value in the balance sheet. This is called **depreciation**.

## Current assets

**3.7** **Current assets** fall into two categories.

(a) **Items owned** by the business (or owed to the business) which will be turned into cash within one year

(b) **Cash**, including money in the bank, owned by the business

These assets are **current** as they are **continually flowing** through the business.

## Stock

**3.8** **Stock** comprises **goods for use or resale**. They can exist either in their original form (for example, as the component parts which when assembled make up the product), or as **work in progress** or as **finished goods** awaiting resale. The basic rule of stock valuation is that stock should be valued at the **lower of cost or net realisable value**.

(a) **Cost** is the amount **paid** for the stock in cash terms to bring it to its current location and condition: raw materials, manufacturing time and labour costs are typical elements of cost.

(b) **Net realisable value** (NRV) is defined as the expected selling price, less any costs still to be incurred getting the stock ready for sale and then selling it.

## Debtors

**3.9** A debtor is a person, business or company who **owes money to the business**. When the debt is finally paid, the debtor disappears as an asset, to be replaced by cash at bank and in hand, another asset. **Most debtors are customers who have bought on credit but have not yet paid**.

**3.10** This is why many firms have **credit control departments**. They assess the creditworthiness of new customers, and monitor their payments record. They chase any late-payers and employ debt collectors. The purpose of any sale is to make a profit, and offering credit has a cost and a risk.

## Current liabilities

**3.11** A **liability** is owed **by** a business **to** another person or organisation (eg to the bank or government). Here are some examples.

- Loans repayable within one year
- A bank overdraft is normally payable on demand
- A **trade creditor** (owed money for debts incurred in the course of trading)
- Taxation payable
- Accrued charges (expenses incurred, for which no bill has yet been received)

## Long-term liabilities

**3.12** Long-term liabilities include:

- Loans which are repayable after one year, such as a bank loan
- A mortgage loan, which is a loan specifically secured against a freehold property
- Debentures (securities issued at a fixed rate of interest repayable by a specified date)

## Capital and reserves

**3.13** The **capital and reserves** figures in the balance sheet represent the **shareholders' funds**.

(a) The original **capital** contributed by the ordinary shareholders (the cost of the shares).

(b) The **profits** the business has **retained** over the years **which** are accumulated in the profit and loss account balance.

## Brand valuation

**3.14** **Companies expect to derive long-term future economic benefit from the value of their brands**. Some have wished to reflect the value of the brands on their balance sheets, since they would then most truly reflect the worth of the company. While not actually illegal, this is frowned upon by auditors and a very strong case would have to be made before it would be permitted.

(a) What **valuation methodology** should be adopted?

(b) Should brands be treated as an **intangible fixed asset**, like patents, in the **published financial statements**?

(c) **How should brands be treated in the internal decision-making processes of the company**?

**3.15** **Carrying out a brand valuation exercise**

(a) A **brand audit** identifies the strength of the brand.

(b) The **current earnings** and **future prospects** are assessed

(c) The brand is given a capital value. **Discounted cash flow (DCF) analysis** might be used to value the brand based on the revenue it is expected to produce in the future. We discuss DCF in the next chapter.

### 3.16 Sources of brand strength

| Source | Weighting | Comment |
|---|---|---|
| **Leadership** | 25% | How dominant is the brand in its sector? High scores are earned for dominance. |
| **Market** | 10% | What are the growth characteristics of the market? |
| **Stability** | 15% | Well established brands that enjoy consumer loyalty will receive higher strength scores. |
| **Internationality** | 25% | International brands are generally worth more than national ones, as they are not vulnerable to one market, and a brand might be in another stage of its life cycle in an overseas market. |
| **Trend** | 10% | A trend indicates a brand's ability to sustain itself. Reductions in sales volume reduce profit, but also make price increases harder to justify. |
| **Support** | 10% | Marketing expenditure can support a brand, but it must be of the right quality (eg a successful re-positioning). |
| **Protection** | 5% | (eg Patent protection, copyright, imitation) |

**Exam Tip**

*Brand valuation is a means of increasing the market value of a company so that it would appear too expensive to be a potential target for takeover. High brand values also enable firms to raise money, by issuing shares.*

# 4 Profit or cash?

**4.1** Businesses aim to make a profit. We can define profit in very simple terms as follows.

$$P = S - E$$

Where P = Profit
S = Sales value (or revenue)
E = Expenses (or costs)

**4.2 EXAMPLE**

(a) As a very simple example, suppose that you buy a book for £8. You then sell it to a friend for £10. Obviously, you are now £2 better off, and this £2 represents your profit.

(b) The relationship between profit and cash in the example above is simple and direct. The £2 profit was represented by £2 in cash.

(c) But what if your friend had given you an IOU for the £10, to be paid in one month's time? You have still made a **profit** of £2 on the sale of your book, but you are £8 worse off in terms of **cash** than you were before you touched the book.

(d) **Profit and cash are not the same in the short term.**

## Key Concepts

**Liquidity**. Liquid assets are cash or assets which can be converted quickly and easily into cash. Limited companies are **not** allowed to continue trading if they cannot pay bills as they fall due. Liquidity is therefore very important to them.

**Profitability**. The excess of revenue over costs.

**4.3** We can demonstrate the significance using a diagram.

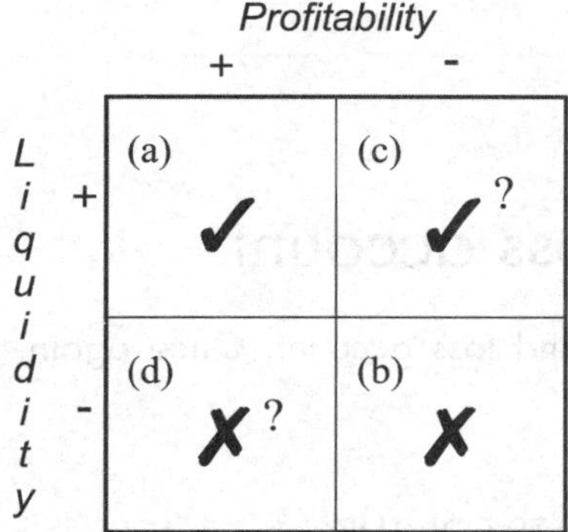


(a) **Profitable and liquid**. Such a firm will survive as it can pay its bills as they fall due and it can attract investment because it is profitable.

(b) **Neither liquid nor profitable**. Such a firm cannot pay bills as they become due and it cannot attract investment because it is not profitable and it therefore will not give a good return to the investor. It will not survive.

(c) **Not profitable but still liquid**. The company has money to pay bills in the short term but it is unprofitable and therefore would not be expected to survive in the long term.

(d) **Profitable but not liquid**. The company in this situation would have difficulty surviving in the **short-term** as it cannot pay its bills. However, its profitability should attract **long-term** investment.

## Sales volume versus profit

**4.4** A business which is **increasing its sales revenue**, perhaps as a result of increased sales effort, is **not necessarily increasingly profitable**. If **new sales are won on the basis of substantially increased costs, or by offering significant discounts**, it is possible to **increase revenue without increasing profits**.

(a) **Period 1**. For example, a business sells its products for £10 each and in **period 1** sales = 10 units and total expenses £80.

Profit = revenue – expenses
£20 £100 £80

(b) **Period 2**

After an increased expenditure on marketing support, costs increase by £20 and sales increase to 12 units.

£20 = £120 – £100

Although revenue has increased by 20% the profit has stayed the same.

**4.5** Alternatively if the additional sales are earned by offering significant **discounts** so that the sales price per unit becomes £8 each, it can be seen that **both** revenue **and** profit can actually fall, despite **sales volume** rising to 12 units each.

£16 = £96 – £80

## Action Programme 2

Why do you think the law now enables businesses to charge interest on overdue debts?

# 5 The profit and loss account

**5.1** We now turn to the profit and loss account. Once again, as an example, let us look at the accounts of ARC Ltd.

ARC LIMITED
PROFIT AND LOSS ACCOUNTS FOR THE
YEARS ENDED 31 DECEMBER

| | *20X0* | *20X1* |
|---|---|---|
| | £'000 | £'000 |
| Turnover | 53,470 | 98,455 |
| Cost of sales | 40,653 | 70,728 |
| Gross profit | 12,817 | 27,727 |
| Distribution costs | 2,317 | 4,911 |
| Administrative expenses | 1,100 | 2,176 |
| Profit on ordinary activities before interest | 9,400 | 20,640 |
| Interest receivable | 100 | 40 |
| Interest payable | - | (280) |
| Profit for the financial year | 9,500 | 20,400 |
| Tax on profit on ordinary activities | 3,200 | 5,200 |
| Profit on ordinary activities after taxation | 6,300 | 15,200 |
| Dividends | | |
| Ordinary: interim (paid) | 1,100 | 2,100 |
| final (proposed) | 3,000 | 6,000 |
| Retained profit for the financial year | 2,200 | 7,100 |

**5.2** The profit and loss account is a statement in which **revenues and expenditure** are compared to arrive at a figure of **profit or loss**.

**5.3** Most of the **marketing expenses** will appear in this section.

(a) **Distribution costs**. These are expenses associated with the process of selling and delivering goods to customers and in published accounts they will **include marketing expenses**.

- Salaries of marketing and sales directors and management
- Salaries and commissions of sales staff
- Travelling and entertainment expenses of sales people
- Marketing costs (eg advertising, market research, sales promotion)
- Costs of running and maintaining delivery vans
- Discounts allowed to customers for early payment of their debts
- Bad debts written off

(b) **Administration expenses**

- Salaries of directors, management and office staff
- Rent and rates
- Insurance
- Telephone and postage
- Printing and stationery
- Heating and lighting

## Capital and revenue items

**5.4 Distinction between capital and revenue items**

(a) **Capital items** are related to financing decisions, such as the purchase of a fixed asset and how the purchase is to be financed.

(b) **Revenue items** are related to trading decisions, that is the sale, purchase and expense, transactions associated with normal trading.

(c) (i) The type of decision-making involved will be very different for revenue and capital items.

(ii) The accounting treatment for capital items is different to that of revenue items.

# 6 Ratio analysis

**6.1** The financial statements provide sources of useful information about the condition of a business. They are in the **public domain** and can be an important feature in a **competitor analysis**. A company which is losing money and has borrowed heavily may behave quite differently in marketing terms than one which has many sources of cash.

**6.2** The analysis and interpretation of these statements can be carried out by calculating certain ratios and then **using the ratios for comparison**.

(a) **One year and the next** for a particular business, in order to identify any trends, or significantly better or worse results than before.

(b) **One business and another**, to establish which business has performed better, and in what ways. You should be very careful, when comparing two different businesses, to ensure that the accounts have been prepared in a similar way.

**6.3** Below we identify some typical ratios used.

## Profitability and performance ratios

### Profit margin

6.4 **Profit margin** is the **ratio of profit before interest and tax over sales turnover**. For example, in 20X0, ARC's profit margin was 17.6% (hence costs as a percentage of sales were 82.4%). **Profit Before Interest and Tax** (PBIT), is also known as the operating profit. In the accounts of ARC Ltd, the PBIT for 20X1 is £20,640,000 and for 20X0, £9,400,000. The profit margins for the two years are:

| *20X0* | *20X1* |
|---|---|
| $\frac{9,400}{53,470} = 17.6\%$ | $\frac{20,640}{98,455} = 21\%$ |

If the ratio of costs to sales goes down, the profit margin will automatically go up. For example, if the cost: sales ratio changes from 80% to 75%, the profit margin will go up from 20% to 25%. What does this mean?

- A **high margin** indicates costs are controlled and/or sales prices are high.
- A **low margin** can mean **high costs** or **low prices**.

### Asset turnover

6.5 **Asset turnover** is the ratio of sales turnover in a year to the amount of **net assets** which should equate to the amount invested in the business. In the accounts of ARC Ltd, the asset turnover for 20X1 and 20X0 is:

| *20X0* | *20X1* |
|---|---|
| $\frac{53,470}{9,000} = 5.9$ times | $\frac{98,455}{16,100} = 6.1$ times |

This means that for every £1 of assets employed in 20X0, the company generated sales turnover of £5.90 per annum. To utilise assets more efficiently, managers should try to create a higher volume of sales and a higher asset turnover ratio.

### Return on capital employed (ROCE)

6.6 **Return on capital employed** (ROCE) is the amount of profit as a percentage of capital employed (net assets). If a company makes a profit of £30,000, we do not know how good or bad the result is until we look at the amount of capital which has been invested to achieve the profit. £30,000 might be a good sized profit for a small firm, but this would not be good enough for a 'giant' firm such as Marks & Spencer. For this reason, it is helpful to measure performance by relating profits to capital employed. The ROCE of ARC Ltd for 20X1 and 20X1 is:

| *20X0* | *20X1* |
|---|---|
| $\frac{9,400}{9,000} = 104.4\%$ | $\frac{20,640}{16,100} = 128\%$ |

6.7 You may already have realised that there is a mathematical connection between return on capital employed, profit margin and asset turnover:

$$\frac{\text{Profit}}{\text{Capital employed}} = \frac{\text{Profit}}{\text{Sales}} \times \frac{\text{Sales}}{\text{Capital employed}}$$

$$\text{ie ROCE} = \text{Profit margin} \times \text{Asset turnover}$$

This is important. If we accept that ROCE is the single most important measure of business performance, comparing profit with the amount of capital invested, we can go on to say that business performance is dependent on two separate 'subsidiary' factors, each of which contributes to ROCE, **profit margin** and **asset turnover**.

### 6.8 EXAMPLE

Company A and Company B both sell electrical goods. Both have £100,000 capital employed (net assets) and both want to make a target ROCE of 20%. Company A is a specialist retailer and Company B is a discount warehouse.

(a) **Specialist Company A** might decide to sell its products at a fairly high price and make a profit margin on sales of 10%. It would then need an asset turnover of 2.0 times to achieve a ROCE of 20%. It would therefore need annual sales of £200,000.

(b) **Discount warehouse Company B** might decide to cut its prices so that its profit margin is only 2½%. Provided that it can achieve an asset turnover of eight times a year, attracting more customers with its lower prices, it will **still make a ROCE of 2½%** × **8 = 20%**. It would need annual sales of £800,000.

## Action Programme 3

What might be the implications for marketing mix decisions of the two approaches to achieving a target ROCE in 6.8 above?

## Action Programme 4

Suppose that Swings and Roundabouts Ltd achieved the following results in 20X6:

| | |
|---|---|
| Sales | £100,000 |
| Profit | £5,000 |
| Capital employed | £20,000 |

The company's management wish to decide whether to raise its selling prices. They think that if they do so, they can raise the profit margin to 10% and by introducing extra capital of £55,000, sales turnover could be increased to £150,000. You are required to evaluate the decision in terms of effect on ROCE, profit margin and asset turnover.

6.9 A single ratio is nearly meaningless. What is important is the movement in that ratio over time and the comparison of that ratio with other companies in a similar business.

6.10 **Earnings per share** shows the return due to the ordinary shareholders. This simply divides profit after tax by the average number of ordinary shares in issue whilst the profit was generated.

6.11 The **price/earnings (P/E) ratio** reflects the investors' view of the future prospects of a share. Share prices depend on expectations of future earnings.

$$P/E = \frac{\text{The market price of a share (in pence)}}{\text{Earnings per share}}$$

## Gearing

**6.12** **Gearing** is a method of comparing how much of the long-term capital of a business is provided by **equity** (ordinary shares and reserves) and how much is provided by long-term **loan capital**.

**6.13** **Why is gearing important?**

(a) If a company's gearing is **too high** (say over 50%), **we might find that it is difficult to raise more loans**.

(b) **Loan capital is cheaper**, because the interest cost diminishes in real terms if secured on company assets and attracts tax benefits.

(c) Interest **must** be paid, whereas the directors of a company can decide **not** to pay a dividend.

(d) High gearing might be considered **risky** for lenders is that the more loan capital a business has, the bigger becomes the size of profit before interest and tax (PBIT) which is necessary to meet demands for interest payments.

## Operational ratios

**6.14** **Operational ratios relate to the cash cycle of a business**.

(a) A business which cannot pay its debts as they fall due is insolvent. **Liquidity** is a critical and urgent issue, which is why working capital is monitored thoroughly. A company facing crises in liquidity has few options.

(b) Often external parties, such a banks, will provide extra funds, but in extreme cases **marketing strategies must be devised to raise as much cash as possible**.

**6.15** Consequently the finance function will monitor **turnover periods**. These ratios, usually expressed in days, measure how long or how many times the business is exchanging cash over a period of time.

**6.16** **Debtors' turnover period**, or **debt collection period**: the length of the credit period taken by customers or the time between the sale of an item and the receipt of cash for the sale from the customer.

(a) This describes the level of debtors compared with the sales turnover. So the ratio for ARC Ltd is:

| | *20X0* | *20X1* |
|---|---|---|
| $\frac{\text{Debtors}}{\text{Sales}}$ | $\frac{8,900}{53,470} = 16\%$ | $\frac{27,100}{98,455} = 28\%$ |

(b) This can be expressed in days. By multiplying our ratio by 365 we recognise that the debtors are on average:

| *20X0* | *20X1* |
|---|---|
| $\frac{8,900}{53,470} \times 365 = 61 \text{ days}$ | $\frac{26,700}{98,455} \times 365 = 99 \text{ days}$ |

**6.17** We can, of course, do similar turnover calculations for **stock turnover period**. This is the length of time an item stays in stores before use.

$$\frac{\text{Average finished goods stocks (use closing stock)}}{\text{Total cost of goods sold in the period}} \times 365 \text{ days}$$

| | *20X0* | *20X1* |
|---|---|---|
| Stock turnover period | $\frac{5,000}{40,653} \times 365 = 45$ days | $\frac{15,000}{70,728} \times 365 = 77$ days |

**6.18** Similarly, the **creditors' turnover period**, or period of credit taken from suppliers, is the length of time between the purchase of materials and the payment to suppliers.

$$\frac{\text{Average trade creditors (use closing creditors)}}{\text{Total purchases in the period*}} \times 365 \text{ days}$$

| | *20X0* | *20X1* |
|---|---|---|
| Creditors' payment period | $\frac{6,000}{40,653} \times 365 = 54$ days | $\frac{10,000}{70,728} \times 365 = 52$ days |

* Cost of sales can be substituted as an approximation

Again these can be expressed in days or months.

**6.19** The **importance** of turnover ratios is their impact on **cash requirements**. An increase in the **stock turnover ratio** or in the **debtor turnover ratio** means that more money is being tied up in funding **working capital** and this may not be desirable.

## Liquidity ratios

**6.20** Liquidity as we have seen is an organisation's ability to convert its assets into cash to meet all the demands for payments when they fall due. They are particularly important for **credit control**.

**6.21** **Current liabilities** are items which must be paid for in the near future. When payment becomes due, enough cash must be available to make the payment.

**6.22** Let us see how some ratios apply.

| | *Current ratio* | *Quick ratio* |
|---|---|---|
| Ratio | $\frac{\text{Current assets}}{\text{Current liabilities}}$ | $\frac{\text{Current assets less stock}}{\text{Current liabilities}}$ |
| ARC 20X0 | $\frac{14,500}{13,000} = 1.1:1$ | $\frac{14,500-5,000}{13,000} = 0.7:1$ |
| ARC 20X1 | $\frac{42,100}{38,400} = 1.1:1$ | $\frac{42,100-15,000}{38,400} = 0.7:1$ |

**6.23** The best way to judge liquidity would be to look at the current ratio at different dates over a period of time. If the trend is towards a **lower current ratio**, we would judge that the **liquidity position is getting steadily worse**.

## Action Programme 5

Calculate liquidity and working capital ratios from these accounts of a manufacturer of products for the construction industry.

| | *2003* | *2002* |
|---|---|---|
| | £m | £m |
| **Turnover** | 2,065.0 | 1,788.7 |
| Cost of sales | 1,478.6 | 1,304.0 |
| Gross profit | 586.4 | 484.7 |
| **Current assets** | | |
| Stocks | 119.0 | 109.0 |
| Debtors (note 1) | 400.9 | 347.4 |
| Short-term investments | 4.2 | 18.8 |
| Cash at bank and in hand | 48.2 | 48.0 |
| | 572.3 | 523.2 |
| Creditors: amounts falling due within one year | | |
| Loans and overdrafts | 49.1 | 35.3 |
| Corporation taxes | 62.0 | 46.7 |
| Dividend | 19.2 | 14.3 |
| Creditors (note 2) | 370.7 | 324.0 |
| | 501.0 | 420.3 |
| Net current assets | 71.3 | 102.9 |
| *Notes* | | |
| 1 Trade debtors | 329.8 | 285.4 |
| 2 Trade creditors | 236.2 | 210.8 |

## Exam Tip

*Many of the analytical techniques in this chapter can be used in evaluation of strategies.*

# 7 Segmental analysis and customer profitability

7.1 **One of the most important tools for market analysis is that of segmentation.** We can approach this firstly by examining what market segments we currently market in and how big a contribution each segment is making to total turnover and profit. Finally we should consider whether each market segment is in growth or decline.

**7.2** A segmental analysis might therefore look as follows.

| *Market segment* | *Turnover* | *Proportion of total turnover* | *Profit* | *Proportion of total profit* |
|---|---|---|---|---|
| | £k | | £k | |
| A | 500 | 14% | 50 | 9% |
| B | 1,000 | 28% | 200 | 36% |
| C | 1,500 | 44% | 150 | 27% |
| D | 500 | 14% | 150 | 27% |

**7.3** The following return on sales apply to each segment.

| *Market segment* | *Turnover* | *Profit* | *Profit as a % of turnover* |
|---|---|---|---|
| | £k | £k | |
| A | 500 | 50 | 10 |
| B | 1,000 | 200 | 20 |
| C | 1,500 | 150 | 10 |
| D | 500 | 150 | 30 |

**7.4** You will note that each segment offers different profit opportunities.

## How to calculate profits on a segmental basis

**7.5** Identifying total turnover is easy. A segment is a collection of customers, and revenue streams from them are fairly easy to identify.

**7.6** Identifying costs is much harder. Here are some different types of cost.

(a) **Fixed vs variable**

(i) **Fixed costs**: you will incur these however many or however few items you produce or sell. Factory rent is an example.

(ii) **Variable costs**: these relate directly to the number of units produced. For example, a variable cost in producing books is paper.

(b) **Controllable vs uncontrollable**

(i) Controllable costs are at management discretion, such as an advertising campaign.

(ii) Uncontrollable costs are those which, in the short run at least, management are committed to.

(c) **Direct vs indirect**

(i) A direct cost relates to a unit of production (eg the amount of material).

(ii) Indirect costs or overheads **cannot** be tied specifically to a unit of production. However, new management accounting techniques such as activity based costing try to set up the link.

(d) **Avoidable vs unavoidable**

(i) Avoidable cost: this cost is affected by a decision.

(ii) Unavoidable cost: this cost will not be affected by a decision.

For example, the cost of the managing director's salary will not be affected by a decision not to serve an individual customer.

### 7.7 Typical marketing costs

| Cost | Comment |
|---|---|
| Direct selling expense | Personal calls by salesperson |
| Indirect selling | Sales admin, supervision |
| Marketing research | Consultancies, primary data collection, analysis |
| Advertising | Media costs |
| Sales promotion | Consumer, trade etc |
| Transport | Carriage costs |
| Storage | Warehousing |
| Order processing | Checking, billing, bad debts |

7.8 These can be allocated, in different ways, to products, customer groups, and sales territories. We are currently interested in segments.

**Step 1.** Identify revenue derived from a segment

**Step 2.** Identify direct product costs (eg materials)

**Step 3.** Identify marketing costs

**Step 4.** Allocate **avoidable** costs to the segment (ie those costs which would be saved if the segment were not serviced)

## *Customer profitability*

**Marketing at Work**

Take the Post Office. A uniform price is paid for a first class stamp irrespective of whether it is to be delivered to an address five miles away or five hundred (in the UK), despite the significant differences in transport costs. Of course the advantages of a uniform price are that there are savings on the costs of administering a wide range of prices, and that people are encouraged to use the postal services.

7.9 It is the case in many industries that the total costs of servicing customers can vary depending on **how** customers are serviced. Here are two examples.

(a) **Volume discounts**. A customer who places **one large order** is given a discount, presumably because it benefits the supplier to do so.

(b) The **different rates** charged by power utilities to domestic as opposed to business users. This reflects the administrative cost of dealing with individual customers.

## Key Concept

**Customer or segment profitability** is the 'total sales revenue generated from a customer or customer group, less all the costs that are incurred in servicing that customer or customer group.'

### 7.10 EXAMPLE

Seth Ltd supplies shoes to Narayan Ltd and Kipling Ltd. Each pair of shoes has a list price of £50 each; as Kipling buys in bulk, Kipling receives a 10% trade discount for every order over 100 shoes. It costs £1,000 to deliver each order. In the year so far, Kipling has made five orders of 100 shoes each. Narayan Ltd receives a 15% discount irrespective of order size, because Narayan Ltd collects the shoes, thereby saving Seth Ltd any distribution costs. The cost of administering each order is £50. Narayan makes ten orders in the year, totalling 420 pairs of shoes. Which relationship is the most profitable for Seth?

### 7.11 SOLUTION

You can see below that the profit earned by Seth in servicing Narayan is greater, despite the increased discount.

| | *Kipling* | *Narayan* |
|---|---|---|
| Number of shoes | 500 | 420 |
| | £ | £ |
| Revenue (after discount) | 22,500 | 17,850 |
| Transport | (5,000) | - |
| Administration | (250) | (500) |
| Net profit | 17,250 | 17,350 |

**7.12** **Customer profitability analysis (CPA)** focuses on profits generated by customers and suggests that profit does not automatically increase with sales revenue.

(a) The benefits of CPA are that a **company can focus its efforts on customers which promise the highest profit**, or at least it can **rationalise its approach to those which do not**. Note that the concern is **relative** differences in profitability.

(b) The obvious problem with CPA is identifying which customers or customer groups generate the most profit.

(c) This is a consideration that must be brought into **market segmentation** decisions. The firm's **existing customer groupings may reflect administrative measures (eg sales force convenience) rather than their strategic value or market realities**.

**7.13** It is necessary to focus on the right costs for comparison.

(a) Costs **common to all customers** (eg sales director's basic salary) would not be avoided by failing to serve **one** of them.

(b) Furthermore, you have to be careful that you **choose the 'right' product cost**. The 'cost' of a product as revealed by the accounting system might include an amount of marketing overhead, which may **not** be avoided by ceasing to serve a customer. Therefore only **avoidable costs** should be taken into account.

**7.14** Ward suggests the following format for a statement of customer or segment profitability.

| | | £'000 |
|---|---|---|
| Sales revenue | | X |
| Less direct product cost | | (X) |
| | | X |
| Customer or segment-specific variable costs: | | |
| – distribution | X | |
| – rebates and discounts | X | |
| – promotion etc | X | |
| | | (X) |
| | | X |
| Other costs | | |
| – sales force | X | |
| – customer service | X | |
| – management cost | X | |
| | | (X) |
| | | X |
| Financing cost | | |
| – credit period | X | |
| – customer-specific inventory | X | |
| | | (X) |
| Customer or segment profitability | | X |

**7.15** Such a report can highlight the differences between the cost of servicing different individuals or firms. This information can be used for the following purposes.

(a) Directing management effort to cutting **customer or segment specific costs**. Installing an EDI system can save the costs of paperwork, data input and so forth.

(b) **Identifying those customers who are expensive to service**, thereby suggesting action to increase profitability.

(c) Using this as part of a **comparison with competitors' costs**. A firm which services a customer more cheaply than a competitor can use this cost advantage to offer extra benefits to the customer.

(d) CPA can indicate cases where **profitability might be endangered**, for example by servicing customers for whom a firm's core competence is not especially relevant.

### Marketing at Work

Pareto's law, or the 80:20 rule applies here. In retail banking, wealthier customers account for a significant proportion of bank's profits. Hence many banks are targeting the 'new affluent' by setting up private bank subsidiaries for customers with assets of over £50,000.

## Market performance ratios

**7.16** An organisation should study information not only about its share of a particular market, but also the performance of the market as a whole.

(a) **Some markets are more profitable than others**. The reasons why this might be so (rivalry among existing firms, the threat of new entrants, the bargaining power of buyers, the bargaining power of suppliers and the threat from substitute products or services) were discussed in an earlier chapter.

(b) Some markets will be new, others growing, some mature and others declining. The stage in the product's life cycle might be relevant to performance analysis.

Information about market performance is needed to enable an organisation to plan and control its product-market strategy.

**7.17** We can, of course, now make projections for these segments to determine where we are likely to be in the future and whether we need to consider moving into **new segments**.

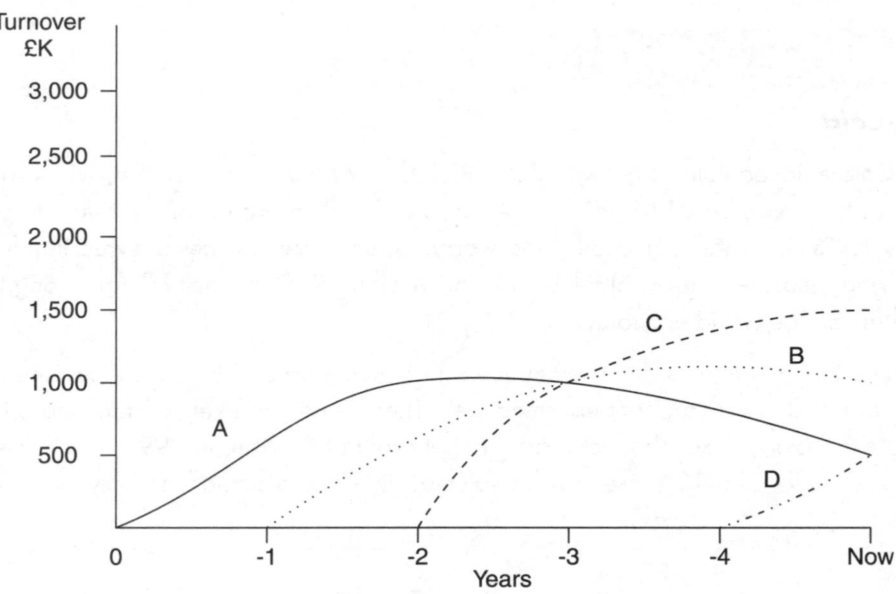


(a) Segment A is in decline and a relatively low contributor to profit.

(b) Segment B is contributing well to turnover and is the major contributor to profit.

(c) Segment C is growing. This is the major contributor to turnover and a relatively high contributor to profit.

(d) Segment D is a relatively new segment for us. Sales to this segment are likely to rise, and so could become our future major contributor to profit.

# 8 Productivity

**Key Concept**

**Productivity** is the ratio of $\frac{\text{Outputs}}{\text{Inputs}}$ or $\frac{\text{Output units}}{\text{Input units}}$

**8.1** For example, a measure of productivity might be revenue/profit per employee.

| | *Revenue* | *Profits* | *Employees* |
|---|---|---|---|
| Deutsche Telecom | $41.8bn | $2.5bn | 179,000 |
| TeleKom Italia | $27.3bn | $2.2bn | 127,000 |
| BT | $25.7bn | $2.8bn | 124,000 |

In this example, BT appears to be most productive generating $22,000 profit per employee compared with $17,000 for TeleKom Italia and $14,000 for Deutsche Telecom.

**8.2** Productivity can be targeted to marketing measures too.

**8.3 Examples of productivity relating to marketing costs**

- Increases in customer recognition of a brand name per £ of advertising
- Number of sales leads generated by an exhibition
- Response rate to direct mailshots
- Number of hits on a website converted into purchases per cost of website

## Marketing at Work

***Coca-Cola***

Coca-Cola enjoyed volume growth of 7 – 8% pa in the 15 years to 1998, with profits rising 18% pa. However, on 21/4/99, it revealed a 13% fall in profits, and a return to shareholders of only 1.4%. The share price fell. Most worrying, unit-case volumes of syrup (the firm's preferred underlying measure of growth) fell by 1% Jan–March 1999, the first fall for a long time. Coca-Cola blamed the world economy.

Coke's recent growth was due to a unique set of circumstances. It had rationalised its bottling operations and *Pepsi* had not performed well. There is now market resistance to price increases. Selling expenses are $6.6bn, compared to net profit of $3.5bn. In 1997, a 4% rise in selling expenses produced a 10% rise in sales volumes. In 1998 a similar rise only increased volumes by 6%.

*Update*

Since that time, Coca-Cola has faced a public relations crisis in Belgium and two changes of chief executive. It is still successful, but is facing yet more changes in direction, and is investing in more brands.

In India, Coca-Cola markets itself and an Indian sub-brand *ThumsUp*

# 9 The components of time series

## Key Concept

A **time series** is a series of figures or values recorded over time.

**9.1** The following are examples of time series.

- Output at a factory each day for the last month
- Monthly sales over the last two years
- Total annual costs for the last ten years
- The Retail Prices Index each month for the last ten years
- The number of people employed by a company each year for the last 20 years

**9.2** The main features of a time series are as follows.

- A trend
- Seasonal variations or fluctuations
- Cycles, or cyclical variations
- Non-recurring, random variations

## The trend

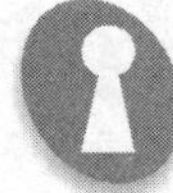

### Key Concept

The **trend** is the underlying long-term movement over time in the values of the data recorded.

**9.3 EXAMPLE: PREPARING TIME SERIES GRAPHS AND IDENTIFYING TRENDS**

| | *Output per labour hour* Units | *Cost per unit* £ | *Number of employees* |
|---|---|---|---|
| 20X4 | 30 | 1.00 | 100 |
| 20X5 | 24 | 1.08 | 103 |
| 20X6 | 26 | 1.20 | 96 |
| 20X7 | 22 | 1.15 | 102 |
| 20X8 | 21 | 1.18 | 103 |
| 20X9 | 17 | 1.25 | 98 |
| | (A) | (B) | (C) |

(a) In time series (A) there is a **downward trend** in the output per labour hour. Output per labour hour did not fall every year, because it went up between 20X5 and 20X6, but the long-term movement is clearly a downward one.

*Graph showing trend of output per labour hour in years 20X4-X9*

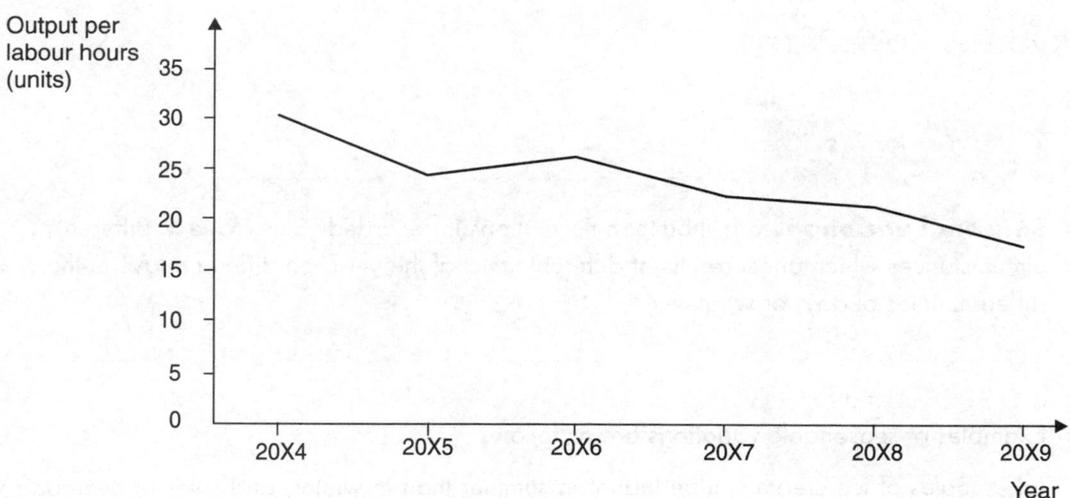


(b) In time series (B) there is an **upward trend** in the cost per unit. Although unit costs went down in 20X7 from a higher level in 20X6, the basic movement over time is one of rising costs.

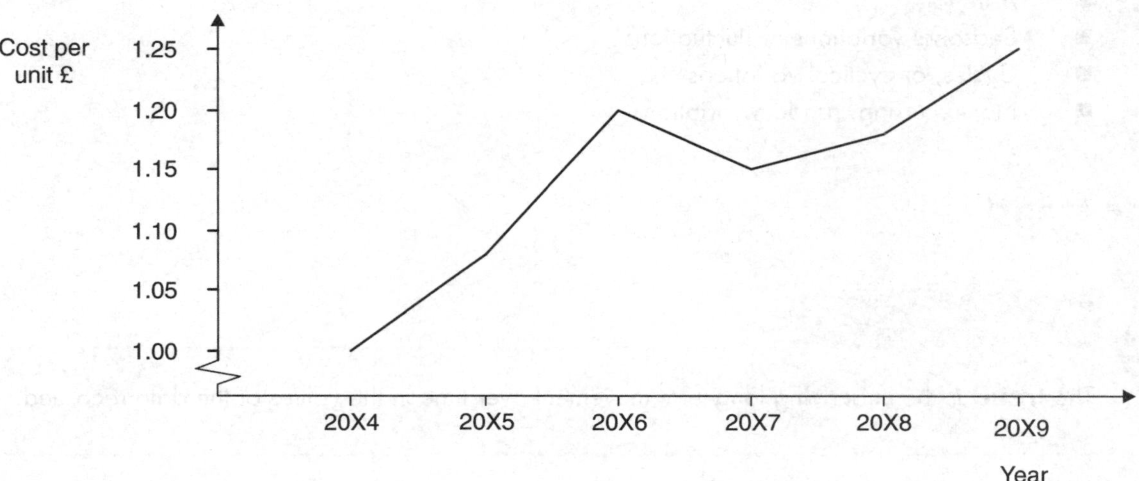


(c) In time series (C) there is no clear movement up or down, and the number of employees remained fairly constant around 100. The trend is therefore a **static**, or **level one**.

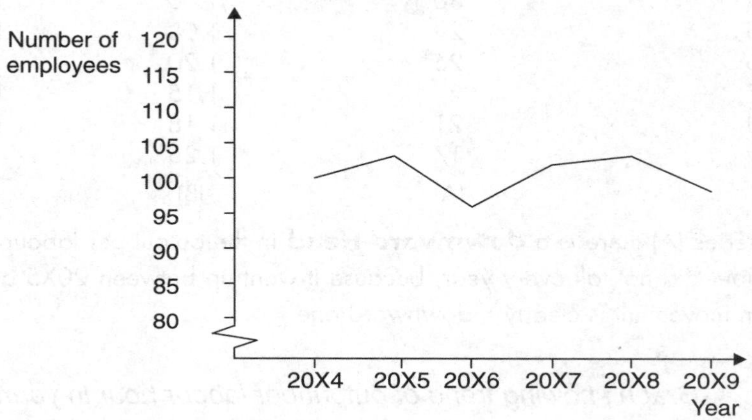


## Seasonal variations

**Key Concept**

**Seasonal variations** are short-term fluctuations in recorded values, due to different circumstances which affect results at different times of the year, on different days of the week, at different times of day, or whatever.

**9.4** Examples of seasonable variations are as follows.

(a) Sales of ice cream will be higher in summer than in winter, and sales of overcoats will be higher in autumn than in spring.

(b) Shops might expect higher sales shortly before Christmas, or in their winter and summer sales.

(c) Sales might be higher on Friday and Saturday than on Monday.

(d) The telephone network may be heavily used at certain times of the day (such as mid-morning and mid-afternoon) and much less used at other times (such as in the middle of the night).

**9.5 EXAMPLE: A TREND AND SEASONAL VARIATIONS**

The number of customers served by a company of travel agents over the past four years is shown in the following **historigram** (time series graph).

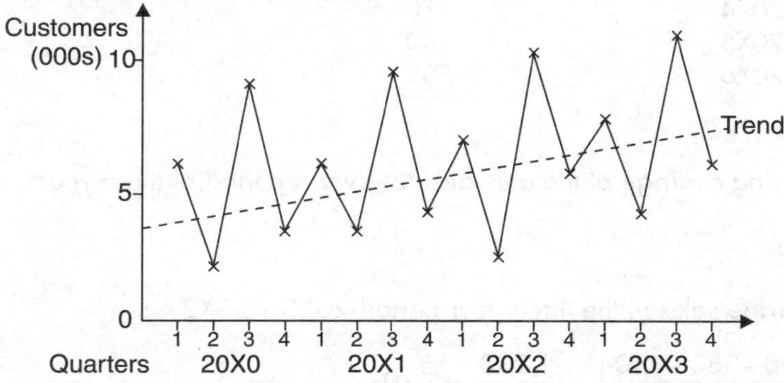


**In this example, there would appear to be large seasonal fluctuations in demand, but there is also a basic upward trend.**

## Cyclical variations

9.6 **Cyclical variations** are medium-term changes in results caused by circumstances which repeat in cycles. In business, cyclical variations are commonly associated with **economic cycles**, **successive booms** and **slumps** in the economy. Economic cycles may last a few years. **Cyclical variations are longer term than seasonal variations.**

## Summarising the components

9.7 The components of a time series can be summarised by the following equation.

$$Y = T + S + C + I$$

where Y = the actual time series
T = the trend series
S = the seasonal component
C = the cyclical component
I = the random or irregular component

# 10 Finding the trend

10.1 The main problem we are concerned with in time series analysis is how to identify the trend and seasonal variations.

## Finding the trend by moving averages

### 10.2 EXAMPLE: MOVING AVERAGES OF AN ODD NUMBER OF RESULTS

| *Year* | *Sales* |
|---|---|
| | Units |
| 20X0 | 390 |
| 20X1 | 380 |
| 20X2 | 460 |
| 20X3 | 450 |
| 20X4 | 470 |
| 20X5 | 440 |
| 20X6 | 500 |

*Required*

Take a moving average of the annual sales over a period of three years.

### 10.3 SOLUTION

(a) Average sales in the three year period 20X0 – 20X2 were

$$\left(\frac{390+380+460}{3}\right) = \frac{1,230}{3} = 410$$

This average relates to the middle year of the period, 20X1.

(b) Similarly, average sales in the three year period 20X1 – 20X3 were

$$\left(\frac{380+460+450}{3}\right) = \frac{1,290}{3} = 430$$

This average relates to the middle year of the period, 20X2.

(c) The average sales can also be found for the periods 20X2 – 20X4, 20X3 – 20X5 and 20X4 – 20X6, to give the following.

| *Year* | *Sales* | *Moving total of 3 years' sales* | *Moving average of 3 years' sales (÷ 3)* |
|---|---|---|---|
| 20X0 | 390 | | |
| 20X1 | 380 | 1,230 | 410 |
| 20X2 | 460 | 1,290 | 430 |
| 20X3 | 450 | 1,380 | 460 |
| 20X4 | 470 | 1,360 | 453 |
| 20X5 | 440 | 1,410 | 470 |
| 20X6 | 500 | | |

Note the following points.

(i) The moving average series has five figures relating to the years from 20X1 to 20X5. The original series had seven figures for the years from 20X0 to 20X6.

(ii) There is an upward trend in sales, which is more noticeable from the series of moving averages than from the original series of actual sales each year.

**10.4** The above example averaged over a three-year period. Over what period should a moving average be taken? The answer to this question is that **the moving average which is most appropriate will depend on the circumstances and the nature of the time series**. Note the following points.

(a) A moving average which takes an average of the results in many time periods will represent results over a longer term than a moving average of two or three periods.

(b) On the other hand, with a moving average of results in many time periods, the last figure in the series will be out of date by several periods. In our example, the most recent average related to 20X5. With a moving average of five years' results, the final figure in the series would relate to 20X4.

(c) When there is a known cycle over which seasonal variations occur, such as all the days in the week or all the seasons in the year, the most suitable moving average would be one which covers one full cycle.

## Action Programme 6

Using the following data, complete the following table in order to determine the three-month moving average for the period January–June.

| *Month* | *No of new houses finished* | *Moving total 3 months new houses finished* | *Moving average of 3 months new houses finished* |
|---|---|---|---|
| January | 500 | | |
| February | 450 | | |
| March | 700 | | |
| April | 900 | | |
| May | 1,250 | | |
| June | 1,000 | | |

## Moving averages of an even number of results

**10.5** In the previous example, moving averages were taken of the results in an **odd number of time periods**, and the average then related to the **mid-point of the overall period**. If a moving average were taken of results in an **even number of time periods**, the basic technique would be the same, but **the mid-point of the overall period would not relate to a single period**. For example, suppose an average were taken of the following four results.

| | | |
|---|---|---|
| Spring | 120 | |
| Summer | 90 | average 115 |
| Autumn | 180 | |
| Winter | 70 | |

**The average would relate to the mid-point of the period, between summer and autumn**. The trend line average figures need to relate to a particular time period; otherwise, seasonal variations cannot be calculated. To overcome this difficulty, we take a **moving average of the moving average**. An example will illustrate this technique.

### 10.6 EXAMPLE: MOVING AVERAGES OVER AN EVEN NUMBER OF PERIODS

Calculate a moving average trend line of the following results.

| *Year* | *Quarter* | *Volume of sales* '000 units |
|---|---|---|
| 20X5 | 1 | 600 |
| | 2 | 840 |
| | 3 | 420 |
| | 4 | 720 |
| 20X6 | 1 | 640 |
| | 2 | 860 |
| | 3 | 420 |
| | 4 | 740 |
| 20X7 | 1 | 670 |
| | 2 | 900 |
| | 3 | 430 |
| | 4 | 760 |

### 10.7 SOLUTION

A moving average of four will be used, since the volume of sales would appear to depend on the season of the year, and each year has four quarterly results.

The moving average of four does not relate to any specific period of time; therefore a second moving average of two will be calculated on the first moving average trend line.

| *Year* | *Quarter* | *Actual volume of sales* '000 units (A) | *Moving total of 4 quarters' sales* '000 units (B) | *Moving average of 4 quarters' sales* '000 units (B ÷ 4) | *Mid-point of 2 moving averages Trend line* '000 units (C) |
|---|---|---|---|---|---|
| 20X5 | 1 | 600 | | | |
| | 2 | 840 | | | |
| | 3 | 420 | 2,580 | 645.0 | 650.00 |
| | 4 | 720 | 2,620 | 655.0 | 657.50 |
| 20X6 | 1 | 640 | 2,640 | 660.0 | 660.00 |
| | 2 | 860 | 2,640 | 660.0 | 662.50 |
| | 3 | 420 | 2,660 | 665.0 | 668.75 |
| | 4 | 740 | 2,690 | 672.5 | 677.50 |
| 20X7 | 1 | 670 | 2,730 | 682.5 | 683.75 |
| | 2 | 900 | 2,740 | 685.0 | 687.50 |
| | 3 | 430 | 2,760 | 690.0 | |
| | 4 | 760 | | | |

**By taking a mid point** (a moving average of two) **of the original moving averages, we can relate the results to specific quarters** (from the third quarter of 20X5 to the second quarter of 20X7).

# 11 Finding the seasonal variations

**11.1** Once a trend has been established, by whatever method, we can find the **seasonal variations**.

**11.2** How do we go about finding the seasonal component?

***Step 1.*** The additive model for time series analysis is Y = T + S + I.

***Step 2.*** If we deduct the trend from the additive model, we get Y – T = S + I.

***Step 3.*** If we assume that I, the random, or irregular component of the time series is relatively small and therefore negligible, then S = Y – T.

Therefore, the seasonal component, S = Y – T (the de-trended series).

## 11.3 EXAMPLE: THE TREND AND SEASONAL VARIATIONS

Output at a factory appears to vary with the day of the week. Output over the last three weeks has been as follows.

| | *Week 1* | *Week 2* | *Week 3* |
|---|---|---|---|
| | '000 units | '000 units | '000 units |
| Monday | 80 | 82 | 84 |
| Tuesday | 104 | 110 | 116 |
| Wednesday | 94 | 97 | 100 |
| Thursday | 120 | 125 | 130 |
| Friday | 62 | 64 | 66 |

*Required*

Find the seasonal variation for each of the 15 days, and the average seasonal variation for each day of the week using the moving averages method.

## 11.4 SOLUTION

Actual results fluctuate up and down according to the day of the week and so a **moving average of five** will be used. **The difference between the actual result on any one day (Y) and the trend figure for that day (T) will be the seasonal variation (S) for the day**. The seasonal variations for the 15 days are as follows.

| | | *Actual* | *Moving total of five days' output* | *Trend* | *Seasonal variation* |
|---|---|---|---|---|---|
| | | (Y) | | (T) | (Y–T) |
| Week 1 | Monday | 80 | | | |
| | Tuesday | 104 | | | |
| | Wednesday | 94 | 460 | 92.0 | +2.0 |
| | Thursday | 120 | 462 | 92.4 | +27.6 |
| | Friday | 62 | 468 | 93.6 | –31.6 |
| Week 2 | Monday | 82 | 471 | 94.2 | –12.2 |
| | Tuesday | 110 | 476 | 95.2 | +14.8 |
| | Wednesday | 97 | 478 | 95.6 | +1.4 |
| | Thursday | 125 | 480 | 96.0 | +29.0 |
| | Friday | 64 | 486 | 97.2 | –33.2 |
| Week 3 | Monday | 84 | 489 | 97.8 | –13.8 |
| | Tuesday | 116 | 494 | 98.8 | +17.2 |
| | Wednesday | 100 | 496 | 99.2 | +0.8 |
| | Thursday | 130 | | | |
| | Friday | 66 | | | |

You will notice that the variation between the actual results on any one particular day and the trend line average is not the same from week to week. This is because **Y – T contains not only seasonal variations but random variations,** but **an average of these variations can be taken**.

| | *Monday* | *Tuesday* | *Wednesday* | *Thursday* | *Friday* |
|---|---|---|---|---|---|
| Week 1 | | | +2.0 | +27.6 | –31.6 |
| Week 2 | –12.2 | +14.8 | +1.4 | +29.0 | –33.2 |
| Week 3 | –13.8 | +17.2 | +0.8 | | |
| Average | –13.0 | +16.0 | +1.4 | +28.3 | –32.4 |

Variations around the basic trend line should cancel each other out, and add up to 0. At the moment they do not. The average seasonal estimates must therefore be corrected so that they add up to zero and so we spread the total of the daily variations (0.30) across the five days (0.3 ÷ 5) so that the final total of the daily variations goes to zero.

| | *Monday* | *Tuesday* | *Wednesday* | *Thursday* | *Friday* | *Total* |
|---|---|---|---|---|---|---|
| Estimated average daily variation | –13.00 | +16.00 | +1.40 | +28.30 | –32.40 | 0.30 |
| Adjustment to reduce total variation to 0 | –0.06 | –0.06 | –0.06 | –0.06 | –0.06 | –0.30 |
| Final estimate of average daily variation | –13.06 | +15.94 | +1.34 | +28.24 | –32.46 | 0.00 |

These might be rounded up or down as follows.

Monday –13; Tuesday +16; Wednesday +1; Thursday +28; Friday –32; Total 0.

## Action Programme 7

Calculate a four-quarter moving average trend centred on actual quarters and then find seasonal variations from the following.

*Sales in £'000*

| | *Spring* | *Summer* | *Autumn* | *Winter* |
|---|---|---|---|---|
| 20X7 | 200 | 120 | 160 | 280 |
| 20X8 | 220 | 140 | 140 | 300 |
| 20X9 | 200 | 120 | 180 | 320 |

## Seasonal variations using the multiplicative model

**11.5** The method of estimating the seasonal variations in the additive model is to use the differences between the trend and actual data. **The additive model assumes that the components of the series are independent of each other**, an increasing trend not affecting the seasonal variations for example.

The alternative is to use the multiplicative model whereby each actual figure is expressed as a proportion of the trend. Sometimes this method is called the proportional model.

**11.6** The additive model example above (in Paragraph 11.3) can be reworked on this alternative basis. The trend is calculated in exactly the same way as before but we need a different approach for the seasonal variations.

**The multiplicative model is Y = T × S × I** and, just as we calculated S = Y – T for the additive model we can calculate **S = Y/T for the multiplicative model.**

| | | *Actual* (Y) | *Trend* (T) | *Seasonal variation* (Y/T) |
|---|---|---|---|---|
| Week 1 | Monday | 80 | | |
| | Tuesday | 104 | | |
| | Wednesday | 94 | 92.0 | 1.022 |
| | Thursday | 120 | 92.4 | 1.299 |
| | Friday | 62 | 93.6 | 0.662 |
| Week 2 | Monday | 82 | 94.2 | 0.870 |
| | Tuesday | 110 | 95.2 | 1.155 |
| | Wednesday | 97 | 95.6 | 1.015 |
| | Thursday | 125 | 96.0 | 1.302 |
| | Friday | 64 | 97.2 | 0.658 |
| Week 3 | Monday | 84 | 97.8 | 0.859 |
| | Tuesday | 116 | 98.8 | 1.174 |
| | Wednesday | 100 | 99.2 | 1.008 |
| | Thursday | 130 | | |
| | Friday | 66 | | |

**11.7** The summary of the seasonal variations expressed in **proportional terms** is as follows.

| | *Monday* | *Tuesday* | *Wednesday* | *Thursday* | *Friday* |
|---|---|---|---|---|---|
| Week 1 | | | 1.022 | 1.299 | 0.662 |
| Week 2 | 0.870 | 1.155 | 1.015 | 1.302 | 0.658 |
| Week 3 | 0.859 | 1.174 | 1.008 | | |
| Total | 1.729 | 2.329 | 3.045 | 2.601 | 1.320 |
| Average | 0.8645 | 1.1645 | 1.0150 | 1.3005 | 0.6600 |

Instead of summing to zero, as with the absolute approach, these should sum (in this case) to 5 (an average of 1).

They actually sum to 5.0045 so 0.0009 has to be deducted from each one. This is too small to make a difference to the figures above, so we should deduct 0.002 and 0.0025 to each of two seasonal variations. We could arbitrarily decrease Monday's variation to 0.8625 and Tuesday's to 1.162.

**11.8** **The multiplicative model is better than the additive model for forecasting when the trend is increasing or decreasing over time**. In such circumstances, seasonal variations are likely to be increasing or decreasing too. The additive model simply adds absolute and unchanging seasonal variations to the trend figures whereas the multiplicative model, by multiplying increasing or decreasing trend values by a constant seasonal variation factor, takes account of changing seasonal variations.

**11.9** We can summarise the steps to be carried out when calculating the seasonal variation as follows.

**Step 1.** Calculate the moving total for an appropriate period.

**Step 2.** Calculate the moving average (the trend) for the period. (Calculate the mid-point of two moving averages if there are an even number of periods.)

**Step 3.** Calculate the seasonal variation. For an additive model, this is Y – T. For a multiplicative model, this is Y/T.

**Step 4.** Calculate an average of the seasonal variations.

**Step 5.** Adjust the average seasonal variations so that they add up to **zero** for an **additive model**. When using the **multiplicative model**, the average seasonal variations should add up to an **average of 1**.

**Action Programme 8**

Find the average seasonal variations for the sales data in Action Programme 7 using the multiplicative model.

# 12 Forecasting and time series analysis

## Making a forecast

**12.1** Time series analysis data can be used to make forecasts as follows.

**Step 1.** **Plot a trend line**: use the line of best fit method or the moving averages method.

**Step 2.** **Extrapolate the trend line**. This means extending the trend line outside the range of known data and forecasting future results from historical data.

**Step 3.** **Adjust forecast trends** by the applicable average seasonal variation to obtain the actual forecast.

(a) **Additive model** – add positive variations to and subtract negative variations from the forecast trends.

(b) **Multiplicative model** – multiply the forecast trends by the seasonal variation.

**12.2 EXAMPLE: FORECASTING**

Use the trend values and the estimates of seasonal variations calculated in Paragraph 11.4 to forecast sales in week 4.

**12.3 SOLUTION**

We begin by plotting the trend values on a graph and extrapolating the trend line.

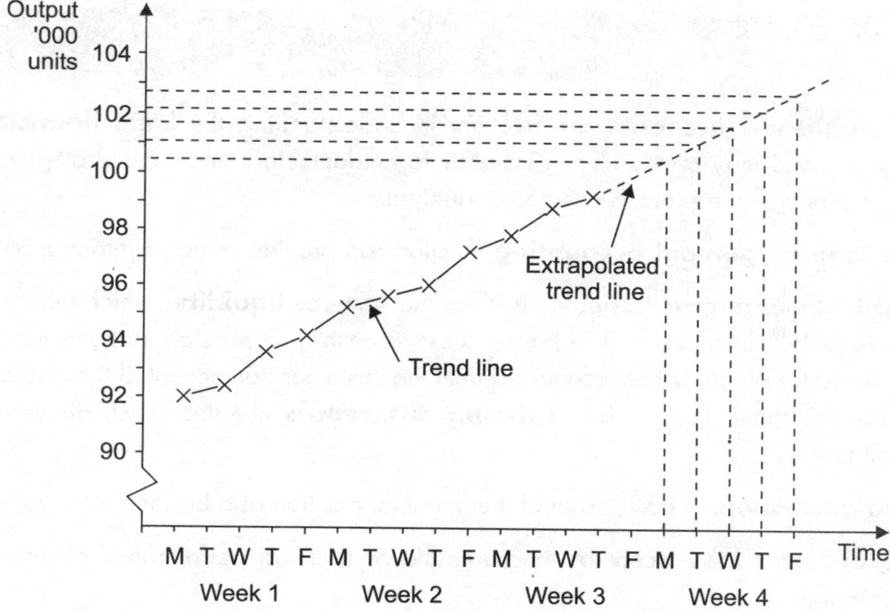


From the extrapolated trend line we can take the following readings and adjust them by the seasonal variations.

| *Week 4* | *Trend line readings* | *Seasonal variations* | *Forecast* |
|---|---|---|---|
| Monday | 100.5 | –13 | 87.5 |
| Tuesday | 101.5 | +16 | 117.1 |
| Wednesday | 101.7 | +1 | 102.7 |
| Thursday | 102.2 | +28 | 130.2 |
| Friday | 102.8 | –32 | 70.8 |

**12.4** If we had been using the multiplicative model the forecast for Tuesday, for example, would be 101.1 × 1.1645 = 117.7 (from Paragraph 11.7).

## Action Programme 9

Unemployment numbers actually recorded in a town for the first quarter of 20X9 were 4,700. The underlying trend at this point was 4,400 people and the seasonal factor is 0.85. Using the multiplicative model for seasonal adjustment, the seasonally-adjusted figure (in whole numbers) for the quarter is

A 5,529 B 5,176 C 3,995 D 3,740

# The reliability of time series analysis forecasts

**12.5** All forecasts are subject to error, but the likely errors vary from case to case.

(a) The further into the future the forecast is for, the more unreliable it is likely to be.

(b) The less data available on which to base the forecast, the less reliable the forecast.

(c) The pattern of trend and seasonal variations cannot be guaranteed to continue in the future.

(d) There is always the danger of random variations upsetting the pattern of trend and seasonal variation.

(e) The extrapolation of the trend line is done by judgement and can introduce error.

## Chapter Roundup

- The **published accounts** are relevant in understanding the basic **financial health** of a company and may provide some insight into fundamental trends and strategies being adopted. This is especially relevant to competitor analysis.
- A firm's **management accounting** function can provide valuable information to the marketer.
- **Profit** is sales revenue less costs. It is not the same as **liquidity**, which denotes a firm's ability to pay its bills on time, and to have access to cash. It is possible to have high profitability but low liquidity. A sale is not recognised until the customer has accepted the goods. It is not secure until the customer has paid. It is **timing differences** like this which differentiate profitability and liquidity.
- A **balance sheet** is a snapshot of the financial position of a business at a point in time.
- A **profit and loss account** measures the operational performance of the company over a period of time.
- Capital items are concerned with financing decisions. Revenue items are concerned with trading decisions.
- The **cash flow statement** is an analysis of where a business gets its cash and how cash is used.
- Financial terms have been defined in this chapter and you should be able to reproduce these definitions to enable you to communicate effectively with financial staff. The main definitions are given briefly here.
  - **Assets** are things of value that a business owns or has use of. **Fixed assets** are assets which are acquired for use within a business with a view to facilitating the generation of revenue (and consequently profits). **Current assets** are assets which are owned by the business which are intended to be turned into cash within one year. **Debts** are financial obligations **to** us. **Brands** are problematic.
  - **Liabilities** are financial obligations to someone else. **Creditors** are people to whom the business has a financial obligation. **Capital** is the money put into a business by the owners and it is therefore owed by the business to the owners.
  - **Gross profit** is the profit shown after the purchase or production cost of the goods sold is deducted from the value of sales.
  - **Net profit** is the gross profit, plus any other income from sources other than the sale of goods, minus other expenses of the business which are not included in the cost of goods sold.
- The **interpretation of financial data** is the key to the understanding of any business, either in a practical application or during your studies. Companies as large as GEC have been effectively managed for many years simply by ensuring that the ratios relevant to their businesses were kept within acceptable limits. These are the important to be lessons learned.
  - **Ratios** are a useful measure when in comparison with something else: either the company's history, or a competitor or an industry norm.
  - **Consistency in calculation** and in the base data is important otherwise we could end up comparing apples and oranges.

## Chapter Roundup (cont'd)

- **Return on capital employed** is the product of two other ratios.

  ROCE = profit margin × asset turnover
- **Gearing** is a measure of how funds have been generated to buy assets.
- Proper control of cash is vital to the continued financial strength of any company. Marketing managers should be aware of the **debt collection periods** (also known as the debtor turnover or day sales outstanding) and other tests of liquidity such as stock turnover.

■ Different **segments** and different **customers** offer different levels of **profit**.

■ A **time series** is a series of figures or values recorded over time. A graph of a time series is called a **historigram**.

■ There are four components of a time series: **trend**, **seasonal variations**, **cyclical variations** and **random variations**.

■ The **trend** is the underlying long-term movement over time in the values of the data recorded. **Seasonal variations** are short-term fluctuations due to different circumstances which affect results at different points in time. **Cyclical variations** are medium-term changes in results caused by circumstances which repeat in cycles.

■ One method of finding the trend is by the use of **moving averages**.

■ Remember that when finding the moving average of an **even number of results**, a second moving average has to be calculated so that trend values can relate to specific actual figures.

■ **Seasonal variations are the difference between actual and trend figures**. An average of the seasonal variations for each time period within the cycle must be determined and then adjusted so that the total of the seasonal variations sums to zero.

■ Seasonal variations can be estimated using the **additive model (Y = T + S + I, with seasonal variations = Y – T)** or the **proportional (multiplicative) model (Y = T × S × I, with seasonal variations = Y/T)**.

■ **Forecasts** can be made by **extrapolating the trend** and **adjusting for seasonal variations**. Remember, however, that all forecasts are subject to error.

## Quick Quiz

1 Why is accounting useful to the marketing manager?

2 What is the purpose of giving a financial value to brands?

3 What is a simple definition of profit?

4 How is liquidity defined?

5 How can ratios be used?

6 What are the four main components of a time series?

7 Time series analysis data can be used to make forecasts by **extrapolating** the trend line. What does extrapolation mean?

## Answers to Quick Quiz

1 It measures the input of their decisions upon the success of the organisation.

2 Investment has been made in order to create them and they can represent important assets. Shareholders should be made aware of their value.

3 Profit equals sales minus costs.

4 Liquid assets can be converted quickly into cash.

5 Generally, ratios are used for making comparisons. The same ratio can be compared year on year to see if progress is being made and different ratios can be compared to give clues to problem solutions.

6 Trend, seasonal variations, cyclical variations and random variations.

7 Extension of the trend beyond the known data in order to make a forecast.

## Action Programme Review

1 Do not be concerned with some of the more technical aspects of financial information but look at the **layout of the accounts**. It would be useful if you could obtain copies of similar documents from a couple of your major competitors or customers and compare the basic layout and information available. You may also note how useful this report has become as a means of communicating a **public relations** message to the shareholders and potential shareholders, to banks and to other users.

2 Many small firms sell to large companies. Large firms have higher bargaining power, as their suppliers **depend** on the sales. **Small firms have fewer financial resources**.

3 (a) Company A – low volume of sales, but high margin on each unit sold. To justify the high profit margin, the firm might have to differentiate its offer in some way, for example, by superior service or another differentiating factor, or by effective segmentation.

(b) Company B – high volume, low margin. This might be similar to the 'Every Day Low Pricing' policy adopted by B&Q. Its explicit aim was to increase sales volume by lowering prices. It is unlikely that A or B would sell exactly the same product/service. Of course, they might sell the same equipment, but augmentation to the product might be made.

Furthermore, Company A and Company B may have little option but to pursue their different strategies, because of the characteristics of the industry and their existing position within it. This is relevant to **strategic group analysis**.

4 Is the increased profit figure necessarily a good thing?

(a) At present, ratios are:

| | |
|---|---|
| Profit margin | 5% |
| Asset turnover | 5 times |
| ROCE (5/20) | 25% |

(b) With the proposed changes, the profit would be 10% × £150,000 = £15,000, and the asset turnover would be:

$$\frac{£150,000}{£75,000} = 2 \text{ times}$$ , so that the ratios might be:

Profit margin × Asset turnover = ROCE

$$10\% \quad \times \; 2 \text{ times} \quad = \quad 20\% \quad \text{ie} \quad \frac{15,000}{75,000}$$

(c) In spite of increasing the profit margin and raising the total volume of sales, the extra assets required (£55,000) only raise total profits by £(15,000 – 5,000) = £10,000. The return on capital employed **falls** from 25% to 20% because of the sharp fall in asset turnover from 5 times to 2 times. In other words, the new investment is not used efficiently.

(d) This does not mean that the management of the company would not raise its prices. However, the financial analysis has provided them with another piece of the decision-making jigsaw. It may be that this is a weakness because the owners of the business, although very happy with the increased profitability, may not be happy with the reduced ROCE. The management must judge which aspect is most acceptable.

**5**

| | *2002* | *2001* |
|---|---|---|
| Current ratio | $\frac{572.3}{501.0} = 1.14$ | $\frac{523.2}{420.3} = 1.24$ |
| Quick ratio | $\frac{453.3}{501.0} = 0.90$ | $\frac{414.2}{420.3} = 0.99$ |
| Debtors' payment period | $\frac{329.8 \times 365}{2,065.0} = 58$ days | $\frac{285.4 \times 365}{1,788.7} = 58$ days |
| Stock turnover period | $\frac{119.0 \times 365}{1,478.6} = 29$ days | $\frac{109.0 \times 365}{1,304.0} = 31$ days |
| Creditors' turnover period | $\frac{236.2 \times 365}{1,478.6} = 58$ days | $\frac{210.8 \times 365}{1,304.0} = 59$ days |

**6**

| *Month* | *No of new houses finished* | *Moving total 3 months new houses finished* | *Moving average of 3 months new houses finished (÷ 3)* |
|---|---|---|---|
| January | 500 | | |
| February | 450 | 1,650 | 550 |
| March | 700 | 2,050 | 683.33 |
| April | 900 | 2,850 | 950 |
| May | 1,250 | 3,150 | 1,050 |
| June | 1,000 | | |

**7**

| | | Sales (Y) | 4-quarter total | 8-quarter total | Moving average (T) | Seasonal variation (Y–T) |
|---|---|---|---|---|---|---|
| 20X7 | Spring | 200 | | | | |
| | Summer | 120 | | | | |
| | | | 760 | | | |
| | Autumn | 160 | | 1,540 | 192.5 | –32.5 |
| | | | 780 | | | |
| | Winter | 280 | | 1,580 | 197.5 | +82.5 |
| | | | 800 | | | |
| 20X8 | Spring | 220 | | 1,580 | 197.5 | +22.5 |
| | | | 780 | | | |
| | Summer | 140 | | 1,580 | 197.5 | –57.5 |
| | | | 800 | | | |
| | Autumn | 140 | | 1,580 | 197.5 | –57.5 |
| | | | 780 | | | |
| | Winter | 300 | | 1,540 | 192.5 | +107.5 |
| | | | 760 | | | |
| 20X9 | Spring | 200 | | 1,560 | 195.0 | +5.0 |
| | | | 800 | | | |
| | Summer | 120 | | 1,620 | 202.5 | –82.5 |
| | | | 820 | | | |
| | Autumn | 180 | | | | |
| | Winter | 320 | | | | |

We can now average the seasonal variations.

| | Spring | Summer | Autumn | Winter | Total |
|---|---|---|---|---|---|
| 20X7 | | | –32.5 | +82.5 | |
| 20X8 | +22.5 | –57.5 | –57.5 | +107.5 | |
| 20X9 | +5.0 | –82.5 | | | |
| | +27.5 | –140.0 | –90.0 | +190.0 | |
| Average variations (in £'000) | +13.75 | –70.00 | –45.00 | +95.00 | –6.25 |
| Adjustment so sum is zero | +1.5625 | +1.5625 | +1.5625 | +1.5625 | +6.25 |
| Adjusted average variations | +15.3125 | –68.4375 | –43.4375 | +96.5625 | 0 |

These might be rounded up or down to:

Spring £15,000, Summer –£68,000, Autumn –£43,000, Winter £96,000

8

| | *Spring* | *Summer* | *Autumn* | *Winter* | *Total* |
|---|---|---|---|---|---|
| 20X7 | | | 0.83* | 1.42 | |
| 20X8 | 1.11 | 0.71 | 0.71 | 1.56 | |
| 20X9 | 1.03 | 0.59 | | | |
| | 2.14 | 1.30 | 1.54 | 2.98 | |

| | *Spring* | *Summer* | *Autumn* | *Winter* | *Total* |
|---|---|---|---|---|---|
| Average variations | 1.070 | 0.650 | 0.770 | 1.490 | 3.980 |
| Adjustment to sum to 4 | + 0.005 | + 0.005 | + 0.005 | + 0.005 | 0.020 |
| Adjusted average variations | 1.075 | 0.655 | 0.775 | 1.495 | 4.000 |

*Seasonal variation $\frac{Y}{T} = \frac{160}{192.5} = 0.83$

9 The correct answer is A.

If you remembered the ruling that you need to **divide** by the seasonal variation factor to obtain seasonally-adjusted figures (using the multiplicative model), then you should have been able to eliminate options C and D. This might have been what you did if you weren't sure whether you divided the **actual results** or the **trend** by the seasonal variation factor.

Seasonally adjusted data = $\frac{\text{Actual results}}{\text{Seasonal factor}} = \frac{4,700}{0.85} = 5,529$

## Now try Question 2 at the end of the Study Text

# Monitoring Performance 3

| Chapter Topic List | |
|---|---|
| 1 | Setting the scene |
| 2 | Marketing audits and marketing effectiveness |
| 3 | Discounting cash flows |
| 4 | Shareholder value analysis |
| 5 | Benchmarking |
| 6 | The balanced scorecard |

## Syllabus content

- Critical, quantitative evaluation of business and marketing performance over current and historic business cycles

## Key Concepts Introduced

- Marketing audit
- Efficiency and effectiveness
- Discounting
- Present value
- Discounted cash flow
- Net present value
- Shareholder value analysis
- Benchmarking
- Balanced scorecard

# 1 Setting the scene

**1.1** In this chapter we take performance evaluation a little further. We start off with the marketing audit, which is a technique fundamental to any discussion of market-related strategic analysis.

**1.2** Shareholder value analysis is a technique specifically named in your syllabus. We consider it in Section 4; however, to understand this subject you must first be able to use **discounting** of cash flows. We therefore cover this financial arithmetic first, in Section 3.

**1.3** Section 5 covers benchmarking and Section 6 the balanced scorecard. These are also mandated by your syllabus and are widely used methods of measuring overall performance.

# 2 Marketing audits and marketing effectiveness

## Marketing audits

**Key Concept**

'A **marketing audit** is a comprehensive, systematic, independent and periodic examination of a company's – or business unit's – marketing environment, objectives, strategies and activities with a view to determining problem areas and opportunities and recommending a plan of action to improve the company's marketing performance.' (Kotler, Gregor and Rodgers, 1977)

**2.1** A marketing audit does not exist in the compulsory formal sense that an external financial audit does. For proper strategic control, however, a marketing audit should have the following features.

(a) **Regular**. It should be conducted **regularly**, for example once a year.

(b) **Comprehensive**. It should take a **comprehensive** look at every product, market, distribution channel, ingredient in the marketing mix etc. It should not be restricted to areas of apparent ineffectiveness (for example, an unprofitable product, a troublesome distribution channel, low efficiency on direct selling and so on).

(c) **Systematic**. It should be carried out according to a set of predetermined, specified procedures.

(d) **Independence**. A consultant might be appointed, or someone else within the organisation.

## The audit procedure

**2.2** A marketing audit should consider the following areas.

- The market environment, macro and micro
- Marketing strategies
- Marketing systems
- Marketing organisation
- Marketing function
- Marketing productivity

**2.3 The marketing environment**

(a) **Micro**. What are the organisation's major markets, and what is the segmentation of these markets? What are the future prospects of each market segment?

(i) Who are the customers, what is known about customer needs, intentions and behaviour?

(ii) Who are the competitors, and what is their standing in the market?

(b) **Macro**. Have there been any significant developments in the broader environment (for example, economic or political changes, population or social changes etc)?

**2.4 Marketing strategy audit**

(a) What are the organisation's marketing objectives and how do they relate to overall objectives? Are they reasonable?

(b) Are enough (or too many) resources being committed to marketing to enable the objectives to be achieved? Is the division of costs between products, areas etc satisfactory?

**2.5 Marketing systems**. What are the procedures for formulating marketing plans and management control of these plans? Are they satisfactory?

**2.6 Marketing organisation**. Does the organisation have the structural capability to implement the plan?

**2.7 Marketing functions**. A review of the effectiveness of each element of the mix (eg advertising and sales promotion activities) should be carried out.

(a) A review of sales and price levels should be made (for example, supply and demand, customer attitudes, the use of temporary price reductions etc).

(b) A review of the state of each individual product (ie its market 'health') and of the product mix as a whole should be made.

(c) A critical analysis of the distribution system should be made, with a view to finding improvements.

**2.8 Marketing productivity**. How profitable are the company's products, markets and channels of distribution? How cost-effective is the marketing programme?

**Exam Tip**

*You may have to explain the purpose, focus and components of a marketing audit. Show how it can be made relevant to the firm, how it can be conducted, and how the results might be used.*

**2.9 Advantages of a marketing audit**

- It should reduce the need for crisis management
- It should identify information needs
- A formal process forces people to think

## Efficiency and effectiveness

**Key Concepts**

(a) **Efficiency**: gaining maximum output for a minimum input and is normally used relatively (ie in comparison to a standard or norm, to competitors, to industry norms, or the PIMS database).

(b) **Effectiveness**: doing the right things rather than doing things right. A firm can be incredibly efficient in producing widgets at the lowest cost but if no one will buy them it is all to no effect and it will soon be out of business.

**2.10** A company that is both efficient and effective will prosper. A company that is inefficient but effective will survive, at least in the short term. A company that is both inefficient and ineffective will die quickly. Let us put this on a grid.

| | | *Effectiveness* | |
|---|---|---|---|
| | | *High* | *Low* |
| *Efficiency* | *High* | THRIVE | DIE SLOWLY |
| | *Low* | SURVIVE | DIE QUICKLY |

Source: Wilson, Gilligan, Pearson

## The importance of marketing effectiveness

**2.11** Although it is obviously true that marketing effectiveness is a vital component of organisational effectiveness, it is not always easy to measure precisely, especially as marketing assets are hard to measure and value.

### *The marketing excellence framework*

**2.12** In *Manufacturing: the Marketing Solution,* the CIM has developed a framework for evaluating companies' marketing operations. A sample of 44 companies from the UK's manufacturing sector was taken, and each company's marketing activities were assessed and scored on a marketing excellence framework. Then, the marketing excellence score was compared with financial results.

**2.13** Most companies in the sample scored badly. The better scorers tended to be large companies. **Correlation with financial performance is not entirely straightforward**.

(a) For many firms, there **is** a link between total score on the marketing excellence framework and profitability and return on capital.

(b) It appears that some companies in particularly demanding markets have 'to run fast to stand still'.

(c) No company earns a high return on capital if it scores **badly** on the framework.

## Measuring marketing capability

**2.14** Kotler has developed the thinking on marketing effectiveness into a general purpose rating tool based upon the following fifteen questions, as adapted in the table below.

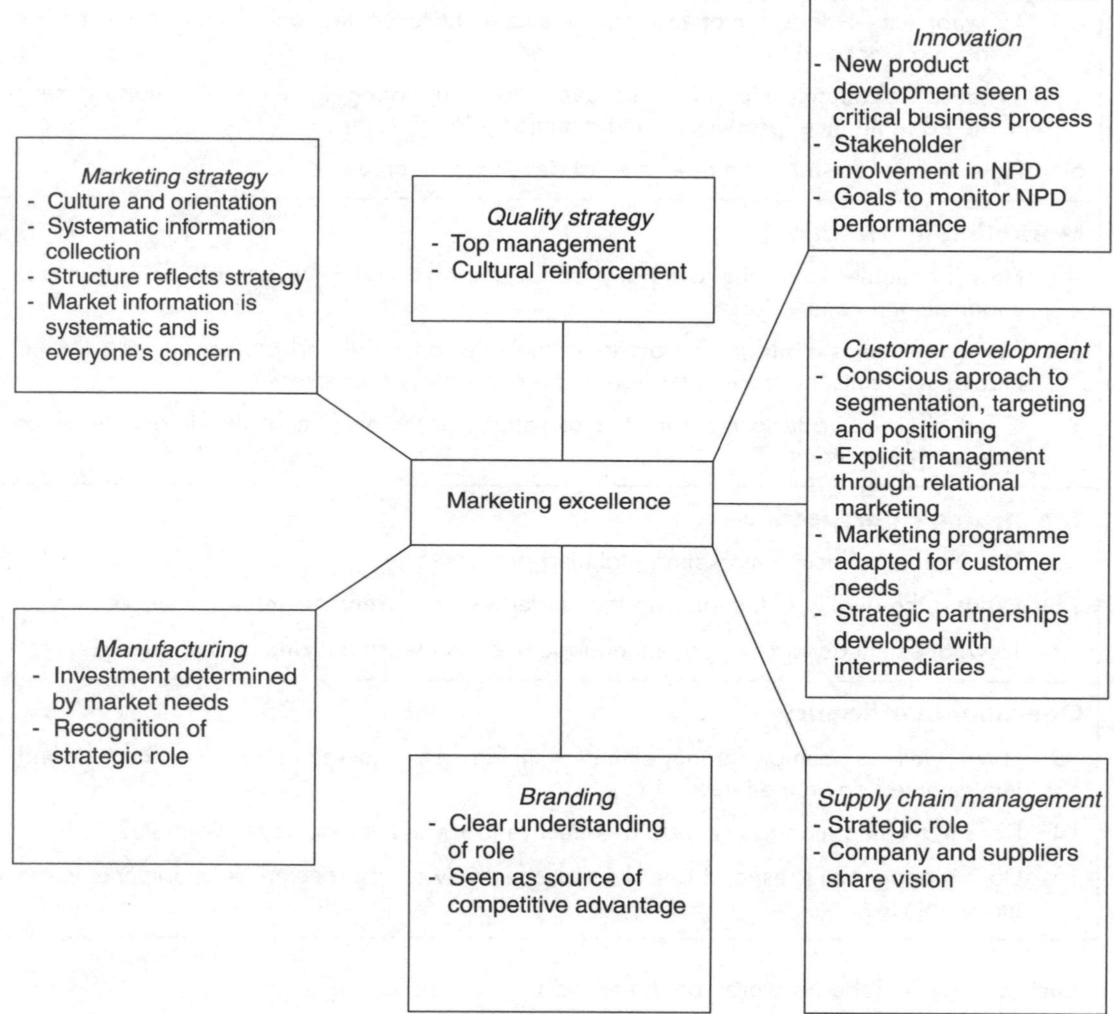

## *Marketing effectiveness rating*

**Customer philosophy**

1 To what extent does management recognise the need to organise the company to satisfy specific market demands?

2 To what extent is the marketing programme tailored to the needs of different market segments?

3 Does management adopt a systems approach to planning, with recognition being given to the interrelationships between the environment, suppliers, channels, customers and competitors?

**Marketing organisation**

4 To what extent does senior management attempt to control and integrate the major marketing functions?

5 What sort of relationship exists between marketing management and the management of the R&D, finance, production and manufacturing functions?

6 How well organised is the new product development process?

**Marketing information**

7 How frequently does the company conduct market research studies of customers, channels and competitors?

8 To what extent is management aware of the sales potential and profitability of different market segments, customers, territories, products and order sizes?

9 What effort is made to measure the cost-effectiveness of different levels and types of marketing expenditure?

**The strategic perspective**

10 How formalised is the marketing planning process?

11 What is the quality of the thinking that underlies the current marketing strategy?

12 To what extent does management engage in contingency thinking and planning?

**Operational efficiency**

13 How well is senior management thinking on marketing communicated and implemented down the line?

14 Does marketing management do an effective job with the resources available?

15 Does management respond quickly and effectively to unexpected developments in the market-place?

**2.15** Each question can be answered on three levels.

(a) Question 1 could have answers:

1.1 To no extent
1.2 To some extent
1.3 To a very high extent

(b) Question 5 could have answers:

| | |
|---|---|
| 5.1 | Extremely poor, antagonism exists, marketing regarded as being too demanding |
| 5.2 | Normally satisfactory although there is an underlying attitude that each department is basically self-serving |
| 5.3 | Extremely good with all departments working together to serve the customer |

(c) Each of these three levels is then allocated a score of 0, 1, or 2:

Poor = 0
Satisfactory = 1
Excellent = 2

(d) Each manager works his way through the fifteen questions in order to arrive at a score. The scores are then aggregated and averaged. The overall measure of marketing effectiveness can then be assessed against the following scale.

| | | | |
|---|---|---|---|
| 0 – 5 | = | None | Firm's survival in doubt |
| 6 – 10 | = | Poor | |
| 11 – 15 | = | Fair | Opportunity to improve |
| 16 – 20 | = | Good | |
| 21 – 25 | = | Very good | |
| 26 – 30 | = | Superior | Beware complacency |

**2.16** The beauty of the Kotler approach is that it can be adapted to suit the purposes of any organisation. Extra questions can be posed as thought fit. For example, if **marketing planning** was considered to be a key attribute of marketing effectiveness than this could be audited and scored using the following schematic approach.

| **AUDITING THE MARKETING PLAN – SCHEMATIC APPROACH** | |
|---|---|
| *Planning* | *Auditing* |
| Corporate mission | Correct? Understood? |
| Corporate objectives | Feasible? Being achieved? |
| Corporate strategies | Appropriate? Have environmental factors changed? What are competitors doing? |
| Marketing objectives | Feasible? Being achieved? |
| Marketing strategies | Appropriate? Working? Competitors? (Direct, indirect) |
| Marketing mix plans | Harmonised? Tailored for each segment? Positioning OK? Check price, place, product/service and promotion. Internal audits, customer audits. |
| Marketing research plan | Is the right data provided at the right time in the right format? |
| Budgets/performance measures | Appropriate? Being achieved? |
| Organisation, integration, co-ordination | Working harmoniously? Is the organisation effective? |
| Overall | How do we compare with last year and the years before? How do we compare with competitors? |

Other more general questions on planning could be devised, for example:

**Marketing planning**

16 To what extent is marketing planning being conducted?

(a) For the short term
(b) For the medium term
(c) For the long term

17 To what extent are marketing plans communicated to other departments?

18 To what extent are marketing plans considered realistic by other departments?

**2.17 Other more obvious ways of reviewing marketing effectiveness and measuring marketing capability**

(a) The extent to which the company has consistently increased **market share**.

(b) **Customer audits**, ideally subcontracted to a marketing research agency to establish objectively the company's standing relative to competitors with regard to:

- Product-service mix
- Pricing policies
- Promotional strategies, in particular customer support and personal selling
- Distribution service including deliveries, stocks etc
- Marketing knowledge/image

(c) **Interfirm comparisons**.

(d) **PIMS database** (comparisons of company's overall product, market and financial effectiveness relative to similar companies).

(e) **Competitor audits** (checking published accounts, competitor intelligence etc).

(f) **Internal audits** of all resources.

# 3 Discounting cash flows

**3.1** In the next section we will discuss shareholder value analysis (SVA). This technique depends on the **discounting** of cash flows, both current and in the future. Discounting is a basic tool of financial analysis that is also widely used in other business techniques, so we will start off by showing you how it works.

**3.2** The **basic principle of compounding** is that if we invest £X now for n years at r% interest per annum, we should obtain £S in n years time, where £S = £X$(1+r^n)$.

**3.3** Thus if we invest £10,000 now for four years at 10% interest per annum, we will have a total investment worth £10,000 × $1.10^4$ = £14,641 at the end of four years (that is, at year 4 if it is now year 0).

**Key Concept**

The basic principle of **discounting** is that if we wish to have £V in n years' time, we need to invest a certain sum *now* (year 0) at an interest rate of r% in order to obtain the required sum of money in the future.

**3.4** For example, if we wish to have £14,641 in four years' time, how much money would we need to invest now at 10% interest per annum? This is the reverse of the situation described in Paragraph 3.2 and, fairly obviously, the answer is £10,000. We can prove this.

Using our formula, $S = X(1 + r)^n$

where X = the original sum invested
r = 10%
n = 4
S = £14,641

$$£14,641 = X(1 + 0.1)^4$$

$$£14,641 = X \times 1.4641$$

$$\therefore X = \frac{£14,641}{1.4641} = £10,000$$

**3.5** £10,000 now, with the capacity to earn a return of 10% per annum, is the equivalent in value of £14,641 after four years. We can therefore say that £10,000 is the **present value** of £14,641 at year 4, at an interest rate of 10%.

**Key Concept**

The **present value** of a future sum is obtained by discounting the future sum at an appropriate discount rate.

**3.6** The discounting formula is

$$X = S \times \frac{1}{(1+r)^n}$$

where S is the sum to be received after n time periods
X is the present value (PV) of that sum
r is the rate of return, expressed as a proportion
n is the number of time periods (usually years).

The rate r is sometimes called a cost of capital.

**3.7 EXAMPLE: DISCOUNTING**

(a) Calculate the present value of £60,000 at year 6, if a return of 15% per annum is obtainable.

(b) Calculate the present value of £100,000 at year 5, if a return of 6% per annum is obtainable.

(c) How much would a person need to invest now at 12% to earn £4,000 at year 2 and £4,000 at year 3?

## 3.8 SOLUTION

The discounting formula, $X = S \times \frac{1}{(1+r)^n}$ is required.

(a)

$$S = £60,000$$
$$n = 6$$
$$r = 0.15$$
$$PV = 60,000 \times \frac{1}{1.15^6}$$
$$= 60,000 \times 0.432$$
$$= £25,920$$

(b)

$$S = £100,000$$
$$n = 5$$
$$r = 0.06$$
$$PV = 100,000 \times \frac{1}{1.06^5}$$
$$= 100,000 \times 0.747$$
$$= £74,700$$

(c)

$$S = £4,000$$
$$n = 2 \text{ or } 3$$
$$r = 0.12$$
$$PV = (4,000 \times \frac{1}{1.12^2}) + (4,000 \times \frac{1}{1.12^3})$$
$$= 4,000 \times (0.797 + 0.712)$$
$$= £6,036$$

This calculation can be checked as follows.

| | £ |
|---|---|
| Year 0 | 6,036.00 |
| Interest for the first year (12%) | 724.32 |
| | 6,760.32 |
| Interest for the second year (12%) | 811.24 |
| | 7,571.56 |
| Less withdrawal | (4,000.00) |
| | 3,571.56 |
| Interest for the third year (12%) | 428.59 |
| | 4,000.15 |
| Less withdrawal | (4,000.00) |
| Rounding error | 0.15 |

### Action Programme 1

The present value at 7% interest of £16,000 at year 12 is £ ☐

## Project appraisal

**3.9** Discounted cash flow techniques can be used to evaluate expenditure proposals such as the purchase of equipment or marketing budgets.

### Key Concept

**Discounted cash flow (DCF)** involves the application of discounting arithmetic to the estimated future cash flows (receipts and expenditures) from a project in order to decide whether the project is expected to earn a satisfactory rate of return.

## The net present method value (NPV) method

### Key Concept

The **net present value (NPV) method** works out the present values of all items of income and expenditure related to an investment at a given rate of return, and then works out a net total. If it is positive, the investment is considered to be acceptable. If it is negative, the investment is considered to be unacceptable.

**3.10 EXAMPLE: THE NET PRESENT VALUE OF A PROJECT**

Dog Ltd is considering whether to spend £5,000 on an item of equipment. The excess of income over cash expenditure from the project would be £3,000 in the first year and £4,000 in the second year.

The company will not invest in any project unless it offers a return in excess of 15% per annum.

*Required*

Assess whether the investment is worthwhile.

**3.11 SOLUTION**

In this example, an outlay of £5,000 now promises a return of £3,000 **during** the first year and £4,000 **during** the second year. It is a convention in DCF, however, that cash flows spread over a year are assumed to occur **at the end of the year**, so that the cash flows of the project are as follows.

| | £ |
|---|---|
| Year 0 (now) | (5,000) |
| Year 1 (at the end of the year) | 3,000 |
| Year 2 (at the end of the year) | 4,000 |

**3.12** The NPV method takes the following approach.

(a) The project offers £3,000 at year 1 and £4,000 at year 2, for an outlay of £5,000 now.

(b) The company might invest elsewhere to earn a return of 15% per annum.

(c) If the company did invest at exactly 15% per annum, how much would it need to invest now to earn £3,000 at the end of year 1 plus £4,000 at the end of year 2?

(d) Is it cheaper to invest £5,000 in the project, or to invest elsewhere at 15%, in order to obtain these future cash flows?

**3.13** If the company did invest elsewhere at 15% per annum, the amount required to earn £3,000 in year 1 and £4,000 in year 2 would be as follows.

| *Year* | *Cash flow* | *Discount factor* | *Present value* |
|---|---|---|---|
| | £ | 15% | £ |
| 1 | 3,000 | $\frac{1}{1.15} = 0.870$ | 2,610 |
| 2 | 4,000 | $\frac{1}{(1.15)^2} = 0.756$ | 3,024 |
| | | | 5,634 |

**3.14** The choice is to invest £5,000 in the project, or £5,634 elsewhere at 15%, in order to obtain these future cash flows. We can therefore reach the following conclusion.

- It is cheaper to invest in the project, by £634.
- The project offers a return of over 15% per annum.

**3.15** The net present value is the difference between the present value of cash inflows from the project (£5,634) and the present value of future cash outflows (in this example, £5,000 × $1/1.15^0$ = £5,000).

**3.16** An NPV statement could be drawn up as follows.

| *Year* | *Cash flow* | *Discount factor* | *Present value* |
|---|---|---|---|
| | £ | 15% | £ |
| 0 | (5,000) | 1.000 | (5,000) |
| 1 | 3,000 | $\frac{1}{1.15} = 0.870$ | 2,610 |
| 2 | 4,000 | $\frac{1}{(1.15)^2} = 0.756$ | 3,024 |
| | | Net present value | +634 |

The project has a positive net present value, so it is acceptable.

## Action Programme 2

A company is wondering whether to spend £18,000 on an item of equipment, in order to obtain cash profits as follows.

| *Year* | £ |
|---|---|
| 1 | 6,000 |
| 2 | 8,000 |
| 3 | 5,000 |
| 4 | 1,000 |

The company requires a return of 10% per annum.

*Required*

Use the NPV method to assess whether the project is viable.

---

## Discount tables

**3.17** Assuming that money earns, say, 10% per annum:

(a) the PV (present value) of £1 at year 1 is £1 × $\frac{1}{1.10}$ = £1 × 0.909

(b) similarly, the PV of £1 at year 2 is £1 × $\frac{1}{(1.10)^2}$ = £1 × 0.826

(c) the PV of £1 at year 3 is £1 × $\frac{1}{(1.10)^3}$ = £1 × 0.751

**Discount tables** show the value of $1/(1 + r)^n$ for different values of r and n. Note, however, that NPV calculations will usually be done using a spreadsheet.

## Project comparison

**3.18** **The NPV method can also be used to compare two or more investment options.** For example, suppose that Daisy Ltd can choose between the investment outlined in Question 2 above *or* a second investment, which also costs £28,000 but which would earn £6,500 in the first year, £7,500 in the second, £8,500 in the third, £9,500 in the fourth and £10,500 in the fifth. Which one should Daisy Ltd choose?

**3.19** **The decision rule is to choose the option with the highest NPV**. We therefore need to calculate the NPV of the second option.

| *Year* | *Cash flow* | *Discount factor* | *Present value* |
|---|---|---|---|
| | £ | 11% | £ |
| 0 | (28,000) | 1.000 | (28,000) |
| 1 | 6,500 | 0.901 | 5,857 |
| 2 | 7,500 | 0.812 | 6,090 |
| 3 | 8,500 | 0.731 | 6,214 |
| 4 | 9,500 | 0.659 | 6,261 |
| 5 | 10,500 | 0.593 | 6,227 |
| | | NPV = | 2,649 |

Daisy Ltd should therefore invest in the second option since it has the higher NPV.

## Limitations of using the NPV method

**3.20** There are a number of problems associated with using the NPV method in practice.

(a) **The future discount factors** (or interest rates) which are used in calculating NPVs can only be **estimated** and are not known with certainty. Discount rates that are estimated for time periods far into the future are therefore less likely to be accurate, thereby leading to less accurate NPV values.

(b) Similarly, NPV calculations make use of estimated **future cash flows**. As with future discount factors, cash flows which are estimated for cash flows several years into the future cannot really be predicted with any real certainty.

(c) When using the NPV method it is common to assume that all cash flows occur **at the end of the year**. However, this assumption is also likely to give rise to less accurate NPV values.

**3.21** There are a number of computer programs available these days which enable a range of NPVs to be calculated for different circumstances (best-case and worst-case situations and so on). Such programs allow some of the limitations mentioned above to be alleviated.

# 4 Shareholder value analysis

**4.1** **Shareholder value analysis** (SVA) was developed during the 1980s from the work of *Rappaport* and focuses on value creation using the discounted cash flow approach. SVA assumes that **the value of a business is the net present value of its future cash flows, discounted at the appropriate cost of capital.** Many leading companies (including, for example, Pepsi, Quaker and Disney) have used SVA as a way of linking management strategy and decisions to the creation of value for shareholders.

**Key Concept**

**Shareholder value analysis** is an approach to financial management which focuses on the creation of economic value for shareholders, as measured by share price performance and flow of dividends.

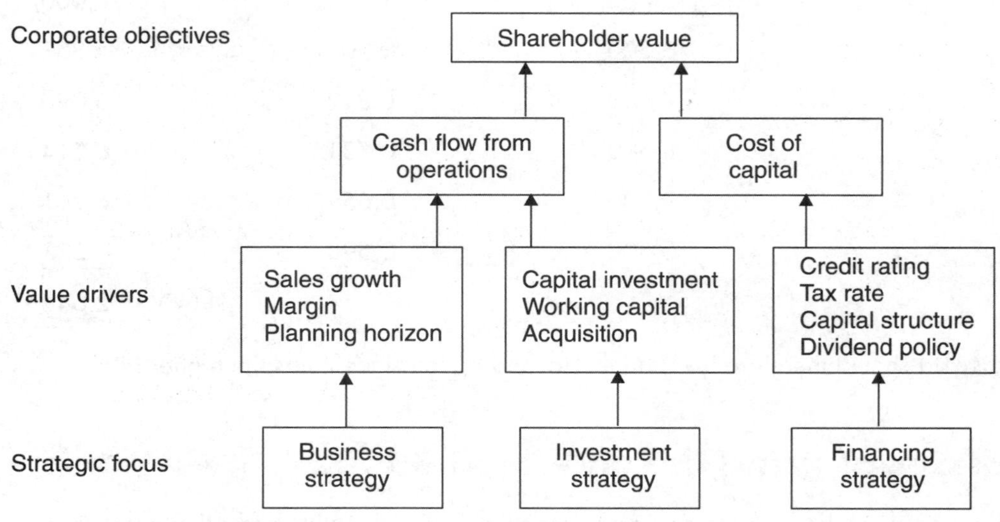


**4.2** SVA takes the following approach.

(a) Key decisions with implications for cash flow and risk are specified. These may be **strategic**, **operational**, **related to investment** or **financial**.

(b) **Value drivers** are identified as the factors having the greatest impact on shareholder value, and management attention is focused on the decisions which influence the value drivers.

**4.3** **Value drivers** are identified as being fundamental to the determination of value.

**4.4** **The model assumes** a constant percentage rate of sales growth and a constant operating profit margin. Tax is assumed to be a constant percentage of operating profit. Finally, fixed and working capital investments are assumed to be a constant percentage of changes in sales.

**4.5** Using the free cash flows, **corporate value** is then computed using a discount rate reflecting the company's **risk.** It will normally be a job for a financial specialist to determine the discount rate to be used. Indeed, it is likely that any financial analysis necessary will be undertaken by such specialists.

**Corporate value = PV of free cash flows + current value of marketable securities and other non-operating investments**

**4.6** **Shareholder value** can then be computed as **corporate value – debt**

**4.7** This approach is relatively **simple to apply**, is **consistent with the concept of share valuation by DCF** and creates management awareness of the **key long-term value variables** (drivers). However, its drawbacks include:

(a) The **constant percentage assumptions** may be **unrealistic**.

(b) The **input data** may **not** be **easily available** from current systems, particularly to outsiders.

(c) It may be **misused in target setting** – giving managers a 12-month target cash flow may discourage longer term profitable investment. On the other hand a longer-term target may be very difficult to set because of uncertainties over future cash flows.

## Economic value added

**4.8** Economic value added is closely associated with shareholder value analysis and gives the economic value or profit added per year. It can be used as a means of **measuring managerial performance,** by assessing the net present value of revenues (profits) less resources used (capital employed). It is **not** a measure of share valuation.

**4.9** **Economic value added = NOPAT – (cost of capital × capital employed)**

where NOPAT = Net operating profit after tax adjusted for non-cash expenses (see below)

(cost of capital × capital employed) = imputed charge for the capital consumed, the cost of capital being the weighted average cost of capital for the firm's **target capital structure**

**4.10** Adjustments may be needed to the profit figures in the accounts to arrive at NOPAT.

(a) **Interest** and **tax relief on interest** should be excluded from NOPAT, as they are taken into account in the imputed capital charge.

(b) **Investing cash flows** should be excluded from NOPAT **but** added to **capital employed.** These include **goodwill, research and development** and **advertising**, and other expenditure designed to build the business up over the next few years. The amount added to capital employed should be a figure that reflects the expenditure that has affected profit this year, say the research and development charge for the last four years or goodwill that has previously been written off. (In some calculations a small charge for research and development is included in the profit and loss account to reflect the economic depreciation of the capitalised value.)

(c) **Lease charges** should be excluded from NOPAT but added in as part of capital employed.

(d) In theory accounting **depreciation** should be added to the profit figures, and economic depreciation subtracted from profit figures to arrive at NOPAT. Economic depreciation is a charge for the fall in asset value due to wear or tear and obsolescence. In practice the depreciation figure in the accounts is often used as an approximation for economic depreciation, so no adjustment is necessary.

## 4.11 Benefits of economic value added

(a) **Net present value**

Economic value added focuses on the **long-term net present value of a company.** Managerial performance will be improved by investing in positive NPV projects, not investing in negative NPV projects and lowering the cost of capital.

(b) **Financing**

By including a financing element, the **cost of capital** is emphasised, and hence managers must have regard for **careful investment** and **control of working capital**. If managers choose negative NPV projects, the imputed capital charge will ultimately be greater than earnings.

(c) **Cash flows**

The adjustments within the model mean that economic value added should be based on **cash flows** rather than accounting data and hence it may be **less distorted** by the **accounting policies** chosen.

(d) **Clarity of measure**

Economic value added is a **monetary figure** rather than a ratio, and one that can be easily **linked to financial objectives**.

## 4.12 Drawbacks of economic value added

(a) **Failure to measure short-term position**

Economic value added does **not measure NPV** in the short-term. Projects with good long-term NPV, but large initial cash investments or poor initial returns, may be rejected by managers who are being judged on their **short-term performance.**

(b) **Use of historical accounts**

Economic value added is based on historical accounts which may be of **limited use** as a guide to the future. In practice also the influences of accounting policies on the starting profit figure may not be completely negated by the adjustments made to it in the economic value added model.

(c) **Other value drivers**

Other value drivers may be important despite being **excluded from the accounts**.

(e) **Adjustments**

Making the necessary adjustments can be **problematic** as sometimes a large number of adjustments are required.

(f) **Cost of capital**

The cost of capital used is based upon **assumptions** such as **no change in risk.**

(g) **Inter-company comparisons**

Companies which are **larger in size** may have larger economic value added figures for this reason. A**llowance for relative size** must be made when inter-company comparisons are performed.

# 5 Benchmarking

**5.1** **Benchmarking** generally involves comparing your operations to somebody else's.

## Key Concept

**Benchmarking**

The establishment, through data gathering, of targets and comparators, through whose use relative levels of performance (and particularly areas of underperformance) can be identified. By the adoption of identified best practices it is hoped that performance will improve.

## 5.2 Types of benchmarking

(a) **Internal benchmarking**, is a method of comparing one operating unit or function with another within the same organisation.

(b) **Functional benchmarking** compares functions with those of the best external practitioners of those functions, regardless of the industry they are in (also known as operational, process or generic benchmarking).

(c) **Competitor benchmarking**, gathers information about direct competitors, through techniques such as reverse engineering.

(d) **Strategic benchmarking** is a type of competitor benchmarking aimed at strategic action and organisational change.

## Marketing at Work

***British Airways***

British Airways used benchmarking from 1987 to help transform itself from a stodgy, state-controlled enterprise to a leading world airline. Apparently BA managers analysed their own business processes to identify the weakest elements, and then visited other airlines with checklists and questions. Problems are often found to be shared and competitors are willing to pool information in pursuit of solutions.

### 5.3 Advantages

(a) **Position audit**. Benchmarking can **assess a firm's existing position.**

(b) The comparisons are carried out by **the managers who have to live with any changes** implemented as a result of the exercise.

(c) Benchmarking **focuses on improvement in key areas** and sets targets which are challenging but **achievable**. What is really achievable can be discovered by examining what others have achieved: managers are thus able to accept that they are not being asked to perform miracles.

(d) If **all firms provide the same standard of quality**, it **ceases to be a source of competitive advantage.**

### 5.4 Dangers of benchmarking

(a) It **implies there is one best way** of doing business – arguably this boils down to the difference between efficiency and effectiveness. A process can be efficient but its output may not be useful. Other measures such as developing the value chain may be a better way of securing competitive advantage.

(b) The benchmark may be **yesterday's solution to tomorrow's problem**. For example, a cross-channel ferry company might benchmark its activities (eg speed of turnround at Dover and Calais, cleanliness on ship) against another ferry company, whereas the real competitor is the Channel Tunnel. In any case, it is a **catching-up exercise** rather than the development of anything distinctive. After the benchmarking exercise, the competitor might improve performance in a different way.

(c) It **depends on accurate information** about competitors, in the case of competitor benchmarking, or an **appropriate analogies** in other industries, in the case of functional benchmarking.

(d) It is not focussed on the **customer**.

**5.5** To make benchmarking work, it is important to **compare like with like**.

### 5.6 Steps in a benchmarking process

***Step 1.*** Identify items to be benchmarked.

***Step 2.*** Identify suitable organisations for comparison.

***Step 3.*** Collect data by an appropriate method.

***Step 4.*** Determine the current performance gap.

***Step 5.*** Project future performance levels.

***Step 6.*** Tell people about benchmark findings.

***Step 7.*** Establish goals for each business function.

***Step 8.*** Develop action plans.

***Step 9.*** Implement action plans.

***Step 10.*** Re-set benchmarks to a higher level to encourage continuous improvement

# 6 The balanced scorecard

**6.1** The balanced scorecard is a technique designed to ensure that the different functions of the business are integrated together in order that they work to achieve the corporate goals.

**Key Concept**

The **balanced scorecard** is 'a set of measures that gives top managers a fast but comprehensive view of the business. The balanced scorecard includes financial measures that tell the results of actions already taken. And it complements the financial measures with operational measures on customer satisfaction, internal processes, and the organisation's innovation and improvement activities – operational measures that are the drivers of future financial performance.' (Kaplan and Norton, January–February 1992, *Harvard Business Review*)

**6.2** 'Traditional financial accounting measures like return on investment and earnings per share can give misleading signals for continuous improvement and innovation'. The balanced scorecard allows managers to look at the business from **four important perspectives**.

- **Customer**
- **Financial**
- **Internal business**
- **Innovation and learning**

## Customer perspective

**6.3** **'How do customers see us?'** The balanced scorecard translates this into specific measures. Here are some examples. You may be able to think of more.

(a) **Time**. Lead time is the time it takes a firm to meet customer needs, from receiving an order to delivering the product.

(b) **Quality**. Quality measures not only include defect levels – although these should be minimised by TQM – but accuracy in forecasting.

(c) **Performance** of the product. (How often does the photocopier break down?)

(d) **Service**. How long will it take a problem to be rectified? (If the photocopier breaks down, how long will it take the maintenance engineer to arrive?)

**6.4** To view the firm's performance through customers' eyes, firms hire market researchers to assess how the firm performs. Higher service and quality may cost more at the outset, but savings can be made in the long term.

## Internal business perspective

**6.5** Findings from the **customers'** perspective must be **turned into the actions the firm must** take to meet these expectations. The **internal business perspective** identifies the **business processes that have the greatest impact on customer satisfaction**, such as quality and employee skills.

(a) Companies should also attempt to identify and measure their **distinctive competences** and the critical technologies they need to ensure continued leadership. Which processes should they excel at?

(b) To achieve these goals, **performance measures must relate to employee behaviour**, to tie in the strategic direction with employee action.

(c) An information system is necessary to enable executives to measure performance. An **executive information system** enables managers to drill down into lower level information.

## Innovation and learning perspective

**6.6** The question is **'Can we continue to improve and create value?'** Whilst the customer and internal process perspectives identify the **current** parameters for competitive success, the company needs to learn and to innovate to **satisfy future needs**. This might be one of the hardest items to measure.

(a) How long does it take to develop new products?

(b) How quickly does the firm climb the experience curve to manufacture new products?

(c) What percentage of revenue comes from new products?

(d) How many suggestions are made by staff and are acted upon?

(e) What are staff attitudes? Some firms believe that employee motivation and successful communication are necessary for organisational learning.

(f) Depending on circumstances, the company can identify measures for training and long-term investment.

Continuous improvement measures might also be relevant here.

## Financial perspective

**6.7** From the financial perspective, the question to be asked is: **'How do we appear to shareholders?'** Financial performance indicators indicate 'whether the company's strategies, implementation, and execution are contributing to bottom line management.'

**6.8** Some analysts consider that financial issues take care of themselves, and that they are only the **result** of the customer, internal process, and innovation and learning issues discussed earlier. This view is rather naive for a number of obvious reasons.

(a) Money is a resource, and financial measures will ultimately effect a firm's ability to obtain that resource (eg by raising the firm's cost of capital, if shareholders perceive greater risk).

(b) Well designed financial control systems can actually assist in TQM programmes (eg by identifying variances).

(c) The balanced scorecard **only measures** strategy. **It does not indicate that the strategy is the right one**. 'A failure to convert improved operational performance into improved financial performance should send executives back to their drawing boards to rethink the company's strategy or its implementation plans.'

## Understanding the balanced scorecard

**6.9** **Disappointing results** might result from a **failure to view all the measures as a whole**. For example, increasing productivity means that fewer employees are needed for a given level of output. Excess capacity can be created by quality improvements. However these improvements have to be exploited (eg by increasing sales). The **financial element** of the balanced scorecard 'reminds executives that improved quality, response time, productivity or new products, benefit the company only when they are translated into improved financial results', or if they enable the firm to obtain a sustainable competitive advantage.

**6.10** The balanced scorecard can help to measure performance. It does not assess strategy. As Kaplan and Norton say 'a failure to convert improved operational performance into improved financial performance should send executives back to rethink the company's strategy or its implementation plans.'

### 6.11 EXAMPLE: A BALANCED SCORECARD

*Balanced Scorecard*

**Financial Perspective**

| GOALS | MEASURES |
|---|---|
| Survive | Cash flow |
| Succeed | Monthly sales growth and operating income by division |
| Prosper | Increase market share and ROCE |

**Customer Perspective**

| GOALS | MEASURES |
|---|---|
| New products | Percentage of sales from new products |
| Responsive supply | On-time delivery (defined by customer) |
| Preferred supplier | Share of key accounts' purchases |
| | Ranking by key accounts |
| Customer partnership | Number of co-operative engineering efforts |

**Internal Business Perspective**

| GOALS | MEASURES |
|---|---|
| Technology capability | Manufacturing configuration vs competition |
| Manufacturing excellence | Cycle time |
| | Unit cost |
| | Yield |
| Design productivity | Silicon efficiency |
| | Engineering efficiency |
| New product introduction | Actual introduction schedule vs plan |

**Innovation and Learning Perspective**

| GOALS | MEASURES |
|---|---|
| Technology leadership | Time to develop next generation of products |
| Manufacturing learning | Process time to maturity |
| Product focus | Percentage of products that equal 80% sales |
| Time to market | New product introduction vs competition |

**6.12** From a marketing point-of-view, the balanced scorecard enables all the vital perspectives – not just the financial ones – to be taken into account. In fact two of the main perspectives – customer and innovation – relate directly to marketing

## Chapter Roundup

- **Marketing audits** examine every aspect of an organisation's marketing strategy and activities. They should be **regular, comprehensive, systematic** and **independent**.
- **Discounting** is a numerical process that determines the **present value** of a future cash flow.
- The **net present value** of a project is the sum of all the future cashflows associated with it.
- Choosing the appropriate **discount rate** is the most difficult aspect of all discounted cash flow techniques.
- **Shareholder value analysis** may be used to measure corporate (and hence management) performance in terms of benefit created for shareholders. **Economic value added** is a simple measure of success in moving towards enhanced shareholder value.
- **Benchmarking** is a widespread technique used to establish standards of best practice. It can be confined to one organisation or be used to make comparisons between competitors.
- The **balanced scorecard** attempts to give a rounded picture of corporate achievement by measuring progress in four 'perspectives':
  - Customer
  - Internal business
  - Financial
  - Innovation and learning

## Quick Quiz

1 Should a marketing audit consider product profitability?

2 If I expect to receive a payment of £10.50 in 6 months time and I can earn 10% by putting money on deposit, what is the payment worth today?

3 A marketing project costing £10,000 is assessed as having a net present value of £147. Should the project go ahead?

4 What, in the context of SVA, are value drivers?

5 In simple terms, what is the formula for EVA?

6 Give two disadvantages of benchmarking.

7 What are the 'perspectives' of the balanced scorecard?

8 How could you use the balanced scorecard to assess strategy?

## Answers to Quick Quiz

1 Yes. Analysis of the product portfolio is an important aspect of marketing management.

2 £10

3 Yes, in theory. Any NPV greater than zero means that wealth is being increased. However, a more robust NPV might be required to allow for the uncertainty of future cashflows.

4 The factors having significant impact on shareholder value. Management attention is focused upon them.

5 Profit minus a charge for the use of capital.

6 Two from:

- Implication that there is a single best approach
- Bias to historical solutions
- Dependency on accurate information about competitors
- Lack of customer focus

7
- Customer
- Financial
- Internal business
- Innovation and learning

8 You can't. It measures performance, not plans.

## Action Programme Review

1 £7,104

*Working*

Using the discounting formula, $X = S \times \frac{1}{(1+r)^n}$

where S = £16,000
n = 12
r = 0.07
X = PV

$PV = £16{,}000 \times \frac{1}{1.07^{12}} = £7{,}104$

2

| | *Cash flow* | *Discount factor* | *Present value* |
|---|---|---|---|
| | £ | 10% | £ |
| 0 | (18,000) | 1.000 | (18,000) |
| 1 | 6,000 | $\frac{1}{1.10} = 0.909$ | 5,454 |
| 2 | 8,000 | $\frac{1}{1.10^2} = 0.826$ | 6,608 |
| 3 | 5,000 | $\frac{1}{1.10^3} = 0.751$ | 3,755 |
| 4 | 1,000 | $\frac{1}{1.10^4} = 0.683$ | 683 |
| | | Net present value | (1,500) |

The NPV is negative. We can therefore draw the following conclusions.

(a) It is cheaper to invest elsewhere at 10% than to invest in the project.
(b) The project would earn a return of less than 10%.
(c) The project is not viable (since the PV of the costs is greater than the PV of the benefits).

**Now try Question 3 at the end of the Study Text**

# Part C

## The internal environment

# 4 Internal Situation Analysis

| Chapter Topic List | |
|---|---|
| 1 | Setting the scene |
| 2 | Resources and limiting factors |
| 3 | Assets |
| 4 | The marketing audit |
| 5 | Innovation audit |
| 6 | The role of culture |

## Syllabus Content

- Techniques and processes for the objective assessment of the internal environment
- Evaluation of the resource-based and asset-based views of the organisation
- Assessment of the fit between culture and strategy
- Evaluation of the core competences, assets, culture and weaknesses of an organisation

## Key Concepts Introduced

- Limiting factor/key factor
- Distinctive competence
- Marketing asset
- Innovation audit
- Culture
- Organisational culture
- Paradigm

# 1 Setting the scene

1.1 A look at the internal environment of an organisation is a way of identifying strengths and weaknesses. It therefore covers all aspects of the organisation. This is because the other functions of the organisation effectively act as constraints over what marketing personnel can achieve.

1.2 A company needs to evaluate its ability to compete and satisfy customer needs. The firm's resources, once identified, must be harnessed to a market orientation to ensure that those resources are directed at satisfying those needs.

1.3 There are a number of approaches to be taken with regard to corporate capability. In this chapter we conduct an overview of resources in the context of organisational effectiveness. The key issues are what resources the organisation has and how they are deployed.

1.4 An analysis of corporate/marketing resources covers:

- What the organisation currently has or owns
- What the organisation has access to, even if it currently does not own the resources
- How effectively it **deploys** its resources

1.5 The culture of an organisation is strategically important. Culture is to some extent formed by past strategic success and influences the development of strategy for the future. An awareness and understanding of the interaction between culture and strategy is therefore an important part of internal strategic assessment. For marketers in particular, the degree of **market orientation** is an important cultural variable.

# 2 Resources and limiting factors

2.1 A **resource audit** is a review of the organisation resources which can be grouped into these categories (Hooley *et al*).

| Resource | Comment |
|---|---|
| **Technical resources** | ■ Technical ability<br>■ Processes for NPD<br>■ Ability to convert new technology into new marketing products |
| **Financial standing** | Firms with a good financial standing find it easier to raise money. |
| **Managerial skills** | Managerial roles and functions were covered in Chapter 2. An effective management is a key organisation resource in planning activities, controlling the organisation and motivating staff. |
| **Organisation** | Organisation structure can be a resource for marketers, for example product divisionalisation or brand management control at brand level. The organisation structure should facilitate communication and decision-making. |
| **Information systems** | The strategic role of information systems is covered at various times throughout this Study Text. |

2.2 **Resources are of no value unless they are organised into systems**, and so a **resource audit** should go on to consider how well or how badly resources have been utilised,

and whether the organisation's systems are **effective** and **efficient** in meeting customer needs profitably.

## Limiting factors

2.3 Every organisation operates under resource **constraints**.

### Key Concept

A **limiting factor** or **key factor** is 'a factor which at any time or over a period may limit the activity of an entity, often one where there is shortage or difficulty of supply'.

*Examples*

- A shortage of production capacity
- A limited number of key personnel, such as salespeople with technical knowledge
- A restricted distribution network
- Too few managers with knowledge about finance, or overseas markets
- Inadequate research design resources to develop new products or services
- A poor system of strategic intelligence
- Lack of money
- A lack of staff who are adequately trained

2.4 Once the limiting factor has been identified, the planners should:

- **Short term**, make best use of the resources available
- **Long term**, reduce the limitation

## Resource use

2.5 Resource use is concerned with the **efficiency** with which resources are used, and the **effectiveness** of their use in achieving the planning objectives of the business.

## Distinctive competences

2.6 To recap from Chapter 1, a strategic approach involves identifying a firm's **competences**. 'Members of organisations develop judgements about what they think the company can do well – its core competence.' These competences may derive from:

- **Experience** in making and marketing a product or service
- The talents and potential of individuals in the organisation
- The **quality of co-ordination**

### Key Concept

The **distinctive competences** of an organisation are what it does better than its rivals.

**2.7 Tests for identifying a core competence**

(a) It provides potential **access to a wide variety of markets**. GPS of France developed a 'core competence' in 'one-hour' processing, enabling it to process films and build reading glasses in one hour.

(b) It **contributes significantly to the value enjoyed** by the customer. For example, in GPS in (a) above, the waiting time restriction was very important.

(c) It should be **hard for a competitor to copy**, if it is technically complex, involves specialised processes, involves complex interrelationships between different people in the organisation or is hard to define.

In many cases, a company might choose to **combine competences**.

**2.8** Bear in mind that **relying on a competence is no substitute for a strategy**. However, distinctive competences are an **important support for competitive positioning**.

# 3 Assets

**Key Concept**

**Marketing asset**: something a firm can use to advantage in the market place.

**3.1** An asset-based approach matches 'marketing assets' with customer requirements. There are four types of marketing assets (Hooley *et al*).

- **Customer-based** assets
- **Distribution-based** assets
- **Internal** assets
- **Alliance-based** assets

**3.2** **Customer-based assets** exist in the customer's mind.

(a) Corporate **image and reputation** can be an asset or a liability, depending on the received wisdom.

(b) A **brand** is an asset. We cover branding in Chapter 9 (the value of brands) and Chapter 14 (in terms of brand building).

(c) **Market domination**. High market share is an asset because of the economies of scale it brings.

(d) **Better products/services** as perceived by the customer.

**3.3 Distribution-based assets**

(a) **Distribution network**. This covers sites and access to customers. For many years banks regarded their branch networks as an asset, but branches are costly to maintain and Barclays in the UK has recently attracted criticism for its decision to close many of its small local branches.

(b) **Distribution control**. Control of distribution constitutes a barrier to entry to other competitors.

(c) **Pockets of strength**. Where a company cannot serve a wide market, it can build strength in specific regions or through selected distribution outlets.

(d) **Uniqueness**. A unique or hard-to-copy distribution channel is an asset. A good example is *Dell Computers*.

(e) **Lead time**. Rapid response to customer orders is an asset. This can be implemented in a just-in-time system.

(f) **Supplier network**. Further up the supply chain, key suppliers can be a marketing asset if they secure supplies of goods or services.

## Marketing at Work

***NXT* speakers**

The difference between a competence and a strategy is illustrated by NXT, a company which 'thinks it has discovered a technology that could change the world. It believes its flat-screen loudspeakers could find their way into everything ... .'

The new speakers came from military research and are based on techniques which show that materials ... radiate sound waves.'

This expertise is the basic competence. But what do they do with it?

They could choose to manufacture speakers themselves, but instead decided to follow *Dolby's* business model by providing its own technology to large companies.

(a) NXT has 1,500 patents in 70 countries, covering the technical workings and several applications.

(b) NXT insists its licensees work with it to adapt its ideas, and even vetoes applications it disagrees with.

(c) NXT aims to ensure its brand name appears on products made by licensees (eg like Dolby or Ontel).

(d) NXT seeks to develop other ideas.

NXT, unlike Dolby, will not continue in manufacturing, to avoid competing with licensees. The strategy is to develop a relationship marketing approach rather than go into manufacturing.

*Financial Times*, 6 February 2001

### 3.4 Marketing assets internal to the firm

(a) **Low costs** give a firm the flexibility to choose low prices or to benefit from better margins.

(b) **Information systems and market intelligence**. Customer databases are built up over time and can enable offers to be targeted.

(c) The **existing customer base**. Satisfied customers are more likely to be repeat customers.

(d) Other assets include **technological skills** which can support marketing activities, production **expertise**, **intellectual property**, partnerships and corporate culture.

3.5 **Alliance based assets**. Many firms are expanding through alliances. For example, airlines have code sharing arrangements. Such assets include:

- Market access
- Management skills
- Shared technology
- Exclusivity (eg shutting out competitors)

**Marketing at Work**

Many airlines have alliances in which they 'share' passengers for flights on certain legs. For example, a passenger flying *BA* might, on certain journeys, be transferred to a *Qantas* flight.

In theory this can be an asset to both companies, provided that customer expectations are met (ie that BA and Qantas offer similar standards of service quality).

# 4 The marketing audit

4.1 A review of marketing effectiveness is carried out in the marketing audit. This important topic has already been discussed.

# 5 Innovation audit

5.1 The chief object of being innovative is to ensure organisational success in a changing world. It can also have the following advantages.

(a) Improvements in quality of **products** and **service**
(b) A **leaner structure** – layers of management or administration may be done away with
(c) Prompt and imaginative **solutions to problems**
(d) **Less formality** in structure and style, leading to better communication
(e) **Greater confidence** inside and outside the organisation in its ability to cope with change

5.2 Innovation and new product development (NPD) is therefore essential for many firms to survive and prosper. It is an increasingly important area.

**Key Concept**

**Innovation audit**: a critical assessment of the firm's innovation record, the internal obstacles to innovation and how performance can be enhanced.

5.3 A firm needs to assess how well it is able to deliver the level and type of innovation necessary to continue to meet customer needs and expectations. Drummond and Ensor (1999) identify **four key areas** for the innovation audit.

- The current **organisational climate**
- Measures of the organisation's **current performance** with regard to innovation
- Review of **policies and practices** supporting innovation and facilitating it
- The balance of **styles** of the management team

**Exam Tip**

*The innovation audit featured in a June 2000 mini-case, in the case of a breakfast cereals producer. Improving the speed and quantity of innovation featured in June 2001. Innovation in a wider sense was a major theme in a June 2002 mini-case.*

## Organisational climate

### 5.4 Barriers to innovation in marketing

(a) **Resistance to change**

Any new method of management thinking can experience some resistance from established managers. This resistance may be due to concern to protect the status quo, or because managers are ignorant of the new thinking. Integrating marketing communications seems so obvious that it may be overlooked or seen as a superficial approach.

(b) **Old planning systems**

Old planning systems have sometimes downgraded marketing decisions to the tactical level. Advertising expenditure is decided on the basis of what the company can afford rather than what is strategically required. Promotion is seen as a series of short-term actions rather than as a long-term investment.

(c) **Old structures/functional specialists**

Complementing traditional planning systems are traditional organisation structures. These structures freeze out new thinking on integrated marketing strategy. Individuals have limited specific responsibilities – just for advertising, say, or just for public relations – and this inhibits new thinking on integration.

(d) **Centralised control**

If the chief executive keeps tight control of the organisation and of its planning and is unconvinced of the benefits of innovation then it will not happen.

(e) **Cost considerations**

Innovation usually requires investment.

### 5.5 Methods of overcoming these barriers

(a) **Top management commitment**

The most effective way of overcoming these barriers to change is through the commitment of top management. The chief executive in particular needs to be convinced of the appropriateness of the new thinking and be enthusiastic about its implementation throughout the organisation.

(b) **Marketing reorganisation**

One way in which the chief executive can take advice is through a reorganisation of the marketing function in the organisation.

(c) **Training and development**

It is one thing to change attitudes. It is another thing to be in a position to know exactly what to do. It needs the services of individuals trained in strategic thinking. The individuals chosen to implement any new programme must be enthusiasts capable of overcoming resistance to change.

(d) **Marketing as a competitive advantage**

Those with responsibility for implementing an integrated marketing programme must do so with the objective of developing it as a sustainable, long-term competitive advantage.

(e) **Producing the results**

Nothing succeeds like success. Producing the business results as a consequence of effective marketing communications will boost confidence and gain management converts to the new thinking on an integrated approach.

## Measures of performance

5.6 This may include measures such as the rate of successful **new product development** and related sales over the past years, or **customer satisfaction ratings**.

5.7 **Customer satisfaction ratings**. An important input to innovation is the degree of customer satisfaction, both from the product itself and service levels.

(a) Customer satisfaction can be measured on a scale (eg from **highly satisfied** to **highly dissatisfied**).

(b) Customers can also be asked to identify which features of a service/product they found most useful.

(c) Firms should **actively measure** customer satisfaction, rather than simply **react to complaints**.

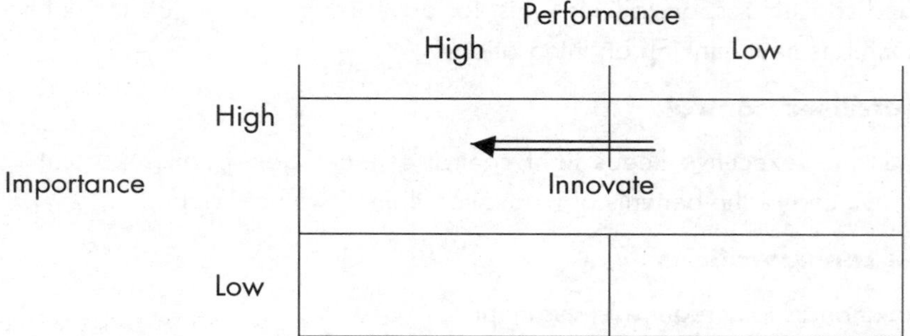


Clearly, a firm should be most concerned about matters of high importance with 'low' performance. Innovation may be necessary to ensure that high performance is achieved on matters of high importance.

5.8 **Innovation/value matrix**

(a) A similar methodology can apply to innovation and its **value** to the customer. Clearly, the best sort of innovation gives highest customer value for the lowest cost or effort. Businesses can be categorised between those that offer the normal level of innovation and market value, those that offer some improvement on the offerings of competition, and finally those that offer significant innovations and value for the customer.

(b) There is a danger that too many innovations can, in fact, confuse the customer. Recent research has encouraged some companies (such as Procter & Gamble) to reduce the variety of goods on offer.

(c) The innovation process should consider both the **technology** and **customer needs**.

(d) For example, once the limitations of the silicon chip are reached, optical computers might be invented. In some cases, instead of technical developments being used to predict future technologies, future social developments can be predicted, in order to **predict future customer needs**. The likely technologies which will satisfy these needs can then be considered.

## Policies to encourage innovation

**5.9** To encourage innovation the objective for management should be to create a more outward-looking organisation.

- People should be encouraged to look for new products, markets, processes and designs
- People should seek ways to improve productivity

**5.10** An innovation strategy calls for a management policy of **giving encouragement** to innovative ideas.

(a) Giving **financial backing** to innovation, by spending on R & D and market research and risking capital on new ideas.

(b) Giving employees the **opportunity** to work in an environment where the exchange of ideas for innovation can take place. Management style and organisation structure can help here.

(i) Management can actively encourage employees and customers to put forward new ideas.

(ii) **Development teams** can be set up and an organisation built up on project team-work.

(iii) **Quality circles** and brainstorming groups can be used to encourage creative thinking about work issues.

(c) Where appropriate, **recruitment policy** should be directed towards appointing employees with the necessary skills for doing innovative work. Employees should be trained and kept up-to-date.

(d) Certain managers should be **made responsible for obtaining information** from outside the organisation about innovative ideas, and for **communicating** this information throughout the organisation.

(e) **Strategic planning** should result in targets being set for innovation, and successful achievements by employees should if possible be rewarded.

## The management team

**5.11** The management team are key in setting the scene for innovation. The management team is also a critical influence on corporate culture. Belbin drew up a list of the characteristics of an ideal team.

| Member | Role |
|---|---|
| **Co-ordinator** | Presides and co-ordinates; balanced, disciplined, good at working through others. |
| **Shaper** | Highly strung, dominant, extrovert, passionate about the task itself, a spur to action. |
| **Plant** | Introverted, but intellectually dominant and imaginative; source of ideas and proposals but with disadvantages of introversion. |
| **Monitor-evaluator** | Analytically (rather than creatively) intelligent; dissects ideas, spots flaws; possibly aloof, tactless – but necessary. |
| **Resource-investigator** | Popular, sociable, extrovert, relaxed; source of new contacts, but not an originator; needs to be made use of. |
| **Implementor** | Practical organiser, turning ideas into tasks; scheduling, planning and so on; trustworthy and efficient, but not excited; not a leader, but an administrator. |
| **Team worker** | Most concerned with team maintenance – supportive, understanding, diplomatic; popular but uncompetitive – contribution noticed only in absence. |
| **Finisher** | Chivvies the team to meet deadlines, attend to details; urgency and follow-through important, though not always popular. |

**5.12** The dynamics of the management team affects how it perceives the work environment.

**5.13** Although the **environment poses strategic questions,** it is **people who make sense of it** and devise strategies. Whilst the recipe provides cultural coherence it can impede strategic renewal. If the corporate strategy is failing, a company will:

**Step 1.** Place tighter **controls** over implementation (eg give tougher performance targets to sales staff); but if **this** fails ...

**Step 2.** Develop a new strategy (eg sell in a new market); but if this fails as well ...

**Step 3.** Only now will the company abandon the recipe (eg realise that the product is obsolete).

**5.14** This is significant if it impacts on the management team's attitude to innovation. A management team might be unbalanced if it has too many 'ideas' people and not enough implementers able to bring projects to fruition.

## Stages of an innovation audit

**5.15** If asked to describe the innovation **audit**, here is a possible approach.

**Step 1.** **Benchmark with leading competitors**. For example, many motor firms regard the rate and speed of NPD as something they must emulate.

**Step 2.** **Assess reactivity: identify performance indicators** for innovation and compare with previous years (Davidson).

- **Rate of NPD**
- Number of innovations
- **Success** rate (more important than quantity)
- Percentage of revenue derived from **innovations** (3M has a target)
- **Incremental** sales resulting from innovation
- Average annual sales per new product/service
- Customer satisfaction ratings
- Staff turnover, if this affects climate of innovation

Note that if a higher percentage of revenue comes from **innovation** then **incremental** products, it looks as if innovatory products are **cannibalising** existing sales.

**Step 3.** Identify obstacles to innovation which typically reside in the corporate cultural structure.

**Step 4.** Recommend innovation objectives.

# 6 The role of culture

## Organisational culture

**Key Concept**

The word **culture** is used by sociologists and anthropologists to encompass 'the sum total of the beliefs, knowledge, attitudes of mind and customs to which people are exposed in their social conditioning.'

**6.1** Through contact with a particular culture, individuals learn a language, acquire values and learn habits of behaviour and thought.

(a) **Beliefs and values**. Beliefs are what we feel to be the case on the basis of objective and subjective information (eg people can believe the world is round or flat). Values are beliefs which are relatively enduring, relatively general and fairly widely accepted as a guide to culturally appropriate behaviour.

(b) **Customs**. Customs are modes of behaviour which represent culturally accepted ways of behaving in response to given situations.

(c) **Artefacts**. Artefacts are all the physical tools designed by human beings for their physical and psychological well-being, including works of art, technology, products.

(d) **Rituals**. A ritual is a type of activity which takes on symbolic meaning; it consists of a fixed sequence of behaviour repeated over time.

The learning and sharing of culture is made possible by **language** (both written and spoken, verbal and non-verbal).

**6.2** Knowledge of the culture of a society is clearly of value to businesses in a number of ways.

(a) **Marketers** can adapt their products accordingly, and be fairly sure of a sizeable market. This is particularly important in export markets.

(b) **Human resource managers** may need to tackle cultural differences in recruitment. For example, some ethnic minorities have a different body language from the majority, which may be hard for some interviewers to interpret.

**6.3** We consider the broader aspects of culture later in this Study Text. For now, we will confine ourselves to a consideration of the importance of **organisational culture.**

## Key Concept

**Organisational culture** consists of the beliefs, attitudes, practices and customs to which people are exposed during their interaction with the organisation.

**6.4** Culture is both internal to an organisation and external to it. The culture of an organisation is embedded in the culture of the wider society. Its importance to strategy is that it can predispose the organisation towards or away from a particular course of action.

**6.5** All organisations will generate their own cultures, whether spontaneously or under the guidance of positive managerial strategy. *Schein* suggests that three levels of culture can be distinguished in organisations.

(a) **Basic, underlying assumptions** which guide the behaviour of the individuals and groups in the organisation. These may include customer orientation, or belief in quality, trust in the organisation to provide rewards, freedom to make decisions, freedom to make mistakes and the value of innovation and initiative at all levels.

(b) **Overt beliefs** expressed by the organisation and its members, which can be used to condition the assumptions mentioned above. These beliefs and values may emerge as sayings, slogans and mottoes, such as IBM's motto, 'think'. They may emerge in a rich mythology of jokes and stories about past successes and heroic failures.

(c) **Visible artefacts** – the style of the offices or other premises, dress rules, visible structures or processes, the degree of informality between superiors and subordinates and so on.

Management can encourage this by selling a sense of the corporate mission, or by promoting the corporate image. It can reward the right attitudes and punish (or simply not employ) those who are not prepared to commit themselves to the culture.

**6.6** An organisation's culture is influenced by many factors.

(a) **The organisation's founder**. A strong set of values and assumptions is set up by the organisation's founder, and even after he or she has retired, these values have their own momentum. Or, to put it another way, an organisation might find it hard to shake off its original culture. *Peters and Waterman* believed that 'excellent' companies began with strong leaders.

(b) **The organisation's history**. *Johnson and Scholes* state that the way an organisation works reflects the era when it was founded. Farming, for example, sometimes has a craft element to it. The effect of history can be determined by stories, rituals and symbolic behaviour. They legitimise behaviour and promote priorities. (In some organisations certain positions are regarded as intrinsically more 'heroic' than others.)

(c) **Leadership and management style**. An organisation with a strong culture recruits managers who naturally conform to it.

(d) **Structure and systems** affect culture as well as strategy.

**6.7** The **McKinsey 7-S** model was designed to show how the various aspects of a business relate to one another. It is a useful illustration of the way culture fits into an organisation. In particular, it shows the links between the organisation's behaviour and the behaviour of individuals within it. The model was developed by Peters and Waterman while working as McKinsey consultants.

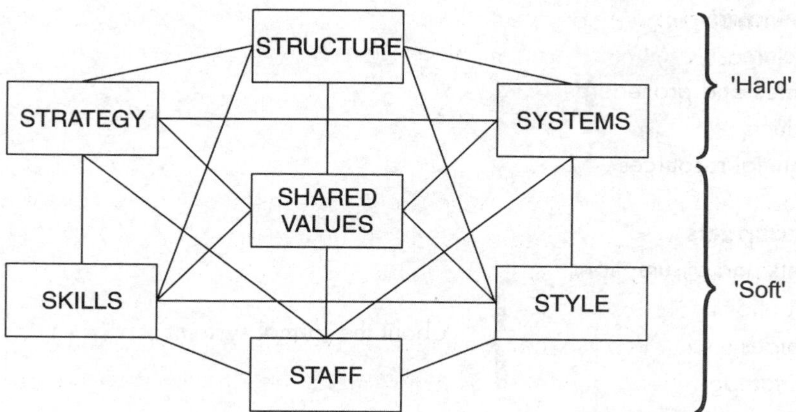


6.8 Three of the elements are considered 'hard'.

(a) **Structure**. The organisation structure determines division of tasks in the organisation and the hierarchy of authority from the most senior to junior.

(b) **Strategy**. Strategy is way in which the organisation plans to outperform its competitors, if it is a business, or how it intends to achieve its objectives.

(c) **Systems**. Systems include the technical systems of accounting, personnel, management information and so forth.

These 'hard' elements are easily quantified or defined, and deal with **facts and rules**.

6.9 However, the McKinsey model suggests that certain 'soft' elements are equally important.

(a) **Shared values** are the guiding beliefs of people in the organisation as to why it exists. (For example, people in a hospital seek to save lives.) It forms part of the corporate culture.

(b) **Staff** are the people in the organisation. They have their own complex concerns and priorities.

(c) **Style** is another aspect of the **corporate culture**, which includes the shared assumptions, ways of working and attitudes of management.

(d) **Skills** refer to those things that the organisation does well. For example, BT is good at providing a telephone service, but even if the phone network is eventually used as a transmission medium for television/film programmes, BT is unlikely to make those programmes itself.

The importance of the 'soft' elements for success was emphasised by Peters and Waterman in their study of 'excellent' companies.

## The organisational iceberg

6.10 *French and Bell* described the **organisational iceberg** in which formal aspects are **overt** and informal aspects are **covert** or hidden, rather as the bulk of an iceberg is underwater. The formal aspects are similar to the McKinsey 'hard' elements while the informal aspects correspond to the 'soft' elements in the 7-S model.

**6.11 Formal aspects**

- Goals
- Terminology
- Structure
- Policies and procedures
- Products
- Financial resources

**6.12 Informal aspects**

- Beliefs and assumptions
- Perceptions
- Attitudes
- Feelings

} about the formal systems

- Values
- Informal interactions
- Group norms

## Paradigm and politics

### Key Concept

The word **paradigm** may be used to signify the basic assumptions and beliefs that an organisation's decision-makers hold in common. Note that this is a slightly different concept from **culture**. The paradigm represents **collective experience** and is used to make sense of a given situation; it is thus essentially conservative and inhibiting to innovation, while an innovative **culture** is entirely feasible.

**6.13** The **politics** of the organisation may also influence strategy.

> 'The political view of strategy development is that strategies develop as the outcome of processes of bargaining and negotiation among powerful internal or external interest groups (or stakeholders).'

**6.14** Johnson and Scholes describe the processes by which paradigm and politics influence the process of strategy development.

**Step 1.** Issue awareness

- Internal results, customer responses or environmental changes can make **individuals** aware of a problem.
- A **trigger** alerts the **formal** information system to the problem, so that organisational activity takes over from the individual's consideration of the problem.

**Step 2.** **Issue formulation**. Managers try to analyse and get to the root of the problem. Information may be used to rationalise, rather than challenge, management's existing view of the situation. **Formal analysis** in practice plays a little role.

**Step 3.** **Solution development**. Some possible solutions are developed and one is selected.

- **Memory search**: solutions which worked in the past.
- **Passive search**: wait for a solution to suggest itself.

Solutions begin with a vague idea, which is further refined and explored by internal discussion.

**Step 4.** **Solution selection**

- **Eliminate unacceptable plans**. This screening process involves bargaining, diplomacy and judgement rather than formal evaluation according to the business case. ('Unacceptable' might mean unacceptable in terms of organisational politics, rather than in terms of business sense.)
- **Endorsements.** Many strategic decisions **originate from management subsystems**, which senior managers authorise. Junior managers might filter strategic information, or ignore certain options, to protect themselves.

## Marketing at Work

***Enron***

Enron is now notorious for its unethical practices. However, its collapse is traceable to a failure of strategic control. In the early 1990s, Enron was extremely successful as a market maker in the supply of gas and electricity. Its strategy was 'asset light': it did not produce gas, or very much electricity, but it used its financial expertise and its control of gas pipe lines and electricity grids to make large profits from the integration of supply and demand.

Unfortunately, early success bred hubris and quite junior executives were allowed to make major investments in industries whose characteristics were totally different from the homogeneity of product and ease of distribution of gas and electricity. In each case, the strategies failed because they made large demands for capital and low utilisation of Enron's core trading competences.

## The paradigm and the cultural web

**6.15** Johnson and Scholes use the term cultural web to mean a combination of the assumptions that make up the **paradigm**, together with the **physical manifestations** of culture. They suggest that the paradigm may be reinforced by such manifestations.

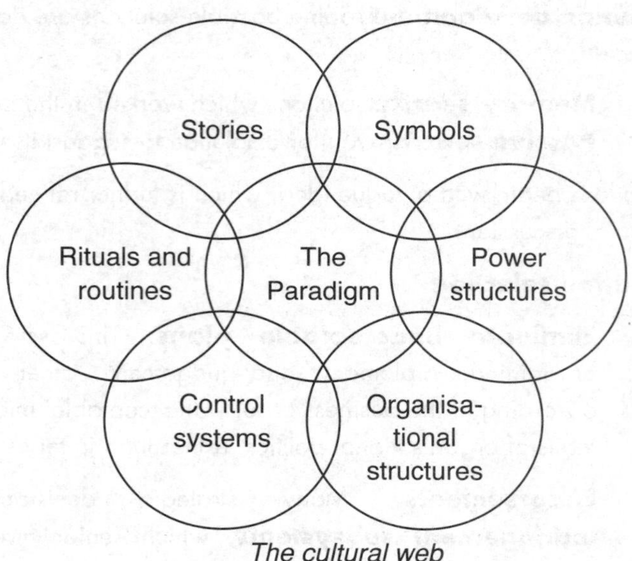


*The cultural web*

## Culture and structure

**6.16** Writing the *Harvard Business Review* in 1972, *Roger Harrison* suggested that organisations could be classified into four types. His work was later popularised by *Charles Handy* in his book 'Gods of Management'. The four types are differentiated by their structures, processes and management methods. The differences are so significant as to create distinctive cultures, to each of which Handy gives the name of a Greek god.

**6.17** **Zeus** is the god representing the **power culture**. Zeus is a dynamic entrepreneur who rules with snap decisions. Power and influence stem from a central source, perhaps the owner-directors or the founder of the business. The degree of formalisation is limited, and there are few rules and procedures, though this does not prevent the power-holders from exercising strict control. Such a firm is likely to be organised on a **functional** basis.

(a) The organisation is capable of adapting quickly to meet change.

(b) Personal influence decreases as the size of an organisation gets bigger. **The power culture is therefore best suited to smaller entrepreneurial organisations, where the leaders have direct communication with all employees**.

(c) Subordinates succeed by successfully guessing how their superiors would want them to act.

**6.18** **Apollo** is the god of the **role culture** or **bureaucracy.** Everything is orderly and legitimate. There is a presumption of **logic and rationality**.

(a) These organisations have a formal hierarchical structure, and operate by well-established rules and procedures. Individuals are required to perform their job to the full, but not to overstep the boundaries of their authority. Individuals who work for such organisations tend to learn an expertise without experiencing risk; many do their job adequately, but are not over-ambitious.

(b) **The bureaucratic style can be very efficient** in a stable environment, when the organisation is large and when the work is predictable.

**6.19** **Athena** is the goddess of the **task culture.** Management is dedicated to achieving the current goal. Performance is judged by results.

(a) The task culture is reflected in project teams and task forces. In such organisations, **there is no dominant or clear leader. The principal concern in a task culture is to get the job done**. Therefore the individuals who are important are the **experts** with the ability to accomplish a particular aspect of the task.

(b) The task culture is well suited to complex, unstable environments.

(c) Task cultures are expensive, as experts demand a market price.

(d) Task cultures also depend on variety, and to tap creativity requires a tolerance of perhaps costly mistakes.

**6.20** **Dionysus** is the god of the **existential culture**. In the three other cultures, the individual is subordinate to the organisation or task. **An existential culture is found in an organisation whose purpose is to serve the interests of the individuals within it**. These organisations are rare, although an example might be a partnership of a few individuals who do all the work of the organisation themselves (with perhaps a little secretarial or clerical assistance).

(a) Barristers (in the UK) work through chambers. The clerk co-ordinates their work and hands out briefs, but does not control them.

(b) Management in these organisations are often lower in status than the professionals and are labelled secretaries, administrators, bursars, registrars and chief clerk.

(c) The organisation depends on the **talent of the individuals;** management is derived from the consent of the managed, rather than the delegated authority of the owners.

**6.21** The descriptions above interrelate four different strands.

- The individual
- The type of the work the organisation does
- The culture of the organisation
- The environment

Organisational effectiveness perhaps depends on an appropriate fit of all of them.

## Marketing at Work

Handy cites a pharmaceutical company which at one time had all its manufacturing subcontracted, until turnover and cost considerations justified a factory of its own. The company hired nine talented individuals to design and run the factory. Result:

(a) The *design team* ran on a task culture, with a democratic/consultative leadership style, using project teams for certain problems. This was successful while the factory was being built.

(b) After its opening, the factory, staffed by 400, was run on similar lines. There were numerous problems. Every problem was treated as a project, and the workforce resented being asked to help sort out 'management' problems. In the end, the factory was run in a slightly more autocratic way. Handy states that this is a classic case of an *Athenian* culture to create a factory being superseded by an *Apollonian* culture to run it. Different cultures suit different businesses.

## Action Programme 1

Which of Handy's cultures would you say is prevalent in your office?

## Action Programme 2

Review the following statements. Ascribe each of them to one of the four approaches.

People are controlled and influenced by:

- The personal exercise of rewards, punishments or charisma;
- The impersonal exercise of economic and political power to enforce procedures and standards of performance;
- Communication and discussion of task requirements leading to appropriate action, motivated by personal commitment, to achieve the goal;
- Intrinsic interest and enjoyment in the activities to be done, and/or concern and caring for the needs of the other people involved.

## Culture, the environment and strategy

**6.22** Culture is an important filter of information and an interpreter of it, as suggested in the diagrams below.

- Ignoring culture

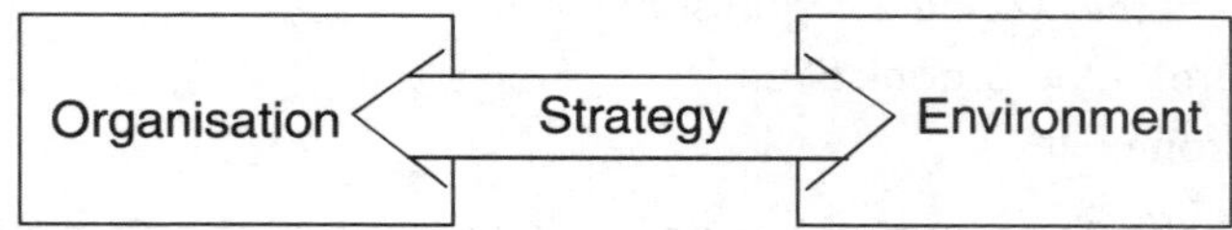


- Including culture

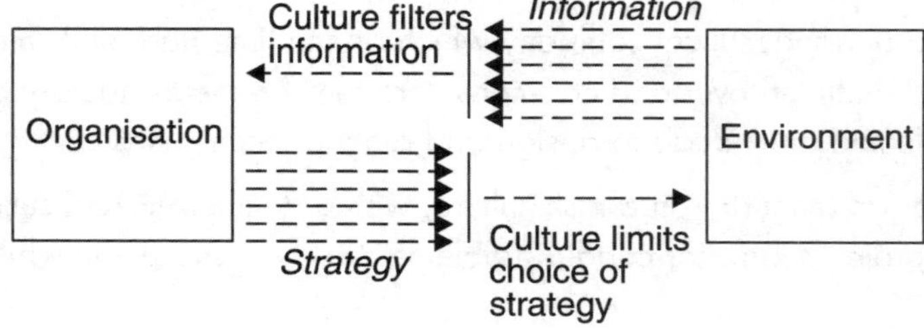


Culture filters and reconfigures environmental information. (A tragic example is the events in Waco, where members of the Branch Davidian cult interpreted environmental information about the FBI as presaging the end of the world.) At the same time culture filters out a number of strategic choices. For example, a firm might have a cultural predisposition against embarking on risky ventures. Another culture might have an ingrained 'Buy British' approach. Finally, **if culture is embodied in *behaviour*, existing behaviour may make a strategy incompatible with the culture and so impossible to implement**.

**6.23** A model of culture which focuses specifically on a firm's approach to strategy was suggested by *Miles and Snow*, who outlined three strategic cultures, and a fourth 'non-strategic' culture.

(a) **Defenders like low risks, secure niche markets, and tried and trusted solutions**. These companies have cultures whose stories and rituals reflect historical continuity and consensus. Decision-taking is relatively formalised. There is emphasis on correct procedure. Personnel are drawn from within the industry.

(b) **Prospectors are organisations where the dominant beliefs are more to do with results** (doing the right things ie effectiveness). They seek to expand and increase market presence, and move into new areas.

(c) **Analysers try to balance risk and profits**. They use a core of stable products and markets as a source of earnings, like defenders, but move into areas that prospectors have already opened up. Analysers follow change, but do not initiate it.

(d) **Reactors**, unlike the three above, **do not have viable strategies**, other than living from hand to mouth.

## Marketing at Work

Miles and Snow's analysis was applied to the responses by the regional electricity companies (RECs) to takeover bids in the Autumn of 1995. (The RECs are responsible for supplying and distributing electricity.) As at October 1995, seven of the 12 RECs in England and Wales had received takeover bids. (*Financial Times,* 4 October 1995).

At privatisation they 'shared a common heritage and hence ... greater similarities than would be found in more well-established private sector market places'.

- The largest REC, Eastern Group, 'embraced' the possibility of an alliance with Hanson. Eastern exhibits the characteristics of a 'prospector'. Its chief executive is 'non-REC' 'with a North American corporate pedigree and a greater interest in activities outside the traditional REC field'.
- Norweb and Midlands were 'cautious prospectors' which allow significant degrees of decentralisation, and a 'willingness to bring in executives with experience external to the industry'. They countenance 'strategic alliances'.
- Many of the RECs 'have demonstrated classical defender strategies'. They have specific features.
  - Hierarchical company structures
  - Board membership drawn from within the industry
  - Incremental growth, rather than more rapid growth by entering new business areas; little enthusiasm for diversification

## Excellence, culture and motivation

**6.24** *Peters and Waterman,* in their book *In Search of Excellence,* found that the 'dominance and coherence of culture' was an essential feature of the 'excellent' companies they observed. A 'handful of guiding values' was more powerful than manuals, rule books, norms and controls formally imposed (and resisted). They commented: 'If companies do not have strong notions of themselves, as reflected in their values, stories, myths and legends, people's only security comes from where they live on the organisation chart.'

**6.25** Peters and Waterman also discuss the central importance of *positive reinforcement* in any method of motivation as critical. 'Researchers studying motivation find that the prime factor is simply the self-perception among motivated subjects that they are in fact doing well ... Mere association with past personal success apparently leads to more persistence, higher motivation, or something that makes us do better.'

**6.26** Peters and Waterman argue that employees can be 'switched on' to extraordinary loyalty and effort in the following cases.

(a) **The cause is perceived to be in some sense great**. Commitment comes from believing that a task is inherently worthwhile. Devotion to the *customer,* and the customer's needs and wants, is an important motivator in this way.

(b) **They are treated as winners**. 'Label a man a loser and he'll start acting like one.' Repressive control systems and negative reinforcement break down the employee's self-image.

(c) **They can satisfy their dual needs, both to** be a conforming, secure part of a successful team to be stars in their own right.

**6.27** This means applying control (through firm central direction, and shared values and beliefs) but also allowing maximum individual autonomy (at least, the illusion of control) and even competition between individual or groups within the organisation. Peters and Waterman call this ***loose-tight* management**. Culture, peer pressure, a focus on action, customer-orientation and so on are 'non-aversive' ways of exercising control over employees. In other words, the control system used is **cultural control**.

## Chapter Roundup

- The **resource audit** covers technical resources, financial resources, managerial skills, the organisation and information systems.
- Resources should be used **efficiently and effectively**, and this is determined by the organisation's strategy, style, systems, structure, staff, skills and shared values.
- Resources are deployed as **competences** which support a competitive position. A distinctive competence is hard to imitate.
- An **asset-based** approach identifies the types of assets the marketer will use: customer; distribution and internal assets.
- An **innovation audit** identifies a firm's record of innovation and how it can be enhanced. It covers the organisation climate and culture, the value to the customer, the management team and the 'recipe'.
- Culture is important both in organisations and in the wider world. It is the knowledge, beliefs, customs and attitudes which people adhere to. In wider society it is affected by factors such as age, class, race and religion, while in organisations it is defined by assumptions, beliefs and artefacts. These, in turn, are influenced by history, management, structure and systems. The McKinsey 7-S model shows how culture relates to other aspects of the organisation.
- Harrison's four-fold classification of organisations, popularised by Handy, is a useful analysis of some common aspects of culture.
  - The **power** culture depends on the holder of centralised power.
  - The **role** culture is associated with bureaucracy and emphasises rules and procedures.
  - The **task** culture is focused on delivering the current goal.
  - The **existential** culture supports individual independence and aspiration.
- Culture colours the organisation's view of its environment and hence influences its strategy. **Defenders** like low risk solutions and niche markets. **Prospectors** are more adventurous and concerned with results. **Analysers** try to balance risk and profits. **Reactors** do not have viable strategies.

## Quick Quiz

1. What is a limiting factor?
2. What is a distinctive competence? How would you identify one?
3. Identify four types of marketing asset.
4. What are some advantages of being innovative?
5. What is an innovation audit?
6. What are some organisational barriers to innovation?
7. What influences organisational culture?
8. Draw the cultural web.
9. How did Miles and Snow analyse strategic culture?

## Answers to Quick Quiz

1 A constraint upon activity, usually a facility or resource of limited capacity.

2 Things an organisation does better than its rivals.

3
- Customer-based
- Distribution-based
- Internal
- Alliance-based

4
- Improved quality
- Problem solutions
- Improved morale
- Leaner structure
- Improved communication

5 A critical assessment of an organisation's record of innovation.

6 Resistance to change; old planning systems; centralised control; cost considerations.

7 Founder; history; leadership and management style; structure and systems.

8

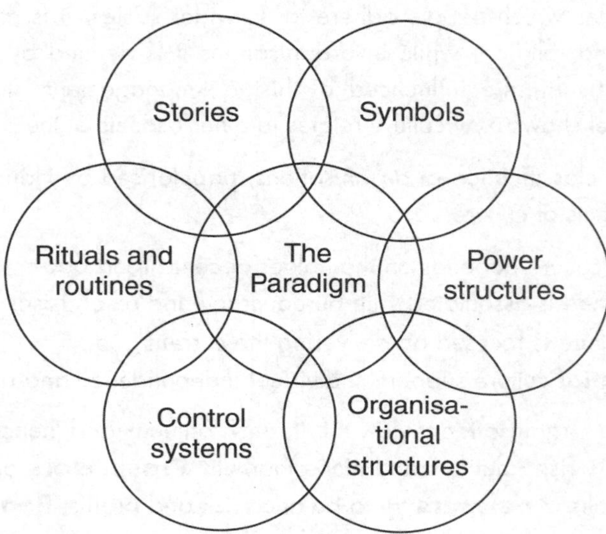


The cultural web

9 Defenders; prospectors; analysers; reactors.

## Action Programme Review

1 Thinking about the way the office is organised, how power is used and how people relate to one another will help you decide.

2
- Power
- Role
- Task
- Existential

### Now try Question 4 at the end of the Study Text

# Auditing Tools 5

| Chapter Topic List | |
|---|---|
| 1 | Setting the scene |
| 2 | The product life cycle |
| 3 | New products and the diffusion process |
| 4 | Experience curves, market share and PIMS |
| 5 | Portfolio analysis |
| 6 | The value chain |

## Syllabus Content

- Techniques and processes for the objective assessment of the internal environment
- Evaluation of the core competences, assets, culture and weaknesses of an organisation

## Key Concepts Introduced

- Product class, form and brand
- Adoption process
- Economies of scale
- Market share
- Portfolio
- Activities; value activities

# 1 Setting the scene

**1.1** The tools discussed in this chapter can be used at many stages in the process of strategic marketing planning. None of the models can be used uncritically, as we shall see.

**1.2** In **international marketing**, you may find that the product is at a different stage of the life cycle in each market. However such timing differences may shrink with speedier communications and growing prosperity in some customer segments.

**1.3** It is not enough to know by heart the theory of each of these tools, so do not spend all your study time on that. At the post-graduate level, you are expected to be able to deploy **higher skills**. These include the sensible selection of a tool and the interpretation of the results it produces. Both depend totally on an understanding of and familiarity with the strengths, weaknesses and applications of a given tool in a **given context**.

# 2 The product life cycle

**2.1** Many firms make a number of different products or services. Each product or service has its own **financial, marketing and risk characteristics**. The combination of products or services influences the profitability of the firm.

### Marketing at Work

Note the difference between the life cycle of the product and its value to the company. **Copyrights** and **patents** are only granted for a restricted time period to enable the holders of intellectual property to benefit from their investment.

**2.2** The profitability and sales of a product can be expected to change over time. The **product life cycle** is an attempt to recognise distinct stages in a product's sales history. Marketing managers distinguish between product class, form and brand.

### Key Concepts

(a) **Product class**: this is a broad category of product, such as cars, washing machines, newspapers, also referred to as the generic product.

(b) **Product form**: within a product class there are different forms that the product can take, for example five-door hatchback cars or two-seater sports cars, twin tub or front-loading automatic washing machines, national daily newspapers or weekly local papers etc.

(c) **Brand**: the particular type of the product form (for example *Ford Escort, Vauxhall Astra; Financial Times, Daily Mail, Sun*).

**2.3** The product life cycle applies in differing degrees to each of the three cases. A **product class** (eg cars) may have a long maturity stage, but a particular make or brand within the class might have an erratic life cycle. **Product forms**, however, tend to conform to the classic life cycle pattern, which is illustrated by the diagram below.

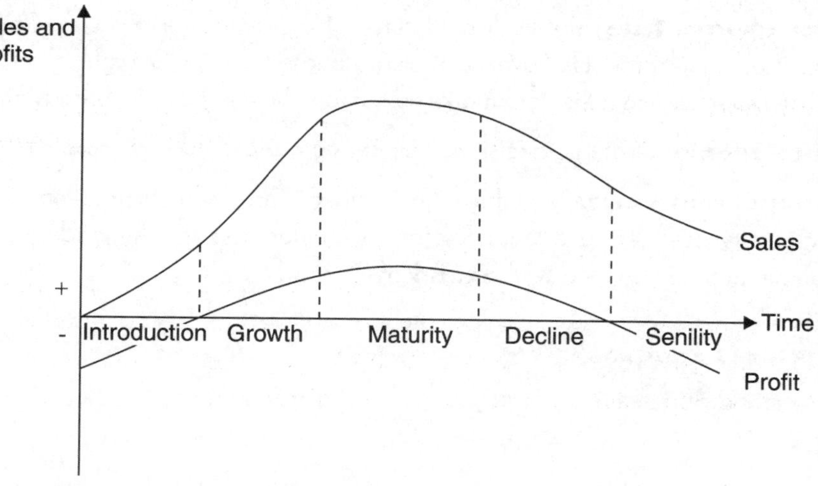


**2.4 Introduction**

(a) A new product takes time to find acceptance by would-be purchasers and there is a slow growth in sales. Unit costs are high because of low output and expensive sales promotion.

(b) There may be early teething troubles with production technology.

(c) The product for the time being is a loss-maker.

**2.5 Growth**

(a) If the new product gains market acceptance, sales will eventually rise more sharply and the product will start to make profits.

(b) Competitors are attracted. As sales and production rise, unit costs fall.

**2.6** **Maturity**. The rate of sales growth slows down and the product reaches a period of maturity which is probably the longest period of a successful product's life. Most products on the market will be at the mature stage of their life. Profits are good.

**2.7** **Decline**. Some products reach a stage of decline, which may be slow or fast. Eventually, sales will begin to decline so that there is over-capacity of production in the industry. Severe competition occurs, profits fall and some producers leave the market. The remaining producers seek means of prolonging the product life by modifying it and searching for new market segments. Many producers are reluctant to leave the market, although some inevitably do because of falling profits.

## *The relevance of the product life cycle to strategic planning*

**2.8** In reviewing outputs, planners should assess the following.

(a) The **stage of its life cycle** that any product has reached

(b) The **product's remaining life**, ie how much longer the product will be able to contribute significantly to profits

(c) How **urgent is the need to innovate**, to develop new and improved products in time?

### *Difficulties of the product life cycle concept*

**2.9** (a) **Recognition**. How can managers recognise where a product stands in its life cycle?

(b) **Not always true**. The traditional curve of a product life cycle does not always occur in practice. Some products have no maturity phase, and go straight from growth to decline. Some never decline if they are marketed competitively (eg certain brands of breakfast cereals).

(c) **Changeable**. Strategic decisions can change or extend a product's life cycle.

(d) **Competition varies** in different industries. The financial markets are an example of markets where there is a tendency for competitors to copy the leader very quickly, so that competition has built up well **ahead** of demand.

### Marketing at Work

***Airbus***

Airbus is a consortium of four partners, and commands about 30% of the airliner market outside the EU. Airbus has launched a range of aircraft which compete with *Boeing* in every sector of the market, save the Boeing 747, and it is now going to build a 'super-jumbo'.

Airbus is expected to be very profitable. It has a relatively modern range of aircraft in an industry with product life cycles of 25 years or more.

The carrot Airbus offers to potential partners is that it will be able to introduce new technology.

## The PLC and cash generation

**2.10** It is essential that firms plan their portfolio of products to **ensure that new products are generating positive cash flow** before existing 'earners' enter the decline stage.

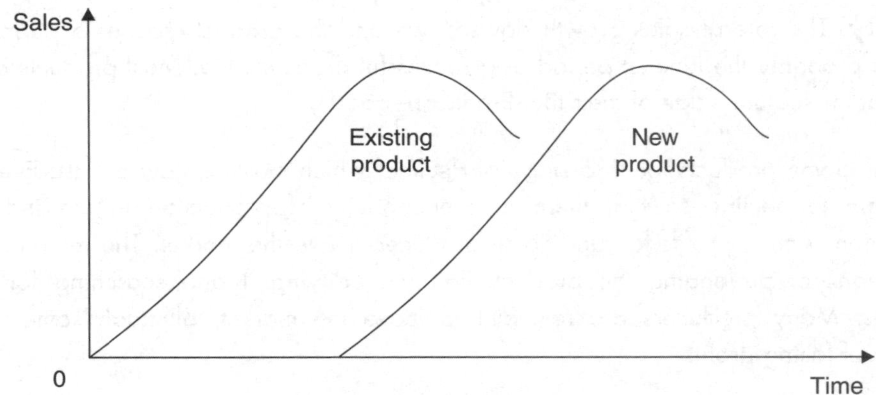


In the situation above the company is likely to experience cash flow problems.

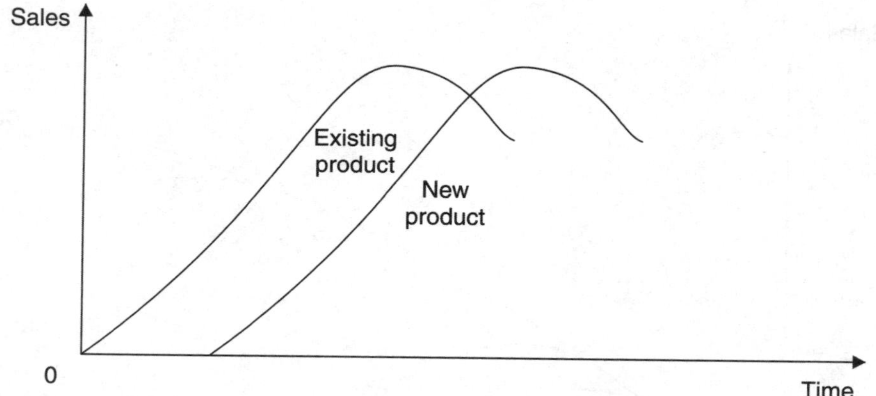


By considering the product life cycle of the existing product when planning the timing for launch of a new product, cash flow problems can be avoided.

**2.11** It is perhaps easy enough to accept that products have a life cycle, but it is not so easy to sort out how far through its life a product is, and what its expected future life might be.

(a) There ought to be a **regular review** of existing products, as a part of marketing management responsibilities.

(b) **Sources of PLC predictions**

- An analysis of past sales and profit trends
- The history of other products
- Market research
- If possible, an analysis of competitors
- A review of technological developments

(c) The future of each product should be estimated in terms of both sales revenue and profits.

**2.12 Decisions for each product**

- **Continue selling**, with no foreseeable intention yet of stopping production
- **Prolong the product's life**, perhaps by adjusting the mix or finding new customers
- **Stop producing** the product

Possible implications of each stage are on the following page.

## *The product life cycle and the marketing orientation*

**2.13** Does the PLC promote a product orientated focus when in fact a 'market orientated' focus is necessary? Ansoff extends the PLC concept to encompass the **demand/technology life cycle** (DLC), and the technology life cycle (TLC). The diagram below illustrates how a **demand life cycle** is made up of a number of **technology life cycles** which in turn are composed of PLCs.

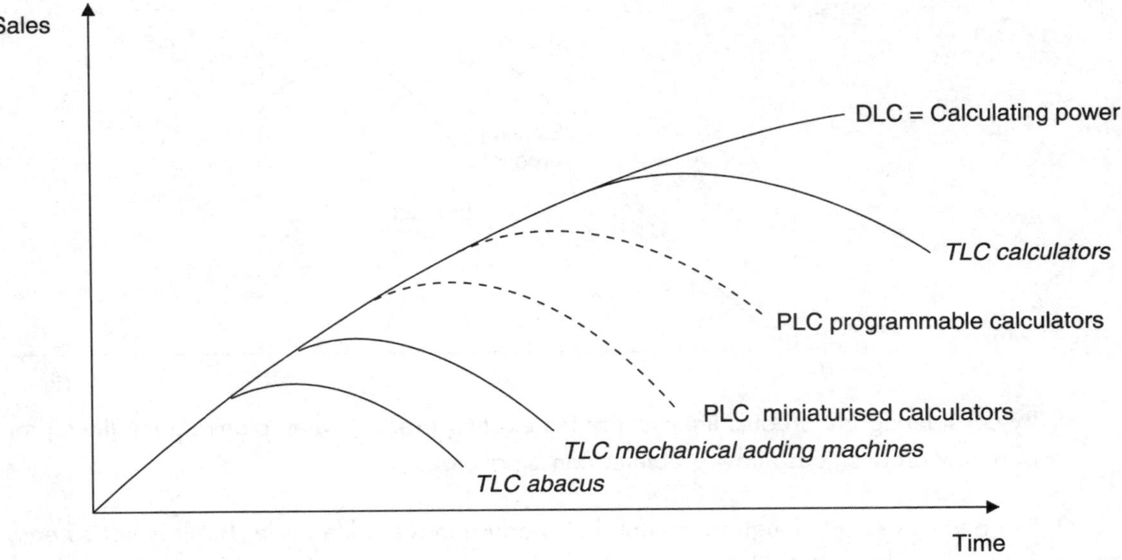


**2.14** For example, 'calculating power' represents a human demand that is probably in the growth stage of the DLC. This has been composed of a number of TLCs – finger counting, abacuses, slide rules, adding machines, calculators, computers. Each new technology usually satisfies the **generic need** in a **superior way**.

**2.15** The TLC indicates that for many products, death will eventually transpire through **technology** and **competitive innovation**.

## Marketing at Work

Going back to the Airbus example, Airbus assumed continued demand for long-haul air travel when developing its super jumbo, and believes that this is best satisfied by large planes flying to major destination hubs. Much of this is deemed accounted for by growth in long-haul tourism, although this theory is likely to be tested by the worldwide downturn in travel (caused for example by terrorism and the SARS virus) that has affected some of the international carriers so badly.

| | Phase | | | |
|---|---|---|---|---|
| | *Introduction* | *Growth* | *Maturity* | *Decline* |
| 1 *Products* | Initially, poor quality.<br><br>Product design and development are a key to success.<br><br>No standard product and frequent design changes (eg microcomputers in the early 1980s). | Competitors' products have marked quality differences and technical differences.<br><br>Quality improves.<br><br>Product reliability may be important. | Products become more standardised and differences between competing products less distinct. | Products even less differentiated. Quality becomes more variable. |
| 2 *Customers* | Initial customers willing to pay high prices.<br><br>Customers need to be convinced about buying. | Customers increase in number. | Mass market.<br><br>Market saturation.<br><br>Repeat-buying of products becomes significant. Brand image also important. | Customers are `sophisticated' buyers of a product they understand well. |
| 3 *Promotion* | High advertising and sales promotion costs. | High advertising costs still, but as a % of sales, costs are falling. | Markets become segmented.<br><br>Segmentation and extending the maturity phase of the life cycle can be key strategies. | Less money spent on advertising and sales promotion. |
| 4 *Competition* | Few or no competitors. | More competitors enter the market.<br><br>Barriers to entry can be important. | Competition at its keenest:<br>on prices, branding, servicing customers, packaging etc. | Competitors gradually exit from the market.<br><br>Exit barriers can be important. |
| 5 *Prices and costs* | High prices but losses due to high fixed costs. | High prices.<br>High contribution margins, and increasing profit margins.<br><br>High P/E ratios for quoted companies in the growth market. | Falling prices but good profit margins due to high sales volume.<br><br>Higher prices in some market segments. | Still low prices but falling profits as sales volume falls, since total contribution falls towards the level of fixed costs.<br><br>Some increase in prices may occur in late decline stage. |
| 6 *Manufacturing* | Over-capacity.<br><br>High production costs. | Under-capacity.<br><br>Move towards mass production and less reliance on skilled labour. | Optimum capacity.<br>Low labour skills. | Over-capacity because mass production techniques are still used. |
| 7 *Distribution* | Few distribution channels. | Distribution channels flourish and getting adequate distribution channels is a key to marketing success. | Distribution channels fully developed, but less successful channels might be cut. | Distribution channels dwindling. |

## Action Programme 1

Try to apply some of your knowledge of the PLC consumer electronics equipment in recent years.

**2.16** The product life cycle concept probably has more value as a **control tool** than as a method of **forecasting** a product's life. Control can be applied to speeding up the growth phase, extending the maturity phase and recognising when to cease making a product altogether.

## Exam Tip

Exam questions are likely to concentrate on the marketing strategies relevant to individual stages of the life cycle, as each stage involves different strategic choices. Each stage involves configuring the marketing mix in a particular way, to meet the firm's objectives.

The examiner is unlikely to want mere descriptions of the model. In the past exam questions have focused on specific stages of the life cycle and their implications for marketing strategy.

(a) Introduction and launch

  (i) Does the firm lead in NPD or copy competitors?

  (ii) Penetration or skimming: should the firm seek to get as much market share as early as possible or should it seek to recoup as much profit as possible?

(b) Growth stage

  (i) What competitive strategy is most appropriate in the market place? Will the firm have to differentiate its offer?

  (ii) How long should the firm continue the intense marketing support needed at this stage to build a market?

(c) Maturity. Higher profits can be achieved by segmenting the market and modifying the product. Market share objectives and distribution are strategically important. Should you rejuvenate a mature product or finish it off? If so, what strategies can you use for rejuvenation: product enhancement, segmentation and so on?

(d) Decline is probably the hardest to negotiate.

  (i) Manage decline. Sales will be falling, so costs should be cut to maintain dealer loyalty. Decline needs to be managed slowly and smoothly, so that the firm can redirect its resources elsewhere.

  (ii) Rejuvenation involves 'finding new needs or uses for the product and fitting the product to them to produce new sales.' This involves modifying the mix, producing new versions of the product or positioning the product for another group. For example Campbell's condensed soups have been additionally positioned as ingredients for cooking sauces.

(e) As a general rule, any answers about the PLC should cover its drawbacks as well as its merits.

---

## Control

**2.17** The management of a product should fit its prevailing life cycle stage, as each stage has different financial characteristics.

(a) **Development**. Money will be spent on market research and product development. Cash flows are negative and there is a high business risk.

(b) **Launches** require expensive promotion campaigns.

(c) **Growth**. The market grows, as does the demand for the product. Risks are competitor action.

   (i) The market price mix might turn out to be inappropriate for the product (eg the price is set too high).

   (ii) Competitors will enter, thereby reducing the profits that can be earned.

(d) **Maturity**. Few new competitors will enter the market. Risk is low, so the concentration is on profit.

**2.18** At all stages, the **risk and return profile** of the product can be managed.

(a) Appropriate product-market strategies, such as innovation, new advertising, changing the product, finding new markets

(b) Raising entry barriers.

Increased marketing expenditure may have the effect of reducing risk, commensurate with the decreased return.

**2.19 Information and financial control needs of different stages of the product life cycle.**

| | *Launch* | *Growth* | *Maturity* | *Decline* |
|---|---|---|---|---|
| **Characteristics** | High business risk. Negative net cash flow. DCF evaluation for overall investment | High business risk. Neutral net cash flow | Medium business risk. Positive cash flow | Low risk. Neutral-positive cash flow |
| **Critical success factors** | Time to launch | Market share growth. Sustaining competitive advantage | Contribution per unit of scarce resource. Customer retention. | Timely exit |

| | Launch | Growth | Maturity | Decline |
|---|---|---|---|---|
| **Information needs** | Market research into size and demand | Market growth, share. Diminishing returns. Competitor marketing strategies | Comparative competitor costs. Limiting factors | Rate of decline; best time to leave; reliable sale values of assets |
| **Financial and other controls** | Strategic 'milestones'. Physical evaluation. Mainly non-financial measures owing to volatility (eg rate of take up by consumers) | Discounted cash flow<br>Market share<br>Marketing objectives | ROI<br>Profit margin<br>Maintaining market share | Free cash flow (for investment elsewhere) |

# 3 New products and the diffusion process

**3.1** An important issue to planners is how quickly a new product will be adopted by the market, in other words what sort of time scale is expected along the horizontal axis of the PLC.

**3.2** **Factors influencing the speed at which new ideas and product innovations will spread or be diffused through the marketplace**

(a) The **complexity** of the new product

(b) The **relative advantages** it offers

(c) The degree to which the innovation fits into **existing patterns** of behaviour/needs

(d) The **ability to try** the new product, samples, test drives or low value purchases entailing little risk

(e) The ease with which the product's benefits can be **communicated** to the potential customer

**3.3** The market segments attitude to change, accessibility to channels of communication and the time frame involved in the **adoption process** are all critical factors in assessing the diffusion process.

## Key Concept

The **adoption process**, sometimes referred to as the decision-making process refers to the stages a customer goes through before making a purchase decision, or a decision not to purchase or repurchase. The five stages identifiable in most models of this process are: awareness → interest → evaluation → trial → adoption. There can be a considerable time lag between awareness and adoption.

**3.4** In *Consumer Behaviour* Schiffmann and Kanuk offer a modified version of Everett Rogers' analysis in *Diffusion of Innovation* (1995).

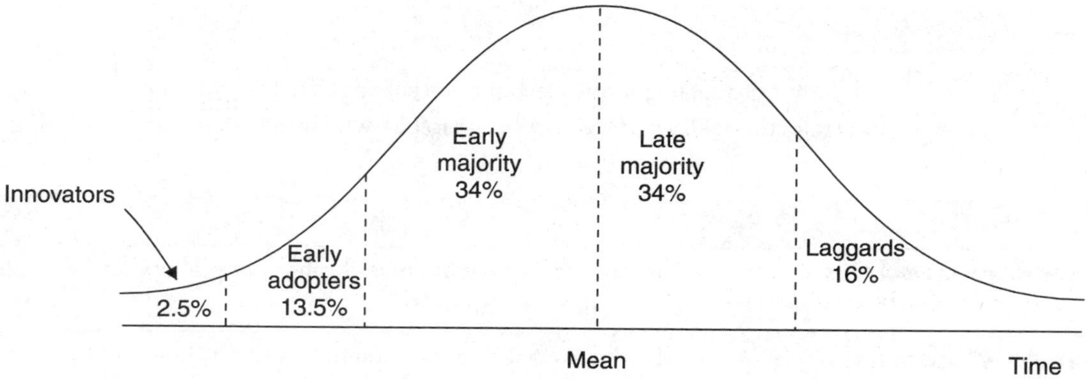


3.5 The characteristics of consumers in these adopter categories varies and so the marketing planner wishing to get the best from a new product, encourage its diffusion and avoid wasting budget, will focus market attention on these different segments, as the product passes through the life cycle.

(a) **Innovators**

These are eager to try new ideas and products and often in close contact with change agents like sales staff and other opinion leaders. Often perceived to be risk takers, prepared to try and willing to pay often premium prices for 'being the first'.

(b) **Early adopters**

They too are willing to change and are often opinion leaders themselves. They are likely to have greater exposure to the mass media than later adopters and certainly more willing to change. They are likely to seek out information actively about new products in specialist journals etc.

(c) **Early majority**

A more conservative segment who tend to purchase a new product just ahead of the average time, but who will have given it some thought before the purchase.

(d) **Late majority**

These are slower than the average and sceptical about new products. They are very cautious purchasers likely to need some persuading.

(e) **Laggards**

These are the smaller group of traditionalists actually unwilling to change. They may actually be forced to change only when their previous choice is obsolete and no longer available.

3.6 **Diffusion and marketing strategy**. Marketers usually want to ensure a rapid diffusion or rate of adoption for a new product. This allows them to gain a large share of the market prior to competitors responding.

(a) A **penetration strategy** associated with low introductory pricing and promotions designed to facilitate trial are associated with such a strategy.

(b) However in some markets, particularly where R & D cost has been high, where the product involves new technology or where it is protected from competition perhaps by patent, a **skimming** policy may be adopted. Here price is high initially usually representing very high unit profits and sales can be increased in steps with price reductions, in line with available capacity or competitors' responses.

## Speed of diffusion

3.7 Needless to say, different products get adopted at different speeds. The marketer will want rapid acceptance, to forestall competition. Here is a list of issues which influence the speed of market penetration.

| Issue | Comment |
|---|---|
| **Network externalities** | The product is only of value if other people have it – such as telephones, the Internet |
| **Common standards** | CD players operate to a common standard owned by Phillips. For DVD (the successor to CDs), acceptance will be delayed because of disputes over standards. Mobile phones operate to two standards globally. Digital TV in the UK is delivered by competing intermediaries |
| **Complementary products** | Computer games consoles need computer games to play on them |
| **Switching costs** | It will cost a lot to change to certain products |
| **Experimentation** | For groceries, it is easy to try something new, as the expense is small. Film companies introduce 'trailers' as part of a marketing campaign to give potential audiences a feel for the film. |

# 4 Experience curves, market share and PIMS

## Economies of scale

4.1 There is a relationship between the quantity of products produced and the cost per unit.

**Key Concept**

**Economy of scale**. The more you produce and sell, the cheaper each successive unit will be.

4.2 **EXAMPLE**

Let us take an example of a publisher contracting with a printer to print Study Texts. (Note: the prices below are notional only. Printers' charges vary according to paper prices, paper quality, turnaround times, volume of work and so on.)

| *Quantity printed* | *Cost* | *Cost per book* |
|---|---|---|
| 100 | £500 | £5.00 |
| 1,000 | £2,500 | £2.50 |
| 2,000 | £4,720 | £2.36 |

The reason for the difference is that there are the same **fixed costs** incurred (for example, in setting up the press) no matter how many or few books you print.

4.3 This shows that the quantity produced affects the cost per unit. From the above example, if customers were unwilling to pay more than £3 for their books, and the publishers wanted to make £0.50p profit on top of print cost, then the publisher would have to sell **at least** 1,000 books.

4.4 How is this relevant to market share? It shows that high market share can, by spreading fixed costs over many units of production, be more profitable. Higher sales volumes can mean lower costs per unit, hence higher profits. The Boston Consulting Group estimated that as production volume doubles, cost per unit falls by up to 20%. **High market share therefore gives cost advantages**.

## Experience curves

4.5 The experience curve takes this further. The more units **over time** that a firm produces, the cheaper will each unit be to produce. Why?

(a) **Economies of scale**, as identified above.

(b) **Learning**: the more people do a task, the more efficient they become (up to a point), and it takes them less time.

(c) **Technological** improvements: firms can improve their production operations and make better use of equipment.

(d) **Simplifying products can cut costs**. For example, car manufacturers are cutting costs by ensuring that the same components can be used in different marques.

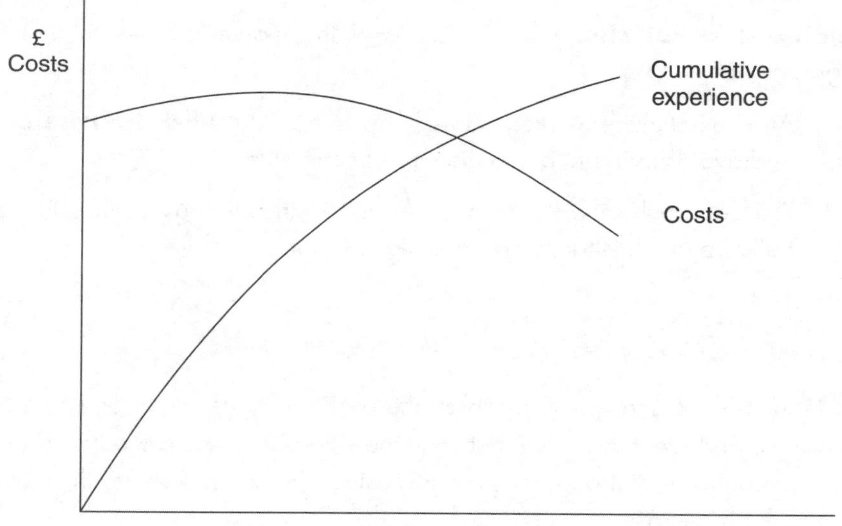


4.6 **Working with the experience curve**

(a) The experience curve is not automatic.

(b) Technological changes can render a particular process obsolete.

(c) Low costs do not have to mean lower prices, although many firms have used the experience curve to buy market share.

(d) Marketing people should focus on the customer not on the process, and so the experience curve should not detract from **customer focus**.

## Marketing at Work

Japanese firms pioneered target costing. They identified a customer need and specified a product to satisfy that need.

The production department and its accountants then worked out:

- How the product could be built
- The volume needed to reach the market price
- How quickly costs could be driven down.

## Market share and PIMS

### Key Concept

**Market share** is 'one entity's sales of a product or service in a specified market expressed as a percentage of total sales by all entities offering that product or service'. Thus, a company may have a 30% share of a total market, meaning that 30% of all sales in the market are made by that company.

4.7 **Relative market share** as the share of the market relative to that of the manufacturer's largest competitor.

(a) An evaluation of market shares helps to identify **who the true competitor really is**, and avoids trying to outdo the wrong competitor.

(b) The approach serves as a basis for marketing strategy, with a firm seeking as a target to build up an x% share of a particular market.

## Profit Impact of Market Strategies (PIMS)

4.8 **PIMS analysis** attempts to establish the profitability (ie return on capital) of various marketing strategies, and identifies a link between the size of **return on capital** and **market share** so that companies in a strong competitive position in the markets for their base products would be earning high returns.

4.9 In general, profits increase in line with market share.

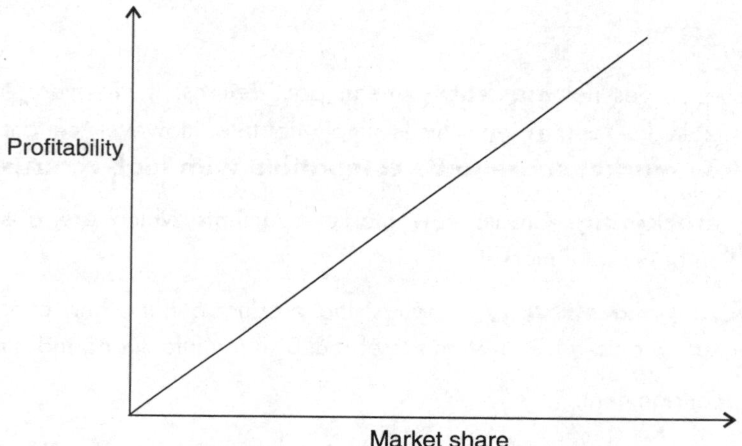


Three possible reasons were put forward for this correlation.

(a) **Economies of scale** and experience curve effects enable a market leader to produce at lower unit costs than competitors, and so make bigger profits. A company with the highest market share, especially if this company is also the innovator with the longest experience, will enjoy a considerable competitive advantage. This is referred to as the experience curve.

(b) **Bargaining power**. A strong position in the market gives a firm greater strength in its dealings with both buyers and suppliers.

(c) **Quality of management**. Market leaders often seem to be run by managers of a high calibre.

**4.10** The linear relationship above does not always hold true. Some industries display a V-shaped relationship.

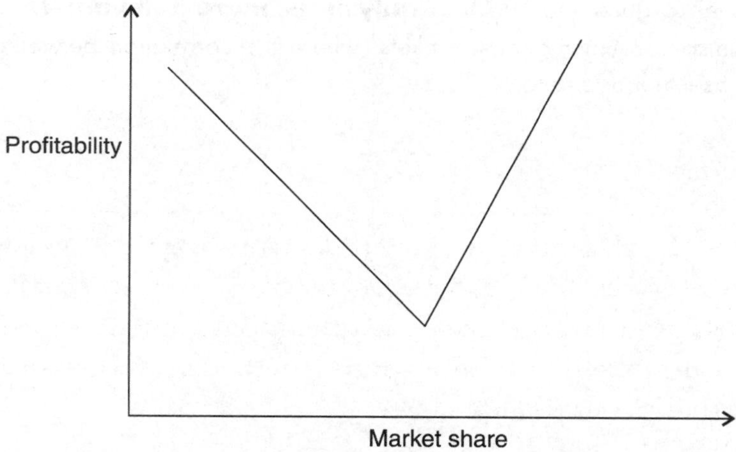


Profitability falls until a certain critical market share is reached, which makes it more likely that there will be a polarisation between large firms and small players. SME's (small and medium sized enterprises) find it very difficult to maintain their position.

**4.11** PIMS researchers would argue that since profitability is a key objective, and since profitability depends on market share, companies should formulate market share objectives. There are four broad groups of market share strategies.

- Building
- Holding
- Harvesting
- Withdrawal

## Low market share

**4.12** Low market share does not **inevitably** mean poor returns. If this were so, small businesses would always make low returns, and this is simply not true. However, certain **conditions must exist for a low market share to be compatible with high returns**.

(a) **Niche marketing**. Create new market segments which are a small but profitable proportion of the total market.

(b) **Premium price strategy**. Emphasising product quality, and charging higher prices. (Efficient use would have to be made of R & D in manufacturing industries.)

(c) Strong management.

(d) When there is a **large, stable market**, where product innovations and developments are uncommon, and where **repeat-buying by customers is frequent**, a company can earn good profits with only a low market share.

## Problems with PIMS

**4.13** (a) **Identifying each market segment properly**. An up-market producer is in a different market segment to a down-market cheap-goods producer, and it would be wrong to classify them as competitors in the same market. In Porter's terminology, they may not exist in the same **strategic group**

(b) **Measuring the actual size of the market**, and so the company's own market share in proportional terms.

(c) **Establishing what returns** are available from a particular market share.

It has also been argued that **PIMS analysis is more relevant to industrial goods markets** than to consumer goods markets, where the correlation between high market share and high returns is not as strong.

### Exam Tip

*An old syllabus question asked why market share is important and when it might not be appropriate as an objective. Consider for example market leaders with near monopolies. Increasing market share and driving out competitors would lead to government action and regulation. Furthermore, the cost of increasing market share might exceed its value in profit terms.*

*PIMS was examined in June 2001 and again in June 2002.*

## Strategic implications of market share

**4.14** Implications of market share should be considered in product-market development planning.

(a) **How easy will it be to build up a market share?** This will depend on the rate of sales growth in the market. Obviously, it is easier to penetrate a growing market than a static one.

(b) **What share of the market will be needed to earn the target profit and return on capital?** Depending on costs, sales prices and total sales volume in the market, the size of market share needed to make a profit will vary.

## Marketing at Work

***Reebok***

Reebok was a best-selling trainer brand but competition from *Nike* and *Adidas* saw its market share plummet and its share price fall from over $50 in 1997 to $7 at the start of 2001.

Reebok is seeking to bounce back as a 'sports brand that operates' in a fashion market, and has designed advertising to appeal to 16–24 year olds.

Other outdoor brands, such as *Timberland* and *Caterpillar*, have also eaten away Reebok's market share. In 2000, Timberland had 2.9% of the US trainer market (2.1% in 1999). Fashion brands such as *Hermes* and *DKNY* have also entered the market.

# 5 Portfolio analysis

5.1 **Portfolio planning** analyses the current position of an organisation's products on SBUs in their markets, and the state of growth or decline in each of those markets. Several matrices have been developed over the years to analyse market share, market growth and market position.

## Key Concept

**Portfolio**: A collection of products/SBUs reporting to one entity. Each product SBU can be separately identified for decision-making and performance measurement.

## Exam Tip

A draft version of the Specimen Paper for this subject included a three-part question on the portfolio analysis as its Part A mini-case study. The three parts of the question reflected the approach the Examiner is likely to take in any question based on a theoretical model.

- Part (a) required you to carry out a portfolio analysis and to summarise the advantages and disadvantages of your chosen model. This was worth a maximum of 20 marks, so even a quite detailed knowledge of, say, the BCG model and its application would not have earned you enough marks to pass Part A.
- Part (b) was also for 20 marks: it required you to discuss the strategic implications of the analysis you had carried out in Part (a). This is typical of the requirements you will encounter at this level. You must be able to think sensibly about the wider implications of the facts you are presented with and the models you use.

- *Part (c) asked you what other information you would need before making resource allocation decisions. This was worth 10 marks. This part of the question allows you to range even wider in your response and demonstrate your awareness of the way businesses work.*

---

## Market share, market growth and cash generation: the Boston classification

5.2 The **Boston Consulting Group** (BCG) developed a matrix, based on empirical research, which classifies a company's products in terms of potential cash generation and cash expenditure requirements. This is related to **market share relative to competitors**.

5.3 You should also note that BCG analysis can be applied to:

- Individual products
- Whole strategic business units (SBUs)

5.4 **EXAMPLE**

To illustrate how to evaluate a portfolio a simulated company example will be provided. An industrial equipment company has five products with the following sales and market characteristics.

| *Product* | *Sales £m* | *£m sales Top 3 firms* | *Market growth rate %* | *Relative share* |
|---|---|---|---|---|
| A | 0.5 | 0.7 0.7 0.5* | 15% | 0.71 |
| B | 1.6 | 1.6 1.6* 1.0 | 18% | 1.0 |
| C | 1.8 | 1.8* 1.2 1.0 | 7% | 1.5 |
| D | 3.2 | 3.2* 0.8 0.7 | 4% | 4.0 |
| E | 0.5 | 2.5 1.8 1.7 | 4% | 0.2 |

* Company sales within the market

This information can then be plotted on to a matrix. The circles indicate the contribution the product makes to overall turnover. The centre of circles indicates their position on the matrix:

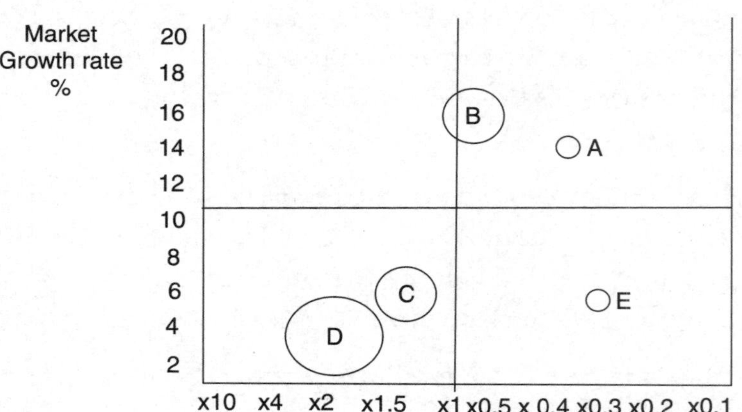


5.5 This growth/share matrix for the classification of products into cash cows, cash dogs, stars and question marks is known as the **Boston classification** (or the **Boston Matrix**).

(a) **Stars** are products with a high share of a high growth market. In the short term, these require capital expenditure in excess of the cash they generate, in order to maintain their market position, but promise high returns in the future.

(b) In due course, stars will become **cash cows**, with a high share of a low-growth market. Cash cows need very little capital expenditure and generate high levels of cash income. Cash cows generate high cash returns, which can be used to finance the stars.

(c) **Question marks** are products in a high-growth market, but where they have a low market share. Do the products justify considerable capital expenditure in the hope of increasing their market share, or should they be allowed to die quietly as they are squeezed out of the expanding market by rival products? Because considerable expenditure would be needed to turn a question mark into a star by building up market share, question marks will usually be poor cash generators and show a negative cash flow.

(d) **Dogs** are products with a low share of a low growth market. They may be ex-cash cows that have now fallen on hard times. Dogs should be allowed to die, or should be killed off. Although they will show only a modest net cash outflow, or even a modest net cash inflow, they are **cash traps** which tie up funds and provide a poor return on investment, and not enough to achieve the organisation's target rate of return.

There are also **infants** (ie products in an early stage of development), **warhorses** (ie products that have been cash cows in the past, and are still making good sales and earning good profits even now) and even **cash dogs**, which are dogs still generating cash.

**5.6** The evaluation and resulting strategic considerations for the company in the diagram above Paragraph 5.5 are these.

(a) There are two cash cows, thus the company should be in a cash-positive state.

(b) New products will be required to follow on from A.

(c) A is doing well (15%) but needs to gain market share to move from position 3 in the market – continued funding is essential. Similar for B.

(d) C is a market leader in a maturing market – strategy of consolidation is required.

(e) D is the major product which dominates its market; cash funds should be generated from this product.

(f) E is very small. Is it profitable? Funding to maintain the position or selling off are appropriate strategies.

## Action Programme 2

The marketing manager of Juicy Drinks Ltd has invited you in for a chat. Juicy Drinks Ltd provides fruit juices to a number of supermarket chains, which sell them under their own label. 'We've got a large number of products, of course. Our freshly squeezed orange juice is doing fine – it sells in huge quantities. Although margins are low, we have sufficient economies of scale to do very nicely in this market. We've got advanced production and bottling equipment and long-term contracts with some major growers. No problems there. We also sell freshly squeezed pomegranate juice: customers loved it in the tests, but producing the stuff at the right price is a major hassle: all the seeds get in the way. We hope it will be a winner, once we get the production right and start converting customers to it. After all the market for exotic fruit juices generally is expanding fast.'

What sort of products, according to the Boston classification, are described here?

---

**5.7** The **product life cycle** concept can be added to a market share/market growth classification of products, as follows.

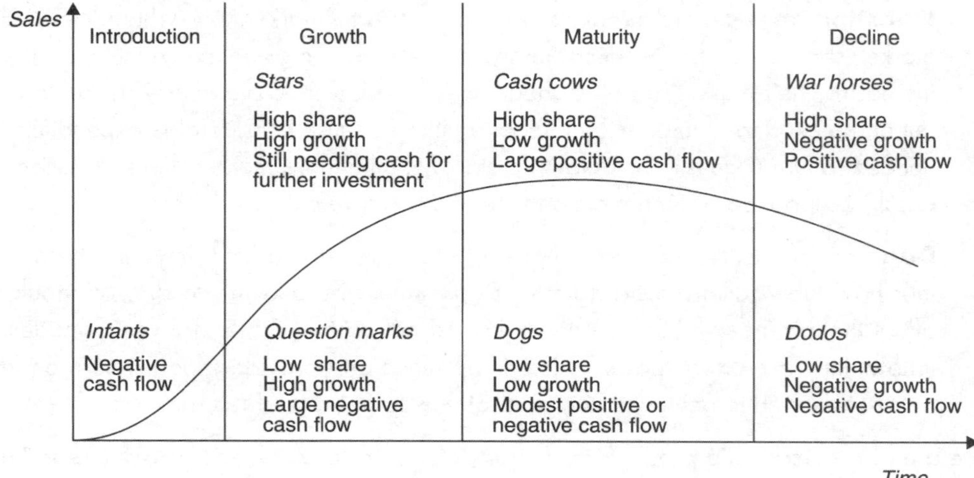


The BCG portfolio analysis is useful because it provides a framework for planners to consider and forecast potential market growth and to evaluate the competitive dimension through an evaluation of market share and the likely changes in cash flow.

**5.8 Shortcomings of BCG**

(a) **Factors besides market share and sales growth affect cash flow**.

(b) Many firms still use **return on investment when assessing the attractiveness of a business opportunity**, despite the opportunity it gives for accounting manipulation and the fact that it ignores the time value of money.

(c) The model provides **no real insight into how to compare one opportunity with another** when considering which opportunity should be allocated investment resources, eg how does a star compare with a question mark?

(d) As we have seen **in the right conditions a firm can profit from a low share of a low-growth market**.

(e) The techniques do not tell you how to generate new businesses.

(f) A tendency to invest too heavily in dogs.

(g) An over-concentration on turning question marks into stars, as opposed to managing the cash cows effectively. In other words, cash cows do not get the money they need.

(h) Expenditure needed to maintain cash cows is not provided.

## Competitiveness of products

**5.9** As a result of some of these weaknesses in the BCG model variations have evolved. Johnson and Scholes cite **General Electric's Business Screen**

(a) This compares **market attractiveness** with **business strength**.

(i) **Determinants of industry/market attractiveness**

- Market factors (eg size, growth)
- Competitors
- Investment factors
- Technological change
- Other PEST factors

(ii) **Determinants of business strength**

- Product quality
- Distribution
- Brand reputation
- Production capacity
- Management skill

(iii) These factors can then be scored and weighted. For example, a market with a low size and intense competition based on price might receive a lower weighting than a market with high growth and limited competition. The **GE matrix** is based on Return on Capital Employed.

(iv) Business strengths and market attractiveness are thus plotted on a grid, and a strategy appropriate to each can be considered.

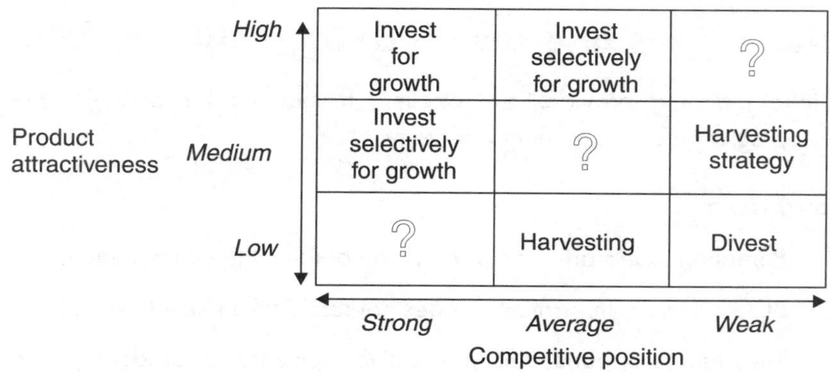


(b) Each 'cell' requires a different management approach.

(i) Each SBU can be plotted in one of the cells and the appropriate management approach adopted.

(ii) It is possible that SBUs might move around the matrix. Changes in PEST factors may change an industry/market's attractiveness.

(iii) The matrix ignores the possibility of **knowledge generation** and **competence** sharing between SBUs. Applications in one SBU may be of value elsewhere.

## Shell Directional Policy Matrix

**5.10** Another example is the Shell Directional Policy Matrix which comprises:

- Prospects for sector profitability
- The enterprise's competitive capabilities

| Enterprise's competitive capabilities \ Prospects for sector profitability | Unattractive | Average | Attractive |
|---|---|---|---|
| Weak | Disinvest | Phased withdrawal | Double or quit |
| Average | Phased withdrawal | Custodial<br>Growth | Try harder |
| Strong | Cash generation | Growth<br>Leader | Leader |

**5.11 Contrasts between BCG and policy matrices**

(a) The BCG looks at individual products and markets in a portfolio

(b) The other matrices look at a company's competences in market sectors, without reference to individual products.

## The advantages and disadvantages of portfolio planning

**5.12** Portfolio planning provides an excellent framework for analysis, and a starting point for developing a product-market mix strategy.

**5.13 Drawbacks**

(a) Portfolio models are simple: they do not reflect the uncertainties of decision-making.

(b) BCG analysis, in particular, does not really take risk into account.

(c) They ignore opportunities for creative segmentation or identifying new niches.

(d) They assume a market is given rather than something that can be created and nurtured. After all, markets may be unattractive because customer needs have not been analysed sufficiently.

(e) A lot of complicated analysis is needed to come up with relevant data. How do you decide whether an industry is attractive or not?

### Exam Tip

*The weakness of the BCG model is that it only covers products and markets.*

### Marketing at Work

***Nokia***

In early 2004, Nokia was undertaking a major re-alignment of its products and strategies. Its revenues were flat, it was facing increased competition and its main markets were saturated.

The company decided that future growth would come from new products in new markets, with software becoming more important than hardware. New product/market ventures include imaging, media, music, gaming and corporate solutions. It does not expect 3G telephony to be particularly important for it because manufacturers in Asia are already producing large volumes and mobile phone networks are manoeuvring to capture a greater slice of mobile phone revenue by offering enhanced services.

---

# 6 The value chain

**Exam Tip**

*The value chain is a very useful model and a favourite with examiners. Make sure you tackle the value chain related questions in your BPP Practice and Revision Kit.*

**6.1** The **value chain** model of corporate activities, developed by Michael Porter (*Competitive Advantage,* 1998), offers a bird's eye view of the firm and what it does. Competitive advantage, says Porter, arises out of the way in which firms organise and perform **activities**. (In other words, this describes **how an organisation uses its inputs and transforms them into the outputs that customers pay for**.)

## Activities

**Key Concept**

**Activities** are the means by which a firm creates value in its products. (They are sometimes referred to as **value activities**.)

**6.2** Activities incur costs, and, in combination with other activities, provide a product or service which earns revenue. 'Firms create value for their buyers by performing these activities.'

**6.3 EXAMPLE**

Let us explain this point by using the example of a **restaurant**. A restaurant's activities can be divided into buying food, cooking it, and serving it (to customers). There is no reason, in theory, why the customers should not do all these things themselves, at home. The customer however, is not only prepared to **pay for someone else** to do all this but also **pays more than the cost of** the resources (food, wages etc). The ultimate value a firm creates is measured by the amount customers are willing to pay for its products or services above the cost of carrying out value activities. A firm is profitable if the realised value to customers exceeds the collective cost of performing the activities.

(a) Customers **purchase value**, which they measure by comparing a firm's products and services with similar offerings by competitors.

(b) The business **creates value** by carrying out its activities either more efficiently than other businesses, or combine them in such a way as to provide a unique product or service.

## Action Programme 3

Outline different ways in which the restaurant can create value.

6.4 Porter (in *Competitive Advantage* 1985) grouped the various activities of an organisation into a **value chain**. Here is a diagram.

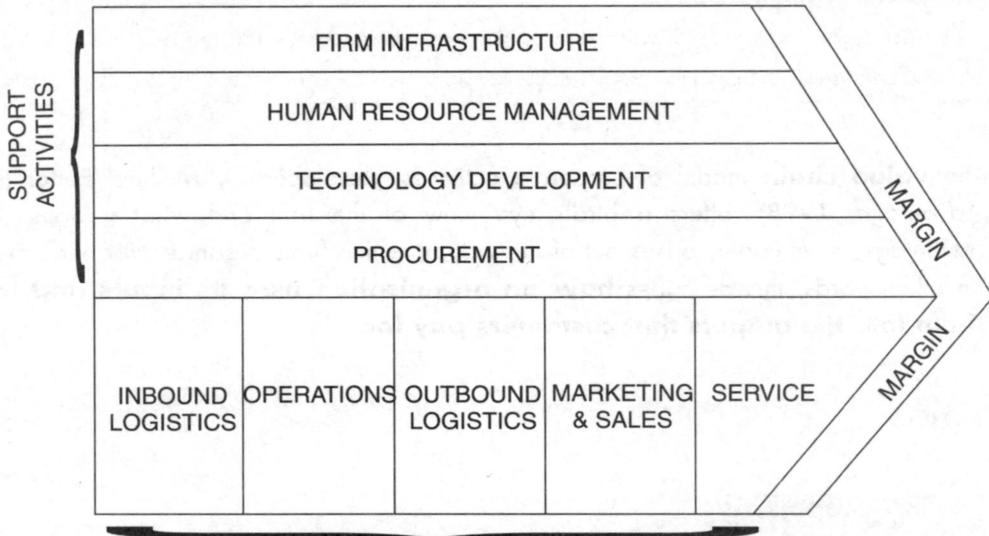


The **margin** is the excess the customer is prepared to **pay** over the **cost** to the firm of obtaining resource inputs and providing value activities.

6.5 **Primary activities** are directly related to production, sales, marketing, delivery and service.

| Activity | Comment |
|---|---|
| **Inbound logistics** | Receiving, handling and storing inputs to the production system (ie warehousing, transport, stock control etc). |
| **Operations** | Convert resource inputs into a final product. Resource inputs are not only materials. People are a resource especially in service industries. |
| **Outbound logistics** | Storing the product and its distribution to customers: packaging, warehousing, testing etc. |
| **Marketing and sales** | Informing customers about the product, persuading them to buy it, and enabling them to do so: advertising, promotion etc. |
| **After-sales service** | Installing products, repairing them, upgrading them, providing spare parts and so forth. |

6.6 **Support activities** provide purchased inputs, human resources, technology and infrastructural functions to support the primary activities.

| Activity | Comment |
|---|---|
| **Procurement** | Acquire the resource inputs to the primary activities (eg purchase of materials, subcomponents equipment). |
| **Technology development** | Product design, improving processes and/or resource utilisation. |
| **Human resource management** | Recruiting, training, developing and rewarding people. |
| **Management planning** | Planning, finance, quality control: Porter believes they are crucially important to an organisation's strategic capability in all primary activities. |

6.7 **Linkages** connect the activities of the value chain.

(a) **Activities in the value chain affect one another**. For example, more costly product design or better quality production might reduce the need for after-sales service.

(b) **Linkages require co-ordination**. For example, just-in-time requires smooth functioning of operations, outbound logistics and service activities such as installation.

## Exam Tip

*The draft Specimen Paper included a Part B question requiring you to apply the value chain model to a company with which you are familiar. The question also asked for recommendations for action. To answer this question you would not only need a good knowledge of the value chain model and a familiarity with a company, You would also have to be able to make sensible strategic comments.*

## Value system

6.8 Activities that add value do not stop at the organisation's **boundaries**. For example, when a restaurant serves a meal, the quality of the ingredients – although they are chosen by the cook – is determined by the grower. The grower has added value, and the grower's success in growing produce of good quality is as important to the customer's ultimate satisfaction as the skills of the chef. A firm's value chain is connected to what Porter calls a **value system**.

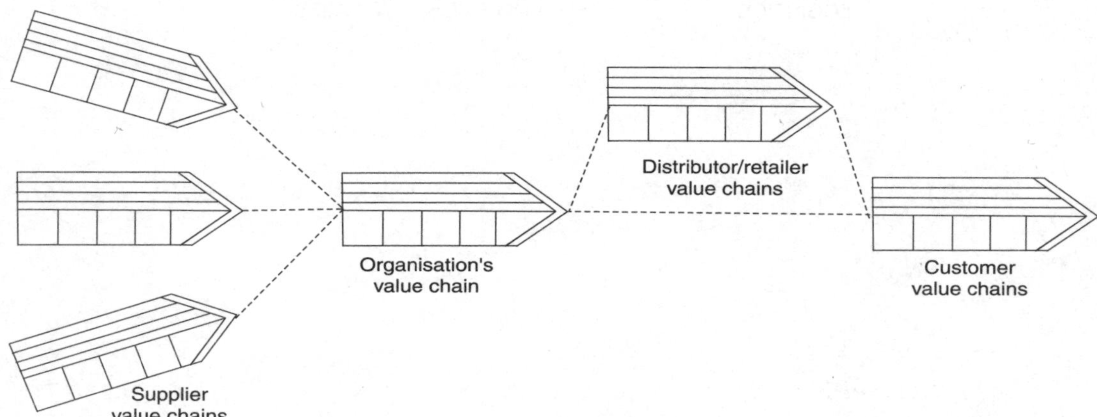

**6.9** **Using the value chain**. A firm can secure competitive advantage by:

- Inventing new or better ways to do activities
- Combining activities in new or better ways
- Managing the linkages in its own value chain
- Managing the linkages in the value system

## Action Programme 4

Sana Sounds is a small record company. Representatives from Sana Sounds scour music clubs for new bands to promote. Once a band has signed a contract (with Sana Sounds) it makes a recording. The recording process is subcontracted to one of a number of recording studio firms which Sana Sounds uses regularly. (At the moment Sana Sounds is not large enough to invest in its own equipment and studios.) Sana Sounds also subcontracts the production of records and CDs to a number of manufacturing companies. Sana Sounds then distributes the disks to selected stores, and engages in any promotional activities required.

What would you say were the activities in Sana Sounds' value chain?

---

**6.10** The examples below are based on two supermarket chains, one concentrating on low prices, the other differentiated on quality and service. See if you can tell which is which.

(a)

| | INBOUND LOGISTICS | OPERATIONS | OUTBOUND LOGISTICS | MARKETING & SALES | SERVICE |
|---|---|---|---|---|---|
| Firm infrastructure | Central control of operations and credit control | | | | |
| Human resource management | Recruitment of mature staff | Client care training | Flexible staff to help with packing | | |
| Technology development | | Recipe research | Electronic point of sale | Consumer research & tests | Itemised bills |
| Procurement | Own label products | Prime retail positions | | Adverts in quality magazines & poster sites | |
| | Dedicated refrigerated transport | In store food halls<br>Modern store design<br>Open front refrigerators<br>Tight control of sell-by dates | Collect by car service | No price discounts on food past sell-by dates | No quibble refunds |

(b)

| | | | | | |
|---|---|---|---|---|---|
| Firm infrastructure | Minimum corporate HQ | | | | |
| Human resource management | | De-skilled store-ops | Dismissal for checkout error | | |
| Technology development | Computerised warehousing | | Checkouts simple | | |
| Procurement | Branded only purchases big discounts | Low cost sites | | | Use of concessions |
| | Bulk warehousing | Limited range<br>Price points<br>Basic store design | | Low price promotion<br>Local focus | Nil |
| | INBOUND LOGISTICS | OPERATIONS | OUTBOUND LOGISTICS | MARKETING & SALES | SERVICE |

**6.11** The two supermarkets represented are based on the following.

(a) The value chain in 6.10(a) is based on a firm which seeks to differentiate on quality and service. Hence the 'no quibble' refunds, the use of prime retail sites, and customer care training.

(b) The value chain in 6.10(b) is similar to that of a 'discount' supermarket chain which differentiates on price, pursuing a cost leadership, or perhaps more accurately, a cost-focus strategy. This can be seen in the limited product range and its low-cost sites.

## Marketing at Work

***Caterpillar***

Caterpillar is the world's biggest manufacturer of diesel generators. Owing to problems in California's electricity supply market, demand has been growing.

- Technology development: Caterpillar is investing in innovative energy technology such as fuel cells, for the long term.
- Caterpillar is moving into after sales service, to operate and service generators on-site.

*Website address*: www.cat.com

## *IT and the value chain*

**6.12** IT can be used at each stage in the value chain.

(a) **Operations**

IT can be used to **automate and improve physical tasks** in the operating core. It also **provides information** about operational processes.

(b) **Inbound and outbound logistics**

(i) **Warehousing**. **Parcelforce** uses IT to track the progress of different parcels through the system.

(ii) Create **virtual warehouses** of stock actually held at **suppliers**. For example an organisation with several outlets might have each connected to a system which indicates the total amount of stock available at different sites.

(iii) Planning procedures to schedule production such as MRPII.

(c) **Sales and marketing**

(i) **Internet websites** can be used as an advertising medium and to gather information about customers.

(ii) **Customer databases** enable firms to monitor consumers' buying habits and to identify new segments.

(iii) Supermarkets use **EPOS** systems to give them a precise hour-by-hour idea of how products are selling to enable speedy ordering and replenishments.

(d) **Services**

(i) IT can be used to plan and schedule after-sales service, and to support service staff on the ground

## Chapter Roundup

- This chapter contains analytical and planning tools which can be used throughout the planning process.
- The **product life cycle** assumes that the marketing and financial characteristics of a product change over time, in relation to the market and in relation to other products.
- Market characteristics partly determine the speed by which **innovations** are diffused and adopted, and buyers can be segmented by their attitudes to innovation.
- Increasing **market share** is a desirable objective as there is sometimes a correlation between market share and profit, owing to **economies of scale** and the **experience curve** effect.
- **Portfolio analyses** compare the marketing and financial performance of a firm's products and/or SBUs with a view to decision-making. BCG analyses products according to market growth and relative market share.
- The **value chain** models how an organisation creates 'value' through managing value activities and the linkages between them. These can be deployed to give distinct customer benefits.

## Quick Quiz

1. Distinguish between product class, form and brand.
2. What are the problems of the PLC?
3. How is the product life cycle related to marketing orientation?
4. Identify five market segments with different attitudes to innovation.
5. What impedes diffusion?
6. Identify four strategies for market share.
7. How do question marks differ from stars?
8. What qualities does the GE Business Screen use to assess products?
9. What is the value chain?
10. How might a firm use value chain analysis?

## Answers to Quick Quiz

1. 'Class' is a broad category; form is an example within a class' 'brand' is the offering (or group of offerings) from a particular supplier.
2. Recognising the PLC stage a product has reached; not all products pass through all phases; strategic decisions can affect progress through the plc; the influence of competition varies significantly between industries.
3. It may be that over-attention to the plc produces a product orientation.
4. Innovators; early adopters; early majority; late majority; laggards.
5. Network externalities; common standards; complementary products; switching costs; experimentation.

6 Building, holding, harvesting, withdrawal.

7 Both are in the high growth markets, but the star has a high market share while the question mark does not.

8 Market attractiveness and business strength.

9 A comprehensive model of corporate activities.

10 Improving methods within activities; combining activities in new or better ways; managing the linkages in its own value chain and its value system more effectively.

## Action Programme Review

1 The compact disc player, and its almost total replacement of the turntable, is in part indicative of the product life cycle. Initial high prices meant that it took a while to be accepted, but its benefits have led to considerable growth in sales. CD players have come down considerably in price and the market is reaching maturity. Consequently, turntables and vinyl records are in decline although vinyl is important in the club market.

Interestingly, the relative performance of CD players and turntables varied for a while according to market segment. CDs dominated the market for classical music earlier than they did for popular music. CDs have had less success in replacing tapes, as tapes are recordable. The Sony mini-disc has had some, limited, success. Furthermore the whole future of recorded music might be threatened by MP3.

In the video market, DVD offers higher quality reproduction, but until these are easily recordable, they will not replace home video.

2 (a) Orange juice is a cash cow.
(b) Pomegranate juice is a question mark, which the company wants to turn into a star.

3 Here are some ideas.

(a) It can become more efficient, by automating the production of food, as in a fast food chain.

(b) The chef can develop commercial relationships with growers, so he or she can obtain the best quality fresh produce.

(c) The chef can specialise in a particular type of cuisine (eg Nepalese, Korean).

(d) The restaurant can be sumptuously decorated for those customers who value atmosphere and a sense of occasion, in addition to a restaurant's purely gastronomic pleasures.

(e) The restaurant can serve a particular type of customer (eg celebrities).

Each of these options is a way of organising the activities of buying, cooking and serving food in a way that customers or chosen customers will value.

4 Sana Sounds is involved in the record industry from start to finish. Although recording and CD manufacture are contracted out to external suppliers, this makes no difference to the fact that these activities are part of Sana Sounds' own value chain. Sana Sounds earns its money by managing the whole set of activities. If the company grows then perhaps it will acquire its own recording studios. A value chain of activities is not the same as an organisation's business functions.

**Now try Question 5 at the end of the Study Text**

# Part D

## The external environment

# The Macro-Environment 6

| Chapter Topic List | |
|---|---|
| 1 | Setting the scene |
| 2 | Environmental influences |
| 3 | The political and legal environment |
| 4 | The economic environment |
| 5 | Social factors |
| 6 | Technological factors |
| 7 | The environment: ecological aspects |
| 8 | Globalisation and hostility to it |

## Syllabus Content

- Objective assessment of the external environment
- Acquisition and use of appropriate information and tools to evaluate the organisation's current competitive position

## Key Concepts Introduced

- Environment
- Demography
- Culture

# 1 Setting the scene

**1.1** Business plans cannot be produced in a vacuum. They must be developed within the context of the wider environment in which the organisation is operating. They need to take into account the opportunities and threats which are emerging as these external factors change.

**1.2** A key issue to keep in mind is **environmental change**. Some organisations face more complex and changing environments than others; the fashion industry is in a 'fast-moving' environment, but this speed of environmental change does not exist for all industries.

**1.3** In this chapter we deal with the wider or macro-environment. This aspect of the business environment lies at a remove from the organisation and might be perceived as being of less importance than the immediate or task environment. However, it is from the macro-environment that major pressures emerge; these have the potential to overwhelm a business or to provide it with huge new profitable markets. The effects of these pressures may well be further away in time than the impact of current market conditions, but they are likely to be far more significant.

# 2 Environmental influences

**2.1** As we saw in Part A, planning is a central part of the management task wherever you are working in the organisation and the first stage should always be to clarify the current position.

(a) **Controllable**. Different managers need to review different aspects of the business. The factors which can be controlled by the **marketing** manager can be primarily represented by the 7 Ps of the marketing mix.

(b) **Not controllable**. Issues of production capacity and sources of supply are of interest and of indirect importance to the marketing manager, but outside the area of direct control. That said, marketing mix decisions and marketing activities do have a significant impact on these other departments.

## Action Programme 1

Choose a business/market with which you are familiar. How has it changed over the last five years? Produce a list of all the external factors (things which the organisation cannot control) which have had a significant impact on the organisation in that time. Refine your list as you work through the rest of this chapter.

## Key Concept

The **environment** of an organisation is everything outside its boundaries. All the factors affect the organisation's performance, but the organisation cannot control them.

**2.2** Organisations have a variety of relationships with the environment.

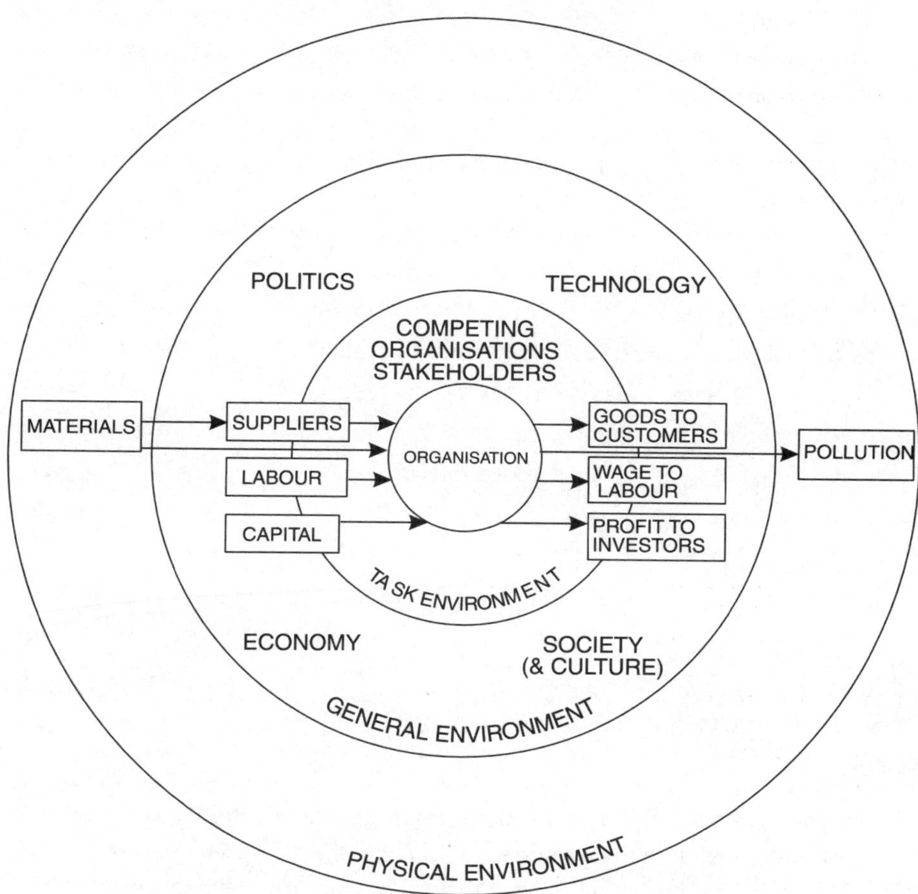


## 2.3 Classifying the environment

(a) The **micro-environment (or task environment)** is of immediate concern, and is uniquely configured for each organisation: no organisation has a network of suppliers, customers, competitors or stakeholders identical to another's.

(b) The **macro-environment (or general environment)** relates to factors in the environment affecting all organisations.

- **P**olitical-legal factors
- **E**conomic factors
- **S**ocial and cultural factors
- **T**echnological factors

} **PEST**

Another acronym you will come across is **SLEPT**, which stands for social, legal, economic, political and technological factors. Yet another is PESTEL, in which the second E stands for **ecological**, or green, concerns.

## Exam Tip

When you answer an examination question that is a case study problem, you might be expected to think about the specific environmental influences that might be relevant to the particular situation. You are expected to bring to bear your general knowledge and general business and marketing awareness. This is particularly evident when dealing with case examples set in an international context.

A Part B question in the draft Specimen Paper asked you to analyse the impact of major trends in the global environment affecting an industry of your choice and how the industry might respond to them. This emphasises an important point about your exam preparation: You need to have a couple of examples up your sleeve. Make sure at the very least that you understand the industry you work in and its characteristics. Learn the basics of its environment and markets. When you are familiar with this, choose another simple example such as the telecomms or oil industry and learn all you can about it from such publications as *The Economist* and the *Financial Times*.

## Marketing at Work

**GM Food**

For many years, *Monsanto* has been developing genetically modified foods, and these new substances have been marketed very successfully in the USA, with no public disquiet. In the UK and the EU generally, a combination of factors has led to public concern.

(a) Suspicion of industrial food production processes, especially after the BSE crisis
(b) Concern about ecology
(c) Trends towards organic food
(d) The relative success of the UK's biotechnology industry
(e) Trade friction between the UK and US

Many UK food producers have decided not to use GM foods.

*Website addresses*

www.monsanto.co.uk
www.ncbe.reading.ac.uk

## Action Programme 2

Choose an industrial product, a consumer durable, a fast moving consumer good and a service business. For each of them identify **how** you think the environmental factors identified in the following paragraphs might affect a business operating in that market.

## Environmental analysis

**2.4** *Johnson and Scholes* suggest that a firm should conduct an **audit of environmental influences**. This will identify the environmental factors which have had a significant influence on the organisation's development or performance in the past.

1 Assess the nature of the environment (eg is it changing?)

2 Identify those influences which have affected the organisation in the past or which are likely to do so in future.

3 A structural analysis will be prepared, identifying the 'key forces at work in the immediate or competitive environment'.

These steps should identify important developments.
Then the following questions should be asked.

↓

4 What is the organisation's position in relation to other organisations?

5 What threats and/or opportunities are posed by the environment?

**2.5** Strategic decisions are made in partial ignorance, as we have seen, because the environment is uncertain. Uncertainty relates to the **complexity and dynamism** of the environment.

(a) **Complexity** arises from:

(i) The **variety of influences** faced by the organisation. The more open an organisation is, the greater the variety of influences. The greater the number of markets the organisation operates in, the greater the number of influences to which it is subject.

(ii) The amount of **knowledge** necessary. All businesses need to have knowledge of the tax system, for example, but only pharmaceuticals businesses need to know about mandatory testing procedures for new drugs.

(iii) The **interconnectedness** of environmental influences. Importing and exporting companies are sensitive to exchange rates, which themselves are sensitive to interest rates. Interest rates then influence a company's borrowing costs.

(b) **Dynamism**. Stable environments are unchanging. Dynamic environments are in a state of change. The computer market is a dynamic market because of the rate of technological change.

**2.6** It is not always easy to detect which environmental factors will be relevant in future.

### Marketing at Work

***CISCO***

CISCO Systems, which provides a lot of the hardware structure of the Internet, announced a 30% drop in quarterly sales to 31/3/2001 – in common with other companies in the industry. This resulted from weak demand and excess optimism that the industry would continue to grow rapidly – only in 2000, orders regularly exceeded forecasts, and long lead times were not uncommon. It has over a year's supply of some components and will have to write off $2.5 billion of stock and reduce its workforce by 8,500. This change has been sudden.

*Website address:* www.cisco.com

## Action Programme 3

How do you consider that Johnson and Scholes' model can be easily applied to the scare about genetically modified foods?

### 2.7 Types of information collected

| Category | Example |
|---|---|
| **Market tidings** | ■ Market potential<br>■ Structural change<br>■ Competitors and industry<br>■ Pricing<br>■ Sales negotiations<br>■ Customers |
| **Acquisition leads** | ■ Leads for joint ventures<br>■ Mergers or acquisitions |
| **Technical tidings** | ■ New products, processes and technology<br>■ Product problems<br>■ Costs<br>■ Licensing and patents |
| **Broad issues** | ■ General conditions<br>■ Government actions and policies |

In the past, many companies have collected information in an unsystematic and haphazard way, perhaps because the costs of collecting information were too high. Nowadays with the Internet, there is a problem with **information overload**.

# 3 The political and legal environment

**3.1** We will outline in **general** terms some key issues to keep in mind. Laws come from common law, parliamentary legislation and government regulations derived from it, and obligations under EU membership and other treaties.

### 3.2 Legal factors affecting all companies

| Factor | Example |
|---|---|
| **General legal framework: contract, tort, agency** | Basic ways of doing business, negligence proceedings |
| **Criminal law** | Theft, insider dealing, bribery, deception |

| Factor | Example |
|---|---|
| **Company law** | Directors and their duties, reporting requirements, takeover proceedings, shareholders' rights, insolvency |
| **Employment law** | Trade Union recognition, Social Chapter provisions, possible minimum wage, unfair dismissal, redundancy, maternity, Equal Opportunities |
| **Health and Safety** | Fire precautions, safety procedures |
| **Data protection** | Use of information about employees and customers |
| **Marketing and sales** | Laws to protect consumers (eg refunds and replacement, cooling off period after credit agreements), what is or isn't allowed in advertising |
| **Environment** | Pollution control, waste disposal |
| **Tax law** | Corporation tax payment, collection of income tax (PAYE) and National Insurance contributions, VAT |

3.3 Some legal and regulatory factors affect **particular industries**, if the public interest is served. For example, electricity, gas, telecommunications, water and rail transport are subject to **regulators** (Ofgem, Oftel, Ofwat, Ofrail) who have influence over:

- Competition and market access
- Pricing policy (can restrict price increases)

3.4 This is because either:

- The industries are, effectively, monopolies: competition removes the need for regulation
- Large sums of public money are involved (eg in subsidies to rail companies)

## Marketing at Work

**Gas and electricity deregulation in the UK**

**Government policy**. Gas used to be a state monopoly. The industry was privatised as one company, *British Gas*. Slowly, the UK gas market has been opened to competition.

**Regulators**. Ofgem regulates the gas and electricity industry. Ofgem has introduced a Code of Conduct requiring gas suppliers to train sales agents, allow for a cooling off period during which customers can change their minds and so on. However, as competition intensifies more and more activities are moved out of the regulated environment.

**New markets**. The government has also deregulated the electricity market. Companies such as British Gas can now sell electricity, and electricity companies can now sell gas.

What happened to the once-monopoly supplier, British Gas? As a result of competition, it demerged some of its operations into two separate companies, *Transco* and *Centrica*. These are part of two separate businesses providing services, in Transco's case mainly to other businesses, in Centrica's case to end-users.

- Transco is a gas transporter. It does not sell gas itself but does maintain the pipeline infrastructure and some emergency services. Transco is now the principal activity of *Lattice*, which 'provides, manages and services infrastructure networks'. Lattice is currently investigating how metering services can be supplied to other utilities. Lattice has recently set up *186k*, a telecomms subsidiary. Lattice Energy Services aims to support other utilities. It is not a gas or energy supplier. *Advantica*, another subsidiary, exports the skills it acquired supporting Transco to overseas markets.

- Centrica provides energy and other services at home and on the road, through three consumer brands: British Gas, the *Automobile Association* and *Goldfish* (a credit card company). Centrica has a substantial business in the US and Canada. Centrica supplies energy, telecomms, roadside energy and financial services.

*Website addresses*

www.lattice-group.com
www.centrica.co.uk

---

### 3.5 Anticipating changes in the law

(a) The governing party's election **manifesto** is a guide to its political priorities, even if these are not implemented immediately.

(b) The government often publishes advance information about its plans (**green paper** or **white paper**) for consultation purposes.

(c) The **EU's single market programme** indicates future changes in the law.

## *Political risk and political change*

3.6 The political environment is not simply limited to legal factors. Government policy affects the whole **economy**, and governments are responsible for enforcing and creating a **stable framework** in which business can be done. A report by the World Bank indicated that the quality of **government policy is important in providing the right**:

- **Physical infrastructure** (eg transport)
- **Social infrastructure** (education, a welfare safety net, law enforcement)
- **Market infrastructure** (enforceable contracts, policing corruption)

3.7 However, it is **political change** which complicates the planning activities of many firms. Here is a checklist for case study use.

| Factor | Example: minimum wage |
|---|---|
| **Possibility of political change** | ■ Concern with social inequality |
| **Nature of impact** | ■ Minimum wage |
| **Consequences** | ■ Level of minimum wage |
| **Coping strategies** | ■ Cash flow planning, increase productivity |
| **Influence on decision making** | ■ Business lobbied to keep it low; trade unions lobbied to keep it high |

## *Political risk*

3.8 The political risk in a decision is the risk that political factors will invalidate the strategy and perhaps severely damage the firm. Examples are:

- Wars

- Expropriation ('rationalisation') of business assets by overseas governments
- Other forms of political influence in local decision making
- Local political chaos making business difficult

3.9 **A political risk checklist** is outlined by Jeannet and Hennessey (*Global Marketing Strategies*, 2002). Companies should ask the following six questions.

1. How **stable** is the host country's political system?
2. How **strong** is the host government's commitment to specific rules of the game, such as ownership or contractual rights, given its ideology and power position?
3. How **long** is the government likely to remain in **power**?
4. If the present government is **succeeded**, how would the specific rules of the game change?
5. What would be the effects of any expected **changes** in the specific rules of the game?
6. In light of those effects, what **decisions and actions should be taken now**?

There are many sources of data. The **Economist Intelligence Unit** (www.eiu.com) offers assessment of risk. Management consultants can also be contacted.

## Government policy and the particular industry

3.10 The government may intervene to protect specific sectors.

### Marketing at Work

The UK film industry has recently been blessed with tax breaks. Successive lobbying had finally paid off. Business and industries can put their case to government and EU officials.

# 4 The economic environment

4.1 The economic environment is an important influence at local and national level.

| Factor | Impact |
|---|---|
| **Overall growth or fall in Gross Domestic Product** | Increased/decreased demand for goods (eg dishwashers) and services (holidays). |
| **Local economic trends** | Type of industry in the area, office/factory rents, labour rates, house prices. |
| **National economic trends:** | |
| ■ Inflation | Low in most countries; distorts business decisions; wage inflation compensates for price inflation. |
| ■ Interest rates | How much it costs to borrow money affects **cash flow**. Some businesses carry a high level of debt. How much customers can afford to spend is also affected as rises in interest rates affect people's mortgage payments. |

| Factor | Impact |
|---|---|
| ■ Tax levels | Corporation tax affects how much firms can invest or return to shareholders. Income tax and VAT affect how much consumers have to spend, hence demand. |
| ■ Government spending | Suppliers to the government (eg construction firms) are affected by spending. |
| ■ The business cycle | Economic activity is always punctuated by periods of growth followed by decline, simply because of the nature of trade. The UK economy has been characterised by periods of 'boom' and 'bust'. Government policy can cause, exacerbate or mitigate such trends, but cannot abolish the business cycle. (Industries which prosper when others are declining are called **counter-cyclical** industries.) |
| ■ Share prices | In the US, an increasing proportion of people's wealth is held in the form of shares. If share prices fall, people perceive they have less money to spend, and thus start saving. |

4.2 The **forecast state of the economy** will influence the planning process for organisations which operate within it. In times of boom and increased demand and consumption, the overall planning problem will be to **identify** the demand. Conversely, in times of recession, the emphasis will be on cost-effectiveness, continuing profitability, survival and competition.

### 4.3 Key issues for the UK economy

(a) The **service sector** accounts for most output. Services include activities such as restaurants, tourism, nursing, education, management consultancy, computer consulting, banking and finance. Manufacturing is still important, especially in exports, but it employs fewer and fewer people.

| | 1981 | 1998 |
|---|---|---|
| Men | 33 | 25 |
| Women | 18 | 10 |

(b) The **housing market** is a key factor for people in the UK. Most houses are owner-occupied, and most people's wealth is tied up in their homes. UK borrowers generally borrow at variable rates of interest, so are vulnerable to changes in interest rates. If house prices rise, people feel wealthier, so they spend more.

(c) **Tax and welfare**. Although headline rates of tax have fallen, people have to spend more on private insurance schemes for health or pensions. The government aims to target welfare provision on the needy and to reduce overall welfare spending by getting people into work.

(d) **Productivity**. An economy cannot grow faster than the underlying growth in productivity, without risking inflation.

(i) UK manufacturing productivity is still lower than that of its main competitors, but in services the UK is relatively efficient.

(ii) UK businesses are high in capital productivity, in other words output earned per £ of capital expenditure.

These measures need to be looked at carefully. For example, countries with high unemployment may have low labour productivity simply because there are more people in work (in less productive jobs). A good measure is GDP per head.

(e) **Inequality**. The government is committed to spending more on health and education, and on reducing presumed inequality, by targeting benefits to those most in need. It has done so by reducing tax breaks for the better off.

(f) **Public spending** as a proportion of GDP is lower in the UK than in some countries. The **private finance initiative** aims to increase public spending by involving the private sector.

**4.4 Impact of international factors**

| Factor | Impact |
|---|---|
| **Exchange rates** | Cost of imports, selling prices and value of exports; cost of hedging against fluctuations |
| **Characteristics of overseas markets** | Desirable overseas markets (demand) or sources of supply |
| **Different rates of economic growth prosperity and tax** | Affects attractiveness of markets (levels of consumer demand, distribution infrastructure, government attitude, religion, post-tax profitability and repatriation of those profits) |
| **Capital, flows and trade** | Investment opportunities, free trade, cost of exporting |

## Marketing at Work

Growth in trade has affected the logistics industry (worth US $130bn of which $31.6bn is outsourced).

The major problem is congestion. The EU is planning to spend €350bn on trans-European networks (road, rail and air links) with possible extensions into Eastern Europe. Despite the single market, goods are still being held up at national borders. There are particular concerns as to environmental impact of logistics activities.

## The single European currency

**4.5** Most countries in the EU now use the Euro. Interest rates are set by the European Central Bank whose goal is price transparency. Implications are these.

(a) **Price transparency**: it will be obvious that prices differ in various markets. Cars are known to be priced higher in the UK than elsewhere. Markets may become harder to segment. Even so, the Internet and activities of the Consumers' Association have publicised 'unjustified' price differentials.

(b) **Interest rates** are now set for the whole of Europe, not by country. What may be suitable for the Netherlands, say, will not be suitable for Portugal. However, this effect may become less important as the EU economics become more integrated.

## Marketing at Work

***Rio Tinto* and the US dollar**

Rio Tinto is the world's second largest mining group. In early 2004 it reported a 10% fall in its underlying profits in the previous year, despite a 9% rise in turnover. This was largely due to the weakness of the US dollar against the Australian and Canadian currencies, which inflated costs.

However, an encouraging economic development was the 30% rise in demand from China for iron ore to support its rapid growth.

# 5 Social factors

## Demography

### Key Concept

**Demography** is the study of population and population trends

**5.1** The following demographic factors are important to organisational planners. A very good source of information about demography is *Social Trends*, published each year by the *Office of National Statistics.* Visit www.statistics.gov.uk.

| Factor | Comment |
|---|---|
| **Growth** | The rate of growth or decline in a national population and in regional populations. |
| **Age** | Changes in the age distribution of the population. In the UK, there will be an increasing proportion of the national population over retirement age. In developing countries there are very large numbers of young people.<br>■ Elderly people have unique needs.<br>■ As a segment they will become increasingly powerful. |
| **Geography** | The concentration of population into certain geographical areas. |
| **Ethnicity** | In the UK, about 5% come from ethnic minorities, although most of these live in London and the South East. |
| **Household and family structure** | A household is the basic social unit and its size might be determined by the number of children, whether elderly parents live at home etc. In the UK, there has been an **increase in single-person households** and lone parent families. Obviously, this impacts on the relevance of models such as the **family life cycle** |

| Factor | Comment |
|---|---|
| **Social structure** | The population of a society can be broken down into a number of subgroups, with different attitudes and access to economic resources. Social class, however, is hard to measure (as people's subjective perceptions vary).<br>■ Social classification systems are changing. The old systems based on the registrar-general grades (I, II, III etc) are to be replaced, from the 2001 census. The new grading covers occupations more closely: 1 Higher managerial and professional; 2 Lower managerial and professional; 3 Intermediate; 4 Small employers and own account workers; 5 Lower supervisory craft and related occupations; 6 Semi-routine occupations; 7 Routine occupations.<br>■ Social status generally passes from generation to generation, despite evidence of social mobility in individual cases. |
| **Employment** | Many people believe that there is a move to a casual flexible workforce; factories will have a group of **core employees**, supplemented by a group of **peripheral employees**, on part-time or temporary contracts, working as and when required. Some research indicates a 'two-tier' society split between **'work-rich'** (with two wage-earners) and **'work-poor'** households. However **most employees are in permanent, full-time employment**. |
| **Wealth** | Rising standards of living lead to increased demand for certain types of consumer good. This is why developing countries are attractive as markets. |

### 5.2 Implications of demographic change

(a) **Changes in patterns of demand**. An ageing population suggests increased demand for health care services. A young, growing population has a growing demand for schools, housing and work.

(b) **Location of demand**: people are moving to the suburbs and small towns.

(c) **Recruitment policies**: there are relatively fewer young people so firms will have to recruit from less familiar sources of labour.

(d) **Wealth and tax**.

## Culture

**Key Concept**

**Culture** is used by sociologists and anthropologists to encompass 'the sum total of the beliefs, knowledge, attitudes of mind and customs to which people are exposed in their social conditioning.'

**Exam Tip**

*Social change may generate new segmentation possibilities, or changes to the marketing mix. It may be provided in the mini-case data. Bear in mind culture when dealing with buyer behaviour, particularly where overseas markets are concerned.*

**5.3** Through contact with a particular culture, individuals learn a language, acquire values and learn habits of behaviour and thought.

(a) **Beliefs and values**. Beliefs are what we feel to be the case on the basis of objective and subjective information (eg people can believe the world is round or flat). **Values** are beliefs which are relatively enduring, relatively general and fairly widely accepted as a guide to culturally appropriate behaviour. Beliefs shape attitudes and so create tendencies for individuals and societies to behave in certain ways.

(b) **Customs**: modes of behaviour which represent culturally accepted ways of behaving in response to given situations.

(c) **Artefacts**: all the physical tools designed by human beings for their physical and psychological well-being: works of art, technology, products.

(d) **Rituals**. A ritual is a type of activity which takes on symbolic meaning, consisting of a fixed sequence of behaviour repeated over time.

The learning and sharing of culture is made possible by **language** (both written and spoken, verbal **and** non-verbal).

**5.4 Underlying characteristics of culture**

(a) **Purposeful**. Culture offers order, direction and guidance in all phases of human problem solving.

(b) **Learned**. Cultural values are 'transferred' in institutions (the family, school and church) and through on-going social interaction and mass media exposure in adulthood.

(c) **Shared**. A belief or practice must be common to a significant proportion of a society or group before it can be defined as a cultural characteristic.

(d) **Cumulative**. Culture is 'handed down' to each new generation. There is a strong traditional/historical element to many aspects of culture (eg classical music).

(e) **Dynamic**. Cultures adapt to changes in society: eg technological breakthrough, population shifts, exposure to other cultures.

**Marketing at Work**

Islamic banking is a powerful example of the importance of culture. The Koran abjures the charging of interest, which is usury. However whilst interest is banned, profits are allowed. A problem is that there is no standard interpretation of the sharia law regarding this. Products promoted by Islamic banks include:

(a) Leasing (the Islamic Bank TII arranged leases for seven Kuwait Airways aircraft)
(b) Trade finance
(c) Commodities trading

The earlier Islamic banks offered current accounts only, but depositors now ask for shares in the bank profits.

---

5.5 Knowledge of the culture of a society is clearly of value to businesses.

(a) **Marketers** can adapt their products accordingly, and be fairly sure of a sizeable market. This is particularly important in export markets.

(b) **Human resource managers** may need to tackle cultural differences in recruitment. For example, some ethnic minorities have a different body language from the majority, which may be hard for some interviewers to interpret.

5.6 Culture in a society can be divided into **subcultures** reflecting social differences. Most people participate in several of them.

| Subculture | Comment |
|---|---|
| **Class** | People from different social classes might have different values reflecting their position in society. |
| **Ethnic background** | Some ethnic groups can still be considered a distinct cultural group. |
| **Religion** | Religion and ethnicity are related. |
| **Geography or region** | Distinct regional differences might be brought about by the **past** effects of physical geography (socio-economic differences etc). Speech accents most noticeably differ. |
| **Age** | Age subcultures vary according to the period in which individuals were socialised, to an extent, because of the great shifts in social values and customs in this century. ('Youth culture'; the 'generation gap' etc.) |
| **Sex** | Some products are targeted directly to women or to men. |
| **Work** | Different organisations have different corporate cultures, in that the shared values of one workplace may be different from another. |

## Marketing at Work

Consider the case of a young French employee of *Eurodisney*.

(a) The employee speaks the French language – part of the national culture – and has participated in the French education system etc.

(b) As a youth, the employee might, in his or her spare time, participate in various 'youth culture' activities. Music and fashion are emblematic of youth culture.

(c) As an employee of Eurodisney, the employee will have to participate in the corporate culture, which is based on American standards of service with a high priority put on friendliness to customers.

*Website*: www.2000.disneylandparis.com

You can look at the employment opportunities on this website to see how a global services firm aims to recruit.

---

5.7 Cultural change might have to be planned for. There has been a revolution in attitudes to female employment, despite the well-publicised problems of discrimination that still remain.

## Action Programme 4

Club Fun is a UK company which sells packaged holidays. Founded in the 1980s, it offered a standard 'cheap and cheerful' package to resorts in Spain and, more recently, to some of the Greek islands. It was particularly successful at providing holidays for the 18–30 age group. What do you think the implications are for Club Fun of the following developments?

(a) A fall in the number of school leavers.
(b) The fact that young people are more likely now than in the 1980s to go into higher education.
(c) Holiday programmes on TV which feature a much greater variety of locations.
(d) Greater disposable income among the 18–30 age group.

---

### *Business ethics*

5.8 The conduct of an organisation, its management and employees will be measured against **ethical standards** by the customers, suppliers and other members of the public with whom they deal.

5.9 **Types of ethical problem a manager may meet with in practice**

(a) **Production practices**. Attempts to increase profitability by cutting costs may lead to dangerous working conditions, inadequate safety standards in products or reprehensible practices (eg child labour). This is a problem for firms which outsource production to low-cost factories overseas.

(b) **Gifts**. There is a fine line to be drawn between gifts, accepted as part of a way of doing business, and bribes.

(c) **Social responsibility**. Companies are being held to account for pollution and human rights issues.

(d) **Competitive behaviour**. There is a distinction between competing aggressively and competing unethically and illegally.

## Action Programme 5

The Heritage Carpet Company is a London-based retailer which imports carpets from Turkey, Iran and India. The company was founded by two Europeans who travelled independently through these countries in the 1970s. The company is the sole customer for carpets made in a number of villages in each of the source countries. The carpets are hand woven. Indeed, they are so finely woven that the process requires that children be used to do the weaving, thanks to their small fingers. The company believes that it is preserving a 'craft', and the directors believe that this is a justifiable social objective. Recently a UK television company has reported unfavourably on child exploitation in the carpet weaving industry. There were reports of children working twelve hour shifts in poorly lit sheds and cramped conditions, with consequent deterioration in eyesight, muscular disorders and a complete absence of education. The examples cited bear no relation to the Heritage Carpet Company's suppliers although children are used in the labour force, but there has been a spate of media attention. The regions in which the Heritage Carpet Company's supplier villages are found are soon expected to enjoy rapid economic growth. What social and ethical issues are raised for the Heritage Carpet Company?

---

# 6 Technological factors

## 6.1 Technology

(a) **Apparatus or equipment**: for example a TV camera.

(b) **Technique**: how to use the TV camera to best effect, perhaps in conjunction with other equipment such as lights.

(c) **Organisation**: the grouping of camera-operators, producers, floor managers and so on into teams, to work on a particular project.

(d) **The way in which markets are identified**. Database systems make it much easier to analyse the market place.

(e) **The way in which firms are managed**. IT encourages delayering of organisational hierarchies, home-working, and better communication.

(f) **The means of communications** with clients, via website, e-mail and so on.

**6.2** **Technology contributes to overall economic growth**. Technology can increase total output.

- Gains in productivity (more output per units of input)
- Reduced costs (eg transportation technology, preservatives)
- New types of product

## 6.3 Effects of technological change on organisations

- The **type of products or services** that are made and sold
- The **way** in which **products are made** (eg robots, new raw materials)
- The way in which **services are provided**

## Marketing at Work

**Mail order/Internet**

(a) Companies selling easily transportable goods – for instance, books and CDs – can offer much greater consumer choice and are enjoying considerable success in attracting revenue. However, whether this business is profitable is a different issue entirely, because many e-businesses depended on old economy skills in logistics and distribution.

(b) The financial sector is rapidly going electronic – call centres are now essential to stay in business, Internet banking has taken off, and the Internet and interactive TV are starting to feature in business plans.

A key issue is the role of the website: is it just another promotional tool or a fundamentally new way of doing business?

---

## Marketing at Work

The Internet has implications for the structure and strategies of some industries and their marketing mixes. Take telecommunications. The telephone tariff system is 'fundamentally a fixed cost system, but we pay for it on the basis of a variable – mainly voice minutes. What is more, where the charges are levied bears no relation to where the costs occur'.

The Internet threatens to undermine this. Access to the Internet is normally charged at local call rates. It will soon be possible to hold conversations over the Internet, which 'will undermine the "price per distance" business model' which allows telephone companies to charge more for long distance calls.

---

**6.4** The impact of **recent** technological change also has potentially important social consequences, which in turn have an impact on business.

(a) **Home-working**. Whereas people were once collected together to work in factories, home-working will become more important.

(b) **Intellective skills**. Certain sorts of skill, related to interpretation of data and information processes, are likely to become more valued than manual or physical skills.

(c) **Services**. Technology increases manufacturing productivity, releasing human resources for service jobs. These jobs require **greater interpersonal skills** (eg in dealing with customers).

## Database marketing

**6.5** Databases can be compiled of people's spending habits and social profiles enabling more precise targeting of marketing communications.

(a) On the **quantitative** side, database marketing is becoming more popular. It is, after all, **real behaviour as opposed to simulated behaviour**.

(b) This also makes it more attractive than **qualitative research**. What people say in **focus groups** or to market researchers does not necessarily reflect their actual purchase behaviour.

**6.6** Firms use databases to keep up-to-date information on their product lines and the behaviour of customers. The danger with database information is that it can rapidly go out of date. '**Dirty data**' as this is called, is a major problem: some estimates suggest that data accuracy deteriorates by about 30% a year.

**6.7** In practice, the data is only as good as firms' use of it. An example of how the different types of data are used is provided below.

## Using the Internet

**6.8** The Internet enables:

(a) New software or information-based products, such as computer games or even distance learning products, to be created or distributed in new ways

(b) Firms to sell other types of product more effectively and to mould customer relationships

**6.9 Key implications of the Internet for the market place**

(a) **Blurred boundaries** between businesses: a competitor's website is a few mouse-clicks away.

(b) **Information is less asymmetrical**. Customers can now compare prices more easily, leading to a greater balance of information than in the past where, typically, the supplier knew more than the customer. The **Internet reduces 'search costs'**.

(c) It is becoming harder to reach a mass market over the net.

(d) Internet shopping operates on a 24-hour basis. Customers can be serviced remotely via e-mail.

(e) Competition can appear from anywhere.

(f) Marketing can be interactive as a customer 'enters an advert'.

**6.10 Within companies**

- Information is available in **real-time**.
- Access to information does not have to be restricted in the organisation.
- Innovative businesses can exploit the rich information provided by IT.

### Marketing at Work

**Supermarket shopping**

UK supermarket groups offer two ways of applying Internet technology to their retailing business.

*Tesco* is one of the world's largest Internet supermarket. Customers log on to its website. The goods are picked at the customer's local store and delivered for £5.

Its competitors, such as *ASDA*, have invested heavily in dedicated warehouses and distribution sectors, for Internet orders.

It remains to be seen which will be more profitable. Tesco adds a £5 delivery charge: does employing a packer and incurring all the driving and van costs only come to this amount for delivery, or is Tesco's service a means to get a market share?

*Website addresses*

www.tesco.com
www.asda.co.uk

# 7 The environment: ecological aspects

**7.1 The importance of physical environmental conditions**

(a) **Resource inputs**. Managing physical resources successfully (eg oil companies, mining companies) is a good source of profits.

(b) **Logistics**. The physical environment presents logistical problems or opportunities to organisations. Proximity to road and rail links can be a reason for siting a warehouse in a particular area.

(c) **Government**. The physical environment is under the control of other organisations.

(i) Local authority town planning departments can influence where a building and necessary infrastructure can be sited. Zoning regulations prohibit the siting of commercial developments in some residential districts.

(ii) Governments can set regulations about some of the organisation's environmental interactions.

(d) **Disasters**. In some countries, the physical environment can pose a major threat to organisations.

## An interrelationship between environmental factors and strategic planning

**7.2** Issues relating to the effect of an organisation's activities on the physical environment have come to the fore in recent years for a number of reasons.

(a) The **entry into decision-making** or political roles of the generation which grew up in the **1960s**.

(b) **Growth in prosperity** might have encouraged people to feel that quality of life is more than just material production and consumption.

(c) Expansion of **media coverage** (eg of famines, global warming) has fuelled public anxiety.

(d) **Disasters** (eg floods, forest fires in Asia, BSE) have aroused public attention.

(e) **Greater scientific knowledge**. The scientific consensus is developing the view that global warming is not only a real phenomenon but also is caused by human activity.

**7.3 How environmental issues will impinge on business**

- **Consumer demand** for products which appear to be ecologically friendly
- Demand for **less pollution** from industry
- Greater **regulation** by government and the EU
- **Polluter pays**. Businesses will be charged with the external cost of their activities
- Possible requirements to conduct **ecology audits**
- Opportunities to develop **products and technologies** which are ecologically friendly

**7.4** The consumer demand for products which claim environmental soundness has waxed and waned, with initial enthusiasm replaced by cynicism about such claims.

(a) **Marketing**. Companies such as Body Shop have exploited environmental friendliness as a marketing tool.

(b) **Bad publicity**. Perhaps companies have more to fear from the impact of bad publicity (relating to their environmental practices) than they have to benefit from positive ecological messages as such.

(c) **Lifestyles**. There may be a limit to which consumers are prepared to alter their lifestyles for the sake of ecological correctness.

(d) Consumers may be **imperfectly educated** about ecological issues. (For example, much recycled paper has simply replaced paper produced from trees from properly managed (ie sustainably developed) forests). In short, some companies may have to educate consumers as to the relative environmental impact of their products.

**7.5** As far as pollution goes, there has been a longish history on ecological legislation and it is likely that governments will take an increased interest in this area.

(a) **Government taxes and fees**. A **Landfill Tax** was introduced in the UK from October 1996. Companies can improve their waste handling. The EU has been considering an energy or carbon tax for some time: such a tax would have to be agreed by the member states, however.

(b) **Government regulations**. Fines might be imposed for persistent breach of pollution guidelines, and pollution might be monitored by government inspectors. The UK government has stated **targets** for **recycling** and reducing **carbon dioxide emissions**.

(c) **Tradable pollution permits** (USA). Every year, the government issues pollution permits to relevant firms for a certain price. These permits can be sold. It might be cheaper for a company to reduce its pollution than do nothing, as the cost could be recouped by the revenue gained by selling the permit. There is talk about introducing this scheme globally.

(d) **Commercial opportunities**. Companies can benefit from the commercial opportunities proposed by the new concern for ecological issues. Chemicals companies have been able to benefit from the development of safe alternatives to CFC gases.

(e) Finally, a firm can **relocate** its activities to a country where ecological standards are less strict, or have a lower priority in relation to other economic and social objectives, such as economic growth.

# 8 Globalisation and hostility to it

**8.1** Globalisation can mean many things.

(a) Relaxation of trade barriers for goods and services
(b) Free flow of investment capital with no restrictions
(c) International co-operation and standardisation

It is covered in detail in your BPP *International Marketing Strategy* Study Text.

**8.2** For companies and marketers, globalisation offers the opportunity to enter new markets. Sound marketing principles still apply but there is no doubt that global marketing is more complex (and risky) than marketing at home.

**8.3** Conversely, globalisation offers increased competitors to domestic producers.

**8.4** **Key issues for marketers**

(a) Characteristics of overseas markets

(b) Can the same segmentation and positioning strategies be adopted?
(c) Is there a global market, or equivalent segments within each country market?
(d) Impact of culture and regulation on resourcing, distribution, advertising and promotion
(e) Management and structure of overseas operations

## Marketing at Work

**Global hotel chains**

The hotel industry is embracing globalisation. International chains are encircling the world, swallowing local operations on an almost daily basis.

Tom Oliver, chief executive of *Bass Hotels and Resorts*, says: 'Brands are everything – as travel becomes increasingly trans-border, hotels which aren't carrying international brands simply don't deliver the same rate of revenue per room'.

Bass was unwittingly pushed into hotels by trade secretary Margaret Beckett, who thwarted the group's ambitions to become a global brewer by blocking its purchase of Carlsberg-Tetley. Fellow brewer Whitbread realised that it, too, could not go much further in beer, and began building its Travel Inn chain and its British franchise for *Marriott Hotels*, snapping up *Swallow Hotels* for £578m in November 1999.

All these deals have been motivated by a recognition that the **market is changing**. In the US, 75% of hotels have a well-known brand, compared with just 35% in Europe. Lesley Ashplant, a hotels expert at PricewaterhouseCoopers, says: 'Europe is the single largest tourist destination in the world. It has 6m hotel rooms under fragmented ownership. There are clear **opportunities in scale**, in taking advantage of **branding** and **advanced technology**'.

Size is becoming important as **expectations rise** – international business travellers want Internet connections, widescreen televisions and push-button blinds in every room, all of which requires investment. They want faxes delivered to their rooms at all hours of the night and the ability to order *foie gras* at four o'clock in the morning – which means employing more staff than most independent operators can afford.

**Hi-tech reservations** systems are also emerging as a crucial factor. In an industry where 75% of costs are staff wages, any savings elsewhere are precious.

Between a third and half of hotels' revenue comes from food and drink, but these only contribute 20% to 30% of profit. Attempts to make hotel restaurant more attractive have generally failed.

Much more profitable are the rooms themselves. The main thrust, therefore, for most operators, is on improving **occupancy**. **Loyalty card** schemes are becoming increasingly elaborate.

Even the most ardent advocates of consolidation accept, however, that there will be limits to the creeping internationalisation of European hotels. Mr Abramson says: 'The US is a wide-open country – if you want a hotel, you can just build it. In Europe, there's much less opportunity for new-builds, so you get a lot of conversions. They're harder to fit into the specific model of the US chain.'

It is difficult to turn a 17th century Provençal château into a Holiday Inn, so some independent operators still prosper. This is bad news for the ideal guest of a multinational chain, who likes to wake up anywhere in the world in the knowledge that the bathroom is on the left, the blinds are blue and the phone is on the wall, six and a half inches above the bedside table.

*Website address*: www.sixcontinentshotels.com *The Guardian*, 18 April 2001

## Hostility to globalisation as a cultural factor

8.5 A number of pressure groups have emerged, linked in their hostility to global capitalism. Thanks, possibly, to better communications and the Internet, they are able to co-ordinate their activities on a world-wide scale. These groups participated in recent protests in Seattle (when the global trading was being discussed by members of the World Trading Organisation) and at the Davos economic forum (a regular gathering of the world's business and political elite).

8.6 Indeed, the anti-globalisation brigade has spawned its own anti-marketing literature. *Naomi Klein's* book, *No Logo*, is a key text on the anti-capitalist reading list. In particular she attacks **brands**. Perhaps marketers need to go back to fundamentals as to what brands actually promise.

8.7 Globalisation is blamed for environmental degradation and global inequality, standardisation and the destruction of local cultures – all under the control of multinational firms which, it is said, are greedy and are not democratically accountable.

8.8 Successful global brands such as *McDonald's* or *Starbucks* are subjects of particular hostility.

## Chapter Roundup

- Organisations exist in an **environment**. For many firms, this environment is **constantly changing**. These changes can often happen with little warning, as with sudden political unrest and conflicts. Although changes in the external environment are outside the control of managers they must be **monitored** and **responded** to if the organisation is to maximise the **opportunities** and minimise the damaging impact of **threats.**
- The **external environment** is made up of a number of variables. Managers need to know which factors are critical to their own markets and monitor these carefully. A mnemonic is **PEST** (political and legal, economic, social and cultural, technological).
- Uncertainty in this context results from **complexity** and **dynamism**.
- If planners ignore the external influences on the business, they are operating in the dark and the risks of being unprepared for an unexpected **environmental threat** are immense. The ability to produce plans in the context of a realistic **appraisal** of the **current** and **forecasted** business environment is dependent on **adequate information** being available to the planners at the right time and in a usable format. Johnson and Scholes suggest a five stage process.
  - Assess the **environment**
  - Identify **influences**
  - Analysis **key** influences
  - Identify **relative position**
  - Identify **threats and opportunities**
- For your CIM examinations you need to bear in mind that the external factors at **corporate level** influence how the business operates and the nature of the market. At **marketing planning** level the main focus of external changes is on how environmental factors influence and change **consumer demand**.

## Quick Quiz

1. What are the main categories of external influences which affect the organisation?
2. What is the source of environmental complexity?
3. List the types of information that can be collected.
4. How does the legal framework potentially affect an organisation?
5. Why do planners need to monitor the political environment?
6. Give two examples of economic change.
7. How has the changing age structure affected business plans?
8. Why is culture important?
9. In what three ways does technological change affect business?

## Answers to Quick Quiz

1 Political-legal factors; economic factors; social factors; technological factors.

2 The variety of influences faced by the organisation; the amount of knowledge necessary; the interconnectedness of environmental influences.

3 Market tidings; acquisition leads; technical tidings; broad issues.

4 Law affects basic ways of doing business, establishes directors' duties and reporting requirements, lays down conditions for employment contracts, sets standards for health and safety requirements, regulates use of data, polluting substances, consumer terms and taxation.

5 Political factors could invalidate a business's strategy and make it impossible to remain profitable. For example, a minimum wage could damage cash flow and force prices to an uncompetitive level.

6 Any two from: growth or full in GDP, inflation, interior rates, tax levels, government spending, business cycle, share prices, property prices, labour rates.

7 Business plans have had to change because of changes in the pattern of demand; the location of demand; the age profile of the available workforce and the relative distribution of wealth in different age groups.

8 To adapt products to appeal to different markets; for communication, particularly, accepted business practice to meet ethical standards; to understand how gestures, such as gifts, will be interpreted.

9 It affects the types of product or service that are offered and the way they are made or delivered.

## Action Programme Review

1 You should have identified **specific** examples of how PEST factors affect your business.

2 This exercise requires you to use your imagination. Identify the characteristics of the product and market and then think of the type of influences. You will need to make a similar systematic leap of the imagination in the exam.

3 **Uncertainty** is caused by inadequate knowledge as to risk. The **variety** of influences include technological factors, the animal feed industry, the EU, the media, environmentalists.

4 The firm's market is shrinking. There is an absolute fall in the number of school leavers. Moreover, it is possible that the increasing proportion of school leavers going to higher education will mean there will be fewer who can afford Club Fun's packages. That said, a higher disposable income in the population at large might compensate for this trend. People might be encouraged to try destinations other than Club Fun's traditional resorts if these other destinations are publicised on television.

5 **Many**. This is a case partly about boundary management and partly about enlightened self-interest and business ethics. The adverse publicity, although not about the Heritage Carpet Company's own suppliers, could rebound badly. Potential customers might be put off. Economic growth in the area may also mean that parents will prefer to send their children to school. The Heritage Carpet Company as well as promoting itself as preserving a craft could reinvest some of its profits in the villages (eg by funding a school), by enforcing limits on the hours children

worked. It could also pay a decent wage. It could advertise this in a 'code of ethics' so that customers are reassured that the children are not simply being exploited. Alternatively, it could not import child-made carpets at all. (This policy, however, would be unlikely to help communities in which child labour is an economic necessity.)

**Now try Question 6 at the end of the Study Text**

# The Task Environment 7

| Chapter Topic List | |
|---|---|
| 1 | Setting the scene |
| 2 | Industry analysis: the competitive forces |
| 3 | Market analysis |
| 4 | Competitor analysis |
| 5 | Customer analysis |
| 6 | SWOT analysis |

## Syllabus Content

- Objective assessment of the external environment
- Acquisition and use of appropriate information and tools to evaluate the organisation's current competitive position
- Development of customer insights by analysis of potential and current customer bases
- Quantification of opportunities and threats
- Summary of salient factors and insights emerging from the external analysis
- Summary of the analysis of the internal and external environment

## Key Concepts Introduced

- Competitive forces
- Market
- Strategic group
- Mobility barriers
- Corporate appraisal

# 1 Setting the scene

1.1 The general factors in the previous chapter affect all organisations equally. However, each firm is positioned differently in each particular market and in the industry as a whole.

1.2 Each industry contains companies aiming to offer similar satisfaction to customers. However, each company has a unique profile compared to its competitors.

1.3 Market analysis and customer analysis shows what companies and industries are competing for: the managing director of a fast food chain spoke about competing for 'share of stomach'.

1.4 Identifying who your competitors are is easier said than done as competition exists outside any particular industry. While competitors are important, only paying customers can determine which firms have competitive advantage.

1.5 We round off this part of the Study Text with a brief discussion of SWOT analysis. This is the technique that draws together the threads of the strategic appraisal so that informed strategic decisions may be made.

# 2 Industry analysis: the competitive forces

2.1 In discussing competition Porter (*Competitive Strategy*) distinguishes between factors which characterise the nature of competition:

(a) **In one industry compared with another** (eg in the chemicals industry compared with the clothing retail industry) and make one industry as a whole potentially more profitable than another (ie yielding a bigger return on investment).

(b) **Within a particular industry**. These relate to the competitive strategies that individual firms might select.

**Key Concept**

Five **competitive forces** influence the state of competition in an industry, which collectively determine the profit (ie long-run return on capital) potential of the industry as a whole. **Learn them**.

(a) The threat of **new entrants** to the industry
(b) The threat of **substitute** products or services
(c) The bargaining power of **customers**
(d) The bargaining power of **suppliers**
(e) The **rivalry** among current competitors in the industry

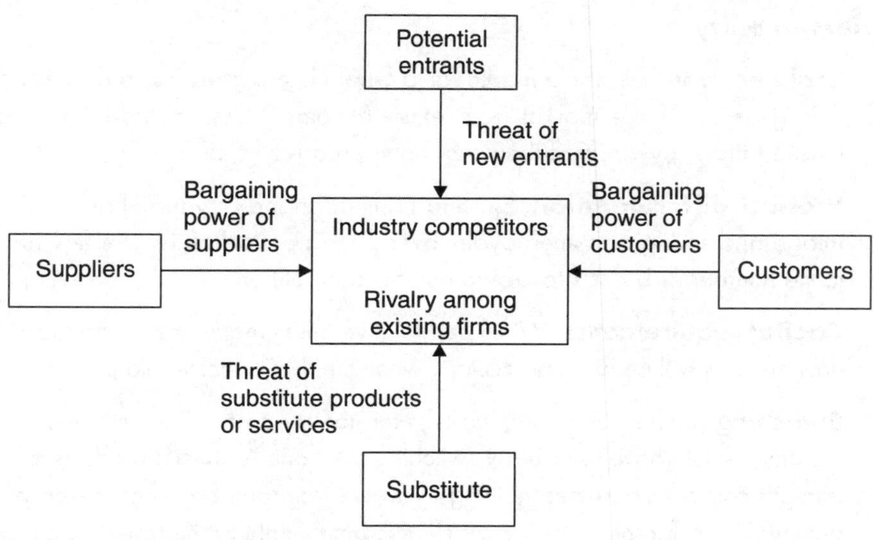


Source: adapted from Porter *(Competitive Strategy)*

## The threat of new entrants (and barriers to entry to keep them out)

2.2 **A new entrant into an industry will bring extra capacity and more competition.** The strength of this threat is likely to vary from industry to industry, depending on:

(a) The strength of the **barriers to entry**. Barriers to entry discourage new entrants.

(b) The likely **response of existing competitors** to the new entrant.

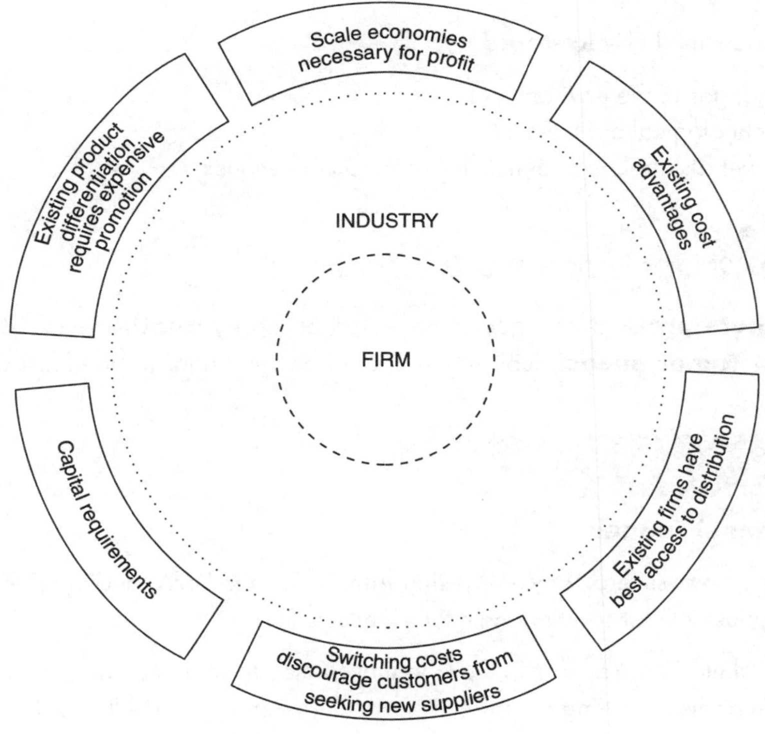

**2.3 Barriers to entry**

(a) **Scale economies**. If the market as a whole is not growing, a new entrant has to capture a large slice of the market from existing competitors, in order to cover its fixed costs. Existing firms, by virtue of their size have an advantage.

(b) **Product differentiation**. Existing firms in an industry may have built up a good brand image and strong customer loyalty over a long period of time. A few firms may promote a large number of brands to crowd out the competition.

(c) **Capital requirements**. When capital investment requirements are high, the barrier against new entrants will be high, particularly when the investment would possibly be high-risk.

(d) **Switching costs**. Switching costs refer to the costs (time, money, convenience) that a customer would have to incur by switching from one supplier's products to another's. Although it might cost a **consumer** nothing to switch from one brand of frozen peas to another, the potential costs for the **retailer or distributor** might be high. As far as consumer marketing is concerned, switching costs can include 'emotional' as well as functional costs.

(e) **Access to distribution channels**. Distribution channels carry a manufacturer's products to the end-buyer. New distribution channels are difficult to establish, and existing distribution channels hard to gain access to.

(f) **Cost advantages of existing producers, independent of economies of scale**

- Patent rights
- Experience and know-how
- Government subsidies and regulations
- Favoured access to raw materials

**2.4** Entry barriers might be **lowered** by:

- Changes in the environment
- Technological changes
- Novel distribution channels for products or services

## The threat from substitute products

**2.5** A **substitute product** is a good/service produced by **another industry** which satisfies the **same customer needs**. Substitutes put a lid on what firms in an industry can charge.

### Marketing at Work

**The Channel Tunnel**

Passengers have several ways of getting from London to Paris, and the pricing policies of the various industries transporting them there reflects this.

(a) 'Le Shuttle' carries cars in the Channel Tunnel. Its main competitors are the ferry companies, offering a substitute service. Therefore, you will find that Le Shuttle sets its prices with reference to ferry company prices, and vice versa.

(b) Eurostar is the rail service from London to Paris/Brussels. Its main competitors are not the ferry companies but the airlines. Prices on the London-Paris air routes fell with the commencement of Eurostar services, and some airlines have curtailed the number of flights they offer.

---

## The bargaining power of customers

**2.6** Customers want better quality products and services at a lower price. Satisfying this want might force down the profitability of suppliers in the industry. Customer strength depends upon the following.

(a) How much the **customer buys**.

(b) How **critical** the product is to the customer's own business.

(c) **Switching costs** (ie the cost of switching supplier).

(d) Whether the products are **standard items** (hence easily copied) or **specialised**.

(e) The **customer's own profitability**: a customer who makes low profits will be forced to insist on low prices from suppliers.

(f) The customer's **ability to bypass** the supplier or **take over** the supplier.

(g) The **skills** of the customer's **purchasing staff**, or the price-awareness of consumers.

(h) When **product quality** is important to the customer, the customer is less likely to be price-sensitive, and so the industry might be more profitable as a consequence.

### Marketing at Work

Although the Ministry of Defence may wish to keep control over defence spending, it is likely as a **customer** to be more concerned that the products it purchases perform satisfactorily than with getting the lowest price possible for everything it buys.

---

## The bargaining power of suppliers

**2.7** Suppliers can exert pressure for higher prices, depending upon the following factors.

(a) Whether there are just **one or two dominant suppliers** to the industry, able to charge monopoly or oligopoly prices.

(b) The threat of **new entrants** or substitute products to the **supplier's industry**.

(c) Whether the suppliers have **other customers** outside the industry, and do not rely on the industry for the majority of their sales.

(d) The **importance of the supplier's product** to the customer's business.

(e) Whether the supplier has a **differentiated product** which buyers need to obtain.

(f) Whether **switching costs** for customers would be high.

## Marketing at Work

Food products in the UK are largely sold through supermarket chains, and it can be difficult for a new producer to get supermarket organisations to agree to stock its product. As retailers become more powerful, they are placing more and more demands on food producers: failure to comply can mean exclusion from the channel of distribution. Supplier bargaining power is low. Sophisticated marketing firms try to get round this by using advertising, for example, to stimulate customer demand by implementing 'pull strategies'. Such strategies can extend to point of sale advertising. *Safeway* in the UK now features LCD screens in supermarket aisles, which may promote one or more products. For example, the merits of Barilla pasta are forcibly promoted in a short film in the aisle where *Barilla* and other pasta products are being marketed.

Other suppliers try to restrict distribution outlets to maintain high prices, particularly in the case of perfumes and cosmetics, by banning sales of these items in 'undesirable' outlets.

## The rivalry amongst current competitors in the industry

**2.8** The **intensity of competitive rivalry** within an industry will affect the profitability of the industry as a whole. Competitive actions might take the form of price competition, advertising battles, sales promotion campaigns, introducing new products for the market, improving after sales service or providing guarantees or warranties. Competition can:

(a) **Stimulate demand**, expanding the market.

(b) **Leave demand unchanged**, in which case individual competitors will make less money, unless they are able to cut costs.

**2.9 Factors determining the intensity of competition**

(a) **Market growth**. Rivalry is intensified when firms are competing for a greater market share in a total market where growth is slow or stagnant.

(b) **Cost structure**. High fixed costs are a temptation for firms to compete on price, as in the short run **any** contribution from sales is better than none at all.

(c) **Switching**. Suppliers will compete if buyers switch easily (eg Coke vs Pepsi).

(d) **Capacity**. A supplier might need to achieve a substantial increase in output **capacity**, in order to obtain reductions in unit costs.

(e) **Uncertainty**. When one firm is not sure what another is up to, there is a tendency to respond to the uncertainty by formulating a more competitive strategy.

(f) **Strategic importance**. If success is a prime strategic objective, firms will be likely to act very competitively to meet their targets.

(g) **Exit barriers** make it difficult for an existing supplier to leave the industry.

(i) Fixed assets with a low **break-up value** (eg there may be no other use for them, or they may be old).

(ii) The cost of **redundancy payments** to employees.

(iii) If the firm is a division or subsidiary of a larger enterprise, the **effect of withdrawal on the other operations** within the group.

(iv) The **reluctance of managers** to admit defeat, their loyalty to employees and their fear for their own jobs.

(v) **Government pressures** on major employers not to shut down operations, especially when competition comes from foreign producers rather than other domestic producers.

## Action Programme 1

The tea industry is characterised by oversupply, with a surplus of about 80,000 tonnes a year. Tea estates 'swallow capital, and the return is not as attractive as in industries such as technology or services'. Tea cannot be stockpiled, unlike coffee, keeping for two years at most. Tea is auctioned in London and prices are the same in absolute terms as they were 15 years ago. Tea is produced in Africa and India, Sri Lanka and China. Because of the huge capital investment involved, the most recent investments have been quasi-governmental, such as those by the Commonwealth Development Corporation in ailing estates in East Africa. There is no simple demarcation between buyers and sellers. Tea-bag manufacturers own their own estates, as well as buying in tea from outside sources.

Recently tea prices were described in India at least as being 'exceptionally firm'. The shortage and high prices of coffee have also raised demand for tea which remains the cheapest of all beverages in spite of the recent rise in prices. Demand from Russia, Poland, Iran and Iraq are expected to rise.

(a) Carry out a five forces analysis.

(b) Thinking ahead, suggest a possible marketing strategy for a tea-grower with a number of estates which has traditionally sold its tea at auction.

# Information technology and the competitive forces

## Marketing at Work

The Internet has had a variety of impacts.

Recently, The *Financial Times* reported that German companies were losing lucrative niche markets because the Internet made it easier for customers to **compare prices** from other suppliers by obtaining other information over the Internet. High prices made German retailers vulnerable in an age when 'a shopper with a credit card and computer could sit at home and could order from around the world'.

### 2.10 Barriers to entry and IT

(a) **IT can raise entry barriers** by increasing economies of scale, raising the capital cost of entry (by requiring a similar investment in IT) or effectively colonising distribution channels by tying customers and suppliers into the supply chain or distribution chain by technologies such as **electronic data interchange**.

(b) **IT can surmount entry barriers**. An example is the use of Internet and telephone banking, which sometimes obviates the need to establish a branch network.

**2.11 Bargaining power of suppliers** and IT

(a) **Increasing the number of** accessible **suppliers**. Supplier power in the past derived from various factors such as geographical proximity and the fact that the organisation requires goods of a certain standard in a certain time. IT enhances supplier information available to customers.

(b) **Closer supplier relationships**. Suppliers' power can be **shared**. Computer aided design can be used to design components in tandem with suppliers. Such relationships might be developed with a few key suppliers. The supplier and the organisation both benefit from performance improvement, but the relations are closer.

(c) **Switching costs**. Suppliers can be integrated with the firm's administrative operations, by a system of electronic data interchange.

**2.12 Bargaining power of customers**. IT can 'lock customers in'.

(a) **IT can raise switching costs**.

(b) **Customer information systems** can enable a thorough analysis of marketing information so that products and services can be tailored to the needs of each segment. We discussed **database marketing** in the previous chapter.

**2.13 Substitutes**. In many respects, **IT itself is 'the substitute product'**. Here are some examples.

(a) Video-conferencing systems might substitute for air transport in providing a means by which managers from all over the world can get together in a meeting.

(b) IT is the basis for new leisure activities (eg computer games) which substitute for TV or other pursuits.

(c) E-mail might substitute for some postal deliveries.

**2.14 IT and the state of competitive rivalry**

(a) IT can be used in support of a firm's **competitive** strategy of cost leadership, differentiation or focus. These are discussed later in this text.

(b) IT can be used in a **collaborative** venture, perhaps to set up new communications networks. Some competitors in the financial services industry share the same ATM network.

## Marketing at Work

**Digital jukeboxes**

The structure of an industry can be radically changed by technical developments. Music can now be downloaded over the Internet in MP3 files and e-mailed.

The big five record companies command 80% of the global market (£22.6bn). They hope to produce a 'pirate-proof' technical standard to ensure protection of intellectual property.

However, piracy is only one issue. Many bands might bypass the existing record companies altogether: digital jukeboxes enable unsigned acts to post recordings on the net without the support of a big label. In the past, the 'big five' used their commercial clout to enforce dominance. In the new digital market place, size is far less important, as barriers to entry are significantly lower.

'Digital jukeboxes are the online version of independent labels, but with such smaller cost bases that they may prove more resilient. These problems pale beside the risk that established superstars – suppliers, as it were – will bypass record companies and retailers by controlling their own online distribution following in the footsteps of Frank Zappa who ran his own mail order catalogue in the 1970s. The big labels are fighting for their contracts.'

*The music industry: Napster*

More fundamental is technology that allows unlimited digital-to-digital copying on users own PCs. This threatened royalties and earnings of copyright holders, and may have contributed to a 46% fall in sales of CD supplies in the US in 2000 (*Financial Times*, 19 April 2001).

Napster was forced to shut down its service after failing to comply with a court injunction requiring it to prevent its 72m users downloading copyright material. There was also a marked increase in illegal copying.

*Yes, but ...*

This implies that all that bands need is a website – what about the marketing support, PR, concert tours?

---

# 3 Market analysis

**Key Concept**

A **market** is a group of actual and potential customers, who can make purchase decisions.

3.1 Businesses also talk about the market for a product (eg the confectionery market) as well as other classifications such as the youth market.

3.2 Many firms compete in several markets, if they are diversified or if they have a distinctive competence or brand which can be exploited.

3.3 A **market analysis** will be made up of a range of factors. Here is a checklist (adapted from Dibb and Simkin, 1996).

| **Statistical data** | **2003** | **2004** | **2005 (forecast)** |
|---|---|---|---|
| *Company/SBU data* | | | |
| Market name | | | |
| Unit sales | | | |
| £ sales | | | |
| Profitability | | | |
| *Market data* | | | |
| Market size | | | |
| Market share | | | |
| No. of main customers | | | |
| No. of dealers/distributors | | | |
| Concentration ratio | | | |
| **Qualitative data** | | | |
| Environmental factors | | | |
| Critical success factors | | | |
| Growing/stable/declining | | | |
| Key competitors and their strategies | | | |
| Future competitors | | | |
| Segmentation opportunities | | | |
| Ease of entry | | | |

**3.4** We can expand upon some elements of the above checklist.

(a) **Market size**. This refers to both actual and potential (forecast) size. A company cannot know whether its market share objectives are feasible unless it knows the market's overall size. Forecasting areas of growth and decline is also important.

(b) **Customers**. The analysis needs to identify who the customers are, what they need, and their buying behaviour (where, when and how they purchase products or services). This will help to point out opportunities.

(c) **Distributors**. The company will need to evaluate its current arrangements for getting goods or services to the customer. Changes in distribution channels can open up new fields of opportunity (eg the Internet).

**3.5** Often these factors overlap and PEST factors will affect many areas. For example, at the present time the UK government is considering how best to free the country's postal systems from monopoly. Parliamentary bills will eventually need to be passed. Here the major driving force could be said to be political, triggered by economic necessity, facilitated by law. The markets will cease to be a monopoly. They might fragment into public and private sectors.

## Marketing at Work

*Marketing Week* (15 April 1999) reported that *Argos*, the catalogue retailer, is to enter the PC market, 'taking on established players such as *Dixons* and *PC World* and direct sellers such as *Time*, *Tiny* and *Gateway*'.

Since 1994, sales volumes in the UK PC sector have grown by 67%, and the market is now valued at £4.6bn. One segment of this market is the small office/home office (Soho) segment, worth £2bn and predicted to grow by 51% (in volume) from 1998 to 2003.

Although Argos does not have the after-sales service expertise, first-time buyers go to recognised retailers, and Argos is well known. Prices are falling, and Argos can offer some good deals.

Mintel suggests that the sector will polarise between those who want PCs with bells and whistles and those who require only a very basic model.

# 4 Competitor analysis

**4.1** Many firms identify key competitors and plan their strategies with competitors in mind.

**4.2** **Key questions for competitor analysis**

- Who are they?
- What are their goals?
- What strategies are they pursuing?
- What are their strengths and weaknesses?
- How are they likely to respond?

## Who are our competitors?

## Marketing at Work

***South Western Airlines***

South Western Airlines is one of the most profitable in the US, partly because it defined its competition carefully.

Most airlines in the US have a 'hub' airport and 'spokes' from it. They compete with each other heavily on matters such as air miles, price and so on.

South Western does not use this arrangement and instead it flies 'point to point' over short distances. It has defined its competitor as the motor car – a substitute product – and has designed its marketing mix so as to minimise the time the customer takes travelling. This has meant flying from smaller, less congested airports, speeded-up check-in times and so on.

**4.3** Identifying current competitors is easy. Identifying **potential** competitors is harder as potential competitors might be:

- Smaller companies attacking the market segment
- Companies operating in other markets wishing to expand
- Companies wishing to diversify

4.4 Finally a firm can **define** who its competitors actually are. Coca-Cola, for example, competes against:

- Pepsi in the Cola market
- All other soft drinks
- Tea and coffee
- Tap water: Coca-Cola's chief executive has declared that 'the main competitor is tap water: any other share definition is too narrow'

## What are competitors' goals?

4.5 Next, you need to discern what the competitors' goals and objectives are.

(a) **Relevant goals and objectives**

(i) Goals and objectives of the **parent company**, if the competitor is part of a larger group.

(ii) The competitors' assessment of risk; a higher risk will require a higher return from a market.

(iii) The personal goals of key managers. For example, a new chief executive may be brought in to 'turn the company round'. The new chief executive may have made a **public commitment** to one set of goals and may have invested a lot of prestige in achieving these goals.

(iv) A company facing cash flow problems may do anything to maximise cash inflow.

(v) The competitors' history, position and the underlying assumptions of their management. For example, some firms consider themselves to be 'market leaders'.

(vi) **How dependent** the competitor is on the current business? A competitor with one main business will fight much harder to defend it than a competitor exposed to several sectors.

(b) **Types of goals**

- Profit
- Market share
- Cash flow
- Technological leadership
- Service leadership

We cover goal-setting later. Suffice it to say that competitors' goals can be taken into account. Different competitors put different weights on certain goals, particularly with regard to time horizons. Some might sacrifice profit, in the short term, for market share.

## Current competitor strategies

4.6 Assessing current competitor strategies is relatively simple, as competitors send out signals to the same customer base. A company's closest competitor is one competing in the same target market.

## Strategic group analysis: a constraint on competitive choice

4.7 **Strategic group analysis** tries to show how firms are positioned in a particular market or segment. Porter identifies a number of dimensions in which firms can differ.

- **Specialisation**. (Limited number of segments? Does it have a narrow product range?)
- **Brand**. Does the firm promote a brand or compete on price?
- **Distribution**. What channels are used?
- **Push** or **pull** approach to distribution?
- **Quality**
- Technological **leader** or follower?
- Degree of vertical **integration**
- **Cost structure**
- **Add-on services**
- **Price policy**
- **Indebtedness**
- Degree of **control** by holding company
- **Government involvement**

4.8 Any firm can be defined according to these dimensions. Firms with **low relative prices** are usually **able to control costs**, but **do not have superior product quality**.

**Key Concept**

In any industry, especially with a large number of firms, some will pursue similar strategies in which case they can be considered a **strategic group**.

4.9 For any two of the attributes above it should be possible to map how firms relate to each other. The number of dimensions of course is very large, so a strategic group is best identified by taking the two most significant dimensions in the industry.

4.10 **Mobility barriers** constrain organisational endeavours and function as barriers to entry.

**Key Concept**

**Mobility barriers** make it hard for a firm in one strategic group to develop or migrate to another.

(a) **Market factors**

(i) Some supermarket chains have a low presence in the South-East of England, where there is substantial competition.

(ii) The brand name may be a mobility barrier, if it is unknown in the particular segment.

(iii) The product line may not be extensive enough.

(iv) Other factors include user technologies and selling systems.

(b) **Industry characteristics**. To move into a mass volume end of the market might require economies of scale and large production facilities. To move to the quality end might require greater investment in research and development.

(c) The organisation may lack the **distinctive skills** and competences in the new market area.

(d) **Legal barriers** might exist.

## Competitors' strengths and weaknesses

**4.11** SWOT analysis is covered in a later chapter, but it is relatively easy to assess a competitor's **strengths** and **weaknesses**. Here are some examples.

- Brand strengths, customer loyalty
- Market share
- Quality of management team
- Resources, financial and otherwise
- Intellectual property
- Distribution network
- Relative cost structure
- Distinctive competence

**4.12** *Kotler* (1999) suggests the following table for consideration for **marketing strengths and weaknesses.**

- Customer awareness
- Product quality
- Product availability
- Technical assistance
- Sales staff
- Market share
- Mind share (% of customers who had heard about the company)
- Share of benefit

### *Analysing competitors' costs*

**4.13** Clearly the strategic response of competitors can vary significantly on the cost profile of the competitor. **Relative costs** are more important than absolute costs: Ward believes that it took Western firms too long to understand that Japanese firms had **sustainable cost advantages**, and hence were able to compete on price on a sustained basis.

**4.14** Furthermore, even if the competitor is not competing on price, despite having a lower cost base, the competitor is:

- Under no pressure to raise prices, thus limiting the firm's ability to raise its own
- More profitable, and hence can invest more

## Competitor reaction and response

**4.15** Kotler identifies the following types of competitor response.

| Predictable | Unpredictable |
|---|---|
| (i) **Laid-back**: competitor does not respond | **Stochastic**: impossible to predict **how** competitor will react |
| (ii) **Selective**: competitor only responds to certain types of attack | |
| (iii) **Tiger**: competitor reacts to any attack | |

### Action Programme 2

Why might a competitor be 'laid-back'?

## Action Programme 3

Jot down a list of items of information that might be obtained from an environmental analysis of competitors.

**4.16 Good competitors**

Monopolies are hard to come by, but some competitors are definitely easier to deal with than others. A **good competitor**:

- Deters new entrants (assuming you are not a new entrant)
- Shares similar assumptions about the industry
- Prefers differentiation and focus to competing on price

## Exam Tip

*In December 2000, you had to describe how competitor analysis would be carried out by a cosmetics company and how relevant it could be. Branding is probably an issue here.*

*In December 2002, the focus was on a consumer goods manufacturer and candidates were asked to outline the content and structure that a competitor analysis would adopt, and, more importantly for this level of your studies, how it could be used to enhance strategic decision making.*

# 5 Customer analysis

## Strategic importance

**5.1** This section is all about **understanding** customers.

**5.2** Marketing is about satisfying customers – but **some customers (or segments) are more important than others**. The factors you should consider in assessing the strategic importance of a customer are outlined below. The list has been adapted from an article by Gary Hamel in the *Harvard Business Review* (July/August 1996).

| *Strategic importance evaluation guide* | *High* | *Medium* | *Low* | *N/A* |
|---|---|---|---|---|
| 1 Fit between customer's **needs** and our **capabilities**, at present and potentially. | | | | |
| 2 **Ability to serve** customer compared with our major competitor, at present and potentially. | | | | |
| 3 **Health** of customer's industry, currently and forecast. | | | | |

| *Strategic importance evaluation guide* | *High* | *Medium* | *Low* | *N/A* |
|---|---|---|---|---|
| 4 **Health** of the customer, current and forecast. | | | | |
| 5 Customer's **growth prospects**, current and forecast. | | | | |
| 6 What can we **learn** from this customer? | | | | |
| 7 Can the customer **help us attract** others? | | | | |
| 8 Relative **significance:** how important is the customer compared **with other** customers? | | | | |
| 9 What is the **profitability** of serving the customer? | | | | |

**5.3** To satisfy customers we need to know how they behave and why they take the purchasing decisions they do.

**5.4** A number of models and theories exist to explain the dynamics of the 'not always rational' customer's behaviour. You will probably already be familiar with them, but the key aspects are included here for your review. These aspects of behaviour are also critical in the process of segmentation. But first, an example.

## Marketing at Work

**'Generation X'**

A segment is a group of customers who might behave in a particular way. In February 1997, *Marketing Business* identified Generation X. This indicates how buyer behaviour and segmental analysis can be related.

'New consumers, Generation X, call them what you will, youth in the 1990s are a cynical and disillusioned bunch. They eschew eighties-style consumerism, laugh in the face of brands which try to woo them and yet paradoxically remain loyal to brands they deem cool. Tap into this illusive but hugely influential demographic and you are onto a winner. Get it wrong and you will miss a golden opportunity.

In 1991 a novel was published called Generation X. It was by an American – Douglas Copeland – and therefore prone to exaggerated generational claims (the country's favourite pastime since the 1960s). But it touched a nerve: today's young adults, it suggested, were terminally disillusioned and cynical. Unemployed and underexploited, they were wasting away in Mc-jobs, serving burgers instead of bettering themselves. They were the first generation in America to realise that they would not enjoy a higher standard of living than their parents.

Bleak stuff. Whether or not Generation X was fact or fiction, its supposed attributes are certainly an important aspect of today's young consumer. However, the apocalyptic tone is not so accurate.

While young consumers have metamorphosed considerably in recent years, they remain very much consumers. Their cynicism and knowingness cannot be ignored, but it should not be taken as a sign that they have rejected capitalism lock, stock and barrel. Targeting them means recognising their outlook as more than just a passing fad. Marketers must first acknowledge certain fundamental changes which have affected all consumer behaviour, and which will become increasingly part of the mainstream as this generation ages.

First people became brand literate. Then, in the 1980s they became advertising-literate, very much into badges and conspicuous consumption. Now they have become marketing-literate.

"The single most important element of our whole media targeting is attitude", says Simon Soothill, brand manager of top tequila brand Jose Cuervo. His activity centres on the 25–34 age group, who "don't want to be sold to and expect to see very dynamic advertising. We try to find ways of talking to them that they find relevant and involving." Soothill believes this age group has younger tastes than in previous generations.

Just as age is no longer the all-powerful defining factor of consumer behaviour, so gender is not the great divider it once was. This magazine has already commented in detail on the blurring of gender boundaries among younger consumers, as exemplified by the Calvin Klein campaigns.

Marketers climbing the corporate ladder are also managing to find new ways of talking to today's young – and tomorrow's mainstream – consumer.

While young consumers can be said to have some homogenous characteristics, it is not enough to define them by age alone. The concept of the teenager is now looking quite staid and indeed rather 1950s.'

*'Kidults'*

As opposed to this, there is anecdotal comment that older people are not assuming the cultural attributes of their previous generational roles, for example, in terms of music or clothing or even some lifestyle activities.

---

## What influences customer behaviour?

5.5 Understanding customer behaviour assists effective marketing management. However, there are many influences on customer behaviour and so the outcome in terms of purchasing decisions can be very difficult to understand from a rational viewpoint. **Emotional and rational influences** intertwine and lead to purchase outcomes which can seem illogical even to the buyer.

## Physiological and psychological influences

5.6 Marketers aim to satisfy customer needs. Maslow's hierarchy of needs is a useful checklist of the needs each person is supposed to have.

**Maslow's hierarchy of needs**

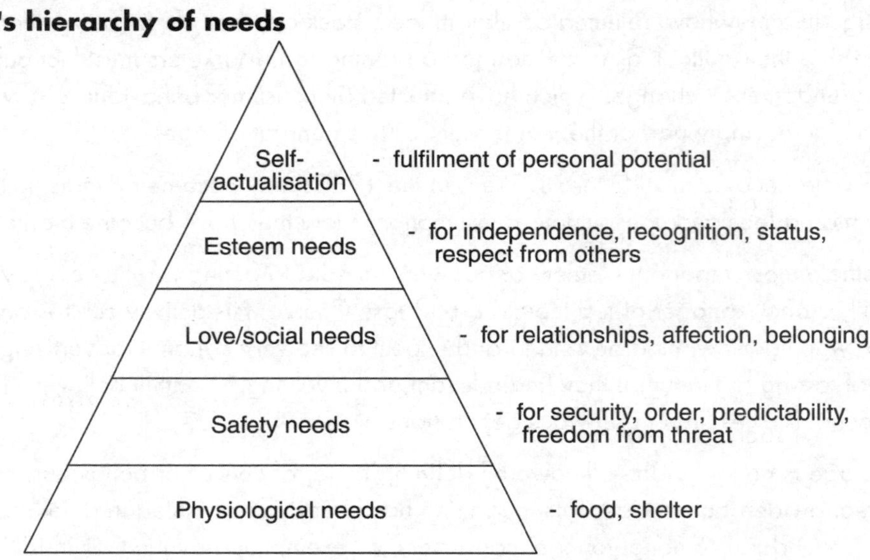


Maslow argued that lower order needs such as physiological needs must be satisfied before higher order ones such as self-actualisation needs (making the most of your potential). These ideas are very appealing, but there are major criticisms in practice.

5.7 **Motives** sit between **needs** and **action**. A need motivates a person to take action. However, motives do not tell us **how consumers choose from the options available** to satisfy needs. Other influences are clearly at work.

## *Attitudes to risk*

5.8 Many purchase decisions involve a degree of risk. People's perceptions of risk differ from objective statistical risks. For example, smoking is a far riskier activity than eating beef on the bone. Examples of risk are **physical risk** (eg BSE in food) and **financial risk** (eg pensions). Some researchers believe that:

(a) **Fear** is a stronger motivator than pleasure.

(b) People's feelings about risk are **irrational**.

(c) Any purchaser of a service runs the **risk of disappointment**.

(d) If marketers understand how consumers perceive risk, then they can design products and services accordingly to reduce risk. For example the 'risk' of wasted time is lessened, in supermarkets, by opening new check-outs if queues longer than a certain length develop.

## *Cultural influences*

5.9 Culture varies widely and has many influences on marketing practice. For example, language differences raise obvious marketing implications when brand names have to be translated, often leading to entirely different (and sometimes embarrassing) meanings in the new language. There are many sub-cultures.

5.10 **How cultural and sub-cultural differences affect purchasing**

- **What** is bought (style, colours, types of goods/service)?
- **When** are things bought (for example, is Sunday shopping approved of)?
- **How** are things bought (bartering, haggling about price)?
- **Where** are things bought (type of retail outlet)?
- **Why** are things bought (influence of culture on needs and hence motives)?

We will discuss cultural influences in more detail in Chapter 9.

### *Social influences*

**5.11** Members of specific groups have **similar** lifestyles, beliefs and values which can and do affect their purchasing behaviour.

(a) **Socio-economic status** indicates a person's disposable income and ability to spend.

(b) People can **aspire to a different socio-economic status**, and some products satisfy these aspirations.

(c) **Psychographics** (lifestyle) and **geodemographic segmentation** (ACORN) provide more sophisticated analysis.

## Marketing at Work

Socio-economic status can be related to buying patterns in a number of ways, both in the amount people have to spend and what they spend it on.

(a) The wealthier professionals spend less of a proportion of their total income on food and housing, and more on leisure, than do unskilled manuals. This does not imply they spend any less in absolute terms of course: they just have more available to spend on other things.

(b) Interestingly, the consumption of alcohol and tobacco is significantly different: in 1990 only 18% of men and women in the professional category smoked, as opposed to 48% of unskilled manual men and 36% of unskilled manual women.

(c) The effect on social class on leisure and services is an example of how discretionary spending varies from class to class. In 1991 over 80% of members of social class AB took at least one holiday, compared with under 60% of class C2. In classes DE, over half took no holiday at all.

### *Personal circumstances and reference groups*

**5.12** Family background is a very strong influence on purchasing behaviour.

(a) It is in family groups that we learn how to be members of society and how to behave in different settings. Having learnt, it is difficult to forget. Family influences remain strong throughout the rest of our lives.

(b) The family is important in purchasing behaviour because it is often a 'purchasing unit' with one member (the buyer) buying on behalf of all members (users) but others in the family influencing the decision (influencers). Joint husband and wife purchasing decisions for major items are common.

**5.13** A person may identify with or aspire to membership of a reference group of other people. This is particularly true of youth culture and the market for fashion goods.

## Marketing at Work

***Audi***

An advertisement for *Audi cars* playing recently profiled members of a reference group (members of an exclusive, backward-looking golf club) that the typical Audi purchaser would not want to belong to, cleverly exploiting the subtle snobberies in the English class system.

# Models of buying behaviour

**5.14** Buyer behaviour models aim is to help the marketing manager to understand the buying process so as to use a marketing strategy which is most applicable to the specific situation. A simple model might attempt to simplify and clarify the purchase decision process by showing it as a series of sequential steps.

| Step | Activity | Marketing |
|---|---|---|
| 1 | Felt need | Market research |
| 2 | Pre-purchase activity (eg information search) | Advertising |
| 3 | Purchase decision | Selling, promotion |
| 4 | Usage behaviour | Customer service |
| 5 | Post-purchase feelings and evaluation | Customer service |

This type of model is useful to the marketing manager in trying to influence the buying process. For example, advertising and promotional activity is aimed at the **information search** stage and customer service is aimed at the post-purchase evaluation stage.

**5.15** Some models try to show the **interrelationship** between the various behavioural and economic factors to give the marketing manager a better understanding of the buying process. The Howard-Sheth model is a good example.

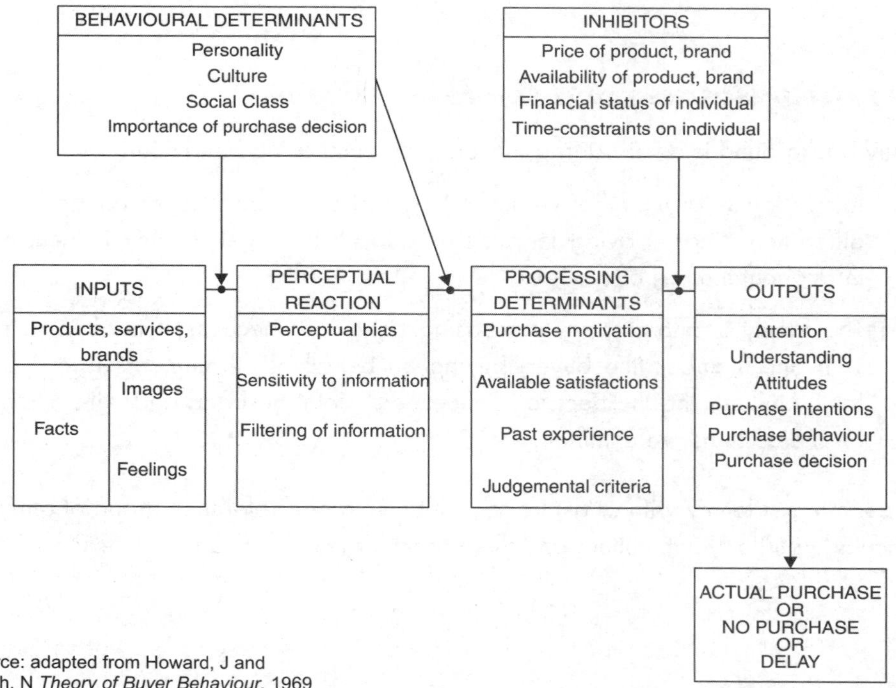


Source: adapted from Howard, J and Sheth, N *Theory of Buyer Behaviour*, 1969

### 5.16 Elements in the Howard-Sheth model

(a) **Inputs**. Information inputs about the alternative services available include both rational and emotional elements.

(b) **Behavioural determinants**. These elements include the existing predispositions of the purchaser which have been influenced by culture, socio-economic group, family and personality factors, amongst others. This element will have a larger role for big or otherwise significant purchase decisions.

(c) **Perceptual reaction**. Information from inputs is not accepted at face value but interpreted. For example, an individual is likely to value information more highly if it has been actively sought than if it has been passively received (from TV advertisements for example).

(d) **Processing determinants**. These are the factors affecting how the information gathered is evaluated.

(e) **Inhibitors**. There are external constraints on actual or potential purchase behaviour.

(f) **Outputs**. The outcome of the complex process of interacting elements may be a purchase decision, a decision not to buy or a decision to delay buying.

### 5.17 Advantages of the Howard-Sheth model

(a) It has been **validated** for practical examples of purchases.

(b) It **indicates the complex nature** of the buying process.

(c) It emphasises the need for marketing managers to **analyse the satisfactions** which customers seek in relation to the purchase of goods or services.

(d) It emphasises the need to gain a **clear understanding of individual purchase motivations**.

(e) It points to the importance of **external constraints** on the process.

(f) It suggests that **customer satisfactions occur on a number of levels** and in a number of forms at the same time. For example, both rational and emotional satisfactions are likely to be sought.

Thus the Howard-Sheth model can help the marketing manager to obtain useful and practical insights into customer behaviour.

## Action Programme 4

Eleanor Plantagenet works for Mast, Rick, Tree and Tee, an advertising agency which is beginning to fall on hard times. For example, Bill Mast (the MD) has had to make do with a cheaper company car. There are ominous rumours about making the agency 'leaner and fitter', 'optimising the agency's human resources' and 'delayering'. Eleanor assumes that all this means possible redundancy for people like her, although the managing director has denied all such rumours.

Mortgage payments account for 25% of Eleanor's post-tax monthly salary. Her husband is a freelance financial journalist. His earnings are erratic, but he has recently been commissioned to write a book for the non-specialist reader about the single European currency. They have two children. They invested an inheritance of £15,000 in the Carlowe Bowes saving scheme but the scheme was run by a fraudster, and they lost all their money. Both Eleanor and her husband are hard-working individuals with severe demands on their time. Eleanor earns significantly more than her husband.

One evening, Eleanor's husband tells her of a new financial services product offered by the International Bank of Canonbury. It offers redundancy insurance. This means that Eleanor will be paid £100 per month of unemployment (up to 12 months) for every £5 invested per month, to a maximum monthly benefit of £1,000. No benefit will be paid if Eleanor becomes unemployed within six months of taking out the policy.

Identify the behavioural determinants, inhibitors, inputs, possible perceptual reactions processing determinants and outputs (as in the Howard-Sheth model) in the above situation.

---

**Exam Tip**

*In this exam, questions on buyer behaviour are likely to concern their implications for marketing planning. The implications of culture, social change and so forth are clearly relevant to segmentation, targeting and positioning. They are also relevant to each element of the mix: how can customers be persuaded to part with their money?*

---

## The organisational buyer behaviour process

**5.18** Organisations are buyers too. Organisational buyer behaviour is more complex than individual buyer behaviour.

(a) There are **many people** influencing the purchase decision.

(b) In theory, organisational purchase decisions are supposed to be driven by **rational** criteria, relating to the **objectives of the business**.

**Webster and Wind's model of organisational buyer behaviour**

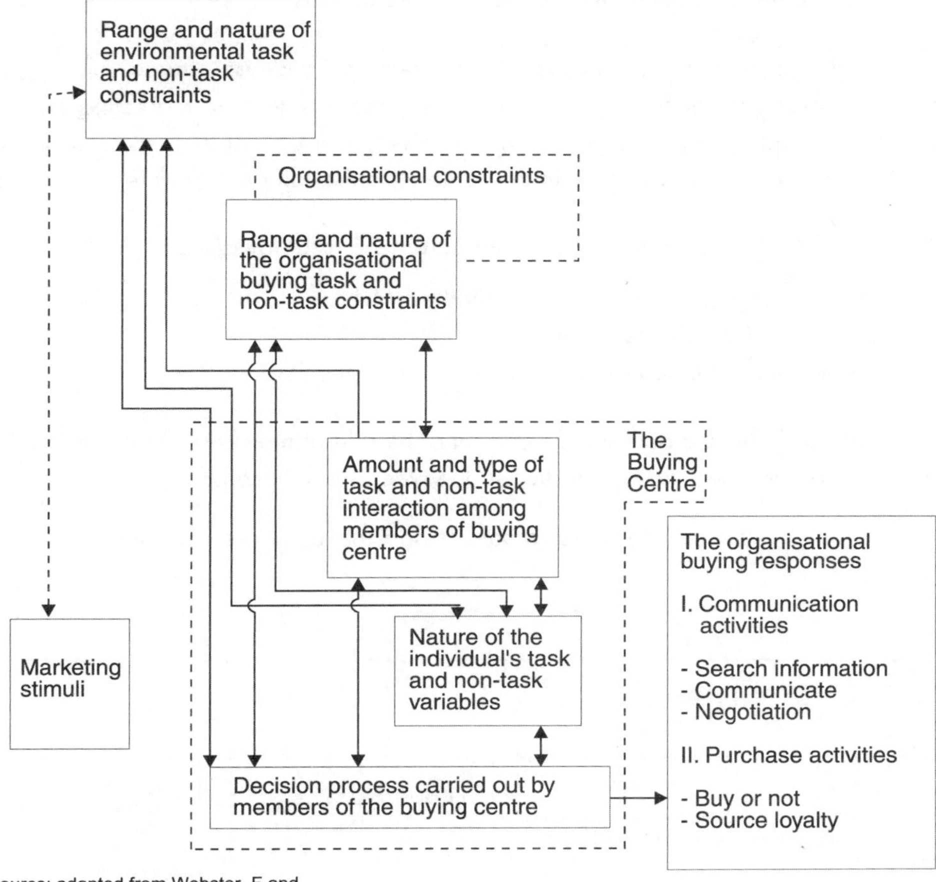


Source: adapted from Webster, F and Wind, Y *Organisational Buyer Behaviour*

5.19 Webster and Wind together see the organisational **buyer (the decision making unit (DMU))** as influenced by a number of sets of variables.

(a) The **individual characteristics** of the members of the DMU, such as personality and preference, are similar to personal buying processes.

(b) The **relationships** between members of the buying centre are also important.

(i) The **user** may have influence on the technical characteristics of the equipment (and hence the cost) and on reliability and performance criteria.

(ii) The **influencer** is particularly useful where the purchase relies on **technical knowledge**.

(iii) The **buyer** or **decider**. These individuals have personal idiosyncrasies, social pressures and organisational and environmental pressures. Thus each has a set of rational factors (task variables) and non-economic factors (non-task variables).

(iv) The **gatekeeper** who controls the flow of information about the purchaser may be senior or junior but is important because he/she influences the communication flow within the organisation.

(c) **Organisational characteristics** include the buying and organisational task, the size and structure of the organisation, the use of technology and so on. The relationships of the buyer within the organisation are particularly important. This post can be senior or junior and can involve power struggles with user departments.

(d) **Environmental factors** such as the physical, technological, economic and legal factors which affect general competitive conditions.

**5.20** These four sets of variables interact in the decision process carried out by members of the **decision making unit** (DMU) of the buying organisation. In marketing terms the DMU is a vital target for the supplier's marketing initiatives. The size and structure of the DMU will vary between organisations, over time in the same organisation and for different types of purchase.

**5.21** People marketing to corporate clients therefore need to be aware of:

- How buying decisions are made by the DMU
- How the DMU is constructed
- The identities of the most influential figures in the DMU

**5.22** The diagram shows the decision process and the role of members of the DMU at each stage. Of course the process will vary according to the type of purchase being made.

*A decision process model of industrial purchase behaviour*

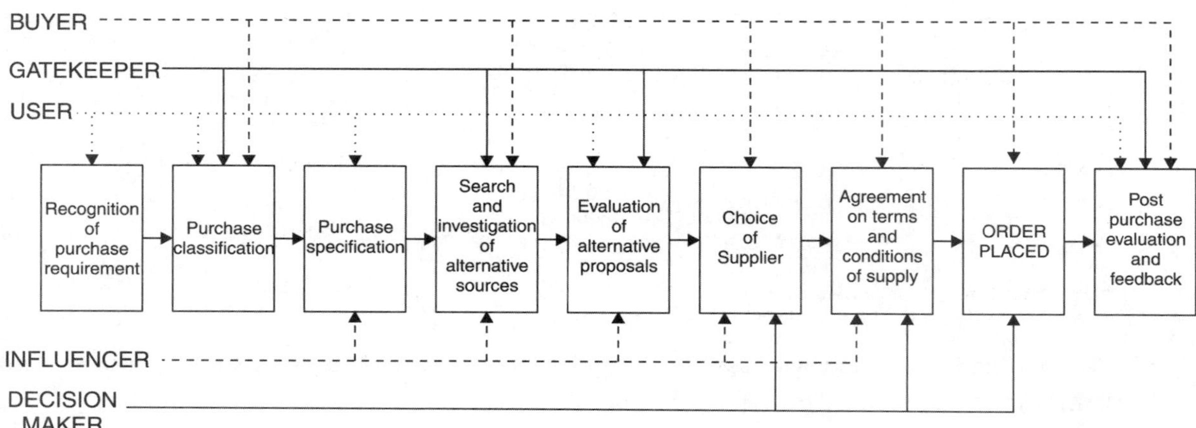


**5.23** The organisational buying process is complex and needs careful marketing action if the outcome is to be influenced favourably. Becoming 'close to customers' is an important step towards satisfying and even delighting them.

**Exam Tip**

*Organisational buying appeared frequently in the old syllabus Analysis & Decision paper which has featured business-to-business marketing on a number of occasions. Clearly any marketing strategy must take the characteristics and concerns of DMU members into account.*

# 6 SWOT analysis

**6.1** The purpose of **corporate appraisal**, or SWOT analysis, is to **combine** the assessment of the environment and the analysis of the organisation's internal resources and capabilities.

## Key Concept

**Corporate appraisal**: 'a critical assessment of the strengths and weaknesses, opportunities and threats in relation to the internal and environmental factors affecting the entity in order to establish its condition prior to the preparation of a long-term plan.'

6.2 A **strengths and weaknesses** analysis expresses which areas of the business have:

- Strengths that should be exploited
- Weaknesses which should be improved

It therefore covers the results of the position audit.

6.3 **Opportunities**

- What opportunities exist in the business environment?
- Their inherent profit-making potential
- The organisation's ability to exploit the worthwhile opportunities

6.4 **Threats**

- What threats might arise?
- How will competitors be affected?
- How will the company be affected?

The opportunities and threats might arise from PEST and competitive factors.

## Bringing the SWOT elements together

6.5 The internal and external appraisals will be brought together, and perhaps shown in a cruciform chart.

6.6 **EXAMPLE**

| Strengths | Weaknesses |
|---|---|
| £10 million of capital available | Heavy reliance on a small number of customers |
| Production expertise and appropriate marketing skills | Limited product range, with no new products and expected market decline. Small marketing organisation. |
| **Threats** | **Opportunities** |
| A major competitor has already entered the new market | Government tax incentives for new investment |
| | Growing demand in a new market, although customers so far relatively small in number |

The company is in imminent danger of losing its existing markets and must diversify its products and/or markets. The new market opportunity exists to be exploited, and since the number of customers is currently small, the relatively small size of the existing marketing force would not be an immediate hindrance. A strategic plan could be developed to buy new equipment and use existing production and marketing to enter the new market, with a view to rapid expansion. Careful planning of manpower, equipment, facilities, research and development would be required and there would be an objective to meet the threat of competition so as to obtain a substantial share of a growing market. The cost of entry at this early stage of market development should not be unacceptably high.

**6.7** The SWOT technique can also be used for specific areas of strategy such as IT and marketing.

**6.8** Effective SWOT analysis does not simply require a categorisation of information, it also requires some **evaluation of the relative importance** of the various factors under consideration.

(a) These features are only of relevance if they are **perceived to exist by the customers**. Listing corporate features that internal personnel regard as strengths/weaknesses is of little relevance if customers do not perceive them as such.

(b) In the same vein, threats and opportunities are conditions presented by the external environment and they should be independent of the firm.

**6.9** The SWOT can now be used to guide strategy formulation. The two major options are **matching** and **conversion**.

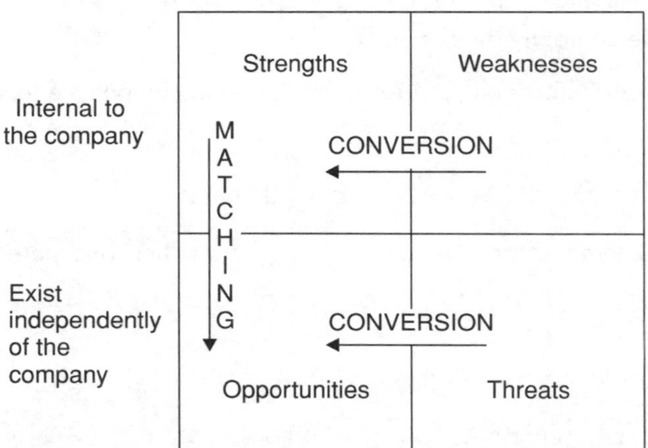


(a) **Matching**

This entails finding, where possible, a match between the strengths of the organisation and the opportunities presented by the market. Strengths which do not match any available opportunity are of limited use while opportunities which do not have any matching strengths are of little immediate value.

(b) **Conversion**

This requires the development of strategies which will convert weaknesses into strengths in order to take advantage of some particular opportunity, or converting threats into opportunities which can then be matched by existing strengths.

## Action Programme 5

Hall Faull Downes Ltd has been in business for 25 years, during which time profits have risen by an average of 3% per annum, although there have been peaks and troughs in profitability due to the ups and downs of trade in the customers' industry. The increase in profits until five years ago was the result of increasing sales in a buoyant market, but more recently, the total market has become somewhat smaller and Hall Faull Downes has only increased sales and profits as a result of improving its market share.

The company produces components for manufacturers in the engineering industry.

In recent years, the company has developed many new products and currently has 40 items in its range compared to 24 only five years ago. Over the same five-year period, the number of customers has fallen from 20 to nine, two of whom together account for 60% of the company's sales.

Give your appraisal of the company's future, and suggest what it is probably doing wrong.

**6.10** In practice it helps if you rank the items of the SWOT in order of **importance** and **urgency**. Marketers have to concentrate their limited resources on the essentials.

## Chapter Roundup

- Most companies are **competing** with other companies for customers. They have to identify or create a position in the customer's mind.
- Within the industry there are **five competitive forces**, determining the profitability of the industry as a whole.
  - New entrants
  - Substitute products or services
  - Customer bargaining power
  - Supplier bargaining power
  - Intensity of competition
- Firms also need to analyse the market (or the customer and customer needs that they must satisfy). A **market analysis** covers statistical and qualitative data relating to customers, influences on customers, trends and buying power.
- An **analysis of individual competitors** will cover who they are, their objectives, their strategies, their strengths and weaknesses and how they are likely to respond.
- **Competitor responses** can be classified as laidback, selective, 'tiger' or stochastic (ie unpredictable).
- Models of **buyer behaviour** consider the influences (rational and emotional) on the buying decisions and the process of decision making (eg individual or group as in a DMU).
- **SWOT analysis** is a useful technique for organising information about an organisation's strengths and weaknesses (**internal** appraisal) and the opportunities and threats (**external** appraisal) which it encounters.
- SWOT can be enhanced by **ranking** items in order of significance, and it is always important not to confuse the level at which the analysis is conducted (eg corporate SWOT and marketing SWOT).
- The SWOT can be used to identify possible **strategies**.

## Quick Quiz

1. List the competitive forces.
2. What are substitute products?
3. How can IT raise barriers to entry?
4. When analysing a market, what basic data about the market are needed?
5. Give three examples of potential competitors.
6. Identify types of competitor response.
7. Why is the family unit an important influence on behaviour?
8. Why are buyer behaviour models useful?
9. How should marketers take the DMU into account?
10. What is SWOT analysis and when would you use it?

## Answers to Quick Quiz

1. Threat of new entrants; threat of substitute products; bargaining power of customers; bargaining power of competitors; rivalry among current competitors.
2. A product produced by a different industry that satisfies the same customer needs.
3. By increasing economies of scale; by tying the supply and distribution chains to the company; by raising the capital cost of entry.
4. Actual and potential size; and areas of growth and decline.
5. Smaller companies operating on the fringe of the market; companies operating in other markets that might wish to expand; and companies that might wish to diversify.
6. Laid back; selective; tiger; stochastic.
7. Much behaviour is learned in childhood; the family is an important purchasing unit.
8. They help in the design of marketing strategies.
9. The DMU is the target of marketing strategies: marketers should know how it is structured and how it takes its decisions.
10. SWOT analysis brings together the findings of the internal and external analyses in order to provide guidance in the formulation of corporate strategy.

## Action Programme Review

1. (a) Here are some ideas. Barriers to entry are high. There are plenty of substitute products (coffee), competitive rivalry is high because of the difficulty of stockpiling products. Customer bargaining power is high, but supplier power is low: all it needs is capital, the right sort of land and labour.

   (b) Williamson and Magor has begun to switch from tea at auction to consumer marketing. The firm is aiming to build up its own brand image in the UK and Germany, by offering – by mail order – unblended, specialist teas from its Indian estates. It advertised via Barclays Premier Card magazine; replies were used to set up a customer database. When the company's Earl Grey tea was recommended on BBC2's *Food and Drink*, these existing customers were targeted with a letter and a sample.

2. A 'laid back' competitor may be:
   - Unable to respond: lack of capability
   - Unwilling to respond owing to differing assumptions about the segment
   - Unconcerned about the threat, which is does not take seriously

3. (a) Who are the existing competitors? How much of the market do they hold in each segment of the markets (eg in each particular region or country)?

   (b) Who are potential competitors? How soon might they enter the market?

   (c) How profitable are existing competitors? What is their EPS, dividend yield, ROCE etc?

   (d) What do the goals of each competitor appear to be, and what strategies have they adopted so far?

   (e) What products/services do they sell? How do they compare with the organisation's own products or services?

(f) How broad is their product line? (eg Are they up-market high quality, or down-market low quality, low price and high volume producers?)

(g) What is their distribution network?

(h) What are their skills and weakness in direct selling, advertising, sales promotions, product design etc?

(i) What are their design skills or R & D skills? Do they innovate or follow the market leader with new product ideas?

(j) What are their costs of sale and operational capabilities, with respect to:

- Economies of scale
- Use of advanced technology equipment
- Patents, trademarks, know-how
- Quality control
- Location
- Transportation costs
- Labour skills and productivity
- Supply advantages (ie special access to raw materials at a low cost)
- Industrial relations and industrial disputes
- Reliability in servicing customers

(k) What are their general managerial capabilities? How do these compare with those of the organisation?

(l) Financial strengths and weaknesses. What is the debt position and financial gearing of each competitor? Do they have easy access to sources of new finance? What proportion of profits do they return in the business in order to finance growth?

(m) How is each competitor organised? How much decentralisation of authority do they allow to operating divisions, and so how flexible or independent can each of the operating divisions be?

(n) Does the competitor have a good spread or portfolio of activities? What is the risk profile of each competitor?

(o) Does any competitor have a special competitive advantage – eg a unique government contract or special access to government authorities?

(p) Does any competitor show signs of changing strategy to increase competition to the market?

4 **Behavioural determinants**. Eleanor and her husband work in service industries. They are used to the concept of investing (even if unsuccessfully), and have financial interests to protect. The family is perhaps slightly unusual in that the female is the breadwinner, and her husband's income is unlikely to be large.

**Inputs**. Only one product is detailed. As a financial journalist, Eleanor's husband might know of more. He is likely to be interested in the small print, rather than images and feelings.

**Inhibitors**. If Eleanor feels she is likely to be made redundant within the next six months, she is unlikely to take out the policy as it would not be of much use to her.

**Perceptual reaction**. Having lost £15,000 in a previous investment, Eleanor and her husband are possibly very risk averse. They will be sensitive to information regarding the status and reputation of the service provider.

**Processing determinants**. There is a perceived risk that Eleanor will be made redundant, and she is looking for a product which will reduce the financial impact.

**Outputs**. They will want a benefit which will cover at least the mortgage and regular bills.

5 A general interpretation of the facts as given might be sketched as follows.

(a) Objectives: the company has no declared objectives. Profits have risen by 3% per annum in the past, which has failed to keep pace with inflation but may have been a satisfactory rate of increase in the current conditions of the industry. Even so, stronger growth is indicated in the future.

(b)

| Strengths | Weaknesses |
|---|---|
| Many new products developed.<br><br>Marketing success in increasing market share. | Products may be reaching the end of their life and entering decline.<br><br>New product life cycles may be shorter.<br><br>Reduction in customers.<br><br>Excessive reliance on a few customers.<br><br>Doubtful whether profit record is satisfactory. |
| **Threats** | **Opportunities** |
| Possible decline in the end-product.<br><br>Smaller end-product market will restrict future sales prospects for Hall Faull Downes. | None identified. |

(c) Strengths: the growth in company sales in the last five years has been as a result of increasing the market share in a declining market. This success may be the result of the following.

- Research and development spending
- Good product development programmes
- Extending the product range to suit changing customer needs
- Marketing skills
- Long-term supply contracts with customers
- Cheap pricing policy
- Product quality and reliable service

(d) Weaknesses:

(i) The products may be custom-made for customers so that they provide little or no opportunity for market development.

(ii) Products might have a shorter life cycle than in the past, in view of the declining total market demand.

(iii) Excessive reliance on two major customers leaves the company exposed to the dangers of losing their custom.

(e) Threats: there may be a decline in the end-market for the customers' product so that the customer demands for the company's own products will also fall.

(f) Opportunities: no opportunities have been identified, but in view of the situation as described, new strategies for the longer-term would appear to be essential.

(g) Conclusions: the company does not appear to be planning beyond the short-term, or is reacting to the business environment in a piecemeal fashion. A strategic planning programme should be introduced.

(h) Recommendations: the company must look for new opportunities in the longer-term.

(i) In the short term, current strengths must be exploited to continue to increase market share in existing markets and product development programmes should also continue.

(ii) In the longer term, the company must diversify into new markets or into new products and new markets. Diversification opportunities should be sought with a view to exploiting any competitive advantage or synergy that might be achievable.

(iii) The company should use its strengths (whether in R & D, production skills or marketing expertise) in exploiting any identifiable opportunities.

(iv) Objectives need to be quantified in order to assess the extent to which new long-term strategies are required.

## Now try Question 7 at the end of the Study Text

# Part E

# The global marketplace

# The Environment of International Trade

8

| Chapter Topic List | |
|---|---|
| 1 | Setting the scene |
| 2 | Understanding international markets |
| 3 | The political and legal framework |
| 4 | Protectionism in international trade |
| 5 | Economic structure and development |
| 6 | Regional trading groups |
| 7 | The single European market |
| 8 | Demographic issues |
| 9 | Technology |
| 10 | E-commerce and the Internet |

## Syllabus Content

- Assessment of the position of an organisation working in an international or global marketplace
- The effectiveness and value of ICT in cross-border marketing
- Techniques and factors to be used in assessing the attractiveness of international markets

## Key Concepts Introduced

- Political risk
- Protectionism
- Classifications of economic development
- Demography
- Internet
- Electronic commerce

# 1 Setting the scene

**1.1** This chapter deals with the **complexities faced in competing internationally**. These topics are relevant to all commercial organisations, including those that might feel they are not active internationally. This is because all companies are likely to have suppliers, customers or competitors who are themselves involved in international business operations.

**1.2** In Section 2, we offer an overview of some of the issues a firm faces when competing overseas. A huge variety of **PEST factors** have to be dealt with. In Sections 3 – 9 we go over these, with a focus on some examples. Some of these will be familiar to you from other CIM syllabuses you have studied or are currently studying, but we give a slant of particular relevance to international marketing. For example, the **importance of new technology** is without doubt – but technology is influential in different ways, depending on the economic development of each market. **Cultural issues** also feature very significantly in the difficulties facing firms seeking to do international business.

**1.3** Section 10 deals with a growing feature of globalisation: the commercial use of the Internet.

# 2 Understanding international markets

**2.1** **PEST** factors are all key issues in a firm's **domestic** environment. The same factors apply when we are discussing a firm's international exposure – they just become more complex.

**2.2** An organisation is subject to the following international influences.

(a) In times of increasing free trade, firms can expect **incoming competition**. That said, the possibility of competing abroad is also available.

(b) A firm can **attract investment** from overseas institutions. Competing firms from overseas can receive investments from domestic institutions. For example, non-UK banks paid large sums to acquire UK stock brokers and investment firms.

(c) The **barrier** between the domestic and international environment is relatively **permeable**.

(d) **Political factors** and **legal factors** include the following.

   (i) **Political conditions** in individual foreign markets (eg package tour firms and Egypt after terrorist shootings of tourists) or sources of supply (eg risk of nationalisation)

   (ii) **Relationships between governments** (eg UK exporters and investors were worried that Anglo-Chinese disputes over Hong Kong would damage their trade with China)

   (iii) Activities of **supra-national** institutions (eg EU regulations on packaging/ recycling)

   (iv) **Laws and regulations** (eg California's new tough emission standards for cars)

(e) **Economic factors**

   - The overall level of **economic activity**
   - The relative levels of **inflation** in the domestic and overseas market
   - The **exchange rate**
   - The **relative prosperity** of individual overseas markets
   - **Economic growth** in newly industrialised countries
   - A shift towards **market economies**

(f) **Social and cultural factors**

- The **cultures and practices** of customers and consumers in individual markets
- The **media and distribution** systems in overseas markets
- The differences of **ways of doing business**
- The degree to which **national** cultural differences matter
- The degree to which a firm can use its own **national culture as a selling point**

(g) **Technological** factors

- The degree to which a firm can **imitate** the technology of its competitors
- A firm's access to domestic and overseas **patents**
- **Intellectual property** protection
- **Technology transfer** requirements
- The relative **cost** of technology compared to labour
- The **competence of potential service contractors** in the target country

**Exam Tip**

*In almost any question in this syllabus, SLEPT factors can be brought in, but be very careful to make them relevant to the context of the question. General analyses are not welcomed by the examiner.*

# 3 The political and legal framework

**3.1** At some time, most companies engaged in international marketing suffer because of the political or legal structure of a country.

## Political risk

**Key Concept**

**Political risk** is the possibility of turbulence (eg civil war, revolution, changes in government policy) in the political environment.

**3.2** The **level of risk** involved will depend on several factors.

- The attitudes of the country's **government**
- The **product** being traded
- The **company** wishing to trade

### *Political government of the country*

**3.3** The development of plans for international marketing will depend on the following factors.

(a) **The stability of the government**. Rapid changes or political unrest make it difficult to estimate reactions to an importer or a foreign business.

(b) **International relations**. The government's attitude to the firm's home government or country may affect trading relations.

(c) The **ideology** of the government and its **role in the economy** will affect the way in which the company may be allowed to trade, and this might be embodied in legislation.

(d) **Informal relations** between government officials and businesses are important in some countries. Cultivation of the right political contacts may be essential for decisions to be made in your favour.

### *The product*

**3.4** The nature of the goods or services being offered may affect the **degree of interest which a government takes** in a particular trading deal. Generally the more important the goods to the economy or the government, the more interest will be taken.

### *The company wishing to trade*

**3.5** The previous relations of the company (and its home country) with the host country can affect the risk to the company. **Factors influencing the company's acceptability** include the following.

- Relations between the company's home government and the overseas government
- Size of company
- The past relations and reputation of the company in dealing with foreign governments
- The degree of local employment and autonomy of operations generated by the activity

### *Expropriation and other dangers*

**3.6** Political risk is still relevant with regard to overseas investment, especially in large infrastructure projects overseas. History contains dismal tales of investment projects that went wrong, and were **expropriated** (nationalised) by the local government.

(a) **Suspicion** of foreign ownership is still rife, especially when prices are raised.

(b) Opposition politicians can appeal to **nationalism** by claiming the government sold out to foreigners.

(c) Governments might want to **renegotiate** a deal to get a better bargain, at a later date, thereby affecting return on investment.

**3.7** In addition to expropriation, there are other dangers.

- Restrictions on **profit repatriation** (eg for currency reasons)
- **Cronyism** and **corruption** leading to unfair favouring of some companies over others
- Arbitrary changes in **taxation**
- **Pressure group** activity

**3.8** There are many sources of data. The *Economist Intelligence Unit* offers assessment of risk. Management consultants can also be contacted. Companies should ask the following six questions (according to Jeannet and Hennessey, *Global Marketing Strategies*, 2002).

| | |
|---|---|
| 1 | How stable is the host country's political system? |
| 2 | How strong is the host government's commitment to specific rules of the game, such as ownership or contractual rights, given its ideology and power position? |
| 3 | How long is the government likely to remain in power? |
| 4 | If the present government is succeeded, how would the specific rules of the game change? |
| 5 | What would be the effects of any expected changes in the specific rules of the game? |
| 6 | In light of those effects, what decisions and actions should be taken now? |

## *Coping with political risk*

**3.9** The approach taken depends on the **degree of risk** and the **level of involvement**.

| *Level of risk* | | *Low* (level of involvement) | *High* (level of involvement) |
|---|---|---|---|
| | *High* | ■ Keep low profile<br>■ Communicate via third parties<br>■ High level contacts<br>■ Short term deals<br>■ Export credit insurance | ■ Contingency plans<br>■ Disinvest?<br>■ Act for stability? |
| | *Low* | No need to worry | No need to worry – but monitor for increasing riskiness |

*Level of involvement*

**3.10** Measures to **reduce political risk** are as follows.

- Use **local partners** with good contacts
- **Vertical integration** of activities over a number of different countries
- **Local borrowing** (although not a good idea in high inflation countries)
- **Leasing** rather than outright purchase of facilities in overseas markets
- Take out **insurance**

## Legal factors

**3.11** In international markets we are interested in legislation which may affect a firm's trade with a particular country.

- Domestic **legal system**
- Structure of **company law**
- Local **laws**

**3.12** Legal implications extend far beyond the marketing mix. Each country may legislate on issue, and these may affect the marketer to a greater or lesser degree. here are some examples.

(a) **Export and import controls** for political, environmental, or health and safety reasons. Such controls may not be overt but instead take the form of bureaucratic procedures designed to discourage international trade or protect home producers.

(b) **Law of ownership**. Especially in developing countries, there may be legislation requiring local majority ownership of a firm or its subsidiary in that country, for example.

(c) **Acceptance of international trademark, copyright and patent conventions**. Not all countries recognise such international conventions.

# 4 Protectionism in international trade

**Key Concept**

**Protectionism** is the discouraging of imports by raising tariff barriers, imposing quotas etc in order to favour local producers.

4.1 Some governments seek to prevent the influence of international trade by making it harder to import from overseas.

- **Tariffs**
- Non tariff **barriers**
- Import **quotas and embargoes**
- **Subsidies** for domestic producers
- Exchange **controls**
- Exchange rate **policy**

## Tariffs

4.2 A **tariff** is a **tax on imports**. The government **raises revenue** and domestic producers may expand sales, but **consumers** pay higher prices if they buy imported goods. They may have to buy domestic goods of a lesser quality.

## Non-tariff barriers

4.3 Paragraph 4.11 outlines some barriers.

### *Import quotas*

4.4 **Import quotas** are **restrictions** on the quantity of product allowed to be imported into a country. The restrictions can be imposed by **import licences** (in which case the government gets additional revenue) or simply by granting the right to import only to certain producers.

### *Minimum local content rules*

4.5 Related to quotas is a requirement that, to avoid tariffs or other restrictions, products should be made **in** the country or region in which they are sold. In the EU the product must be of a specified **minimum local content** (80% in the EU) to qualify as being 'home' or 'EU-made'. This is one of the reasons Japanese and Korean manufacturers have set up factories in Europe.

### Minimum prices and anti-dumping action

4.6 **Dumping** is the sale of a product in an overseas market at a price lower than charged in the domestic market. **Anti-dumping measures** include establishing quotas, minimum prices or extra excise duties.

### Embargoes

4.7 An embargo on imports from one particular country is a **total ban**, a zero quota. An embargo may have a political motive, and may deprive consumers at home of the supply of an important product.

### Subsidies for domestic producers

4.8 An enormous range of government **subsidies** and assistance for exporters is offered, such as **export credit guarantees** (insurance against bad debts for overseas sales), financial help and assistance from government departments in promoting and selling products. The effect of these grants is to make unit production costs lower. These may give the domestic producer a **cost advantage** over foreign producers in export as well as domestic markets.

### Exchange controls and exchange rate policy

4.9 Many countries have **exchange control regulations** designed to make it difficult for importers to obtain the currency they need to buy foreign goods.

4.10 If a government allows its currency to depreciate, imports will become more expensive. Importers may cut their profit margins and keep prices at their original levels for a while, but sooner or later prices of imports will rise. A policy of exchange rate depreciation in this context is referred to as a **competitive devaluation**.

## Unofficial non-tariff barriers

4.11 Some countries are accused of having **unofficial barriers to trade**, perpetrated by government. Here are some examples.

(a) **Quality and inspection procedures** for imported products, adding to time and cost for the companies selling them.

(b) **Packaging and labelling** requirements may be rigorous, **safety and performance** standards difficult to satisfy and **documentation procedures** very laborious.

(c) Standards which are much easier for domestic manufacturers to adhere to.

(d) Restrictions over **physical distribution**.

(e) Toleration of **anti-competitive practices** at home.

### Action Programme 1

Why might a US car manufacturer support protectionist policies, despite the effects of restraining trade, and a Swedish manufacturer choose to oppose protectionist measures?

# 5 Economic structure and development

**5.1** Economic factors affect the demand for, and the ability to acquire, goods and services. Even in **lesser developed countries** (see below) there often exists a wealthy elite who provide a significant demand for sophisticated consumer goods.

**5.2** Countries generally have larger agricultural sectors in the early stages of economic development (for example India and Africa). As the economy develops, the manufacturing sector increases.

## Level of economic development

**5.3** GDP on a **per capita** basis, suitably adjusted for purchasing power, is probably the **best single indicator of economic development**.

**5.4** A danger in using GDP is that it considers only the **average**. The **distribution of wealth** is critical in poor countries, where a market may exist amongst above average sections of the population.

### *Classification of economic development*

**5.5** Generally each country can be classified under one of five headings.

**Key Concepts**

**Lesser developed country (LDC)**. Relies heavily on primary industries (mining, agriculture, forestry, fishing) with low GDP per capita, and poorly developed infrastructure.

**Early developed country (EDC)**. Largely primary industry based, but with developing secondary (manufacturing) industrial sector. Low but growing GDP, developing infrastructure.

**Semi-developed country (SDC)**. Significant secondary sector still growing. Rising affluence and education with the emergence of a 'middle class'. Developed infrastructure.

**Fully developed country (FDC)**. Primary sector accounts for little of the economy. Secondary sector still dominates, but major growth in tertiary (service) sector. Sophisticated infrastructure.

**Former Eastern Bloc country (EBC)**. May be any of the above, but the 'command economy' under communism has left a legacy that defies straightforward classification. For example, Russia, has most of the features of an SDC but lacks a developed infrastructure though it has a well educated middle class.

### *Measuring levels of economic development*

**5.6** Measures that may be used by the international marketer include the following.

- **GDP** per head
- **Source of GDP** (primary, secondary or tertiary sector based economy)
- **Living standards** (ownership of key durables may be used as a surrogate measure)

- **Energy** availability and usage
- **Education** levels

## Identifying market size

**5.7** The economic worth of a consumer market is based on some general factors.

- The **number of people** in the market
- Their **desire to own** the goods
- Their **ability to purchase** the goods

**5.8** Thus in measuring a market, the marketer will obtain information on the following, although they are often crude measures.

(a) **Population**. Its size, growth and age structure, household composition, urban vs. rural distribution. Household size and spatial distribution affect demand for many consumer goods.

(b) **Income**. GDP per head is a crude measure of wealth and account should also be taken of distribution of GDP among various social groups, and their purchasing power.

(c) **Consumption patterns**. The ownership of various goods and the consumption of consumables are indicators of potential demand.

(d) **Debt and inflation**. A high level of debt in a country may indicate import controls (or their possible introduction) or weak currency and currency controls. Inflation may affect purchasing power. In either case ability to pay will be reduced.

(e) **Physical environment**. Physical distance, climate and topography will affect demand in various ways. The availability of natural resources can directly affect demand for equipment and so on to exploit these resources.

(f) **Foreign trade**. The trade relations of a country will affect the attitude towards foreign goods. Factors include economic relations (for example, a member of same economic group such as the EU) and balance of trade.

# 6 Regional trading groups

## Types of trading group

**6.1** Currently, a number of **regional trading arrangements** exist, as well as global trading arrangements. These regional trading groups take three forms.

- Free trade areas
- Customs unions
- Common markets

### *Free trade areas*

**6.2** Members in these arrangements agree to lower barriers to trade amongst themselves. They enable free movement of **goods** and **services**, but not always the factors of production.

## Customs unions

**6.3** **Customs unions** provide the advantages of free trade areas and agree a common policy on tariff and non-tariff barriers to **external countries**. Internally they attempt to harmonise tariffs, taxes and duties amongst members.

## Economic unions/common markets

**6.4** In effect the members become one for economic purposes. There is free movement of the factors of production. The EU has economic union as an aim, although not all members, including the UK, necessarily see this goal as desirable. The EU has a 'rich' market of over 300 million people and could provide a counterweight to countries such as the USA and Japan.

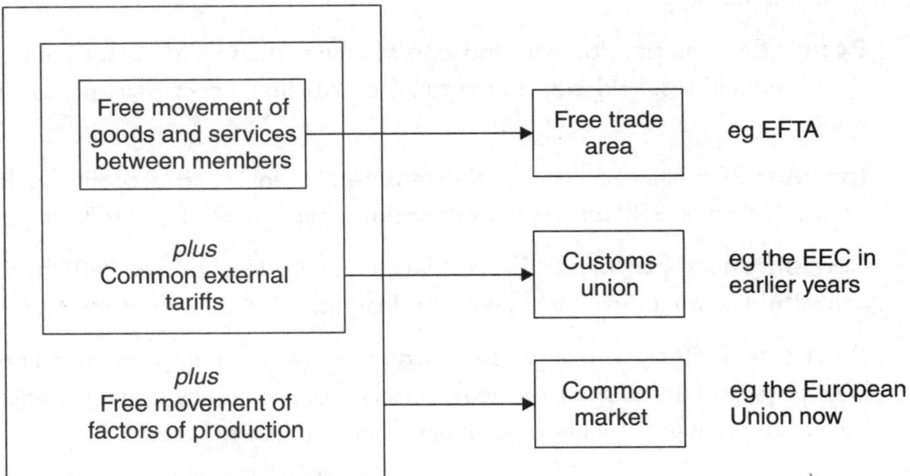


**6.5** The major regional trade organisations are as follows.

(a) North American Free Trade Agreement (**NAFTA**) – US, Canada and Mexico.

(b) European Free Trade Association (**EFTA**) – Norway, Switzerland, Iceland, Liechtenstein.

(c) European Union (**EU**) – Ireland, Britain, France, Germany, Italy, Spain, Portugal, Finland, Sweden, Denmark, Luxembourg, Belgium, the Netherlands, Austria, Greece. A number of other countries have applied to join.

(d) Asean Free Trade Area (**AFTA**) – Brunei, Indonesia, Malaysia, the Philippines, Singapore, Thailand.

(e) Asia-Pacific Economic Co-operation (**APEC**) – Australia, Brunei, Malaysia, Singapore, Thailand, New Zealand, Papua New Guinea, Indonesia, the Philippines, Taiwan, Hong Kong, Japan, South Korea, China, Canada, US, Mexico, Chile.

(f) **Mercosur** – Brazil, Argentina, Paraguay and Uruguay (Chile is an associate).

(g) Southern African Development Community (**SADC**); Angola, Botswana, Lesotho, Malawi, Mozambique, Mauritius, Namibia, South Africa, Swaziland, Tanzania, Swaziland, Zimbabwe.

(h) West African Economic and Monetary Union (**UEMOA**) – Ivory Cost, Burkina Faso, Niger, Togo, Senegal, Benin and Mali.

(i) South Asian Association for Regional Co-operation (**SAARC**) – India, Pakistan, Sri Lanka, Bangladesh, the Maldives, Bhutan and Nepal.

(j) Andean Pact – Venezuela, Colombia, Ecuador, Peru and Bolivia.

(k) Association of Southeast Asian Nations (**ASEAN**) – Indonesia, Malaysia, Philippines, Singapore and Thailand.

## Regional trading agreements and the global market

6.6 Regional trading blocks only extend the benefits of free trade to their members. They may distort **global** trading patterns.

6.7 There is a widely held idea that the industrial world is falling into **three trading blocks**, each led by a lead country. (this is called the 'Triad ' theory.)

- The EU (led by Germany)
- The Americas (led by the USA) and particularly NAFTA
- The Far East and Pacific Rim (led by Japan)

(b) Trading within the blocks would be relatively **liberalised** but there would be **barriers to competition** from outside. The blocs would trade with each other, but this would be more restricted. Countries would have to try and attach themselves to one of the blocks.

(c) **Non-block countries** were not seen as terribly important. Given that some non-block countries (eg India and China) are likely to be some of the world's largest and fastest growing markets, suggestions to restrict trade to block countries are short sighted. The Chinese economy, for example is growing at over 10% per annum.

6.8 The theory of trading blocks does not provide a complete analysis of world trade.

(a) The block theory **works better for some industries** than others.

(i) The EU and US have had extensive programmes to protect agriculture, to the outrage of more efficient producers (such as the Cairns Group representing Australia and some other countries).

(ii) Even in sensitive industries like aerospace, there is free trade.

(b) The block theory does not really take **investment flows** into account.

(c) The block theory does not account for all **trade** flows. The US is Japan's most significant **individual** export market, although East Asia as a region has overtaken the US as a market for Japanese's goods.

(d) The **World Trade Organisation** (WTO) regulates world trade.

### Marketing at Work

**Developing countries and technology**

**India**

Software exports from India are growing at a 'blistering pace'. For eight consecutive years, they have grown by more than 50%, with lots of business coming from year 2000 contracts. The US is the main market (57% of sales), with the EU accounting for 26% and Japan 8%. The top wealth creators in India are now information technology companies, the top three being Satyam Computer, Wipro and Infosys Technologies.

**China**

China knows exactly how many Internet users it has because everyone has to register with the government before opening an account. The number of users grew from 600,000 at the end of 1997 to around 10 million by 2000. This is a very small proportion of its population of around 1,221 million, and with only 540,000 computers currently connected to the Internet it seems that there will continue to be low penetration rates, but a huge potential market.

*Computer Business Review*

---

(e) **Knowledge-based industries** (which many writers such as *Drucker* believe are the motors of future economic growth) are hard to evaluate and control. **Technology** might make ideas as to trading blocks obsolete.

(f) All trading blocks have extensive economic interactions with **third world countries**. They will have a growing relationship with countries in the former Soviet Union which have recently entered the global market.

**6.9** A significant effect of regional trade blocks has been the rush to qualify for **local status** by multinational firms. This has been achieved by the multinationals setting up within one or more member states. Thus France, Germany and the UK have seen considerable inward investment from US and Japanese firms.

# 7 The single European market

**7.1** Since 31 December 1992 there has been a 'single European market'.

(a) The **single European market** is supposed to allow for the free movement of **labour, goods and services** between the member states of the EU.

 (i) **Physical barriers** (eg customs inspection) on goods and service have been removed for most products. Companies have had to adjust to a new VAT regime as a consequence.

 (ii) **Technical standards** (eg for quality and safety) should be harmonised.

 (iii) **Governments should not discriminate** between EU companies in awarding public works contracts.

 (iv) **Telecommunications** should be subject to greater competition.

 (v) It should be possible to provide **financial services** in any country.

 (vi) Measures are being taken to rationalise **transport** services.

 (vii) There should be **free movement of capital** within the community.

 (viii) **Professional qualifications** awarded in one member state should be recognised in the others.

 (ix) The EU is taking a co-ordinated stand on matters related to **consumer protection**.

(b) At the same time, there are many areas where harmonisation is some way from being achieved.

(i) **Company taxation**. Tax rates, which can affect the viability of investment plans, vary from country to country within the EU.

(ii) **Indirect taxation (VAT)**. Whilst there have been moves to harmonisation, there are still differences between rates imposed by member states.

(iii) **Differences in prosperity**. There are considerable differences in prosperity between the wealthiest EU economy (Germany), and the poorest (eg Greece). The UK comes somewhere in the middle.

(1) Grants are sometimes available to depressed regions, which might affect investment decisions.

(2) Different marketing strategies are appropriate for different markets.

(iv) **Differences in workforce skills**. Again, this can have a significant effect on investment decisions. The workforce in Germany is perhaps the most highly trained, but also the most highly paid, and so might be suitable for products of a high added value.

(v) **Infrastructure**. Some countries are better provided with road and rail than others. Where accessibility to a market is an important issue, infrastructure can mean significant variations in distribution costs.

(vi) **Delays**. Single market regulation is still being introduced in some industries (insurance).

(vii) **Social differences**. The UK's welfare state is far less generous than Germany's.

**7.2** Two other points about the EU are worthy of note.

(a) Bear in mind that the EU is much **more than a single market and a free trade area**. It has its own Parliament, elected from throughout the EU, civil service and courts, and it is one of the many political arrangements in which the countries of Western Europe are involved. It has a **political and constitutional dimension** largely absent from other free trading arrangements.

(b) The EU is set to **expand from its current membership**. Candidates for membership include Poland, Hungary, the Czech Republic, Cyprus and Turkey. This expansion will have a significant impact on two areas.

(i) The EU's constitutional arrangements.

(ii) The EU's budgetary arrangements. Already the agriculture budget is being cut. Funds also flow from the EU to economically depressed regions (eg parts of Greece, Merseyside). These may change.

# 8 Demographic issues

**Key Concept**

**Demography** is the 'analysis of statistics on birth and death rates, age structures of populations, ethnic groups within communities etc.' (Bennett, *Dictionary of Personnel and Human Resources Management*).

**8.1** The adjective **demographic** is sometimes used to denote the population-related aspects of an issue.

**8.2** The **purpose** of studying a country's population and trends within it is as follows.

(a) People create a demand for goods and services.

(b) If economic growth exceeds population growth you would expect to see enhanced **standards** of living. **Quality of life** measures would also include pollution measures, life expectancy rates, infant mortality and so on.

(c) Population is a source of labour, one of the **factors of production**.

(d) Population creates demands on the physical environment and its resources, a source of increased international political concern. (The Kyoto conference in Japan at the end of 1997 agreed reductions in carbon dioxide.)

**8.3** The higher rate of population growth in **less-developed countries** compared with developed countries has arisen due to a continuing high birth rate and a declining death rate although some populations are being threatened by the HIV virus (for example in South Africa). Social changes (eg attitudes to large families) have not accompanied medical advances imported from developed societies. People are living longer.

(a) **Growing populations**

- Require fast economic growth just to maintain living standards
- Result in overcrowding on land and/or cities and a decline in the quality of life
- Require more resources for capital investment
- Stimulate investment (as the market size is increasing)
- Lead to enhanced labour mobility

(b) **Falling populations**

- Require more productive techniques to maintain output
- Make some scale economies harder to achieve
- Put a greater burden on a decreasing number of young people
- Exhibit changing consumption patterns

## Age structure and distribution

**8.4** We should now discuss the **age structure** of the population.

(a) The effect of greater life expectancy is that a larger proportion of the population will be senior citizens and unlikely to be working. These offer significant opportunities to international marketers. The UK, Europe and Japan all face an ageing population.

(b) The proportion of old people is lower in developing countries. In Egypt and Iran, over half the population is below the age of 30.

## Geographic distribution

**8.5** Where we live is another important feature of demography. The above arguments have taken the individual country as a homogenous unit. In practice, however this is a vast oversimplification. A country may suffer the problems of overpopulation in some areas and underpopulation in others.

## Action Programme 2

The Republic of Guarana in Latin America is undergoing a number of major changes. Now a democracy, it has re-established links with Western providers of capital, who are investing in the country, to extract its unique resource of Vrillium. In particular, large numbers of Vrillium mines have been opened in the San Serif valley. This comprises about 10% of the country's land area and is the site of Guarana's elegant capital Bosanova. This new economic activity is welcome. The mines and related industries will spur rapid economic growth. Bosanova has a population of 50,000. 80% of Guarana's population are peasant farmers. The prices of their crops on world markets have plummeted and the government of Guarana is alarmed at the growing rural poverty, especially as the population is increasing and agriculture is primitive and inefficient. The government has little money to invest in the countryside.

Jot down what you think are the consequences of the huge increase in industrial and mining activities in Bosanova.

---

**8.6** Demography also deals with the effect of concentration and dispersal of population in particular areas. Industrialisation has traditionally meant a shift from the countryside to the towns and can be seen in the explosive growth of **mega-cities** in Latin America (Mexico City, Sao Paolo in Brazil), and Asia (eg Bombay, Shanghai, Jakarta).

## Sex

**8.7** There is often an imbalance in the population between the numbers of men and the numbers of women. This has arisen for a number of reasons.

(a) Males tend to die younger.

(b) In some countries male children are more valued than female children, and female children are more likely to suffer infanticide.

**8.8** The **work roles** played by males and females in different societies vary, even within the industrial world. In different societies, women and men have distinct purchasing and social powers. This is a key cultural issue.

## Ethnicity

**8.9** Only a few societies are homogenous, with populations of one culture and ethnic background. Japan is an example, although the population includes descendants of Koreans. On the other hand, societies like the USA and the UK have populations drawn from a variety of different areas.

## Buying patterns

**8.10** Buying behaviour is an important aspect of marketing. Many factors influence the buying decisions of individuals and households. Demography and the **class structure** (the distribution of wealth and power in a society) are relevant in that they can be both **behavioural determinants** and **inhibitors**.

(a) **Behavioural determinants** encourage people to buy a product or service. The individual's personality, culture, social class, and the importance of the purchase decision (eg a necessity such as food or water, or a luxury) can predispose a person to purchase something.

(b) **Inhibitors** are factors, such as the individual's income, which will make the person less likely to purchase something.

**8.11** **Socio-economic status** can be related to buying patterns in a number of ways, both in the amount people have to spend and what they spend it on. It affects both the quantity of goods and services supplied, and the proportion of their income that households spend on goods and services.

## Marketing at Work

(a) India has a large peasantry and an industrial proletariat, but its huge population size means that its wealthy middle class is bigger than the populations of many developed countries. With import liberalisation and economic deregulation, this should be an attractive segment for marketers.

(b) The level of inequality in society also influences its attractiveness to the marketer. Brazil has the greatest degree of inequality in the world. Japan, famously, has low inequality.

   (i) In societies of high inequality, wealth is concentrated, hence the buying power of the majority is limited. This might suggest more success in selling luxury goods.

   (ii) Where equality is higher, there may be a higher demand for mass market goods as more people will have access to them.

## Family structure

**8.12** The role of the family and family groupings varies from society to society.

(a) In societies such as India, the **caste system** still exists and family structures can be part of this wider network.

(b) **Extended families** are still strong in many countries, especially where the family is to assume most of the burden of looking after the elderly: many countries do not have a welfare state.

(c) Family size varies.

**8.13** Marketers have often used the model of the **family life cycle** (FLC) to model purchase and consumption patterns. You will have encountered it before.

- Bachelor – single people
- Newly-weds – household and childcare products
- Full nest
- Empty-nest – children have left home
- Solitary survivor

**8.14** This model may not hold.

(a) Quite often, households contain three generations (grand-parents, parents, children).

(b) People leave home later in life. In countries such as Italy and Spain it is common for adult children to live at home.

(c) Purchase and consumption decisions vary.

## Marketing at Work

***Diageo's* blunder**

An advertisement on the London Underground in December 2002 for *Smirnoff* offended the Taiwanese. It showed a picture of an item with the label "Made in Taiwan" and the caption "Warning – this gift will break down on Christmas morning". Taiwan, so long a byword for inferior manufacturing quality, is now one of the leading high-tech manufacturers in the world. The Taiwan government was considering an outright ban on Diageo products.

Diageo was trying to achieve distinctiveness in a 'noisy' market, but this must never come at the expense of social responsibility and international awareness. This is a difficult line to tread – to appeal to one segment, you might risk offending others. Joking is always risky!

So Diageo found itself plunged into crisis management, despite the fact that its marketing code includes the provision: 'Don't use anything likely to be considered gratuitously offensive or demeaning to either gender, or to any race, religion, culture or minority group.'

# 9 Technology

**9.1** The history of the past 200 years has been one of enormous economic growth. Many countries are able to support populations which in the early 19th century would have been inconceivable.

**9.2** Material advances have promoted a large complex of economic, social, political and cultural changes. These changes have included the following.

(a) **Industrialisation** (eg movement of labour and resources from agriculture to industry) which has been a feature of many overseas markets.

(b) **Modernisation** (urbanisation, reduction in death rates, centralising government and so forth).

## Marketing at Work

An example can be based on the effect that a 'new' technology can have on an old one. Different technologies are adopted at different rates. The cinema ('moving pictures') was once a new medium.

(a) In the UK the fall in cinema attendances has largely been caused by television, a new technology which has fallen in cost since its invention. Television itself has been subject to competition from video. New technology has also increased the number of television channels available.

(b) In India, on the other hand, television penetration might be high in urban areas but less so in the poorer villages. Cinema is still India's principal medium for distributing moving pictures, and the Indian film industry is more prolific than Hollywood.

## Technological development and the marketing mix: a cautionary perspective

**9.3** Technology, or investment in it, in the narrow sense, cannot on its own promote economic growth. The first use of **steam** power was discovered, not in 18th century England, but almost 2,000 years before: there was, however, no 'use' for it. Societies with large pools of slave labour had little need for 'labour-saving' inventions.

**9.4** Modern apparatus and techniques have had very uneven success in 'modernising' underdeveloped countries.

(a) The **environmental consequences** of introducing western technology to underdeveloped countries have been ill thought out.

(b) The **economic consequences** have not been as beneficial as might at first be supposed. 'The prestigious new production technologies have not worked optimally or even satisfactorily.' The problems are two-fold.

(i) **Technological dependency** leading to a heavy foreign currency payments burdens. The country has to import **spare parts**, and even raw materials, to run machinery. It might have to pay for **expatriate technicians**. This is expensive, and so the costs of the technology might be greater than anticipated, thus reducing any economic benefit.

(ii) The inappropriateness of Western technology. **Climatic** conditions can affect performance. **Infrastructural** deficiencies such as naturally poor roads affect, for example, the 'good design' of a car. The **labour/capital** mix means that in poor countries, with surplus labour, labour intensive industries rather than labour saving capital equipment might be a better use of resources.

### Action Programme 3

The Republic of Rukwa is a largely agricultural society. For foreign exchange, it is dependent on the exports of kwat. Kwat is a grain which can only be grown in Rukwa's climate. It is, however, widely in demand in Western markets as a 'health' food. Kwat is grown by peasant farmers on small plots of land on banks of the River Ru. At present, the harvested Kwat is transported by ox-drawn barges down the River Ru to port Ruk for export. The process is slow, owing to bottlenecks on the river. The government is thinking of several alternatives to ease this situation. Rukwa has no other natural resources.

1 Build a high speed road, and use foreign loans to buy lorries and four-wheel drive vehicles for farmers.

2 Build a railway, with imported steel and engines.

3 Widen the River Ru at key points, and purchase outboard motors for the barges.

What do you think is right or wrong with all these alternatives?

**9.5** The relevance of this to international marketers is as follows.

(a) **How do you define customer needs?** Elite groups sometimes 'need' products which are not economically beneficial for society.

(b) To what extent do you apply the societal marketing concept to overseas markets?

(c) The marketing mix may presuppose a level of **technological development** which is in fact non-existent for large parts of the population.

## Level of technological development

**9.6** The level of technological development in a country is important in the marketing of many products.

- Understanding **how the product is used**
- The provision of **support services** for the product
- The existence of an appropriate **distribution network**
- **Communication** with the customer

### *How to use the product*

**9.7** Many products are technically sophisticated and require a level of **technological awareness** that may not be widely available. Technologically aware cultures recognise switches and buttons and instructions almost instinctively.

### *Support services*

**9.8** Many products require maintenance and spare parts which may be unavailable outside the most technologically advanced economies. The classic solution is known as the **'backward invention'** in which the product is simplified to either the level of support available or, ultimately, the point at which the owner can support the product himself.

### *Distribution network*

**9.9** Certain products require an **infrastructure for their distribution** and use. Thus a TV requires both electricity and a TV transmission service. Telephones require a carrier network. Distribution of medicines and foodstuffs require careful handling and temperature conditions in transit, necessitating specialised and sophisticated transport.

### Action Programme 4

A firm has developed a drug which can cure Alzheimer's disease. What factors do you think would distinguish its export marketing efforts to a country in the EU from its export marketing efforts to a country in the Third World?

# 10 E-commerce and the Internet

## Electronic commerce

**10.1** Electronic commerce is the latest example of the impact of technology on global markets.

## Key Concepts

**Electronic commerce** (e-commerce, e-business, e-biz) can be defined as using a computer network to speed up all stages of the business process, from design to buying, selling and delivery. The process is fairly familiar between companies, but less so between retailer and customer.

The **Internet** is the sum of all the separate networks (or stand-alone computers) run by organisations and individuals alike. (It has been described as an **international telephone service** for computers.)

## Growth of the Internet

**10.2** 60% of households in the USA and 50% of households in the UK had Internet access by the end of 2002. A critical factor in the long-run expansion of the Internet is its use today by children, the adult consumers of tomorrow. The Internet is not expanding at the same rate in every sphere of business. The rate of growth is influenced by a number of factors.

(a) The degree to which the customer can be persuaded to believe that using the Internet will **deliver some added-value** – in terms of quickness, simplicity and price

(b) Whether there are 'costs' which the **customer** has to bear – not exclusively 'costs' in the financial sense, but also such psychological 'costs' as the isolated online shopping experience

(c) The **market segment** to which the individual belongs. The Internet is largely the preserve of younger, more affluent, more technologically competent individuals with above-average amounts of disposable income.

(d) The frequency of supplier/customer **contact** required

(e) The availability of **incentives** which might stimulate Internet acceptance. For example, interest rates on bank accounts which are higher than those available through conventional banks (Egg), the absence of any charges (Freeserve), the creation of penalties for over-the-counter transactions (Abbey National), and the expectations of important customers (IBM's relationships with its suppliers)

## Marketing at Work

In many areas, users are proactively switching to the Internet. When *Lloyds TSB* first developed Internet banking facilities, they were not publicised but customers were seeking it out and joining at the rate of 380 accounts per day. At the same time, customers are not yet ready to abandon the channels they used in the past: even with Internet and telephone banking, many still visit their bank branches regularly.

**10.3** Arguably, the most profitable pure Internet companies, as well as the most influential, will be **business-to-business 'infomediaries'** (the term coined by John Hagel of McKinsey), because they can exploit the Internet's most salient characteristics.

(a) **The Internet shifts power from sellers to buyers by reducing switching costs**. Buyers may feel overwhelmed by this power, but they typically want one-stop shopping, with information they believe and advice they can trust.

(b) **The Internet reduces transaction costs and thus stimulates economic activity**. According to one US calculation, a banking transaction via the Internet costs 1 cent, 27 cents at an ATM (automated teller machine) and 52 cents over the telephone. Infomediaries can enable significant savings to be enjoyed by small-scale or even single customers.

(c) **The speed, range and accessibility of information on the Internet, and the low cost of capturing and distributing it, create new commercial possibilities**. Infomediaries can focus on particular product/service supply issues; by doing so, they attract specialised buyers and sellers; in turn they acquire more expertise which generates continued customer loyalty and participation.

**10.4** The major growth so far in the field of e-commerce has concentrated on the **Business-to-Business** (B2B) sector.

(a) **Major companies** are setting themselves up as e-businesses. In November 1999, both Ford and General Motors announced that they were switching a major portion of their procurement and supply chain management to the web.

(b) IBM now requires **all its suppliers to quote and invoice electronically** – no paper documentation is permitted.

(c) Many firms are using the Internet to exploit the **transparency of supplier prices**, and to maximise their purchasing benefits from the availability of world-wide sourcing. Robert Bosch, the German kitchen appliance manufacturer, **requires all its suppliers to have web-based catalogues** and prices.

(d) Companies are also increasing their customer service through the web. Dell, the computer company, has created **extranets for its major business customers**, enabling them to receive personalised customer support, their own price lists, and some free value-added services.

## Exam Tip

*The development of a Web-based strategy in the business-to-business context was examined in December 2002. This was essentially a question about supply chain management in the electronic age.*

## Marketing at Work

The Internet has the potential to turn business upside down and inside out, to fundamentally change the way companies operate, whether in high-tech or metal-bashing. This goes far beyond buying and selling over the Internet, or e-commerce, and deep into the processes and culture of an enterprise.

Some companies are using the Internet to make direct connections with their customers for the first time. Others are using secure Internet connections to intensify relations with some of their trading partners, and using the Internet's reach and ubiquity to request quotes or sell off perishable stocks of goods or services by auction.

The Internet is helping companies to lower costs dramatically across their supply and demand chains, take their customer service into a different league, enter new markets, create additional revenue streams and redefine their business relationships.

Some writers argue that companies can be either 'brick' or 'click' businesses, but they can't be both: if they are a 'brick' operation – ie they have real premises, real shops, real factories and warehouses – then their culture will make it impossible for them fully to assimilate the drastic changes required in order to operate successfully in a 'click' environment. It is no accident, therefore, that companies like Prudential Assurance have initiated their Internet activities through stand-alone enterprises, using newly-recruited people situated in geographically-distinctive locations.

---

10.5 The Internet provides opportunities to automate tasks which would previously have required more costly interaction with the organisation. These have often been called low-touch or zero-touch approaches.

## Problems with the Internet

10.6 To a large extent the Internet has grown **without any formal organisation**. There are specific communication rules, but it is not **owned** by any one body and there are no clear guidelines on how it should develop. Inevitably, the **quality** of much of the information on the Internet leaves much to be desired.

10.7 Speed is a major issue. Data only downloads onto the user's PC at the speed of the slowest telecommunications link. However, future developments will mean that speeds will improve. A number of **faster services** have recently become available.

(a) **Integrated Services Digital Network (ISDN)** is an international communications standard for sending voice, video, and data over digital telephone lines or normal telephone wires. ISDN supports data transfer rates three times faster than modems.

(b) **ADSL** (Asymmetric Digital Subscriber Line) offers data transfer rates of up to **8 Mbps**, considerably faster than ISDN. ADSL allows information to be sent out over ordinary copper wires and simultaneous use of the normal telephone service.

## How does the Internet and e-commerce challenge traditional business thinking?

10.8 There are several features of the Internet which make it radically different from what has gone before.

(a) It **challenges traditional business models** – because, for example, it enables product/service suppliers to interact directly with their customers, instead of using intermediaries (like retail shops, travel agents, insurance brokers, and conventional banks).

(b) Although the Internet is global in its operation, its benefits are not confined to large (or global) organisations. **Small companies** can move instantly into a global market place, either on their own initiative or as part of what is known as a 'consumer portal'.

(c) It offers a **new economics of information** – because, with the Internet, much information is free. Those with Internet access can view all the world's major newspapers and periodicals without charge.

(d) It supplies an almost incredible **level of speed** – virtually instant access to organisations, plus the capacity to complete purchasing transactions within seconds.

(e) It has created **new networks of communication –** between organisations and their customers (either individually or collectively), between customers themselves (through mutual support groups), and between organisations and their suppliers.

(f) It stimulates the appearance of **new intermediaries** and the disappearance of some existing ones. Businesses are finding that they can cut out the middle man, with electronic banking, insurance, publishing and printing as primary examples.

(g) It has led to **new business partnerships** through which small enterprises can gain access to customers on a scale which would have been viewed as impossible a few years ago.

## Marketing at Work

A university can put its reading list on a website and students wishing to purchase any given book can click directly through to an online bookseller such as Amazon.com. The university gets a commission; the online bookseller gets increased business; the student gets a discount. Everyone benefits except the traditional bookshop.

(h) It promotes **transparent pricing** – because potential customers can readily compare prices not only from suppliers within any given country, but also from suppliers across the world.

(i) It facilitates **personalised attention** – even if such attention is actually administered through impersonal, yet highly sophisticated IT systems and customer database manipulation.

(j) It provides sophisticated **market segmentation** opportunities. Approaching such segments may be one of the few ways in which e-commerce entrepreneurs can create **competitive advantage**.

(k) The web can either be a **separate** or a **complementary** channel.

(l) A new phenomenon is emerging called **dynamic pricing**. Companies can rapidly change their prices to reflect the current state of demand and supply.

**10.9** These new trends are creating **pressure** for companies. The main threat facing companies is that **prices will be driven down by consumers' ability to shop around**.

## Marketing at Work

(1) **Airlines**

The impact of the web is seen clearly in the transportation industry. Airlines now have a more effective way of bypassing intermediaries (ie travel agents) because they can give their customers immediate access to flight reservation systems. British Airways aims to sell at least half of its tickets on-line by the year 2003; one of the low-cost airlines in the UK, EasyJet, has become the first airline to have over half of its bookings made online.

(2) **Travel agents**

The web has also produced a new set of online travel agents who have lower costs because of their ability to operate without a High Street branch network. Their low-cost structure makes them a particularly good choice for selling low margin, cheap tickets for flights, package holidays, cruises and so forth.

These low-cost travel agents have been joined, furthermore, by non-travel-agents who simply specialise in opportunistic purchasing (eg lastminute.com).

(3) ***Tesco***

In another arena, Tesco is already the UK's largest Internet grocery business, but other companies are rapidly developing new initiatives. Waitrose@work allows people to order their groceries in the morning (typically through their employer's intranet communication system) and then have them delivered to the workplace in the afternoon: this approach achieves significant distribution economies of scale so far as Waitrose is concerned.

(4) **Financial services**

The impact of the Internet is especially profound in the field of financial services. New intermediaries enable prospective customers to compare the interest rates and prices charged by different organisations for pensions, mortgages and other financial services. This means that the delivering companies are losing control of the marketing of their services, and there is a downward pressure on prices, especially for services which can legitimately be seen as mere commodities (eg house and contents insurance).

## Disadvantages of e-commerce

**10.10** E-commerce involves an unusual mix of people – security people, web technology people, designers, marketing people – and this can be very difficult to manage. The e-business needs supervision by expensive specialists.

**10.11** In spite of phenomenal growth the market is still fuzzy and undefined. Many e-businesses have only recently reported making any **profit**, the best-known example being **Amazon.com** the Internet book-seller.

**10.12** Unless the e-business is one started completely from scratch, any new technology installed will **need to link up with existing business systems**, which could potentially take years of programming. Under-estimating the time and effort involved is a common obstacle.

**10.13** The international availability of a website means that the **laws of all countries** that transactions may be conducted from have to be considered. The legal issues surrounding e-commerce are complex and still developing.

## Marketing at Work

For some the Internet is a necessary evil – others browse and surf the net with that obsessive drive that is peculiar to any new technology. But the Internet is not just any new technology. It is the most important communications development since the advent of the telephone, and like the telephone it has created its own culture and given birth to new businesses and new possibilities.

Early confusion about the Internet meant that many companies built their own websites after learning the rudiments of HTML. They had registered their company name and done everything by the book. The website went online and they all waited with bated breath. Nothing happened. No new business arrived and nothing changed, and they couldn't understand why.

E-commerce is a tidal wave; if you choose to participate you either 'sink or swim'. You must be daring enough in design to achieve something quite different from the ways things have been done in the past.

A website is a shopfront that must be located in the centre of town in the full gaze of everyone. A good one can make a small business as powerful and competitive as some of the largest players. It just needs flair and commitment to succeed. But to do so there are some measures that must be used. Marketing outside the web, in the press or even on the radio can alert the market to the website. The site itself should be properly identified by name, registered competently with the appropriate search engines and it must look good.

| WEBSITE ESSENTIALS |
|---|
| ■ Integration with all company systems (ie back office) |
| ■ Speedy implementation |
| ■ Quick and easy updating by own staff to retain topicality |
| ■ Self producing audit records |
| ■ Promotion via the Internet |
| ■ Press and PR for website |
| ■ Attractive design but appropriate for the web |
| ■ Scope to interact with visitors |
| ■ Planned structure to include profitable business concept |
| ■ Control and maintenance by owner, without developer involvement |

The appearance of a website is extremely important. Attractive and easy to fill interactive forms can lure a sales prospect into being a buyer. One has seconds in which to achieve this end. Too many graphics slow down the procedure. The experience of visiting and browsing through the shop and responding to the goods on offer must be clever, intriguing, quick and efficient. Millions of pounds worth of business is lost on the Internet every day as a result of so-called interactive websites that are difficult to operate and dull.

Adapted from *Management Accounting*, February 2000

## Action Programme 5

Up to now, many companies have ignored e-commerce. They have watched as a succession of much-publicised ventures have failed to get off the ground and even the best have struggled to translate success into profits, especially after the 'dotcom bubble' burst fairly spectacularly. This has created an impression that the Internet is a confusing and dangerous sales channel that can, for now, be left to others.

Why, do you think, is this view increasingly untenable?

---

## The Internet in context

**10.14** Commentators highlight so-called 'megatrends' which, coupled with the Internet, are changing the face of organisations:

(a) New **distribution channels**, revolutionising sales and brand management.

(b) The continued **shift of power** towards the consumer.

(c) **Growing competition** locally, nationally, internationally and globally.

(d) An acceleration in the **pace of business**.

(e) The **transformation of companies** into 'extended enterprises' involving 'virtual teams of business, customer and supplier' working in collaborative partnerships.

(f) A re-evaluation of how companies, their partners and competitors **add value** not only to themselves but in the wider environmental and social setting.

(g) Recognition of '**knowledge**' as a strategic asset.

**10.15** Most observers and experts agree that a successful strategy for e-commerce cannot simply be bolted on to existing processes, systems, delivery routes and business models. Instead, management groups have, in effect, to start again, by asking themselves such **fundamental questions** as:

- What do customers want to buy from us?
- What business should we be in?
- What kind of partners might we need?
- What categories of customer do we want to attract and retain?

**10.16** In turn, organisations can visualise the necessary changes at three interconnected levels.

**Level 1** The simple **introduction of new technology** to connect electronically with employees, customers and suppliers (eg through an intranet, extranet or website).

**Level 2** **Re-organisation** of the workforce, processes, systems and strategy – in order to make best use of the new technology.

**Level 3** **Re-positioning** of the organisation to fit it into the emerging e-economy.

**10.17** So far, very few companies have gone beyond levels (1) and (2). Instead, pure Internet businesses such as Amazon.com and AOL have emerged from these new rules: unburdened by physical assets, their competitive advantage lies in knowledge management and customer relationships.

## Marketing at Work

Conventional thinking says that a company should pay no more to bring in a customer than the net present value of the stream of profits that the customer will subsequently generate. Yet in the e-commerce context, investors have often rewarded companies for customer acquisition without asking any questions about how quickly those customers may disappear. The evidence suggests that many 'dot.com' enterprises remain unable to achieve sustained profitability or indeed any profitability at all.

## Chapter Roundup

- **International markets** offer firms opportunities to trade, to acquire resources and investment, but also offer threats in that other companies from overseas can do the same.
- We can analyse environmental factors using the mnemonic **SLEPT** (social, legal, economic, political, technological).
- Although trade has benefits, many countries have sought to limit its effects in order to **protect** local producers. In the long term this serves to harm economic welfare as resources are not allocated where they are most productive.
- **Regional trading blocks** promote trade between countries in groups. The environment of world trade is becoming freer, globally, with the influence of the World Trade Organisation.
- **Social factors** include overall global population growth, and the disparity between the ageing and stable (in numbers) populations of the developed world, with the young and growing populations of lesser developed countries. In individual markets, **culture** can be a determining factor of marketing success.
- **Political factors** offer extra risks to the exporter, in terms of the stability of the country, the attitude of the government to trade generally and to the company in particular.
- **Legal factors** in individual markets include product regulations and control over the marketing mix generally. Human resource usage is also determined by legal factors.
- **Economic factors** include the overall level of growth and stage of development, frequently measured by GDP. The balance of payments is an influence on government policy.
- **Technology** creates new products and industries, and enhances productivity and growth. That said, countries need an infrastructure to cope with technology.
- **E-commerce** is revolutionising the way most business is conducted.

## Quick Quiz

1. What factors does the level of political risk depend on?
2. Draw up a checklist for companies to consider when dealing with the political environment.
3. List some protectionist measures.
4. What is meant by LDC, EDC, SDC?
5. How do you measure economic development?
6. What is the Triad? How relevant is Triad theory?
7. Why study demography?
8. What is the effect of growing populations?
9. What is the significance of age structure?
10. What is electronic commerce?

## Answers to Quick Quiz

1 Government attitudes; the nature of the product; the company involved.

2
- How stable is the country politically?
- Are the local rules of the game known and enforced?
- How long is the government likely to be in power?
- How would a new government change the rules?
- What would be the effects of expected changes to the rules?
- What decisions and actions should be taken now?

3 Tariffs; barriers; import quotas and embargoes; domestic subsidies; exchange controls; exchange rate policy.

4 Lesser developed country; early developed country; semi-developed country.

5 Several measures are used including: GDP/head; sector source of GDP; living standards; energy usage; education level.

6 The Triad is three trading blocs: EU, NAFTA and the informal East Asian bloc led by Japan.

The Triad approach has some merit but it does not take into account the WTO, investment flows and much trade.

7 Markets are made up of people: demographic changes produce important changes in markets.

8 Demand increases, as does the labour force. Other resources are required to provide economic growth, though they may not be available.

9 The proportion of the population is of working age impacts on output; age distribution also affects relative levels of demand for a range of products.

10 Commerce that depends on the use of computer networks generally and the Internet in particular.

## Action Programme Review

1 Protectionism is about the relative benefits and drawbacks to countries of restraining trade. For commercial organisations, however, protectionism has some short run advantages.

The USA is the largest market for automobiles. US car manufacturers produce overseas for foreign markets, generally speaking, as opposed to exporting from the US itself. Free trade in motor vehicles automatically means a great deal of competition at home (particularly from Japan).

A closed market would allow them to raise prices. On the other hand, Swedish car manufacturers, such as Volvo, depend on successful exports since the home market is too small to support them. The benefits of protection would be exceeded by the disadvantages.

2 Here is one possible answer. The existence of the new wealth will encourage:

(a) mass urbanisation
(b) potential rural depopulation

as the new industries will encourage peasants to move in from the land in the hope of a better life. Bosanova's resources will become more and more strained. At the same time it is possible that, without parallel increases in agricultural efficiency, the ageing rural workforce, who cannot move, will become less productive.

3 There is often no right answer, but here are some ideas.

(a) Will the foreign exchange earnings from Kwat justify the infrastructural investment at all? After all, the government will have to use the foreign exchange earnings to pay interest on loans. Option (3) might be the least risky here.

(b) Does the country have an educational and technical infrastructure to support the technology. Road vehicles need spare parts and trained service personnel. Spare parts might be an additional drain on foreign exchange. Again option (3) might be the least risky.

4 Hints. You could write reams here, but there are a few preliminary ideas.

**Western countries**

(a) Attitudes to elderly.

(b) Distribution: over the counter? Prescribed by doctors?

(c) Current health care of elderly.

(d) Demographic trends: is the age structure of the country becoming more heavily weighted towards older people?

(e) Drug testing and certification regime.

**Third World country**

(a) Is Alzheimer's seen as a major problem, compared to other medical conditions (eg diseases from poor sanitation)?

(b) Would the drug be affordable?

(c) Attitudes to elderly.

(d) Age structure of the country (fewer old people than in the West).

You will doubtless think of more.

5 Relevant points include:

(a) The likely scale and speed of development is immense: pundits predicted by the end of 2002, Internet business between, for example, US businesses, would exceed $300bn, rising from only $4.5bn in 1997.

(b) Every part of the value chain is up for grabs. Any participant in the value chain could usurp the role of any other participant.

(i) The free flow of information about buyers and sellers undermines the role of intermediaries.

(ii) A book publisher could bypass retailers or distributors and sell directly.

(iii) A book seller could decide to publish books, based on the information it has obtained about readers' interests.

**Now try Question 8 at the end of the Study Text**

# Culture

| Chapter Topic List | |
|---|---|
| 1 | Setting the scene |
| 2 | What is culture? |
| 3 | Sources of culture |
| 4 | Culture and international marketing |
| 5 | Motivation and buyer behaviour |
| 6 | Consumer buyer behaviour |
| 7 | Business and government buyer behaviour |
| 8 | Buyer behaviour in other sectors |
| 9 | Culture and the organisation |

## Syllabus content

- Using information and tools to evaluate the core competences, assets, culture and weaknesses of an organisation
- Assessing the fit between an organisation's culture and its current strategy
- Understanding customers' needs, preferences and buying behaviour
- Developing a detailed understanding of customers and markets in a foreign marketing environment
- Techniques and factors to be used in assessing the attractiveness of international markets

## Key Concepts Introduced

- Buyer behaviour
- Not-for-profit organisation

# 1 Setting the scene

**1.1** **Culture** was introduced in Chapter 4, and is one of the most sensitive areas in international marketing. Culture refers to ways of feeling, behaving and 'seeing the world': people's basic beliefs and assumptions about who they are, what is important in life, and how they feel about themselves and their fellow humans. In marketing terms, **culture has a major effect upon buyer behaviour**.

**1.2** Culture is particularly important for the **promotion** and the **product** elements of the mix. It is also relevant to **international marketing management**, in that doing business overseas requires the manager successfully to negotiate all the issues that exist behind outward business behaviour.

**1.3** Of course many firms do negotiate these problems successfully. In some cases, this is because the product is not **culturally specific**, but in other cases, they ensure their managers are **sensitive to cultural difference**.

## Links to other papers

**1.4** Culture is a key issue for **marketing communications**, and of course will be a factor when choosing between strategic alternatives. Cultural differences may provide barriers to effective implementation of marketing strategies and plans.

**1.5** Marketing communications is a key tool in encouraging customers to buy; hence the importance of behaviour models.

# 2 What is culture?

**2.1** The term is used by sociologists and anthropologists to encompass the total of the learned **beliefs, values, customs, artefacts** and **rituals** of a society or group.

**2.2** It is clear that an individual can participate in several different cultures.

(a) The 'national' culture – if such a thing exists

(b) Sub-cultures (such as 'youth culture') can be important in the early stages of product introduction. 'Computer geeks', for example, were among the first to be enthusiastic about the Internet.

(c) Corporate cultures

## Marketing at Work

The *Guardian* carried this following report, translated from an article in the French newspaper *Le Monde* by Jean-Michel Normand.

**"'Sensual couples' joy of sinks hits dishwasher makers"**

The makers and marketers of dishwashers in France are in despair. For the French may object to ironing or dusting, but they don't mind doing the dishes. Washing up is seen as therapeutic by some and a sign of a happy marriage by others.

The French National Institute of Statistics and Economics has found that 80 per cent of men and 75 per cent of women don't see washing up as unpleasant, while one in 20 find it very enjoyable.

These "sensual aquariophiles", as the sociologist Jean-Claude Kaufmann calls them, constitute a lost cause for dishwasher manufacturers. For years they have found it impossible to persuade more than one in three households to buy their products.

"They regard washing up as a purification ritual", dishwasher manufacturer Gifam reports despairingly.

In daily life the washing up often represents a good way to share the household tasks. A dishwasher could endanger a rite that maintains stability between couples.

Gifam is planning a publicity campaign with the emphasis on economy. Dishwashers use three or four times less water than washing up by hand, experts say.'

---

## The development of attitudes and beliefs

2.3 We acquire our feelings about the worth of goods and services through a process of cultural and social development. In international marketing these differences in values may be quite marked, whereas in domestic markets they may be so subtle as to be unnoticeable. For the international marketer differences in attitudes and beliefs may affect the following.

- Attitude towards **ownership** of an item
- **Strength** and **direction** of attitude
- **Reason** for desire/antipathy
- **Perception** of appropriate design/style
- **Meaning** of colours, symbols and words

## Language and symbols

2.4 Another very important element of culture, which makes the learning and sharing of culture possible, is **language**. Without a shared language and symbolism – verbal and non-verbal – there would be no shared meaning.

2.5 **Symbols** are an important aspect of language and culture. Each symbol may carry a number of different meanings and associations for different people. For example, in Western cultures, the colour white symbolises purity, but in some Eastern cultures it symbolises death. Logos, trademarks and brands all have symbolic uses.

## The transfer of cultural meaning

### *Cultural meaning*

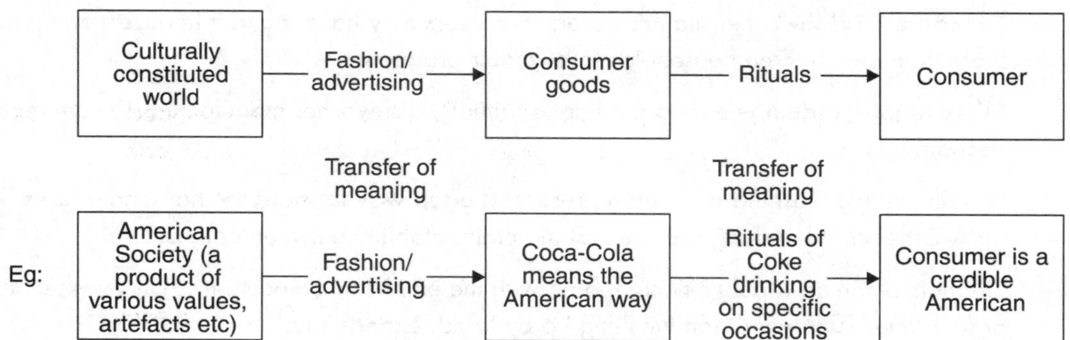


**2.6** We have already noted that each culture establishes its own norms. Often these are derived from **religious observance**. Thus alcoholic drink, beef or pork, unclad females, men doing housework and so on may all be taboo in certain cultures. The book *The Satanic Verses* by Salman Rushdie caused significant offence in Muslim societies.

### Exam Tip

*Culture is a catch-all topic and can be brought into many questions on international marketing.*

*(a) It affects the product area of the mix, as you will see later.*

*(b) Marketing communications are also heavily influenced by culture, for obvious reasons.*

*(c) Distribution might be affected – for example, the role of the shopkeeper in the local society.*

*(d) Even price can be influenced by culture – eg bargaining.*

*(e) Services are probably more affected by culture than other goods.*

*As well as the mix, culture can affect the success of marketing operations and even business negotiations.*

*Consequently, culture has featured regularly in the mini-cases in such diverse contexts as food preferences, selling techniques, shopping habits and internal management.*

*The draft Specimen Paper included a Part B question about the challenges differences of culture can create. This question asked for illustrations either from within organisations or between countries. We discussed organisational culture earlier in this Study Text.*

# 3 Sources of culture

**3.1** There are approximately 200 different countries, each of which contains many different cultures and with a myriad of beliefs, norms and taboos. It is helpful for us to have a framework showing the major categories. This is shown below.

**3.2** Taking the example of religion, this can affect **market entry** (religious conflict) **marketing organisation** (days of prayer) **goods** (type of clothes worn, types of food eaten) **promotion** (images shown), methods of doing **business** (eg Islamic banks) and so forth.

## Marketing at Work

Islamic banking is a powerful example of the importance of culture in an economy. The Koran abjures the charging of interest, which is usury. However whilst interest is banned, profits are allowed. A problem is that there is no standard interpretation of the Sharia law regarding this. Products promoted by Islamic banks include:

(a) Leasing (the Islamic Bank TII arranged leases for seven Kuwait Airways aircraft)
(b) Trade finance
(c) Commodities trading

The earlier Islamic banks offered current accounts only, but depositors now ask for shares in the bank profits. To tap this market, Citibank, the US bank, has opened an Islamic banking subsidiary in Bahrain.

*A Cultural Framework*

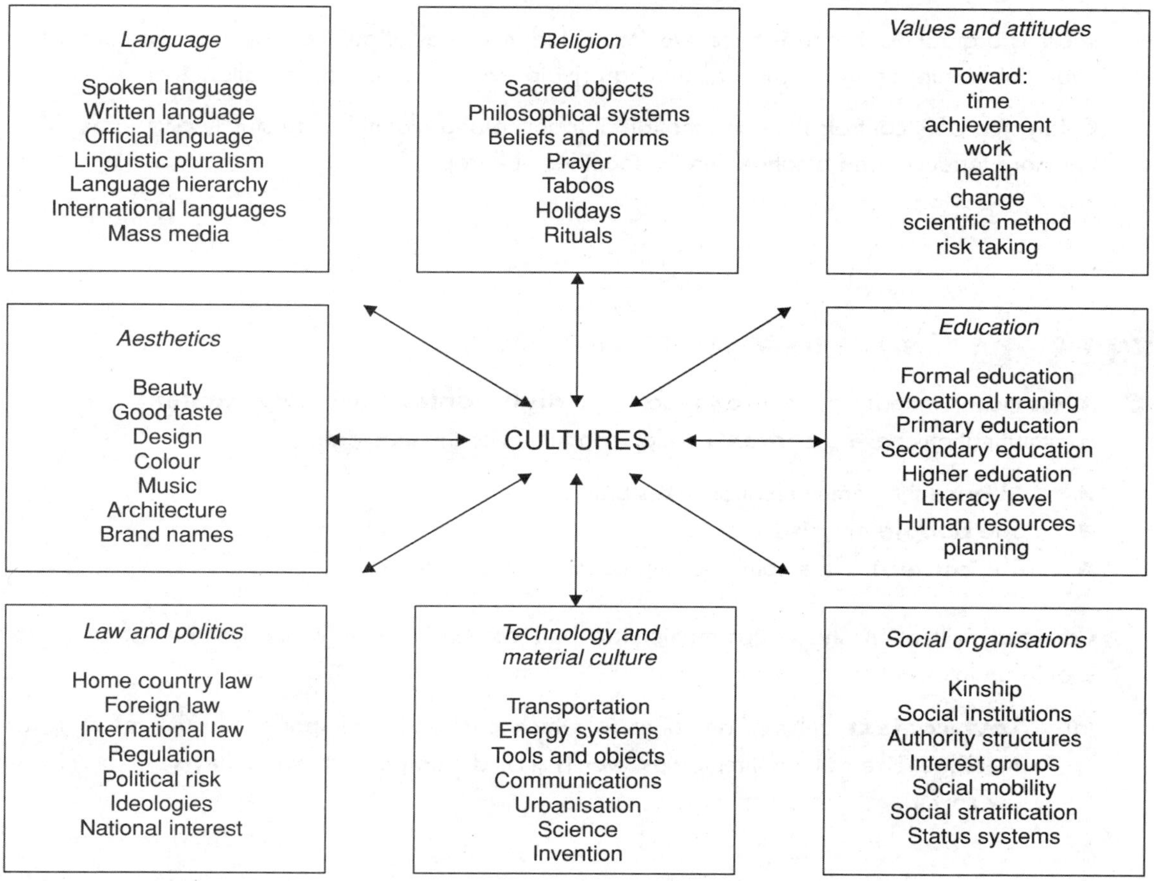

*Language*
Spoken language
Written language
Official language
Linguistic pluralism
Language hierarchy
International languages
Mass media

*Religion*
Sacred objects
Philosophical systems
Beliefs and norms
Prayer
Taboos
Holidays
Rituals

*Values and attitudes*
Toward:
time
achievement
work
health
change
scientific method
risk taking

*Aesthetics*
Beauty
Good taste
Design
Colour
Music
Architecture
Brand names

CULTURES

*Education*
Formal education
Vocational training
Primary education
Secondary education
Higher education
Literacy level
Human resources planning

*Law and politics*
Home country law
Foreign law
International law
Regulation
Political risk
Ideologies
National interest

*Technology and material culture*
Transportation
Energy systems
Tools and objects
Communications
Urbanisation
Science
Invention

*Social organisations*
Kinship
Social institutions
Authority structures
Interest groups
Social mobility
Social stratification
Status systems

## National cultures

**3.3** Many cultures can be identified with a nation, but often this does not apply.

(a) The UK is relatively small, with one language, English, predominantly spoken.

(b) A large country like India is home to many language groups, and while Hinduism is shared across many of these language groups, there is a large Muslim minority.

**3.4** Some countries combine two more or less equal linguistic cultural groups. Switzerland is a nation state that is 'explicitly multi-cultural'.

**3.5** Many of the world's **nation states**, with defined borders and central institutions, are relatively recent creations, resulting not from ethnicity or cultural homogeneity but from **colonial administration**. This is particularly true of Africa.

### Marketing at Work

A huge cultural difference between the US and most other countries of similar economic development is the role of guns and firearms.

Most European states place restrictions on ownership of firearms. In the USA, the right to bear arms is embodied in the constitution and powerful lobby groups such as the National Rifle Association (NRA) seek to keep it that way.

Although hunting as a hobby is often cited as a reason, guns in the US have been given a symbolic role: the American War of Independence started with gun-shots, and the West was 'won' in this way. Even now, ownership of guns is justified as the citizen's last protection against the almighty state, and indeed against other citizens.

There is a great deal of resistance even to limited measures of gun control – quite a contrast to wide public support in the UK for banning private ownership of firearms altogether.

Oddly, the USA controls the consumption of tobacco and alcohol more strictly compared with the more tobacco- and alcohol-friendly countries of Europe.

## High context and low context cultures

**3.6** A distinction needs to be drawn between **high context** and **low context** cultures. All communications have a **context,** which can influence the message.

- **Where** the communication takes place
- The **people** involved
- The **content** of the conversation (eg work, negotiation)

**3.7** **Context** will often shape communication and can indicate how the content of a message should be interpreted.

(a) **Low context** cultures are ones in which context is unimportant to the meaning of a message. Like railway timetables, words should mean exactly what they say. The meaning is explicit.

(b) In **high context** cultures, messages must be interpreted from the context. In a high context culture, communication might be impossible if you do not know the person you are with.

**3.8** Usunier (*Marketing Across Cultures*, 1999) identifies the following groups.

- Low-context and explicit messages: Swiss, Germans, Scandinavians, North Americans
- Medium-context: English, French, Italian, Spanish
- High context: Latin Americans, Arabs, Japanese

## Action Programme 1

Two people, one from a low context and one from a high context culture meet for the first time to discuss a business deal. What will be the main objective of each, and where do you think each will obtain security that the deal will be ok?

# 4 Culture and international marketing

**4.1** **Cultural segmentation** must be considered particularly carefully, therefore, in an international (or **cross-cultural**) context: the marketer needs to understand the beliefs, values, customs and rituals of the countries in which a product is being marketed in order to alter or reformulate the product to appeal to local needs and tastes, and reformulate the **promotional message** to be intelligible and attractive to other cultures.

**4.2** There are two ways of looking at cross-cultural marketing.

(a) **Localised marketing strategy** stresses the diversity and uniqueness of consumers in different national cultures.

(b) **Global marketing strategy** stresses the similarity and shared nature of consumers worldwide.

**4.3** The marketer will be interested in the extent of the cultural differences between two countries with regard to the following.

| | **Potential problems** |
|---|---|
| (a) **Language** | A promotional theme may not be intelligible – or properly translatable – whether in words or symbols. |
| (b) **Needs and wants** | The benefits sought from a product in one country may be different in another. |
| (c) **Consumption patterns** | One country may not use a product as much as another (affecting product viability), or may use it in very different ways (affecting product positioning). |
| (d) **Market segments** | One country may have different demographic, geographical, socio-cultural and psychological groupings to another. |

(e) **Socio economic** — Consumers in one country may have different disposable income factors and/or decision-making roles from those in another.

(f) **Marketing conditions** — Differences in retail, distribution and communication systems, promotional regulation/legislation, trade restrictions etc may affect the potential for research, promotion and distribution in other countries.

**4.4** A **failure to understand cultural differences** may cause problems with each of the elements of the marketing mix.

(a) **The product**. Nestlé coffee, Camay soap and a host of similar products are marketed internationally – with different names, flavours, aromas, and other characteristics. Coffee is preferred very strong, dark and in ground form in Continental Europe – but weaker, milder and instant in the USA.

(b) **Promotion**. Customs, symbols and language do not always travel well. 'Come alive with Pepsi' was translated as 'Pepsi brings your dead ancestors back to life' in one Far Eastern country.

(c) **Price**. Large package sizes may not be marketable in countries where average income is low, because of the cash outlay required.

(d) **Place**. Distribution tastes may vary. Supermarkets are very popular in some countries, while others prefer intimate personal stores for groceries and other foodstuffs. Newly-opening markets such as Eastern Europe exhibit poor distribution systems and very low salesperson effort and productivity – compared to Japan, say, which rates very highly.

(e) **People**. There are differing attitudes to personal service in some countries. Clearly different countries have different service cultures.

(f) **Processes**. A good example of the cultural influence on processes in some industries is the religious requirements regarding slaughtering and cooking of halal and kosher food.

(g) **Physical evidence**. In service industries such as hotels, physical evidence is of the 'essence'. Different people have different expectations as to requirements for comfort.

**4.5** International business activities introduce new products, services and ways of doing business. Some cultures will resist this if no attempt is made to understand the cross-cultural dimensions of global marketing. Consideration has to be given to understanding the impact of the firm's activities. See Chapter 6 for more on this.

**4.6** International marketers need to analyse the different elements of culture in order to develop an effective strategy. They need to think about the following.

- Customer needs and motivations
- Buyer behaviour
- Cultural values relevant to the product
- Decision making in the target market
- Appropriate promotion methods
- Appropriate distribution channels

## Marketing at Work

- The Japanese culture is seen as a difficult one to export to because Japanese people often automatically regard foreign goods as inferior.
- The UK wine market has grown by an enormous amount. UK consumers are prepared to experiment with products from different countries, and the UK supermarkets have taken a large share of the market. The French wine industry has lost UK market share to competitors from Australia, New Zealand, Bulgaria, South America and South Africa.

---

**4.7** The growth of the **service sector**, and the marketing of services, is affected by culture. Services such as travel, culture and health and fitness are becoming status symbols in many European consumer groups. Culture probably affects service products more than goods, and so the marketing of such services has to be aware of regional differences.

## Cultural convergence and divergence

**4.8** For certain product groups, where social exposure is important, and to the social classes where **status** is also important, the acquisition and adoption of an international **lifestyle** has led to international products such as *Walkman* and *Coke*. Two groups seem to be most affected.

- **Young people**, who have an above average need for social acceptance
- **International travellers**, who are exposed to multicultural values

**4.9** This **convergence** process has led to the idea of global products that have an appeal worldwide with little or no modification.

**4.10** In an earlier chapter, we described the globalisation process. To what extent does it apply to culture?

(a) Some products and **brands** are of international appeal, such as those mentioned above: Sony Walkman, Coca-Cola, and so forth.

(b) There has been a revolution in **communications** with radio, television, and now the Internet. Many of these carry American programmes.

(c) There is an argument that a **youth culture** has developed, susceptible to the use of particular brands. After all, many of the key experiences of youth (such as education) are similar across many countries. However the existence of shared tastes among the affluent countries in the west should not be taken to apply globally.

(d) The rise in **nationalism** and religious **fundamentalism** cast doubt on a 'global' culture.

**4.11** In practice, is there such a person as the global consumer? Or even a Euro-consumer? This will only happen where **cultures converge**. We cite the example of wine drinking in the UK.

## Marketing at Work

The establishment of Vinopolis, a 'City of Wine', is just the latest stage in the transformation of British wine-drinking from a hobby pursued by cognoscenti to a mass pursuit. Back in the 1960s, Oxbridge colleges and gentlemen's clubs cultivated fine cellars, but most people stuck firmly to their beer. In the past 30 years, however, wine consumption has soared by over 450%, while it has merely doubled in America and has actually fallen by 50% in France. In 1966 British wine consumption was only about 2% of France's; now the British market is about 25% the size of the French.

As the market has expanded, so the retail trade has been transformed. Specialist off-licences, such as *Victoria Wine* or *Thresher*, each now have around 1,500 stores across the country. But in the past decade, the real story has been the rise of the supermarkets. Safeway, which stocks over 500 wines, claims that seven out of every ten bottles of wine is sold in a supermarket compared with less than four ten years ago.

From *The Economist*

## Self reference

**4.12** Another problem is **self reference**, in other words the tendency to interpret something according to one's own values and experience, rather than on its own terms. It is pointless getting upset about practices which are 'the norms' in the overseas market.

**4.13** To avoid misinterpreting other people in the light of one's own assumptions, some firms analyse their products and promotional messages specifically for their cultural connotations, and how the product relates to them.

## Exam Tip

Convergence and divergence came up in an old syllabus paper, in which candidates were asked to comment whether culture was a 'thing of the past'.

Clearly the answer must be no – even though certain cultural traits might easily cross national boundaries – as a result of industrial development and communications – from culture to culture. Furthermore, some 'cultures' are actively being revived. Welsh is spoken by more people now than a few decades ago and is a language of instruction in schools.

Clearly, 'culture' will never go away – although different cultures might develop and segmentation opportunities will emerge across national boundaries.

# 5 Motivation and buyer behaviour

5.1 Whilst we have examined the effect that culture has on the marketing mix, it might be worth examining in a little more detail why this should be so, with reference to **motivation** and **buyer behaviour**.

**Key Concept**

**Buyer behaviour** is the process a buyer goes through and the weight given to various factors in arriving at a decision to purchase a product.

## Motivation

5.2 We experience a need (eg for water) which motivates us to act (eg drink). Some writers, like Abraham Maslow (*Motivation and Personality,* 1987), believe that all motivation is the result of a desire to satisfy one of several needs. He devised a **hierarchy of needs**. These are outlined below. You will have encountered these before.

- Physiological
- Safety
- Love/social
- Esteem
- Self-actualisation
- Freedom of enquiry and expression
- Knowledge and understanding needs

5.3 The 'ethnocentricity' of Maslow's hierarchy has been noted. It works, possibly, for people in the US, but does not translate well into other cultures.

5.4 However, it is a useful **model** of the sort of needs people might have. Cultural factors in a society influence a number of the needs Maslow identifies.

(a) **Physiological needs** are likely to be powerful in societies where people are poor or where extended families and kinship networks place special demands on the working individual's role as **provider**.

(b) **Safety needs** are powerful in particular social contexts.

(i) For example, the practice of lifetime employment in some Japanese companies began after World War II. Safety was promised as a 'job for life' in return for dedication to work. Economic factors are now taking their toll on this concept and the 'job for life' can not now be guaranteed.

(ii) Just as importantly, perception of 'safety' and 'risk' differ. Some societies have a variety of different attitudes to 'food' and 'health' and the risk of infection, which can have an important effect on the desirability of health products.

(c) Satisfaction of **esteem needs**

- The visible trappings of success
- The respect of the group

(d) **Self-actualisation**, the fulfilment of personal potential may not be seen as a 'need' in some societies, especially those where the success of the 'group' and conformance to its demands is the dominant value system. 'Self-actualisation' implies an individualist philosophy not always present in many cultures.

**5.5** Finally, the same product will satisfy different consumer needs in different countries.

# 6 Consumer buyer behaviour

**6.1** It is worth emphasising that buyer behaviour is influenced by a number of factors, not only motivational issues. Here are some examples.

(a) Who takes **major purchase decisions**? The husband or wife? Or are they reached by group discussion, as might be the case in an extended family? Do people defer to the elders in their family? Is individualism or collectivism the cultural orientation?

(b) What is the **overall buying power** of an individual in a buying situation?

(c) What is the **retailing structure** (eg large out of town supermarkets encourage stocking up once a week)? To what extent is the population urban or suburban?

## Marketing at Work

Consumers in India are acutely price sensitive. They will think nothing of spending an entire morning scouting around to save five rupees. As a result India has the largest 'used goods' market in the world. Most washing machines in the Punjab are used to churn butter, and the average washing machine (conventionally deployed) is over 19 years old.

'What many foreign investors don't understand is that the Indian consumer is not choosing between buying one soft drink and another; he's choosing between buying a soft drink or a packet of biscuits or a disposable razor,' says Suhel Seth of Equus Red Cell, an advertising company.

What this means for foreign investors is that they must price cheaply and therefore source almost everything locally, to keep costs down.

There are other problems. Standard refrigeration becomes pretty useless when acute power shortages occur. Most consumable goods perish quickly in the climate. And the country's fragmented regional culture means that advertisers have to focus on common ground (such as music, Bollywood and cricket).

Is it worth the effort? Investors say that overcoming such obstacles has equipped them for success in any market in the world.

Adapted from the *Financial Times*, April 2002

**6.2** We can see that culture is an important variable in the purchase decision.

(a) Culture can render certain products **unacceptable** in the first place (eg advertising pork or beef in countries where there are taboos against eating pigs or cows).

(b) Culture can also bias a person's **perception** of information.

6.3 Usunier cites **institutions**, social **conventions**, **habits** and **customs** as relevant to buyer behaviour. He gives the example of **eating**. Cultures differ in the following ways.

- The number of meals consumed in a day
- The duration of meal times
- The composition of the meal (cooking style, portion size)
- The extent to which a meal is just a 'refuelling' stop or a family/social event
- Is the food prepared with basic ingredients or is it purchased part-cooked?

6.4 'The list is endless because nothing is more essential, more universal and at the same item more accurately **defined** by culture than eating habits. Eating habits should be considered as the whole process of purchasing food and beverages, cooking, tasting and even commenting. In many countries, commercials advertising ready-made foods (canned or dried soups, for instance) faced resistance in the traditional role of the housewife, who was supposed to prepare meals from natural ingredients for her family. As a result, advertisers were obliged to include a degree of preparation by the housewife in the copy strategy.'

### Cultural change

6.5 Finally, it is as well to bear in mind that culture is not a static thing. Many governments recognise this, and some deplore 'Westernising' attitudes. In the West cultural values have changed.

6.6 A good example is attitudes to debt. Being in debt was regarded as a state to be avoided at all costs, and there were strong moral injunctions in some areas of UK society against indebtedness. This taboo has completely vanished. The financial services sector has been one of the UK's most prosperous industries.

## 7 Business and government buyer behaviour

### Decision making units

7.1 Most models of business buyer behaviour refer to the decision-making unit, in other words the group of people responsible for making the decisions whether to buy a product. We can examine some possible problems below.

(a) **Authority and delegation**. In some organisations, individuals have clearly defined areas of authority and decision-making power. However in some cultures, decisions have to be referred upwards to more senior figures, so the person doing the negotiating may not have the right to make the decision.

(b) **Clarity of authority**. In some cultures, managerial decision making is taken by consensus. The problem is to manipulate this consensus on your behalf. The way in which decisions are taken or can be overridden can be a significant problem.

(c) **The decision process**. Does the DMU judge proposals according to the 'rational model'? In other words, are a number of alternatives evaluated in the cold light of day, or do other 'political' considerations intrude? If the firm is part of a network of other firms, it might be under pressure to buy from a group company.

## 'Doing business'

**7.2** A factor which has an impact on organisations engaging in international industrial marketing is the **management culture**. This comprises the views about managing held by managers, their shared educational experiences, and the 'way business is done'. Obviously, this reflects wider cultural differences between countries, but national cultures can sometimes be subordinated to the corporate culture of the organisation.

**7.3** A 'world leadership survey' conducted by the *Harvard Business Review* asked a variety of questions to managers in different countries. Managers in different countries do not seem to have the same priorities when it comes to business issues. When asked what they thought were the three most important factors in organisational success, these were listed as follows, in order of priority.

- Japan: product development, management, product quality
- Germany: workforce skills, problem solving, management
- USA: customer service, product quality, technology

**7.4** The existence of these different systems of priorities and ways of doing business affects the **competitive environment, international marketing** and the **success of joint ventures** which can be damaged by communication problems.

## Negotiation

**7.5** Cultural differences might affect buying behaviour, especially during negotiations.

(a) How do you establish the salesperson's **credibility**? Many cultural preconceptions can underline the difficulties of assessing which person to believe. For example, frankness is to be avoided in some cultures (if it means someone else is losing face).

(b) Is the **style of negotiation** communicative or manipulative? In other words, do you want to **exchange facts** or **manipulate the other party**?

(c) To what extent are **oral agreements** the basis for business, and to what extent are contracts or written agreements preferred?

## Government buyer behaviour

**7.6** In many countries, government is the biggest buyer and will be responsible for buying a wide range of goods and services. The way government buys is influenced by the extent to which public accountability for expenditure is deemed to be important – so a cultural history of **public service and accountability** is critical.

**7.7** The usual forms of buying procedure are the **open tender** and the **selective tender**. For a selective tender process, the firm needs to be accepted on the appropriate list. In some countries, it takes considerable persistence to get to that stage, since it may take several visits to appropriate government officials to establish a good working relationship.

**7.8** In the EU, most public procurement contracts should be open to any competitor throughout the European Union – and the bidding will normally be to an open tender.

### *Social and cultural factors*

**7.9** It is generally true that in dealing with governments and government departments, the significance lies, perhaps, with **who you know** rather than with **what you know**. The right political contacts are often essential.

**7.10** It is also true that buying decisions may be affected as much by a lowly departmental clerk acting as a gatekeeper in a Decision Making Unit (DMU), as by a senior government official or even a politician acting as a **decision maker** or an **influencer** in the DMU. A clerk in a regional office can make life very difficult, despite support at the centre.

**7.11** A clear understanding of the cultural inter-relationships in **government circles**, hierarchical **relationships** and **political influence** may be critical in some markets and countries.

(a) For example, a **different style** is necessary for dealing with officials from high context cultures than from low context cultures.

(b) Officials may have formal **authority**, but little actual **power**.

(c) Firms suffer if **relationships** between the domestic government and the host country government deteriorate.

(d) Different cultures have different attitudes to **gifts**.

(e) Some cultures prefer a high degree of **legalism**, others do not.

(f) There may be **conflict** between different government departments.

(g) Governments are susceptible to pressure from powerful **interest groups** at home.

# 8 Buyer behaviour in other sectors

**8.1** There are many similarities between buyer behaviour for products and services, but there are important differences.

- Attitudes
- Needs and motives
- Purchase behaviour

**8.2** The **personal elements involved in services** can be key to a customer's decision. Customers are more likely to be dissatisfied with service purchases, because services are often seen as more personal than goods. An unfriendly stewardess on an international flight will affect customer perception of the entire service.

**8.3** Consumers are more likely to be influenced by friends, family and colleagues when purchasing a service. **Word-of-mouth promotion** is therefore frequently relied upon and should be targeted by international marketers.

### Commodity, semi-processed and not-for-profit

**8.4** In commodity, semi-processed products and not-for-profit sectors buyers will display a mix of motives in a range of buying situations. To use the framework outlined in paragraph 8.1 we may be able to say the following. It is not an exhaustive presentation of the issues involved. See if you can think of further examples.

| | Buyer attitudes | Needs and motives | Purchase behaviour |
|---|---|---|---|
| **Commodity** ie raw materials; agricultural products | Goods to be bought in bulk, often from lesser developed (ie primarily agricultural) economies. Prices may vary with season and availability | For example, providing the food for population of the buyer's country. Needs could be satisfied by any one of a number of suppliers | Based upon quality considerations and availability of proper distribution facilities from the point of production. End consumers not involved |
| **Semi-processed** eg picked and frozen fruit for use in jam, yoghurts or pies | Companies may have habitual suppliers and will look to them to provide goods at reasonable price. Price may be subject to availability and seasonality | Quality product required that complies with necessary regulations and can add value ie be converted to final product at a profit. Transport important | Fruit or other products examined for quality, price compared with other suppliers. Contracts may be struck on basis of previous dealings. End consumers not involved |
| **Not-for-profit** eg charities, arts organisations, social services | Might expect some form of recognition of a charity donation; expect to enjoy output of arts/leisure organisations; vulnerable members of society need 'help' from social services. Buyers will want to know that organisation's resources are not being wasted | 'Humanitarian'; leisure time and recreation, basic needs eg for food and shelter, education or protection | Recommendation of friends and colleagues; emotional reaction to charity appeal; 'nowhere else to turn'. End consumer is usually involved |

## Charity and not-for-profit marketing

8.5 Although most people would 'know one if they saw it', there is a surprising problem in clearly delimiting what counts as a **not-for-profit (NFP) organisation**. Local authority services, for example, would not be marketing in order to arrive at a profit for shareholders, but nowadays they are being increasingly required to apply the same disciplines and processes as companies which are oriented towards straightforward profit goals.

## Marketing at Work

Oxfam operates more shops than any commercial organisation in Britain, and these operate at a profit. The Royal Society for the Protection of Birds operates a mail order trading company which provides a 25% return on capital, operating very profitably and effectively.

---

**8.6** Bois suggests that we define NFP enterprises by recognising that their first objective is to be **'non-loss' operations** in order to cover their costs, that profits are only made as a means to an end (eg providing a service, or accomplishing some socially or morally worthy objective).

## Key Concept

Bois proposes that a **not-for profit organisation** be defined as:' ... an organisation whose attainment of its prime goal is not assessed by economic measures. However, in pursuit of that goal it may undertake profit-making activities.'

This may involve a number of different kinds of organisation with, for example, differing legal status – charities, statutory bodies offering public transport or the provision of services such as leisure, health or public utilities such as water or road maintenance.

---

**8.7** **Marketing management** is now recognised as equally valuable to profit orientated and NFP organisations. The tasks of marketing auditing, setting objectives, developing strategies and marketing mixes and controls for their implementation can all help in improving the performance of charities and NFP organisations. Whilst the basic principles are appropriate for this sector, differences in how they can be applied should not be forgotten. Dibb *et al* (*Marketing Concepts and* Strategies, 2000) suggest that four key differences exist, related to **objectives**, **target markets** (and hence buyer behaviour), **marketing mixes** and **controlling marketing activities**.

## Objectives

**8.8** Objectives will not be based on profit achievement but rather on achieving a **particular response** from various target markets. This has implications for reporting of results. The organisation will need to be open and honest in showing how it has managed its budget and allocated funds raised. **Efficiency and effectiveness** are particularly important in the use of donated funds.

## Action Programme 2

List possible objectives for NFP and charitable organisations.

---

**8.9** The concept of target marketing is different in the not-for-profit sector. There are no buyers but rather a number of different **audiences**. A target public is a group of individuals who have an interest or concern about the charity. Those benefiting from the organisation's activities are known as the **client public**. Relationships are also vital with **donors and volunteers** from the general public. In addition, there may also be a need to lobby local and national government and businesses for support.

## Marketing mix issues

**8.10** Charities and NFP organisations often deal more with **services and ideas** than products. In this sense the extended marketing mix of people, process and physical evidence is important.

(a) **Appearance** needs to be business-like rather than appearing extravagant.

(b) **Process** is increasingly important, for example, the use of direct debit to pay for council tax, reduces administration costs leaving more budget for community services.

(c) **People** need to offer good service and be caring in their dealings with their clients.

(d) **Distribution channels** are often shorter with fewer intermediaries than in the profit making sector. Wholesalers and distributors available to a business organisations do not exist in most non-business contexts.

(e) **Promotion is usually dominated by personal selling**. Advertising is often limited to public service announcements due to limited budgets. Direct marketing is growing due to the ease of developing databases. Sponsorship, competitions and special events are also widely used.

(f) **Pricing** is probably the most different element in this sector. Financial price is often not a relevant concept. Rather, opportunity cost, where an individual is persuaded of the value of donating time or funds, is more relevant.

**8.11** Controlling activities is complicated by the difficulty of judging whether **non-quantitative objectives** have been met. For example assessing whether the charity has improved the situation of client publics is difficult to research. Statistics related to product mix, financial resources, size of budgets, number of employees, number of volunteers, number of customers serviced and number and location of facilities, are all useful for this task.

# 9 Culture and the organisation

## The Hofstede model of national cultures

**9.1** A model was developed in 1980 by Professor Geert Hofstede (*Cultures and Organisations)* in order to explain national differences by identifying 'key dimensions' which represent the essential 'programmes' forming a common culture in the value systems of all countries. Each country is represented on a scale for each dimension so as to explain and understand values, attitudes and behaviour.

**9.2** In particular, Hofstede pointed out that countries differ on the following dimensions.

(a) **Power distance**. This dimension measures how far superiors are expected to exercise power. In a high power-distance culture, the boss decides and people do not question.

(b) **Uncertainty avoidance**. Some cultures prefer clarity and order, whereas others are prepared to accept novelty. This affects the willingness of people to **change** rules, rather than simply obey them.

(c) **Individualism/collectivism**. In some countries individual achievement is what matters. A collectivist culture (eg people are supported – and controlled – by extended families) puts the interests of the group first.

(d) **'Masculinity'/'Femininity'**. In 'masculine' cultures, the roles of the sexes are clearly differentiated. In 'feminine' ones they are not. 'Masculine' cultures place greater emphasis on possessions, status, and display as opposed to quality of life and care for the environment.

**9.3** Hofstede grouped countries into eight 'clusters'.

| Group | | Power-distance | Uncertainty avoidance | Individual-ism | 'Masculinity' |
|---|---|---|---|---|---|
| I | 'More developed Latin' (eg Belgium, France, Argentina, Brazil, Spain) | High | High | Medium to high | Medium |
| II | 'Less developed Latin' (eg Portugal, Mexico, Peru) | High | High | Low | Whole range |
| III | 'More developed Asian' (eg Japan) | Medium | High | Medium | High |
| IV | 'Less developed Asian' (eg India, Taiwan, Thailand) | High | Low to medium | Low | Medium |
| V | Near Eastern (eg Greece, Iran, Turkey) | High | High | Low | Medium |
| VI | 'Germanic' (eg Germany) | Low | Medium to high | Medium | Medium to high |
| VII | Anglo (eg UK, US, Australia) | Low to medium | Low to medium | High | High |
| VIII | Nordic (eg Scandinavia, the Netherlands) | Low | Low to medium | Medium to high | Low |

**9.4** There are dangers in using these models. In the management of individual businesses, other factors may be more important.

(a) **Type of industry**: people working in information technology from two countries might have more in common with each other than they might with people working in a different industry.

(b) **Size of company**. Some people may be accustomed to working in a bureaucracy.

## Chapter Roundup

- **Culture** is the complex body of shared beliefs, artefacts and behaviour patterns to which people are exposed in social conditioning.
- Cultures are exemplified in language, religions, customs, value systems, education, law and aesthetics.
- A variety of **frameworks** exist to analyse culture. For example, low context cultures require messages to be clear and direct. High context cultures place more emphasis on body language, and messages are not always explicit.
- Some cultures will resist new products of services if no attempt is made to understand **cross-cultural factors**.
- Culture can be an influence on **buyer behaviour**, but it should be noted that relatively simple models of motivation, such as Maslow's, do not always apply.
- Different types of buyer display different attitudes, needs and purchasing behaviour.
- Different cultures have different ways of doing business and means that people from different cultures have different expectations of a meeting, for example.
- Cultural issues need also to be considered in **organisational terms** to ensure common organisational loyalties.

## Quick Quiz

1. Define culture.
2. Distinguish between high context and low context cultures.
3. What are the two ways of looking at cross-cultural marketing?
4. To what extent has there been a 'globalisation' of culture?
5. Why might a culture resist 'cook-chilled' foods?
6. What are the usual buying procedures of governments subject to public accountability?
7. Where are there differences in buyer behaviour for services as opposed to products?
8. What are the four dimensions of Hofstede's analysis of national cultures?

## Answers to Quick Quiz

1. Learned beliefs, values, customs, artefacts and rituals.
2. In low context cultures, messages have explicit meanings; in high context cultures, meaning depends on context.
3. It is possible to stress either cultural diversity or the similarities between consumers worldwide.
4. This is a matter of opinion – and context.
5. Perhaps if careful preparation of food were an important ritual, significant for family bonding.
6. Open tender and selective tender.

7 In attitudes, needs and motives and in behaviour at the time of purchase.

8 Power distance; uncertainty avoidance; individualism and 'masculinity'.

## Action Programme Review

1 (a) Low-context. Get down to business; security is achieved by a precisely detailed contract.

(b) High context. Establish if the other person is someone one can do business with; security is in the relationship.

2 Possible objectives include the following.

- Surplus maximisation (equivalent to profit maximisation)
- Revenue maximisation (as for a commercial business)
- Usage maximisation (as in leisure centre swimming pool usage)
- Usage targeting (matching the capacity available as in the NHS)
- Full/partial cost recovery (minimising subsidy)
- Budget maximisation (maximising what is offered)
- Producer satisfaction maximisation (satisfying the wants of staff and volunteers)
- Client satisfaction maximisation (the police generating the support of the public)

**Now try Question 9 at the end of the Study Text**

# International Marketing Research

| Chapter Topic List | |
|---|---|
| 1 | Setting the scene |
| 2 | Strategic Intelligence and the MkIS |
| 3 | The role of international marketing research (IMR) |
| 4 | Data sources |
| 5 | The IMR process |
| 6 | The uses of IMR data |
| 7 | Some problems in IMR |
| 8 | Managing the research effort |

## Syllabus Content

- Identification of challenges in collecting and interpreting information on foreign markets
- Processes, techniques and factors used in assessing the attractiveness of international markets
- Definition of the organisation's intelligence needs, research needs and resources required to support an analysis of the external environment

## Key Concepts Introduced

- Strategic intelligence
- Marketing information system
- Marketing research
- Secondary data
- Primary data
- Field research
- Desk research
- Segmentation

# 1 Setting the scene

1.1 Whilst the principle of marketing research remains the same for international markets as for domestic markets, **international marketing research (IMR)** is often different in practice from research in the domestic market, not least because of **sources** (Section 3). Not only are countries different from each other, but there are the major problems of distance and the quality of data to contend with.

1.2 The purpose of IMR is to identify **suitable countries for entry** (section 6), or suitable groups of countries whose populations segment in a way that can be met by a similar marketing mix.

1.3 Much **secondary data** is poor (Section 7), and the company is even more 'in the dark' about what is going on than they might otherwise suppose. There is greater reliance on human as opposed to documentary sources. Even **primary data** has to be used with care.

1.4 The **organisation of the IMR function** (centralised at head office or decentralised) is analogous to most organisational problems in international marketing.

# 2 Strategic intelligence and the MkIS

2.1 In Chapter 1, we identified the **dual role of marketing** as an input to the corporate planning process and as a distinct function in its own right. This also applies to **information gathering**.

**Key Concept**

**Strategic intelligence** according to Donald Marchand (*Information Orientation,* 2002), can be defined as 'what a company needs to know about its business environment to enable it to anticipate change and design appropriate strategies that will create business value for customers and be profitable in new markets and new industries in the future'. Not only must the firm anticipate the future, but it must have the capability to react to it.

2.2 Each function of the organisation collects information relevant to it, without any wider corporate viewpoint.

- The marketing department identifies customer needs.
- The R&D department identifies new technology.
- The production department suggests process innovation.

**2.3 A model of the process of creating strategic intelligence**

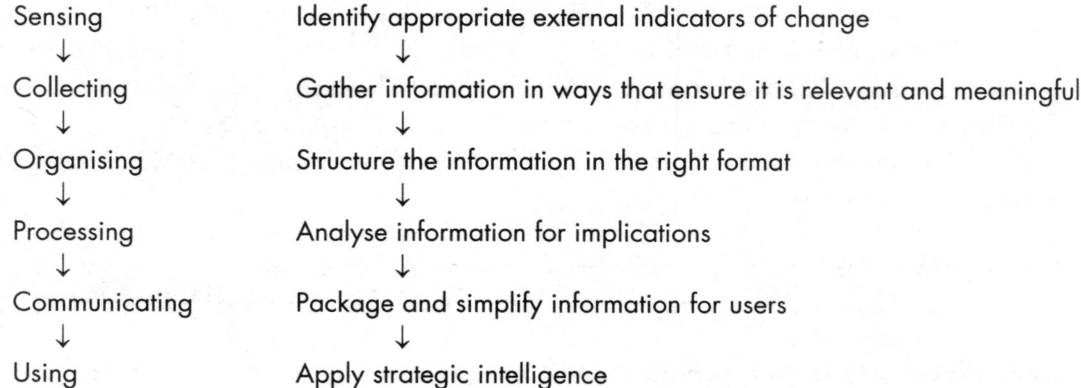


**2.4** A source of strategic intelligence is the MkIS.

**Key Concept**

A **marketing information system** (MkIS) consists of people, equipment and procedures to gather, sort, analyse, evaluate, and distribute needed, timely and accurate information to marketing decision makers.

**2.5 The marketing information system**

*The marketing information system*

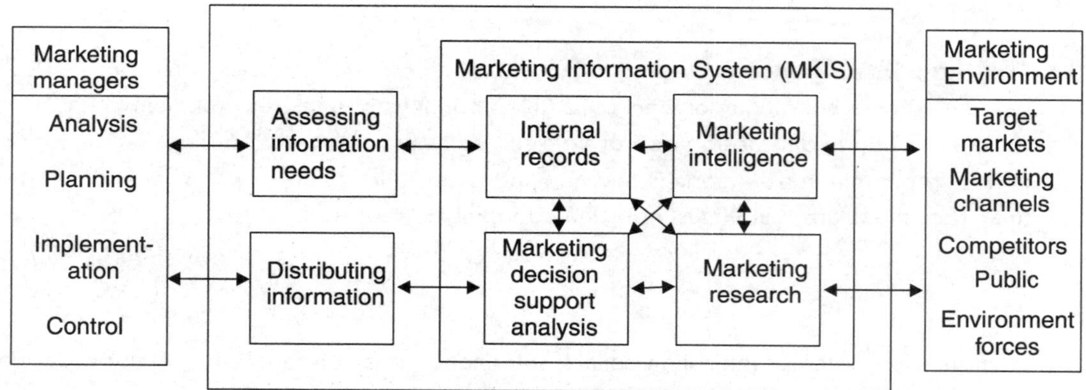


Source: Kotler, *Marketing Management analysis, Planning, Implementation and Control*

(a) **Internal records system**

This includes reports of orders, sales, dispatches, accounts payable and receivable etc which provide a store of historical customer data.

(b) **Marketing intelligence system**

This is the term used for information gathered on the market place by managers on a day-to-day basis. It is derived from **continual monitoring** of the environment to alert managers to new trends.

(c) **Marketing decision support system**

Firms can use regression and correlation analysis, sales forecasting, time series analysis, product design and site selection models.

(d) **Marketing research system**

Marketing research aids management decision making by providing specified information in time for it to be of value.

# 3 The role of international marketing research (IMR)

**Exam Tip**

*Research and the underlying problems involved in researching international markets appears in the exam quite regularly in one form or another. It featured in an old syllabus mini-case where candidates had to advise an American firm on a research programme to help it plan its entry into Continental Europe. You could have used the opportunity to develop an MkIS for the company. Primary research relates to buyers and their attitudes: perhaps buyer behaviour in Europe is different from buyer behaviour in the US. The 12 Cs approach (see paragraph 5.8) would have helped you to identify information needs. Research has also featured in a short question about emerging markets.*

## Reasons for international marketing research

**Key Concepts**

**Marketing research** is the objective gathering, recording and analysing of all facts about problems relating to the transfer and sales of goods and services from producer to consumer or user. It includes market research, price research etc.

Marketing research involves the use of **secondary data** (eg government surveys) in **desk research**, as well as **field research** (which the firm undertakes itself) to acquire **primary data**, maybe by questionnaire.

**3.1** The vast majority of UK companies export less than 10% of their total turnover. They therefore place little priority on what they see as costly market **intelligence gathering** for a minor activity. Where any intelligence is gathered it is usually through intermediaries rather than gleaned directly. However, there are a number of reasons why a company which is seriously intent on international trade should consider devoting more effort to intelligence gathering. If only a few small or medium-sized enterprises made greater commitment to exporting, the impact on national finances could be significant.

**3.2** The most important requirement of effective international marketing is thorough **market analysis**, both before entering the market and also once the market has been entered, in order to maintain continuous awareness of opportunities, threats and trends.

## Marketing at Work

**Wal-Mart in Japan**

*Wal-Mart* buys in such huge volumes and its logistics are so efficient that it can sell much more cheaply then other retailers. However, its low price policy is unsuited to Japan where shoppers expect low price to mean low quality. Wal-Mart has also had problems with Japan's complex and expensive distribution system and, after four years spent studying the market, concluded it needed a partner. It now owns 37% of Seiyn, Japan's fifth largest supermarket chain.

---

**3.3** Specific objectives of international marketing research include the following.

- Identify attractive **new markets**
- Enhance profitability by pinpointing **opportunities and threats**
- Facilitate awareness of **general market trends**
- Monitor changes in **customer needs and preferences**
- Knowledge of **competitor plans and strategies**
- Monitor **political, legal, economic, social** and **technological** trends

**3.4** It is obvious that international marketing research is more complex than domestic marketing research because of its focus on more than one country. It requires additional efforts to overcome a **lack of empathy** with a market and the 'foreign-factor' in general. Thus there is a need to gather information about foreign customer preferences, languages, customs, beliefs etc which in a domestic market could be assumed to be largely known and understood.

## Differing IMR objectives of established and new international marketers

**3.5** To a company whose horizons have so far been limited to its domestic market, all international marketing research is a new activity. Since it has no experience in foreign markets it needs **information** to take fundamental decisions. These may be summarised as four questions.

(a) **Should the company look to foreign markets at all?** This will involve an assessment of overseas market demand and the firm's potential share in it compared to domestic opportunities.

(b) **Which market(s) should it enter?** Potential foreign markets need to be ranked according to size, competition, investment and risk.

(c) **How should the company enter the selected markets?** Detailed analysis is required of market size, international trade barriers, transport systems and costs, local competition, government regulations and political stability.

(d) **What marketing programme is best suited to the selected market?** For each selected market a detailed knowledge of buyer behaviour, competitive practices, distribution channels, promotional methods and media will be required.

## Doing research

3.6 In considering researching foreign markets, a firm has a number of options.

- Do **no research** at all
- Use **feedback** and assistance from the distribution channel
- Employ an **international research agency**
- Conduct the research **'in-house'**

3.7 There are a number of criteria that will have a bearing on the decision.

- The company's **resources**
- The company's **experience** in international trade
- The **amount of foreign trade** as a proportion of turnover
- The degree to which the foreign trade is **ongoing**

If the answer to all the above questions is 'very little' then it is probably best that the company puts little of its own resources into researching the market, since the return on investment is likely to be poor.

### *The small company entering a foreign market for the first time*

3.8 Many small firms do not carry out any market research at all. There are a variety of reasons.

(a) Small firms generally use **indirect means** of exporting, and hence tend to rely on the channel intermediary for market intelligence.

(b) They often lack the available **resources** to devote to IMR.

(c) The **amount of foreign business** does not warrant significant expenditure on market research.

3.9 The lack of market knowledge, and reliance on the expertise of an intermediary, will limit the ability of the company to expand. For this reason most countries, including the UK, have **sources of low cost advice** and assistance targeted at the small business to encourage the company to develop and expand international trading operations.

### *The medium sized company wishing to extend its export business*

3.10 A company in this situation will be faced with problems of finding new markets, representation, and distribution. There are several options.

- Use **existing channels of distribution** to obtain intelligence
- Use available **assistance and advice services**
- Engage an **IMR agency**

### *The larger company with overseas presence wishing to increase its foreign market operations*

3.11 Larger companies

- Tend to be exporting on a **regular basis**
- Gain between **10% to 30% turnover** from export operations
- Have some **'in house' expertise**, usually in the form of an export department

### *Major multinationals introducing new products*

**3.12** The multinational corporation generally tries to introduce products that have a global appeal. Generally such products will be either made under contract, licensed, or made by a subsidiary. Local presence means that the multinational can call upon the expert resources of its own employees in that market. All the IMR activities are usually conducted 'in house'.

**Exam Tip**

*The draft Specimen Paper included a question that required you to consider what market research should be undertaken before entry to a new foreign market.*

# 4 Data sources

## Human sources

**4.1** **Human sources** provide the largest source of information to international marketers.

**4.2** For well established international marketing companies, the principal human information source is the **managers** of subsidiaries, branches and associates abroad. Not only do they live in the foreign cultural environments but they also appreciate the company's business objectives.

- They can distinguish relevant from irrelevant information
- They can use **personal contacts** to acquire unpublished information

**4.3** Managerial colleagues do not represent the sole source of human information. **Consumers**, **customers**, **distributors**, **suppliers** and even **competitors** are all important sources of information. These groups are particularly valuable in providing marketing assessments from their own particular standpoint. Collectively they may give a balanced view of a market, its potential and its problems.

**4.4** Friends, acquaintances, consultants and professional colleagues can provide 'headquarters' marketing managers with information that is reliable and objective.

## Documentary sources

**4.5** **Documentary sources** are compiled without any knowledge of the reader or the precise purposes for which the information is required.

**4.6** The biggest problem in using documentary sources is that there are simply so many of them, whilst none may **specifically address** the point of interest. For example, a marketing manager interested in selling shoe laces in India is unlikely to find written material on such a market, but may have access to numerous pieces on India and on the shoe trade. Without other information sources it would be dangerous to conclude that because say, ninety per cent of the population wore shoes there must be a large market for shoe laces. (The norm may be to wear sandals!)

## Direct sources

**4.7** Direct sources are those from which the marketing manager derives information without any intermediate analysis that could reduce its levels of accuracy and relevance. There are three general types.

(a) **Direct observation and specialist knowledge**. For example, in a tour around a plastics factory the marketing manager might be shown a new lightweight durable plastic. He knows that a persistent problem with his kitchen appliances has been that they are too heavy to be carried easily, and sees in the plastic a product that might reduce the weight of some of the motor's metal components without losing durability.

(b) **Direct observation and background information**. For example, an international marketing manager based in the UK may have heard of the French hypermarket, and received written reports about them, but only by visiting one can he properly appreciate the ambience they offer to the customer.

(c) **Personal experience supporting indirect information**. For example, a marketing manager considering the potential of the Norwegian market for the firm's product will note from a map that Norway is a geographically dispersed country with rugged terrain. But a plane trip from Oslo to Tromso will indicate just how rugged is the terrain and drive home the point that Norway extends for over 1,500 miles from north to south. Such information should encourage particular attention to distribution plans.

## Sources of information and assistance to UK firms

**4.8** A UK company is able to obtain considerable help and advice in its attempts to research foreign markets. Contacts may be made with a variety of organisations, including the following.

- Overseas agents and distributors
- Banks
- Trade and professional organisations
- Chambers of Commerce
- Department of Trade and Industry
- UK and foreign embassies and consulates
- Academic institutions
- Business Links

**4.9** Depending on the help and advice sought there may be a charge involved but it is usually a nominal one. Financial assistance may be obtained in certain cases through the **Overseas Trade Services** under the following schemes.

- Export market research scheme
- Outward mission
- Market entry guarantee scheme
- Overseas trade fairs
- Overseas seminars
- Inward missions

## Export data services

**4.10** The **Overseas Trade Service** has export databases, library facilities and publications to enable businesses to conduct preliminary desk research, plus customised export intelligence.

- Export information
- The Export Market Information Centre (EMIC)
- Export publications
- Export intelligence
- Specialist market knowledge

4.11 **Export information**. This gives both first time and experienced exporters access to up-to-date information concerning new opportunities. The DTI maintains a collection of overseas market information. This is complemented by numerous trade publications, directories, statistical material and published market research. This information is a great help to exporters.

- Compare different markets
- Select the best market(s)
- Analyse chosen market(s)
- Understand business methods in chosen markets
- Find out about tariff and legal requirements
- Prepare for a visit
- Identify potential agents
- Keep up with new business opportunities

4.12 **Export Market Information Centre**. EMIC is a self-help research and library facility. Information available in EMIC includes foreign statistics on trade, production, prices, employment, population and transport as well as development plans of many countries which are useful guides to the current and future state of specific economies as well as highlighting specific opportunities.

4.13 **Export publications**. The DTI publishes a wide range of country and sector reports.

4.14 **Export intelligence**. Export success frequently depends on gathering timely information about possible opportunities overseas. Exporters can arrange to be kept up to date with the export intelligence from the DTI, the EU and the World Bank. Export intelligence includes selling opportunities such as enquiries from overseas buyers and agents and market information on tariff changes, forthcoming projects, aid and loan agreements.

4.15 **Specialist market knowledge**.

- The political and economic scene
- Local conditions for doing business
- Market prospects and product suitability
- Local tariffs and other import regulations
- Business contacts
- General help doing business in that market

## Specific export help

4.16 Help related to specific exporting problems is organised through a variety of services listed below.

(a) **Enterprise Initiative**: specialist consultancy advice and financial assistance in key areas.

(b) **Export Development Advisors** (EDA): identification and dissemination of good exporting practice.

(c) **Market Information Enquiry Service** (MIES): tailor-made information on the country/markets chosen.

(d) **Export Marketing Research Scheme** (EMRS): marketing research advice and financial assistance.

(e) **Export Representative Service** (ERS): advice on overseas contracts.

(f) **Overseas Status Report Service** (OSRS): information on agents and distributors.

(g) **New Products from Britain Service**: promotion of products in overseas publications.

**4.17** You may have read in the newspapers about trade deals and government promotions. Overseas promotion aided by the UK government takes a number of forms.

- **Overseas trade fairs** – provide direct contact with buyers and agents
- **Outward missions** – financial and administrative support to visit overseas markets
- **Overseas seminars** – increase overseas awareness of your goods and services
- **Overseas stores promotions** – provides a shop window for the exporter's products
- **Inward missions** – influential contacts invited from overseas
- **Projects export promotion** – co-ordinate government assistance for large projects

**4.18** For companies wishing to expand their business and find new markets, the **DTI Explorer Initiative** offers assistance by organising escorted trips to trade fairs, and helping with such things as interpreters and provision of up-to-date information.

**4.19** Before companies seeking international marketing opportunities do anything else, they should look at the **Internet**. Sites such as 'Market Explorer' can give the first taste of a potential export market, and indicate the more accessible countries.

## Action Programme 1

Why is it important for UK small businesses to consider exporting?

**4.20** Other commonly consulted sources are listed below.

(a) The **Bank of England** and the major UK banks produce booklets on trade prospects for various countries.

(b) The **broadsheet newspapers**, in particular the *Financial Times* produce periodic surveys on various countries.

(c) The **Economist Intelligence Unit** produces reports on various industries, countries and long term developments.

(d) Most **major trade associations** and Chambers of Commerce hold data on trade fairs, visits and market intelligence for various countries.

(e) There are numerous **trade directories** for overseas markets including Kompass, Dun and Bradstreet, Kluwer and Croner.

(f) The **EU** and **OECD** produce numerous reports on trade statistics and prospects for member countries.

(g) The **Department of Trade and Industry** provides many publications, statistical summaries and intelligence reports.

(h) The **CBI** produces a monthly report on foreign markets.

(i) The **Office of National Statistics** produces regular data on international trade.

- Guide to Official Statistics
- Monthly digest of statistics

- Overseas Trade statistics

(j) Many reference libraries subscribe to services including Emerald, Key Note Ltd, Mintel, Extel, and Euromonitor.

**4.21** Various **international bodies** including the United Nations, the European Union, the Organisation for Economic Co-operation and Development and the International Monetary Fund produce statistical publications on a variety of areas.

**4.22** Most of the sources surveyed here have their counterparts in other countries.

(a) Foreign **governments and international bodies** (such as the United Nations) publish reports and statistics.

(b) Foreign **trade associations** and industry bodies publish surveys. Many also have international links.

(c) **International news** and information agencies (such as Reuters) publish world-wide reports.

(d) International **newspapers and journals** are available (in print, and frequently also on the Internet).

(e) **Internet sites** give access to foreign educational and governmental institutions and their databases, and to the websites of commercial organisations around the world. Access is not restricted to working hours (which helps when there are time differences) and information can be downloaded for later translation.

## Documentation

**4.23** The **red tape** of international marketing requires that a great deal of information has to be processed by a wide range of people working in different languages with different systems. **Mistakes** in the information provided by exporters and a lack of management attention often cause problems.

- **Relationships** with overseas customers are harmed by delays
- **Orders and profits** may be reduced or lost

**4.24** **SITPRO** is an independent body which has the prime objective of simplifying and reducing the cost of international marketing. It has gained a worldwide reputation for the development and **standardisation** of international marketing procedures and documents as well as providing advice and guidance to UK traders on effective practices and information systems. Since non-tariff barriers have been reduced, the **complexity** of the export process has surfaced as a major barrier to trade.

### Exam Tip

*Information needs are a constant feature in exam questions.*

## Internet information

**4.25** The term 'information market' reflects the growing view that information is a commodity which can be bought and sold.

**4.26** **Information is a resource** that has many of the characteristics of any other resource. In particular, the growth of the **service sector** of many western economies has led to an increasing importance being attached to information.

**4.27** The amount of **information** in the world is **doubling every seven years**. One half of every thing a college student learned in his or her first year is obsolete by the time they graduate. The amount of knowledge we are asking a typical A level student to learn is more information than their grandparents absorbed in a lifetime.

**4.28** The communication super highway is **destroying old power structures**. As knowledge flows into every home on demand, it **empowers consumers**. Consumers can scan the world's data base for the best bargains. They can instantly order products from their computers. Speciality use groups will band together to apply political pressure, share their experiences, address educational problems and strategies. The Internet allows consumers to self-educate. When consumers do these things they bypass the educational system, the medical system, the publishing system and the current political system.

# 5 The IMR process

**5.1** A diagram of the process of international market research is shown below.

## Stage 1: monitoring international markets

**5.2** **Monitoring** is by far the most widespread activity in international marketing research. It involves **passive information gathering** in which the organisation has identified a particular market on which information needs to be collected but, as yet, does not warrant active measures.

**5.3** If the information that has been acquired indicates the **potential for a new market**, the manager will proceed to the next stage, investigation.

## Stage 2: investigation

### *Market opportunity*

**5.4** The most important aspect of the investigation stage is the accurate assessment of market opportunity.

(a) **Existing demand** concerns current purchases of the type of product. Often, it is this demand that originally attracted the company's management to the market during the 'monitoring phase'. The level of existing demand alone may be enough to justify entry to that market, to win a share.

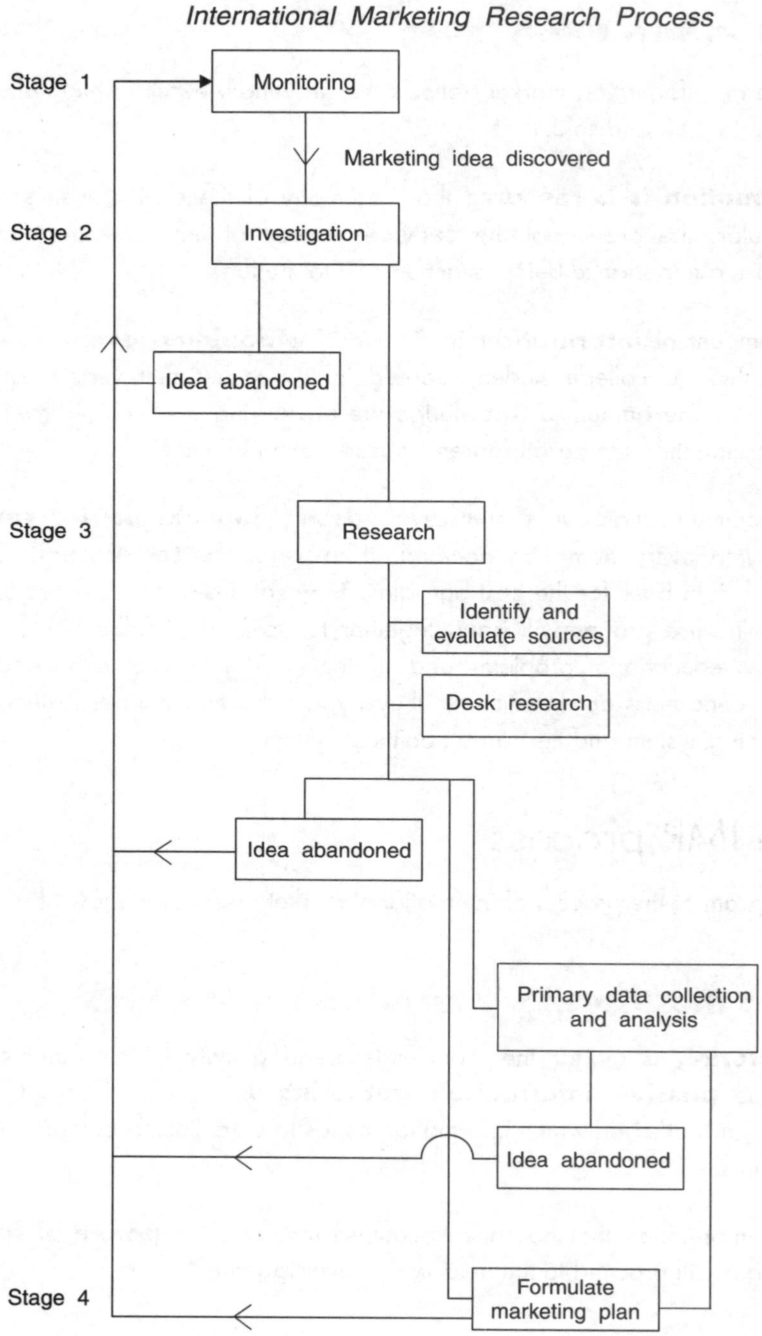

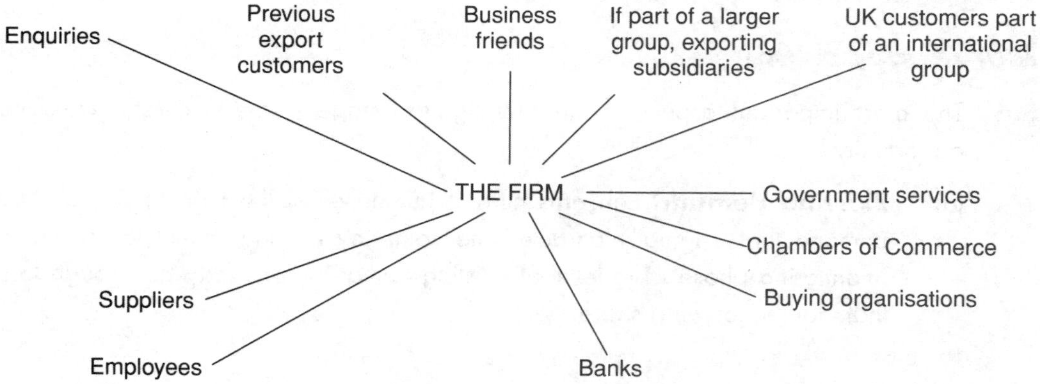

*International Marketing Research Process*





(b) **Latent demand** is demand which exists in the market but is currently **untapped** because of a defect in the marketing mix used by existing suppliers. Often it is simply a question of price but it may be that the distribution channels are not adequate or that the product does not offer features which that market particularly values.

## Marketing at Work

The success of mountain bikes depended on new product features. Although in industrially advanced economies bicycles were regarded as a product of the leisure market rather than as a means of transport, their design gave them a rather 'tame' image, perhaps a two-wheeled version of rambling! The introduction of a more rugged design and other product features (such as styling and colour) designed to appeal to the youth market opened up a whole new segment of the bike market.

---

(c) **Incipient demand** is the demand that depends on trends. It is used most often by manufacturers of goods that require wealth levels in an economy to be above a certain minimum before the volume of demand becomes sufficiently great for the market to become profitable.

**5.5** It is possible to add to these categories three different types of product.

(a) (i) **Competitive**: the product is similar to the competition.

(ii) **Improved**: the product is similar in nature to current products, but demonstrably better in some way.

(iii) **Breakthrough**: the product is completely new.

(b) These can be tracked to the assessment of demand.

(i) An **improved** product makes it easier to enter an **existing** market.

(ii) **Breakthrough** products are useful for entering existing markets, but where demand is latent or incipient, the marketing effort – to create the market – will be high.

## Stage 3: research

**5.6** By this stage of the IMR process the new marketing idea has to look sufficiently promising to be worth **committing** a significant budget to. Whereas during the investigation stage enquiries are often informal and information may be collected as part of other activities, market research proper is proactive. In the international context, this can be expensive.

## Planning

**5.7** A vital part in any research exercise is to plan it properly. Although no entirely standard plan can be drawn up, it is likely to have the following elements.

(a) **Define the scope of the project**

Identify the geographical and political market(s) of interest, the market segments and, not least, the end objective.

(b) **Define the project's information needs**

There must always be a balance struck between the use of information and the cost and difficulty of obtaining it. Posing the following questions will help in finding the correct balance.

(i) **Why** is the information needed?

(ii) If it is obtained, **how** will it be used?

(iii) **Where** may information be obtained from? Is it available directly as a secondary data source, capable of production by analysis of existing secondary data, or does it require primary data collection?

(iv) **What is the information worth** in financial terms?

(v) What is the **cost of not obtaining it**?

(c) **Evaluate the available sources for the required information**

It is no use for the international marketing manager to assume that because data are available they will necessarily be valuable! Often great caution is needed and problems in interpreting data for international marketing purposes are considered later in the chapter.

(d) **Undertake the desk research and evaluate its findings**

Desk research, using documentary sources, should always be done before conducting or commissioning any primary data collection. It is almost invariably cheaper and, if its results are disappointing, the project may be abandoned without any primary data collection being undertaken at all. Even if the project does continue, and primary data is needed, careful analysis of the secondary data can focus attention on the exact primary data requirement and so reduce the costs of the research exercise.

(e) **Undertake field research**

The collection of **primary data** is sometimes known as field research. Field research is carried out 'on the spot' in a number of areas, notably customer research, advertising research, product research, packaging research and distribution research. Techniques involved in the collection and analysis of primary data are as follows.

- Experimentation
- Sampling
- Piloting
- Observation
- Questionnaires
- Consumer panels
- Trade audits, such as retail audits
- Pre-tests
- Post-tests
- Attitude scales

(f) **Knowledge of the culture** of a society is clearly of value to business. Marketers can adapt their products and appeal according to the culture of their intended export market. Multinational companies often establish new subsidiaries in a different country. Much was made of the cultural difficulties which Nissan was supposed to encounter when investing the US and UK. Nissan had to teach its new recruits about the culture of the company.

## Marketing at Work

Both McDonalds and Kellogg's suffered setbacks when trying to penetrate the Indian market. McDonalds has had to come to terms with a market that considers killing cows to be sacrilege, is averse to pork, is 40% vegetarian, hostile to frozen meat and fish, and very fond of spices.

Kellogg's was unsuccessful in persuading Indians that its cereals were a healthier alternative to traditional heavy Indian breakfasts.

## Desk research requirements

**5.8** Phillips, Doole and Lowe (*International Marketing Strategy,* 1995) suggest a '12C' checklist for information which a marketing information system for international markets should contain. This is shown below. Desk research involves work in two main areas.



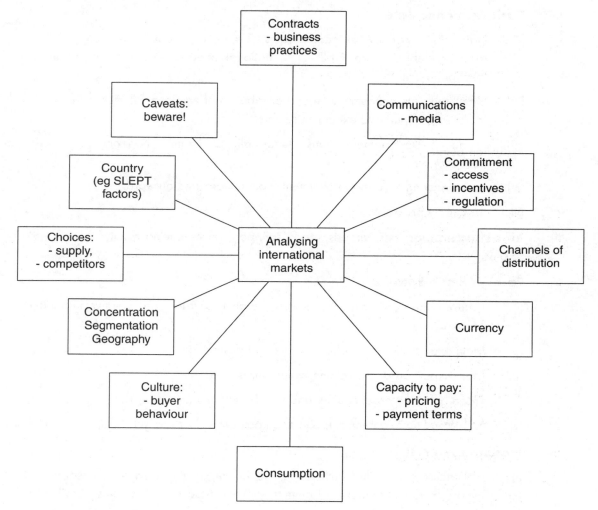

(a) Collecting information

- The business environment as a whole (**general background analysis**)
- The country's economic structure of particular relevance to imports (**market access analysis**)

(b) Beyond this general level, desk research is concerned with obtaining as much information as possible on the structure of the market for the company's goods, the practices of the market and an analysis of competitor's positions. Each of these is considered below.

## General background analysis

**5.9** It is important that the firm has a sound general knowledge of the country. This involves analysing various data.

(a) **Geography**: location, size, topography, climate and so on.

(b) **Population**: size, distribution by location, race, religion, income, education, age, gender etc.

(c) **Language**: official, business and other indigenous languages.

(d) **Government**: type of constitution, roles of central and local government, political climate and attitudes to foreign trade, economic and social policies.

(e) **Basic economic data**

   (i) Indicators: currency exchange rates, balance of payments, foreign currency reserves, debt situation, GNP, GDP, national income, per capita income and price inflation indices.

   (ii) Structure of the economy: rate and distribution of employment, output of the various industrial, service and extractive sectors.

   (iii) Economic Development Plans: funds allocated, time horizon, target sectoral allocations etc.

   (iv) Policy relating to foreign investment: both inward and outward.

   (v) Budgetary provisions.

(f) **Infrastructure**: seaports, airports, roads, rail, postal system, telecommunication system and so on.

(g) **Foreign trade data**

   (i) Total foreign trade: exports, imports, balance of trade, and relative importance to economy.

   (ii) Main export products: volume, value and destination.

   (iii) Main import products: volume, value and source.

   (iv) Trade between target country and the UK: exports and imports.

   (v) Multilateral trade agreements affecting trade between the target country and the UK.

(h) **Trading systems**

   (i) Nationalised: controlling authority, central buying agency, payment procedures.
   (ii) Private sector: Chambers of Commerce, Trade Associations, agents, distributors.

## Market access analysis

**5.10** IMR is also concerned with the **governmental policies and regulations** that specifically affect market entry. These are important because in most countries there are significant variations in the attitude towards, and the regulations imposed upon, a particular importer and the way in which they may be permitted to import. The research may be under various headings.

(a) **General import policy**

(i) Membership of customs union, free trade area, WTO.

(ii) Special trade relationships between the trading countries involved (for example between the UK and Commonwealth countries).

(b) **Restrictive import licensing regulations**: categories, conditions for acquisition, procedures etc.

(c) **Import tariff system**: classification system, tariff rates, bases of assessment for duty.

(d) **Other factors**: foreign exchange controls, import deposit schemes, anti-dumping and minimum price regulations; food, health and safety regulations; selling, promotion, packaging and labelling restrictions; patents and trademark protection in that country; fair trade and anti-trust rules; taxation and shipping documents required.

(e) **Ownership of trading companies** by foreign nationals: restrictions, regulations and imposition of local ownership.

## *Market structure*

**5.11** In order to trade in a foreign market it is vital to have a detailed knowledge of the **market structure and behaviour**. Knowledge of the composition, profile and behaviour of the market is fundamental to marketing, whether domestic or internationally based. Typically in an international context, information is required on the following points.

(a) Who are the **main customers**? How, why, where, when and how much do they buy?

(b) What are the **main channels of distribution** used in such markets? Who are the main distributors, agents etc? Do reciprocal or other possibly limiting trading practices exist that could hamper market entry?

(c) What **product attributes**, specifications and developments are there in the market?

(d) Who are the **main suppliers** to the market? What are their relative positions, shares, strengths and weaknesses, strategies and performance?

(e) Are there significant **geographic variations** in customer requirements, distribution costs, product use, and promotional needs?

(f) What **facilities** are there for promoting the product into the market? What is the effectiveness of the various forms of promotion and media available?

(g) What is the **size** of the total market and potential target segments? How durable is the market? For example is it likely to disappear in adverse economic or political conditions?

## *Competitor analysis*

**5.12** World market competition is intensifying in most products and markets. If a company is interested in anything more than an insignificant niche in world trade it must have an extensive knowledge of **competitors' plans**. A firm should be aware of the following.

(a) **Major competitors**: their number, size, market shares and nationalities.

(b) Do the major competitors have **full market coverage**? Do they instead specialise in certain geographic areas or market segments? Do their product ranges contain gaps?

### *Market practices analysis*

**5.13** It is very rare that the marketing mix relevant to one country can be imported unadapted to another. Hence the international marketer needs to assess the relevant aspects of the mix suitable for the target country. These include the following.

(a) **Transport facilities**: types, prices, reliability and risks (both within and between the relevant countries).

(b) **Distribution channels**: relative costs and benefits; possible alternatives; channel norms and trading behaviour.

(c) **Pricing strategy**: upper and lower limits, competitor prices compared to product features and appeal, discount structures etc.

(d) **Promotional factors**: methods normally used in the market, levels of expenditure and availability.

(e) **Product and services**: required features and facilities before, during and after sale. Warranties, information, credit etc as forms of product enhancement.

# 6 The uses of IMR data

**6.1** Many firms engaged in IMR seek to spread their activities over a number of countries, and so one purpose of IMR must be to ensure that strategic positioning of products and the appropriate marketing mixes are duly identified.

**6.2** IMR data can therefore be used in the following ways to **identify market opportunities**.

(a) To estimate product **patterns** of demand/or consumption in individual markets.

(b) To **compare** patterns of demand or consumption in different markets.

(c) To identify **clusters** of markets with similar characteristics, which can be targeted with similar mix.

(d) To identify **strategically equivalent** segments, across country boundaries.

## Predicting patterns of demand

**6.3** Patterns of demand change over time, for many reasons, such as changes in customer needs and expectations on the one hand, or radical product innovations on the other. Demand for computers is far higher than it used to be, because they are so much cheaper. IMR can identify trends in demand both directly, and also by inference.

### *Demand pattern analysis*

**6.4** **Demand pattern analysis** involves analysing production patterns (as a surrogate for demand) over time. It helps in identifying general marketing opportunities and, because it uses **production** statistics, it can indicate potential markets.

## Income elasticity of demand

**6.5** We can also estimate effective demand from how much people earn. **Income elasticity** studies are concerned with specific products. Income elasticity describes the relative changes in demand for a product with changes in income levels.
Income elasticity of demand is expressed as:

$$\frac{\text{Change in product demand} \div \text{Product demand}}{\text{Change in income} \div \text{Income}}$$

(a) Some goods are **income inelastic**. As people get richer, demand for such goods does not increase proportionately. For example, poor people might spend over 50% of their income on basic foodstuffs. In wealthy countries such as the UK, food accounts for about 11%. British people do not eat less, but food takes up a lower proportion of their income.

(b) Goods which are **income elastic** are very sensitive to changes in people's income. These include leisure products and some consumer durables.

## Multiple factor indices

**6.6** It is commonly the case that data of the kind required for direct analysis of a market is unavailable and thus the market researcher must find alternatives. **Multiple factor analysis** attempts to surmount this problem by using surrogate variables that can be closely correlated with demand for the company's own product.

**6.7** There is clearly much scope for error, but this may be reduced by using variables that are as close as possible to demand for the product. So whereas, for example, growth in total population might be found to have a good statistical correlation with demand for compact disc players, changes in population in the 15–30 age group is likely to be a better indicator. Changes in personal disposable income may be a better indicator again.

## Regression analysis

**6.8** **Regression analysis** takes the ideas of multiple factor indices further and adds some statistical rigour. The usual form the technique takes is **linear regression**, where change in an independent variable (often GNP per head) seeks to explain change in the dependent variable (normally demand for the product in question).

**6.9** A study of the US market in the 1960s showed that changes in GNP per head accounted for nearly 80% of variation in radio set ownership, with a growth rate of approximately 25 sets for every increase of $100 in GNP per head.

**6.10** Care must be taken to use this technique within its limitations. In particular, the predictive ability of the regression may be limited to a narrow band of change in the independent variable. To return to the radio sets example, one might find the situation shown overleaf.

**6.11** The regression line can be extended at will but the growth rate of ownership of radios may fall above a certain income level. This is to be expected by intuition. As average wealth increases there comes a point when the majority of people who wish to own a radio have become rich enough to buy one and thus further increases in average wealth have less and less impact on the numbers owning them.

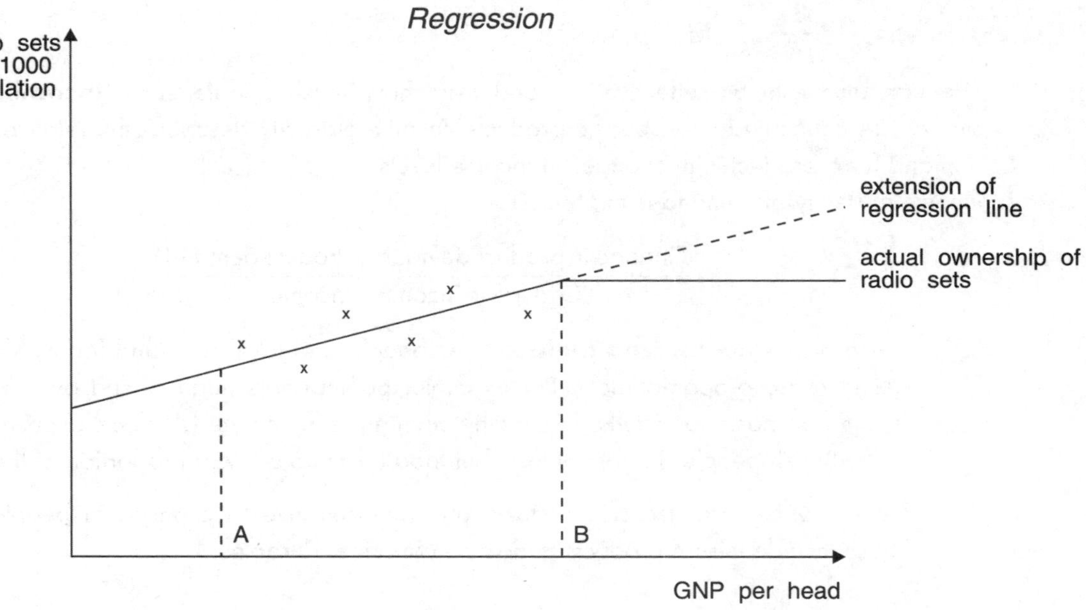


# Comparing patterns of demand/consumption in different markets

## *Comparative analysis*

**6.12** **Comparative analysis** assumes that if market potential is equivalent in two markets then marketing performance should be comparable too. It usually takes the form of comparison of the same company's performance in two (or more) national markets. If the economies are broadly similar but performance is not (or vice-versa) it suggests that marketing performance is not being optimised and thus raises questions to be addressed.

Factors in a comparative analysis include many of the SLEPT factors.

- Size of population
- Age structure
- Geographic distribution
- Incomes
- Lifestyles
- Communications
- Ability to pay
- Barriers to entry

## *Inter-market timing differences*

**6.13** This technique uses the premise that certain markets have **similar demand patterns** for similar goods but that one leads and the other lags. Clearly this technique is useful only for comparing countries that can be assumed to have similar economic, social and cultural conditions. The diagram below shows the similarity in the rate of acquisition of television in the 1950s and 1960s between the UK and West Germany. At its simplest, the technique enabled the prediction of growth or decline in the then West German market by taking that of the UK market a few years earlier and adjusting for the different numbers of households in the two markets.

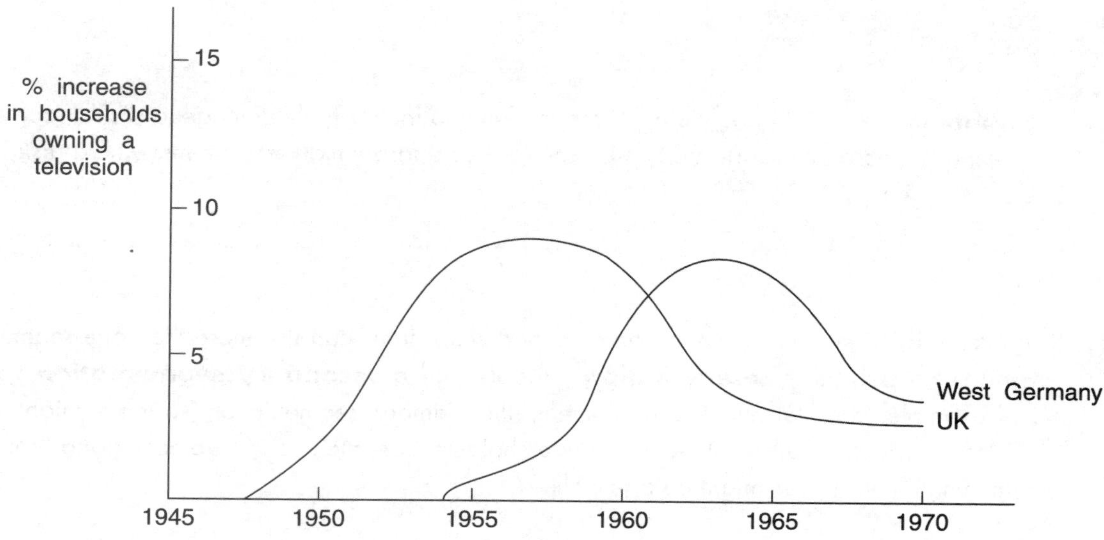


## Identifying clusters of markets with similar characteristics

**6.14** A logical extension of using one market to predict the behaviour of another is to identify **clusters of markets** with the same characteristics. Put another way, this is rather like segmenting groups of customers – instead the countries of the world are being segmented. (Do **not** confuse this with clustering as described by Michael Porter in *The Competitive Advantage of Nations*, 1998). **Cluster analysis** involves mathematical techniques – too complex to describe here – to identify similar markets.

(a) Sethi suggested four sets of variables in which each country could be compared.

- **Production and transportation**
- **Consumption** (income, eg number of cars)
- **Trade data** derived from import or export figures
- **Health and education**

Each of these were scored, and countries were fitted into one of seven groups, with the implication that the similarity of countries within a group was strong enough to justify similar marketing approaches.

(b) **Business International** identified indices covering market size (eg population), market growth rates and market intensity (relative concentration of wealth and purchasing power). For example the former Soviet Union, Poland and Brazil occupied one cluster, having enjoyed similar growth rates between 1986 and 1990 and having a similar 'intensity'.

## Identifying strategically equivalent segments

**6.15** In addition to identifying clusters of countries, it is possible that a firm may wish to segment each market and pursue these segments only.

### Key Concept

**Segmentation** is the subdividing of the market into increasingly homogenous subgroups of customers, where any subgroup can be selected as a target market to be met with a distinct marketing mix.

**6.16** In international marketing, as in domestic marketing, firms can use more than one segmentation variable, a **primary segmentation** variable and a **secondary segmentation** variable. For example, for wet shaving equipment, the primary segmentation variable might be sex (Gillette produces different razor blade holders for men and women), and secondary segmentation variables might be age or lifestyle.

**6.17** In international marketing, using **country** as the **primary** segmentation variable would seem common sense, certainly for consumer products, given the cultural influences, political risk factors and so forth identified earlier. If a firm pursues a multi-domestic strategy it will almost certainly use country as the primary segmentation variable. Even a global firm, to whom the world is a single market, will develop country-based segments in **consumer markets**.

**6.18** Take the example of a firm selling walking sticks in the EU. Using country as the prime segmentation variable may cause confusion. The country markets for walking sticks are each **naturally** segmented by **age**. Consequently, rather than using country as a primary segmentation variable, it might be sensible to use **age** instead to avoid separately targeting segments whose needs are very similar.

**6.19** This leads us to the notion of **strategically equivalent segments**, which transcend national boundaries. Here are some possible examples.

(a) In South East Asia, people of Chinese ethnic extraction form the business elite in many countries (eg Malaysia) despite government attempts to reduce imbalances. Therefore, for certain types of goods and services, overseas Chinese (eg in Malaysia, Singapore, Thailand etc) could be considered a strategically equivalent segment.

(b) Geodemographic segmentation can also be used. Experian analyses ten classifications of European consumers as shown below.

- Wealthy suburbs
- Average-income areas
- Flats – luxury
- Low income inner city
- Municipal/social housing estates
- Industrial communities
- Dynamic families
- Low income families
- Farming/rural
- Holiday/retirement areas

**6.20** Such worries may not exist for many **industrial markets**, where there are fewer buyers, and where purchase decisions are in theory taken according to rational criteria. The market for aircraft engines comprises the world's airlines, and it may not be possible or necessary to segment this market.

## Marketing at Work

Japan's population profile is ageing more rapidly than that of most other countries. Thus, Shiseido, the cosmetics company, launched Acteaheart, a range of cosmetics specially aimed at women over 40. This might also be considered a strategically equivalent segment in other markets which Shiseido may wish to target – the US and the wealthy Asian countries.

# 7 Some problems in IMR

## Researching numerous markets

7.1 In the initial stages, international marketing research may address a hundred or more markets in the broad scan for market opportunities, and certainly concentrate on a minimum of a handful of markets as enquiries become more focused. This generates a number of problems.

(a) **Cost versus profit** considerations. Researching multiple markets can give rise to economies of scale and experience but even so a marginal cost is incurred for each. Moreover many markets are small, heterogeneous and with limited profit prospects. This then justifies only moderate market research expenditure and has forced IMR practitioners to develop methods and techniques geared to limited budgets. It also requires the researcher to exercise judgement as to which countries would be worth investigating. Hence the importance of informal methods of research at the initial stages.

(b) **Differences between countries** gives rise to several problems.

(i) **Definition**: defining the problem with respect to various countries. Bicycles are treated as recreational items in the UK, largely sporting in nature in parts of continental Europe, and as a means of transport in much of the Third World. Thus the definition of research to be carried out and the categories provided in surveys should be sufficiently broad to encompass the variety of uses, reasons and responses that might be evoked.

(ii) **Classification**: meaning and classification problems in surveys and their analysis due to different behavioural and living patterns.

(iii) **Frame**: sources of sampling frames from which to draw samples may not be reliable, especially in under-developed countries.

(iv) **Non-response**: the desire to co-operate with a survey will largely depend on the norms of that culture. It should not be assumed that questions freely answered in one country will be accepted in another.

(v) **Comparability** is weakened by many factors, particularly differing cultural values, consumption patterns, political influences and reliability of data sources.

## Secondary data problems

7.2 There are normally three critical deficiencies regarding secondary data that are important to the international market researcher.

(a) **Lack of data**. Without doubt, the USA has the best documented commercial information. Key economic indicators, compilations of trade statistics and the work of

trade associations, state and local government, and management groups, are readily available to the market researcher. But few countries come close to matching the sheer volume and diversity of data collected in the USA. Until the United Nations began assimilating world economic data, there was often little available other than very rough estimates for many lesser developed countries.

(b) **Poor comparability** and **timeliness**.

(i) This problem is at its most acute in less economically developed countries which, despite recent attempts to remedy the situation, often choose to devote a rather lower proportion of their resources to data collection than advanced economies. As a consequence data is often many years out of date and collected on an infrequent and unpredictable schedule.

(ii) More specific problems involve different definitions used in data collection, the fact that different base years have been used for comparative purposes and that gaps may exist. As an example a television is classified as household furniture in the USA but not in Germany (where it is treated as a recreational purchase) leading to problems of comparability of data collected in different countries.

(c) **Poor reliability** of some of the secondary data that are collected. Much of it has to be analysed with great care.

(i) In many economically underdeveloped countries, national pride takes precedence over statistical accuracy.

(ii) Moreover, companies have been known to reduce their production statistics so that they reconcile to sales reported to the tax authorities!

**7.3** As a practical matter, before basing a marketing strategy on the analysis of secondary data, it is worthwhile asking the following questions.

(a) **Who** collected the data? Would there be any reason for deliberately misrepresenting the facts?

(b) For what **purpose** was data collected?

(c) **How** was the data collected (ie what was the survey methodology used)?

(d) Is the data **consistent with one another** and are they logical (in the light of known data sources or market factors)?

## Marketing at Work

One of the problems of doing market research in Russia is identifying groups of consumers. Official statistics leave a lot to be desired, given the enormous social changes over the past few years.

Researchers have begun, however, to identify new segments, from wealthy entrepreneurs to poorer people dependent on state pensions. Rather than outlining a simple rich/poor divide, a number of groups have been identified.

## Problems in collecting primary data

7.4 Where the informal and secondary sources are inadequate, as a last resort the market researcher must turn to collecting **primary data**. This is both expensive and difficult and the task is often handed over to specialist agencies to carry out. The problems involved in primary data collection include the methods of data collection, non-response, survey control, illiteracy and language.

### *Data collection*

7.5 Except in the most unusual circumstances it is too time-consuming and too expensive for the market researcher to survey the whole of the target population for the product under consideration (even if it can be defined adequately in the first place). Consequently a **sample** needs to be taken.

### *Questionnaires*

7.6 Survey research, to obtain primary data, normally requires a questionnaire. There are three main characteristics of a good questionnaire.

- The questions are easy for interviewees to answer and for the interviewer to record
- It acquires the necessary information but keeps the interview to the point
- It is straightforward

7.7 In order to make sure that the questionnaire achieves these characteristics, a number of **design principles** need to be adhered to. The main ones are as follows.

- Questions should **address** one point only
- Questions that suggest their **own** answer should be avoided
- Ensure that questions **mean** one thing only
- Make the language in which the questions are framed easy to understand
- If at all possible, the questionnaire should list the possible replies to questions
- Avoid asking questions of a personal and potentially embarrassing kind

### Action Programme 2

Design a short questionnaire about a product of your choice. Try it out on a colleague and ask your colleague to give you marks out of ten for questionnaire design.

## Problems in response

7.8 People's unwillingness to provide information is a feature of many countries. Several reasons can be suggested for this.

(a) **Tax evasion and avoidance of responsibility**. Anyone asking questions may be suspected of being a government employee.

(b) **Wish to preserve secrecy**. Many business managers regard data relating to their company or markets as potential help to competitors and accordingly response rates are low when they concern anything that might be regarded as an aid to a competitor.

(c) **Cultural taboos and norms**

(i) Topics that are freely discussed in some countries (for example birth control methods) are taboo for discussion in others except in the most intimate situations.

(ii) Similarly the authority to respond may not be the same in all cultures. Thus whilst in one country a female head of household may feel authorised to discuss a topic with a researcher, in other countries there may be a marked reluctance to give information.

**7.9** In carrying out surveys, firms in the UK take many things for granted that may not exist in other countries, particularly less developed ones.

(a) There may be no suitable lists (**sampling frames**) from which a representative sample can be selected.

(b) In many countries there is a dearth of economic, demographic and social **statistics** on which to base sampling methods.

(c) Inadequate **communication infrastructure** can be a severe practical handicap.

(d) Low levels of **literacy**.

(e) Problems of **language and comprehension** are widespread in IMR. Differences in idiom and problems of precise translation lead to great misunderstandings. In large countries such as India the researcher has to be prepared to deal with some fourteen languages and 200 dialects when planning a survey.

**7.10** This discussion should make it clear that there is a greater necessity for **care, understanding and skill** in IMR data analysis.

(a) Thus the analyst requires an extensive understanding of the cultural environment of the countries being researched and a talent for interpolating data that contains gaps or has other deficiencies.

(b) A final requirement would be a **healthy scepticism** towards both primary and secondary data since they are very likely to be imperfect, resulting in a desire to cross check and substantiate data wherever possible.

# 8 Managing the research effort

**8.1** International marketing intelligence is crucial for a firm's strategic decisions and for the on-going implementation and review of marketing plans. The collection of strategic intelligence has to be co-ordinated.

- At the appropriate level in the organisation
- At the appropriate time

**8.2** Not only does data have to be collected, it has to be **communicated** to the right area of the organisation.

**8.3** For decisions made by local **subsidiaries**, the information will be gathered and stored locally. The international **headquarters**, however, can operate as a clearing house for research studies, actively passing on information to those who might benefit from it.

8.4 **International head office** may conduct research on its own, perhaps on issues relevant to all markets or in areas where there would be duplication if the subsidiaries did all the work themselves.

8.5 Some firms have **regional** HQs as well, covering a number of countries. The advantages of one MR department are economies of scale, and the ability to concentrate efforts.

8.6 Co-ordinating the **timeliness** of information is important. After all, if a product launch is critically dependent on marketing intelligence, any delay can be costly.

8.7 An important management decision is the extent to which firms use **agencies** to conduct their IMR.

## Using external agencies

8.8 IMR managers face considerable problems in obtaining useful information at a reasonable cost. The manager may consider hiring an external agency to carry out IMR. Before hiring such an agency however the firm must make three crucial decisions:

### *Whether to hire an agency or not*

8.9 There are a number of factors favouring the hire of an agency.

(a) The firm may have little or no **marketing research resources**.

(b) The firm does have marketing research resources but these are subject to **peak demands**. Thus it may be more economical to hire agencies to meet peak loads than to increase the firm's permanent resources.

(c) The firm may have little or no **experience of the foreign market** to be analysed. Here an agency with that specific market experience may be of great value.

(d) The research is of a **highly specialised** kind involving skills not present in the firm (for example behavioural studies).

(e) The research is a **'one-off' exercise** and thus it would be uneconomic to develop 'in-house' expertise.

(f) The firm anticipates **language or cultural problems** in carrying out the research that their own expertise cannot cope with.

(g) Management requires an **objective view**, which is often difficult when its own employees are aware of the pressures within the firm for a particular answer.

8.10 On the other hand, there are also several factors that would favour 'in-house' research.

(a) **Lack of suitable marketing research agencies** in the foreign markets to be investigated.

(b) The firm is **well experienced** in IMR and has a good understanding of the cultural and other conditions that might affect the research.

(c) The relevant **resources and skills** already exist in the firm.

(d) The firm needs to develop a **thorough knowledge** of the market. Agencies do provide information, but they may leave the firm without the extensive knowledge which is required to get a 'feel' for the market.

(e) The firm would find it difficult to **brief** the agency adequately on its research objectives and the technical parameters and applications of the product.

(f) The research project is a **small** one, requiring few interviews and relatively little time.

(g) It may be **cheaper** for the firm to execute its own marketing research. It is quite likely that economies of scale and experience can be achieved when studies are duplicated in multiple countries.

## *Which type of agency to select*

**8.11** In general terms the firm may engage any one of three types of agency to execute its IMR.

(a) **Foreign agency domiciled in the target country**. This offers the major benefit of having a comprehensive understanding of the local market, language, culture and business environment. However, it requires costly and time consuming visits by the firm's personnel to select and brief the agency, and then to supervise the project.

(b) **Domestic agency sending competent staff to the target country**. This is beneficial insofar as it permits easy and cheap selection, briefing and supervision of an agency. It should also offer a high standard of marketing research skills and may be less costly than hiring a foreign agency. A serious disadvantage would arise, however, if the agency or its personnel were not in fact thoroughly familiar with the foreign market, its culture or its environment.

(c) **Domestic agency with foreign agency subsidiaries, associates or subcontracting arrangement**. This is the synthesis of the above two alternatives. Here the domestic agency works in conjunction with its overseas associates.

  (i) The benefit for the firm is that it only has to select, brief and supervise the domestic agency which in turn acts on behalf of the firm with the foreign agency. Further it is assumed that the foreign agency will have a thorough understanding of the target market, its culture and its environment.

  (ii) The major disadvantage of such an arrangement is that the firm has little or no control over the selection and supervision of the foreign agency. Additionally there may be some communication problems between the two agencies, and the cost of utilising two agencies may be greater than with direct hiring.

(d) **Global agency** with a worldwide presence.

## *Selecting a particular agency*

**8.12** Whatever type of agency the firm finally decides to hire, it must select an appropriate agency to carry out the research. This involves obtaining information about the various agencies to evaluate their suitability and acquiring a research proposal from each for assessment. Agencies might be invited to tender.

**8.13** **Briefing**. Each agency approached will require certain **guidelines** from the firm to ensure that the proposal which it prepares is appropriately formulated.

- A clear written statement of the **research problem**
- An indication of the **way in which the research findings will be used**
- An indication of the approximate **budget**
- An opportunity for the agency to **discuss** the proposed programme

**8.14 Shortlisting**. In making a shortlist, the firm should take the following factors into account.

(a) Evidence of suitable **background and experience** of the agency staff in IMR and the target markets.

(b) Details of any **specialist staff** (statisticians, analysts, psychologists and so on) used by the agency.

(c) **Agency experience** in relevant IMR areas, foreign markets, products and research techniques.

(d) **Quality and reliability** of field operations including the selection and training of staff, levels of supervision, and control and monitoring procedures.

(e) Where large amounts of data are to be collected, the agency's **facilities for data processing**, analysis and report preparation.

(f) The financial **status** and reputation of the agency.

A **recommendation** from other satisfied users of an agency can be a significant aid in shortlisting a suitable agency. The informal network outlined earlier in this chapter can be utilised here.

**8.15 Final choice**. The agency selected from among the shortlisted and submitted proposals will be the one which puts forward the most appealing blend of the following.

(a) A demonstration of a sound grasp of the research problem and its objectives.

(b) A detailed description of the research including a statement of the scope and nature of preliminary desk research, pilot studies and qualitative research. Where quantitative research is involved, a statement of the data collection method, the population to be sampled, the sample size and the sampling technique.

(c) A statement of the staff involved and their duties.

(d) A statement of the total cost with a detailed breakdown of the component costs, and a reasonably detailed timetable for the research programme, including a final reporting date.

## Chapter Roundup

- **International marketing research** is more complex than domestic marketing research, as there are additional factors to consider. Some foreign markets may be attractive commercially, but there may be legal barriers to entry. Detailed **analysis** of international trade regulations could be appropriate, as would be a general background analysis of the country, its market structure, competitors, market practices and access.
- IMR information can be used to predict patterns of demand, to compare different markets, to cluster countries and to identify strategically equivalent segments.
- **Databases and expert systems** can provide useful information. Expert systems in particular represent a leap in information effectiveness because of their ability to make 'decisions' and promote precision marketing.
- Some **government agencies** offer specific export assistance, often in terms of advice and promotional help.
- International market research is made difficult by the existence of different **cultural assumptions** in the foreign market, which may distort the results of research designed for use in the home country. Moreover, secondary data may be non-existent and unreliable.
- **Cross-cultural differences** must be recognised when undertaking IMR.
- The commissioning of a **research agency** experienced in the overseas market might be advisable, although the market knowledge provided may not be less thorough than it would be if the firm did the research itself.

## Quick Quiz

1. What are the objectives of IMR?
2. What is the main source of marketing information?
3. Outline the process of IMR.
4. Why might latent demand exist?
5. What are the two main areas of desk research?
6. Is demand for basic foodstuffs income elastic or income inelastic?
7. What is the basis of comparative analysis?
8. What are the three common deficiencies in secondary data?
9. What are the characteristics of a good questionnaire?

## Answers to Quick Quiz

1
- Identify new markets, opportunities and threats
- Identify market trends
- Monitor customer needs and preferences
- Monitor competitor plans and strategies
- Monitor the macro-environment

2 Human beings.

3 Monitoring; investigation; research.

4 Because of defects in the marketing mixes used by existing suppliers.

5 General background analysis of the business environment as a whole and market access analysis.

6 Income inelastic.

7 An assumption that if the marketing of two separate markets is similar, then marketing performance should be similar.

8 Lack of data; poor comparability and timeliness; and poor reliability.

9 Questions are easy to answer and record; the required information is acquired efficiently; straightforwardness.

## Action Programme Review

1 Aside from the possibility of increasing sales, exporting provides exposure to more rigorous market disciplines than might be available in the home market. Moreover, it might provide information about competitors' products. The foreign market may also be a source of new ideas.

2 Your colleague could perhaps give you marks out of ten according to the criteria set out in Paragraph 7.7.

**Now try Question 10 at the end of the Study Text**

# Part F

## Mini-cases in the examination

# Mini-cases in the Examination

11

| Chapter Topic List | |
|---|---|
| 1 | Setting the scene |
| 2 | What is a mini-case? |
| 3 | An approach to mini-cases |
| 4 | Other questions in the examination |

# 1 Setting the scene

**1.1** With the obvious exception of the dedicated case study paper, Strategic Marketing in Practice, each exam at Professional Post-Graduate diploma level incorporates a 50 mark mini-case study as Part A. candidates often have difficulty with mini-cases, so this chapter offers detailed guidance on how to tackle them. Question practice can be found in the BPP *Practice & Revision Kit* for this subject – an order form can be found at the end of the Study Text.

# 2 What is a mini-case?

**2.1** A mini-case in the examination is a 500–800 word long description of an organisation at a moment in time. You first see it in the examination room and so you have a maximum of 72 minutes to read, understand, analyse and answer the mini-case. The length of the mini-case is likely to be between one and two pages of A4.

**2.2** The approach is the same for all the subjects and so practice in one area will benefit your other Diploma subjects.

**2.3** The mini-case carries 50% of the available marks in the examination. Students who fail a Diploma paper are often found to have had difficulties with the mini-case. It is worth noting that a good result on the mini-case can be used to compensate for a weaker performance in part B of the paper.

**2.4** As mini-cases are fundamental to your exam success, you should be absolutely clear about what mini-cases are, CIM's purpose in using them, what the examiners seek and then, in context, to consider how best they should be tackled.

## The purpose of the mini-case

**2.5** Diploma examiners require students to demonstrate not only their knowledge of marketing management, but also their ability to use that knowledge in a commercially credible way in the context of a real business scenario.

**2.6** **You cannot pass this part of the paper by regurgitating theory**. You must be able to apply the theory to real problems. The mini-case is included to test your competence in analysing information and making clear and reasonable decisions.

## The examiners' requirements

**2.7** The examiners are the consumers of your examination script. You should remember first and foremost that they need a paper which makes their life easy. That means that the script should be well laid out, with plenty of white space and neat readable writing. All the basic rules of examination technique must be applied, but because communication skills are fundamental to the marketer, the ability to communicate clearly is particularly important.

**2.8** The examination is your opportunity to market yourself to the examiner, in this case as a marketing professional competent in the skills of analysis and evaluation. As actions speak louder than words, a candidate who has failed to plan the answers or who has run out of the resource time, is unlikely to impress.

**2.9** Management skills are commonly ignored by candidates who fail to recognise their importance. Management is more about thinking than knowing, more about decision than analysis. It is about achieving action through persuasive communication. It is about meeting deadlines. It is therefore about clear, logical analysis under time pressure, which leads to decisive recommendations presented in simple, clear business English.

**2.10** The six key factors from the above paragraph are:

- Thinking
- Logical analysis
- Decision
- Action
- Persuasive communication
- Business English

All must be demonstrated to the examiners, especially in the case and mini-case study elements of the Diploma examinations.

**2.11** If you are entering the Diploma by exemption, take particular note of the examiners' requirements. Certificate holders will have encountered mini-cases before. They should note the change in emphasis from the learning of marketing to its management.

**2.12** Examiners' reports note the reasons why candidates fail. It makes depressing reading to go back over a series of reports because year after year the examiners make the same points and year after year many candidates ignore them! No examiner can understand why candidates refuse to take notice of their requirements. In everyday life we do what our manager instructs, or we leave the job (one way or another). If candidates would only think of the examiners as senior managers at work, and address them accordingly, the pass rate would shoot up.

## Examiners' comments

**2.13** Examiners' reports on mini-cases repeatedly stress the same points.

(a) Relate the time allocated to the answer to the marks available.

(b) Answer the question asked. Never use a question as a pretext to answer a different one.

(c) Time planning is crucial to success.

(d) Quality and insight are worth more than quantity and detail.

(e) It is essential to write in role.

(f) Intelligently apply knowledge of theory to a marketing problem.

(g) Do not repeat chunks of the mini-case in the answer.

(h) Do not show any analytical work (for example SWOT) unless specifically requested.

(i) Presentation must be of management quality. Spelling and grammar are important, only a certain laxity will be allowed for the pressures of the exam room.

**2.14** Direct quotes from examiners' reports reinforce the points made in the previous paragraph.

(a) 'The commonest 'self-destruct' faults

- Bad time management
- Using the question as a pretext to answer a different one
- Poor presentation'

(b) 'Your examiners regard badly constructed and unrealistic case solutions as a particularly serious failing among candidates for the professional diploma of a chartered institute.'

(c) 'The gap between question answering and case solving abilities continues to be very marked.'

(d) 'A wider spread of up-to-date knowledge (greater than Coca-Cola and McDonald's) would give the examiner greater confidence in your competence.'

(e) 'Management of any sort, and particularly marketing management, is about thinking rather than knowing. It is for example about selecting the best strategy rather than simply knowing the range of options available.'

(f) 'Preparation time should be spent in practising techniques as much as in learning content.'

(g) 'Diploma candidates not only need to demonstrate their ability to communicate succinctly as a subsidiary test of marketing awareness but in their own interests of scoring higher marks by getting more valid points across in the limited time available in the exam situation.'

(h) 'It is a shame that such basic mistakes mar what are often otherwise diligent and enthusiastic efforts.'

## The expectations of examiners

**2.15** Examiners are experienced marketing managers. They know that mini-cases give only limited information and that candidates are working under a tight time constraint. They do not, therefore, require considered, fully rounded answers. There is insufficient data and time. The successful candidate learns to work with what is available, to make reasonable assumptions that help in the decision making process, and to present an answer cogently and concisely.

**2.16** The examiner can only mark within the criteria that have been established. The requirements are set out very clearly. It is not difficult to satisfy them. The well prepared candidate should not fail the mini-case. Since the information is limited, the time is very constrained, and the examiner is looking for evidence of a managerial approach, any candidate that makes reasonable assumptions about the case, takes clear and sensible decisions, and communicates these succinctly must pass.

**2.17** Also remember that mini-cases are set for all candidates. Some will know absolutely nothing about the industry, some will work in it and be expert. Candidates take the examinations in centres across the world. Therefore the examiner will not ask technical questions about the industry, nor any tied to a specific culture or economy. Questions have to be more general, more open, less specific. However, you will be expected to have acquired a level of business appreciation and marketing knowledge from your other studies.

**2.18** Summary

The requirements are as follows.

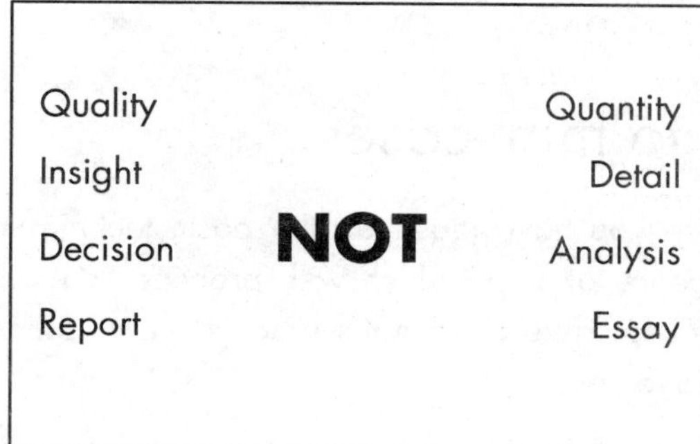

Quality
Insight
Decision
Report
NOT
Quantity
Detail
Analysis
Essay


## Management reports in CIM mini-cases

**2.19** A management report is a specialised form of communication. It is the language used in business. It is not difficult to learn to write in report style, but it does require practice to become fluent. Mini-cases must always be answered in report style.

**2.20** Management reports are action planning documents and are generally written in the third person. Their role is to make positive recommendations for action. Situational analysis is included only if it is needed to clarify an ambiguity. Examiners complain that many candidates do little more than produce a SWOT analysis as their response to a mini-case. Support material is often included, but as appendices to the body of the report. In CIM mini-case work it is exceptional to include an appendix.

**2.21** Management reports: the basic rules

- Always head a report with the name of your organisation.
- State to whom it is addressed, from whom it comes, and give the date.
- Head the report (for example 'Marketing research plan for 2004/05').
- Number and sub-number paragraphs. Head them if appropriate.
- Present the contents in a logical order.
- Include diagrams, graphs, tables only if they have positive value.
- Include recommendations for action that are written as intention against time.

**2.22** If you are forced to use appendices there are two further rules to remember.

- Refer to them within the body of the report (eg 'See Appendix A').
- Indicate when the report concludes (.../ends).

**2.23** Management reports are written in crisp, no-nonsense business English. There is no room for superlatives, flowery adjectives nor flowing sentences. You are not trying to entertain, simply to present facts as clearly as possible. Think about the style you would adopt if writing a report to senior managers at work.

**2.24** As we have already said, presentation is of key importance in CIM examinations. The rules are as follows.

- Use a black or a blue pen, never red or green.
- Start your first answer on the facing page of the answer book, never inside the cover.
- Make the first three pages as neat and well laid out as possible, to impress.

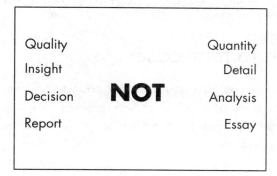

- Use plenty of space. Do not crowd your work.
- Number your questions above your answers. Never write in either margin.
- Leave space (four or five lines) between sections of your report.

# 3 An approach to mini-cases

3.1 Mini-cases are easy once you have mastered the basic techniques. The key to success lies in adopting a logical sequence of steps which with practice you will master. You must enter the exam room with the process as second nature, so you can concentrate your attention on the marketing issues which face you.

3.2 Students who are at first apprehensive when faced with a mini-case often come to find them much more stimulating and rewarding than traditional examination questions. There is the added security of knowing that there is no single correct answer to a case study.

3.3 You will be assessed on your approach, style, creativity and commercial credibility, but you will not be judged against a single 'correct' answer. Treat the mini-case as though it were happening in real life, at work or at a social meeting with a friend. Most of the mini-case is narrative; it tells a story or paints a picture. If a friend says over a drink 'I've got a problem at work' the most usual answer is 'Tell me about it'. The listener will need background information to establish frame reference and to understand the problem. That is what the case narrative is doing. Most of it is background, and it should be read just to grasp the context and flavour of the situation.

3.4 It helps to pretend to yourself that the examiner needs your advice. The questions posed indicate the advice which is being sought.

(a) Just as your friend would not be impressed if you spent half an hour pontificating on how he or she got themselves into this situation, neither will the examiner reward you for analysis of how the situation arose.

(b) Neither will the examiner be impressed with a long list of 'you could do this ....' 'but on the other hand....' Identify the alternatives, but make a clear recommendation if you want to win friends and influence examiners.

3.5 You will be faced with limited information, less than would be available to you in the real world. This is one of the limitations of case study examinations, but everyone is faced with the same constraint. You are able to make assumptions where it is necessary.

3.6 A reasonable assumption is logically possible and factually credible. You may need to make and clearly state two or three assumptions in order to tackle a case.

3.7 Some students feel uncomfortable that there is no bedrock (an easy, well defined question) on which to build. They feel all at sea and panic.

3.8 Preparation is the answer. It is important to practise the technique of handling a mini-case. There are three later in this chapter, and they should be taken individually. For each there are careful instructions and a time guide is given. After you have completed these it will still be necessary for you to develop speed, but the principles needed for success in the examination will have been established. Mini-case scenarios are also included as one of the data sheets in the CIM's *Marketing Success* and these will provide you with regular new material on which to practise.

## An example of a mini-case

3.9 This mini-case example is worked through stage by stage to show you the process. This shows you the methodology. Another mini-case is at the end of this text.

## Direct Lounge Furniture Ltd (DLF)

3.10 DLF is owned by two entrepreneurs each of whom built up a separate direct marketing business, one in the East Midlands and one in the West Midlands over a period of some 15 years, before merging three years ago. The main advantages of the merger were joint advertising, wider product ranges, more flexible production and less reliance upon one person. The two owners are good friends and work well together, meeting at least once a week.

3.11 Both the two constituent businesses comprise showrooms mainly featuring upholstered three-piece suites finished in Dralon cloth, in a wide variety of styles and colours. This furniture is manufactured in two small factories, each of which has an adjoining showroom.

3.12 Sales are achieved by advertising in free newspapers delivered to Midlands households. These advertisements illustrate the furniture on offer, strongly emphasise the lower prices available to the public by buying direct from the manufacturers and of course invite readers to visit the showrooms without obligation.

3.13 Upon visiting the showroom the public can look around the products on offer, discuss their individual requirements with a salesperson and be shown round the factory to emphasise the quality of the workmanship, wooden frames etc.

3.14 This marketing formula works very well and sales/profits are booming. Customers feel they are involved in the design of their own furniture and that they are getting good value. DLF enjoy high proportions of recommendations and repeat sales.

3.15 Buying behaviour patterns are however changing. People are tending to buy individual items rather than the standard three-piece suite (two armchairs plus a 2/3/4 seater settee) and to seek co-ordination with curtains, carpet etc. In partial response to this the East Midlands showroom offers made-to-measure curtains in Dralon to complement or match the upholstery. Another change in the industry is in the foam used for upholstering which was formerly highly flammable and when on fire gave out dense black smoke causing many deaths. Legislation has now been passed enforcing the use of safer foam.

3.16 The media exposure of the fire hazard has caused the public to be more careful when choosing furniture and increasing affluence has also resulted in a move up-market by more households.

3.17 DLF are well aware that their formula appeals mainly to the more price-conscious households, who have been tolerant of the somewhat less than sophisticated showroom and factory conditions associated with direct marketing of this nature.

### *Question*

3.18 You have been called in by DLF as a consultant to advise on expansion options. After conducting a marketing audit and a SWOT analysis you are now evaluating the options for:

- Product development only
- Market development only
- A combination of both product and market development

Submit your report giving the advantages and disadvantages of each of these three options in more detail, stating what control techniques you would recommend in each case.

## Analysis

**3.19** You should immediately identify the following characteristics about the business.

- DLF is a small business.
- They operate in a local market.
- They specialise in the direct marketing of consumer durables.

**3.20** These characteristics should start to inform your thinking about the case and the nature of the business, for example you can now make the following connections.

(a) *Small business:* may mean limited resources.

(b) *Local market:* local communication media.

(c) *Direct marketing:* control over marketing mix but cost of storage and delivery, credit provision etc.

(d) *Consumer durables:* infrequent purchase, influenced strongly by style, colour, not brand names etc.

**3.21** The secret of case study questions is to really play the role you have been given. You need to be able to picture this business, its products and showrooms. As soon as you have a mental picture you will be able to fit easily into the role of marketing consultant.

**3.22** Now read through the case again and identify the key points, strengths, weaknesses etc. You can do this on the examination paper to save time. You need to really think about the narrative and what it is telling you.

**3.23** Alternatively, or in addition, you can convert the information onto a SWOT chart to help clarify the picture. Remember that you are not presenting this to the examiner, so use a page at the back of your answer book and do not waste too much time on it.

> Remember that weaknesses can always be converted into strengths and that threats can usually be turned to opportunities. Do not waste time worrying about how to categorise an element. It is usually more important that you have identified it.

**3.24** *SWOT of Direct Lounge Furniture Ltd*

| *Strengths* | *Weaknesses* |
|---|---|
| ■ Owners are friends | Could be a weakness if they fall out; may imply informal systems and procedures |
| ■ Established | |
| ■ Financially strong; sales and profits high | Resources for expansion limited for a small business |
| ■ Good reputation<br>–price<br>–workmanship | Perceived as bottom end of market |
| | ■ Limited geographic market<br>■ Two unsophisticated showrooms<br>■ Product oriented<br>■ Limited product portfolio<br>■ Little marketing activity |

| *Opportunity* | *Threats* |
|---|---|
| ■ Higher customer incomes<br>■ Safety awareness pushing demand towards higher value products | ■ Legislation<br>■ Changing customer needs and attitudes Increased standard of living amongst current customers |
| ■ New materials and production techniques which may become available | ■ Possibility of increased competition |

**3.25** Marketing audit is an assessment of the current marketing activity of DLF. We have uncovered some clues when developing the corporate SWOT.

(a) The company is product oriented not marketing oriented.

(b) There is advertising activity but no evidence of a co-ordinated marketing function, therefore no marketing procedures, plans etc.

(c) We can do a SWOT on the marketing mix.

(i) *Product*

Strength: good workmanship, low prices, range of suites

Weakness: not a varied product portfolio, one material used, traditional ideas of customer needs

(ii) *Promotion*

Weakness: limited to local advertising, not targeted or controlled. Product oriented by featuring pictures of products

Strength: good local image and reputation for value for money

(iii) *Place*

Weakness: limited to two showrooms. No information on waiting lists etc

(iv) *Price*

Strength: current pricing policy is a strength while market is price conscious, but the market is changing

**3.26** Marketing opportunities do exist and some have been identified for us.

(a) To diversify into new products

- Curtains
- Other furniture

(b) To develop a wider market

(c) To develop new segments in the current geographic market

(d) To reposition DLF as a quality product provider

**3.27** Review the question carefully. We have done the SWOT and the marketing audit. Our response should be based on our analysis of the company. It should not be just a presentation of the analysis.

**3.28** We are required to evaluate three options and to submit a report indicating the advantages, disadvantages and control techniques in each case.

> It is important that you attempt all parts of this question if you want a chance to gain the maximum marks. In this case the question requirements give you an automatic structure to your report.

Before going further you will find it useful to spend 55 minutes preparing your own answer to the question. Compare it with the suggested solution we have provided. Remember that there is no single right answer. Use our solution only as a guide and as an indicator of the process involved.

## *Solution*

**3.29**

Report to: Managing Directors
Direct Lounge Furniture Ltd

From: A Consultant

Date: 5 April 20XX

Subject: Evaluation of product/market opportunities for DLF Ltd.

1 **Background**

1.1 Following our initial analysis of DLF's current situation we have found that although the company is in a secure financial position, with no doubt about short-term survival, the medium-term picture is rather bleak.

1.2 The DLF product range is limited to lounge suites, traditionally configurated and covered in one fabric, Dralon. This type of lounge furniture is probably in the mature stage and possibly in the decline stage of its life cycle. The DLF position has been weakened by the following macroenvironmental changes.

- Changing customer needs and expectations in home furnishings.
- Higher incomes making demand increasingly price inelastic.
- Safety fears encouraging customers to trade up.

1.3 We would therefore confirm your personal assessment that for DLF to thrive in the medium and long term, positive action must be taken to develop new product/market strategies. It is important that this action is undertaken before declining demand has an adverse impact on profitability and erodes the resources necessary for exploiting a new opportunity.

*The options*

2 **Product development only**

2.1 Product development could cover any activity from modification of the existing product (lounge suites), to adding new products to the range. We will assume that the option is basically the former.

2.2 *Advantages*

(a) This would be a market oriented development, allowing products to be designed to meet identified customer needs.

(b) You are experienced in the business, its production and operational requirements, materials etc.

(c) You have an established reputation in the business of lounge furniture.

(d) Product development would allow ranges and lines to be developed to meet the needs of a variety of market segments and would provide a number of opportunities to develop and enhance the business. The workmen have the skills to develop a quality 'made to order' package.

2.3 *Disadvantages*

(a) You are positioned at the value for money end of the market. Repositioning for a new segment of the market would require a considerable marketing effort and may be easier with a new kind of product, for example dining room furniture.

(b) Proliferation of product choice would increase the costs of stockholding, requiring a greater variety of raw materials etc.

(c) Existing showrooms may be unsuitable for attracting a different group of customers.

(d) Product portfolio is limited. Recession and declining demand for lounge furniture affects the whole business.

2.4 *Controls*

(a) Enquiry and sales data by product line would be important to assess the profitability of new products offered.

(b) If the product range was extended to provide all lounge furnishings, for example curtains, cushions, and tables, it would be important to measure the scale of value added sales, by customers purchasing additional items.

(c) Information on customers would help to identify whether target markets are being attracted. As most products will be delivered, it should be relatively easy to monitor geographic locations and possibly develop a simplified process for classifying residential neighbourhoods.

(d) There should be controls on production activities such as average stock levels. Order times etc would also be important to monitor efficiency of the operations as a more customer oriented product policy was developed.

3 **Market development only**

3.1 This would involve looking for new customers for the existing product range. It would imply increasing the geographic spread of the business.

3.2 *Advantages*

(a) It would require no change to the existing operation at production level.

(b) It would allow the profitable value for money target customer base to be extended. These are customers who DLF already know well.

(c) It would require no additional investment in the production resources.

3.3 *Disadvantages*

(a) It would leave the company product oriented, looking for customers for products, instead of developing products for customers. In the long run this approach will make DLF very vulnerable to competition.

(b) Although this strategy may boost sales in the short run, we know that customer needs and wants are changing and that this low price, traditional product is in decline.

(c) It would require investment in distribution to set up either showrooms or agencies in new areas. These may prove difficult to control.

3.4 *Controls*

(a) Controls would need to focus on any new distribution channels and salespeople established. Cost of sales and conversions of enquiries would help DLF establish the rate at which the new market became aware of their products.

(b) Given the indicators of general decline in DLF's market, control information would be needed to monitor average customer purchases (two sofas and no chairs), demand for matched curtains, average spend and other purchase patterns. This would provide valuable control information for sales forecasting.

4 **Product and market development**

4.1 At its extreme, for example moving into high quality kitchen units, product and market developments could be a major diversification, involving not only products but also customers with whom DLF is unfamiliar. However, diversifying into TV cabinets and coffee tables for a made to measure premium market would involve less risk.

4.2 *Advantages*

(a) It allows DLF to have an effective new start, researching the market to identify product/market opportunities which could be developed.

(b) Assuming that the current cash cow business will be retained at least in the short run, this strategy would diversify the business and so reduce the risk of sudden changes in demand caused by external variables.

(c) A product/market development would allow DLF to completely reposition themselves in the furniture market.

4.3 *Disadvantages*

(a) The strategy would be risky. The extent of the diversification would indicate how much risk is involved.

(b) It would be expensive, involving investment in both marketing and production.

(c) There is a danger of attempting to develop too many opportunities simultaneously, losing sight of the core business and over-extending resources.

4.4 *Controls*

(a) Such a major shift in strategy would require close control. New product sales levels would need to be monitored as would the value of business from new market segments.

(b) New distribution channels and promotional activities would probably be needed and these would also require evaluating to assess their effectiveness.

(c) Plans and budgets for the separate parts of the business would need establishing, together with administrative systems and procedures. These are unlikely to exist in the current small scale operation.

5 **Conclusions and recommendations**

(a) Action is needed to ensure the medium-term survival of DLF.

(b) The business has the strengths to extend its product range to meet the needs of new customer segments, in particular high quality, made to order products at premium prices. This extension of the product portfolio should be developed after careful research of the target market.

(c) The company should clearly review its mission and should establish financial objectives for the operation. Corporate and marketing plans must be developed as well as a management information system.

A Consultancy will be happy to offer any further assistance to DLF in this activity.

# 4 Other questions in the examination

**4.1** Although the questions in Section B are of the more traditional examination style, you must still make certain that you do not answer them in a purely academic manner.

**4.2** Ensure that you support theory with real world examples and illustrations, use the introductions and conclusions to comment on the value of the concept in question, disadvantages of a technique and so on. You should evaluate every question in terms not only of its content, but also the context in which it is being asked.

**4.3** Most students will have the knowledge to pass the exam, it is using that information in the 'context' of the question which causes the downfall. A question about the role of planning in the public sector should be answered differently from the same question set in a private sector context.

**4.4** Make sure you answer the questions set out and watch out for variations in mark allocation made within a question.

**4.5** These suggested solutions which follow are just that. There is no single correct answer, but use them as a comparison for your own work and an example of the style, approach and the depth needed in the exam.

**4.6** Remember to practise answers in exam conditions. You will have only 30 minutes per question in the exam room. After allowing planning and review time allow a little over 20 minutes writing time per question. Quality not quantity is required.

## Chapter Roundup

- This chapter has explained the nature and purpose of a mini-case. We have used examples from past examination papers to demonstrate how to use our recommended technique and extracts from examiners' reports have illustrated the examiners' requirements and common mistakes made by candidates.

# Questions and suggested solutions

## 1 Marketing and corporate strategy *45 mins*

What are the characteristics of strategic decisions at the corporate and marketing level, and how can a strategic perspective at the marketing level be developed? **(25 marks)**

## 2 Financial analysis *45 mins*

As a newly appointed marketing manager with profit responsibility for a wide range of consumer durables that are sold though several types of distribution network, draft a memorandum to the financial director explaining types of financial analysis you require and how the results will be used. **(25 marks)**

## 3 Gnome *45 mins*

The Gnome Company produces a variety of high-quality garden furniture and associated items, mostly in wood and wrought iron.

There is potential to expand the business. The directors have identified three main options for a four-year plan.

(a) Expand its flourishing retail outlet to include all products.
(b) Branch out into mail order.
(c) Produce greenhouses and conservatories.

These options would require initial expenditure of (a) £75,000, (b) £120,000 or (c) £200,000. The best information on year-end cash flows is as follows.

| | *Year 1* | *Year 2* | *Year 3* | *Year 4* |
|---|---|---|---|---|
| | £'000 | £'000 | £'000 | £'000 |
| (a) | 40 | 50 | 50 | 50 |
| (b) | 50 | 60 | 80 | 100 |
| (c) | 50 | 100 | 150 | 150 |

*Required*

(a) Using the data on expansion plans, evaluate the three investment options using the net present value (NPV) technique, assuming the cost of capital to be 10%, and recommend, with reasons, one option. (20 marks)

(b) Interpret your results for management. (5 marks)

**(25 marks)**

## 4 Bowland Carpets *27 mins*

Bowland Carpets Ltd is a major producer of carpets within the UK. The company was taken over by its present parent company, Universal Carpet Inc, in 1995. Universal Carpet is a giant, vertically integrated carpet manufacturing and retailing business, based within the USA but with interests all over the world.

Bowland Carpets operates within the UK in various market segments, including the high value contract and industrial carpeting area – hotels and office blocks etc – and in the domestic (household) market. Within the latter the choice is reasonably wide ranging from luxury carpets down to the cheaper products. Industrial and contract carpets contribute 25% of Bowland

Carpets' total annual turnover which is currently £80 million. During the early 1990s the turnover of the company was growing at 8% per annum, but since 1997 sales have dropped by 5% per annum in real terms.

Bowland Carpets has traditionally been known as a producer of high quality carpets, but at competitive prices. It has a powerful brand name, and it has been able to protect this by producing the cheaper, lower quality products under a secondary brand name. It has also maintained a good relationship with the many carpet distributors throughout the UK, particularly the mainstream retail organisations.

The recent decline in carpet sales, partly recession induced, has worried the US parent company. It has recognised that the increasing concentration within the European carpet manufacturing sector has led to aggressive competition within a low growth industry. It does not believe that overseas sales growth by Bowland Carpets is an attractive proposition as this would compete with other Universal Carpet companies. It does, however, consider that vertical integration into retailing (as already practised within the USA) is a serious option. This would give the UK company increased control over its sales and reduce its exposure to competition. The president of the parent company has asked Jeremy Smiles, managing director of Bowland Carpets, to address this issue and provide guidance to the US board of directors. Funding does not appear to be a major issue at this time as the parent company has large cash reserves on its balance sheet.

*Required*

To what extent do the distinctive competences of Bowland Carpets conform with the key success factors required for the proposed strategy change? **(15 marks)**

# 5 Flexible matrix *45 mins*

Several models have been developed to provide a more flexible approach to portfolio analysis than that developed by the Boston Consultancy Group Matrix (BCG). What are the weaknesses of the BCG approach? Using an alternative model of your choice show how it tries to overcome the limitations of the BCG. **(25 marks)**

# 6 Social change *45 mins*

Societies are changing in a wide variety of ways. Identify the nature and significance of two such changes that are taking place within your own society and discuss their implications for the marketing planning and control process. **(25 marks)**

# 7 Information about competitors *45 mins*

Your company's markets are becoming increasingly competitive. Explain how you would develop an effective competitive information system in these circumstances, the nature of the inputs that the system would require and how the outputs from the system might be used to improve the strategic marketing process. **(25 marks)**

# 8 Overseas environment *45 mins*

A clothing company based in the United Kingdom believes that its domestic market is limited and is proposing to expand by the manufacture and sale of its products abroad. At this stage, it has not identified where it will locate its manufacturing facility. The company believes that there are major advantages to be gained by setting up a factory in a country with a low-wage economy.

The company recognises the need to understand the marketing environment of the country within which it establishes its manufacturing facility. It appreciates that besides labour, there are other local environmental issues which need to be fully considered before entering negotiations to build a factory.

*Required*

(a) Compare and contrast the environmental factors which apply in both the UK and the other country. (16 marks)

(b) Explain the possible cultural influences on the effectiveness of the workforce in respect of local education and training, technology, working hours and domestic amenities. (9 marks)

**(25 marks)**

# 9 Culture and IM *45 mins*

Discuss the view that culture lies at the heart of all the problems connected with international marketing.

**(25 marks)**

# 10 Market research in developing countries *45 mins*

What are the problems encountered by companies carrying out international market research in developing countries? How might these companies deal with the issue of information gaps?

**(25 marks)**

# 1 Marketing and corporate strategy

Planning occurs at different management levels.

| Level | Management | Time Scale |
|---|---|---|
| 1 Corporate | Top | Long term |
| 2 Business/Functional | Middle | Medium term |
| 3 Operational/Action | Junior/staff | Short term |

Clarifying the level of analysis within the overall framework of a business plan causes some students and managers alike difficulty. Confusion arises because there are a number of different terms used in the literature for the same thing.

To help understand these levels imagine you are on a staircase, as you move up from one level to another the strategy of the lower level is the tactics of the higher. So for example, marketing strategy is part of corporate tactics. Similarly, sales strategy is marketing tactics.

A **strategic perspective** centres around planning for the future, either planning for the whole organisation or just for the marketing aspects of the organisation.

Johnson and Scholes in *Exploring Corporate Strategy* outline the characteristics associated with the word strategy and strategic decisions at the corporate or 'company wide' level.

(a) **The scope of an organisation's activities**. Does it focus on one area of activity or many? For example should BAe focus on defence?

(b) **The matching of the activities of an organisation to its environment**. In Europe, defence firms are seeking to collaborate to compete internationally, not just serve the home government.

(c) **The matching of an organisation's activities to its resource capability**: strategies need to be rooted in an adequate resource base.

(d) **The allocation of major resources** (often to do with major acquisitions or disposal of resources). BAe significantly rationalised its operations and workforce.

(e) **Affecting operational decisions**. Strategic decisions set off waves of lesser decisions. BAe's decision to rationalise the operation resulted in human resource issues for personnel, revised product and manufacturing plans which inevitably resulted in changes to the sorts of day-to-day problems faced by a production manager or a sales manager.

(f) **The values and expectations of those who have power**. Strategy can be thought of as a reflection of the attitudes and beliefs of those who have most influence in the organisation, this being related to the mission of the organisation. The expectations of the Government to maintain BAe as a major international competitor are influential in its mission.

(g) **The long–term direction of the organisation**. The decision to privatise BAe affected its long-term future.

(h) **Implications for change are thus are likely to be complex in nature**. This arises for three reasons: strategic decisions usually involve a **high degree of uncertainty**, require an **integrated approach** to managing the organisation (including a cross-functional perspective) and thirdly, **involve change**, not only planning change but also in implementing it.

Marketing planning represents the strategic approach to marketing. There are several key reasons for an increasing need for a strategic approach to marketing.

(a) The pace of **change and environmental complexity** – environmental issues, technological change, social change etc.

(b) Increasing **organisation size and complexity** – a move from functionally structured to matrix and strategic business units, internationalisation.

(c) Increased **competition** (deregulation, globalisation, technology).

Kotler (*Marketing Management*) highlights the characteristics of a strategic perspective in his definition of marketing management:

> 'The marketing **management process** consists of analysing market opportunities, researching and selecting target markets, designing marketing strategies, planning marketing programmes and organising, implementing and controlling the marketing effort.'

At the strategic level we see that marketing management involves four processes.

(a) **Analysis**: the antecedent of decision-making and plan formulation.

(b) **Planning**: analysis forms basis of plans, plans represent decision-making.

(c) **Implementation**: having made plans they need to be put into action.

(d) **Control**: this completes the cycle of functional management as it feeds into the analysis and planning stages and the cycle starts again.

The tangible outcome of a strategic perspective to marketing is the **marketing plan**, which outlines the current marketing situation, sets marketing objectives, strategies and tactics and outlines how the plan will be controlled.

Research indicates that very few firms actually have formally written marketing plans, and this is particularly the case within the small business and not-for-profit sectors. Many organisations find it difficult to develop a strategic approach to marketing because of a lack of resources, marketing knowledge, skills, time and probably most importantly a lack of marketing orientation or culture.

Many prescriptive approaches have been developed, often as a checklist of activities needed to be done to write a marketing plan. However, changing an organisation's culture requires top management support, internal communications and training on an on-going basis in marketing skills and cross-function co-ordination.

The reality is that many organisations still do not adopt marketing planning practices at all. Therefore the first challenge for marketers working in these types of companies will be to introduce successfully a simple planning system which has the support of senior management.

# 2 Financial analysis

**Tutorial note**. The finance function produces several different kinds of information. Be sure to cover all of them.

**Examiner's comments**. 'Too many candidates did not use the asked-for format or explain how the results would be used.'

MEMORANDUM

To: Financial Director
From: Marketing Manager
Date: December 200X
Subject: Requirements for Financial Analysis

Can I take this opportunity to outline my current understanding of how you can aid my marketing decision making. I would welcome your comments on this and recommendations on any other types of financial information you think my be useful to me in my new role.

Having taken my Diploma in Marketing I am aware that there are three important accounting roles which produce different forms of output which are relevant to the marketing department.

(a) **Financial accounting** results in the annual report and accounts which includes the key financial statements of the balance sheet, profit and loss and funds flow statement. Whilst important in recording the effects of marketing activities, this information does not aid decision-making.

(b) **Corporate finance** is concerned with financial management and ensuring that enough funds are made available. Marketing activities are not usually funded separately, but are included in the financial plans produced as part of (c) below.

(c) **Management accounting**. Management accounts are produced regularly, usually monthly or quarterly, and aid operational decision-making. I would hope that I can receive monthly information which will include a comparison of financial **performance to date** against my budgeted targets, and assessment of that performance against the budget for the year. In this way financial analysis should aid my marketing analysis, planning and control.

In particular I see financial information being useful in the **review and control process** related to the areas over which I have some or total control, namely marketing costs, revenue and profits by product, product line, product portfolio, pricing strategy, promotional strategy and distribution channel management. This relationship can be shown diagrammatically.

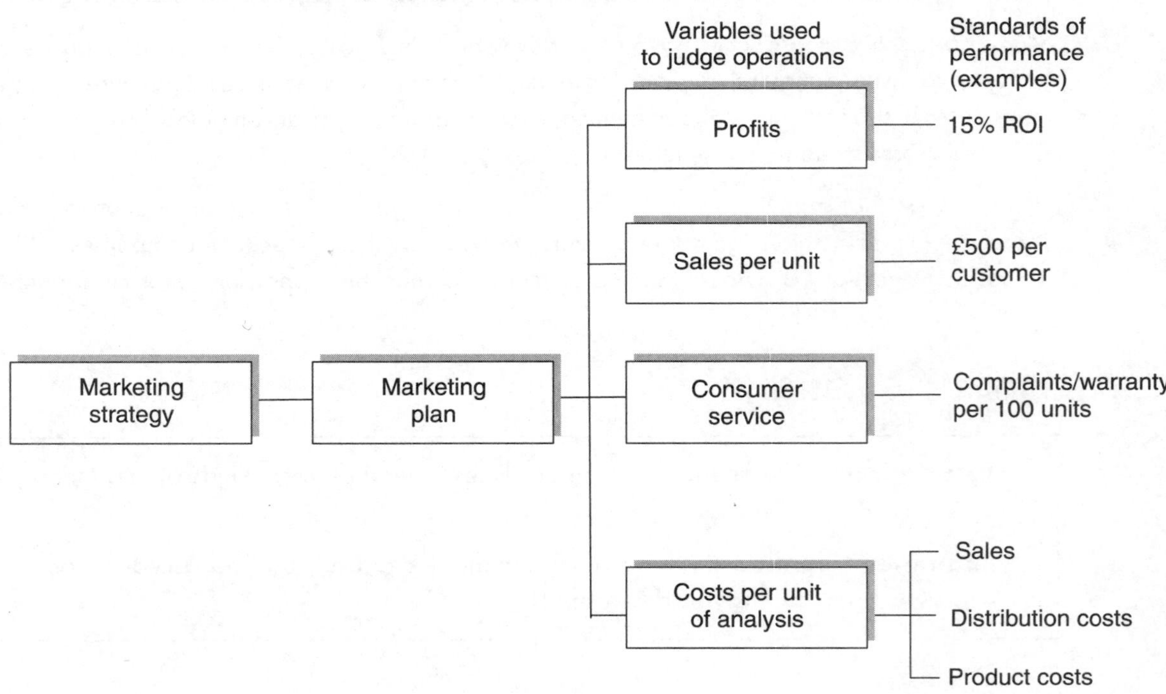

In seeking to control my marketing activities it would be useful for the financial information to conform to the standard characteristics of effective control systems, namely that the information:

- Should be **timely**
- Should measure the essential **nature of the activity** being assessed
- Should provide information on **trends**
- Should **facilitate action**
- Must be **economical and meaningful**

With this in mind, and from the diagram, we can see that as marketing manager I would find financial information relating to the profits, sales and costs of my products useful. More specifically, I need this **information by product and product line**, and by the various **distribution channels** through which we sell our goods. From this variance analysis can be conducted. I should be able to keep close control over my marketing budget each month and be able to assess, longer term, the effectiveness of this expenditure. It would also be useful for me to have **comparative performance data on our major competitors**.

The results of this financial analysis will be used to make both **strategic and tactical decisions**. For example, analysis of sales and profit trends by channel, in conjunction with market share analysis, will inform my distribution channel management strategy and the allocation of trade marketing support.

Looking at financial and market data together, **new product development** and distribution channel development strategies can be formulated. If **specific promotional campaigns** can be isolated, their effectiveness can be assessed by analysis of **sales trend data**. By identification of the most profitable products and channels and in conjunction with the sales manager, **sales force targets and compensation programmes** can be developed, together with sales promotion and advertising support programmes within allocated budgets.

Without this sort of financial information, marketing analysis, planning and control will be less efficient and effective. In view of this, can we arrange a meeting to discuss the exact detail and form in which the financial information will be provided?

# 3 Gnome

> **Pass marks**. Remember that you need to sum all of the individual present values in order to determine the net present value for each of the Options A – C.
>
> The formula for determining the IRR of an investment is not provided in the *exam* – you should therefore make sure that you know it before sitting your Paper 9 examination.

(a) **Option A – Expand retail outlet**

| *Year* | *Cash flow* | *Discount factor* | *NPV* |
|---|---|---|---|
| | £'000 | 10% | £'000 |
| 0 | (75) | 1.000 | (75.00) |
| 1 | 40 | 0.909 | 36.36 |
| 2 | 50 | 0.826 | 41.30 |
| 3 | 50 | 0.751 | 37.55 |
| 4 | 50 | 0.683 | 34.15 |
| | | | 74.36 |

**Option B – Mail order**

| *Year* | *Cash flow* | *Discount factor* | *NPV* |
|---|---|---|---|
| | £'000 | 10% | £'000 |
| 0 | (120) | 1.000 | (120.00) |
| 1 | 50 | 0.909 | 45.45 |
| 2 | 60 | 0.826 | 49.56 |
| 3 | 80 | 0.751 | 60.08 |
| 4 | 100 | 0.683 | 68.30 |
| | | | 103.39 |

**Option C – Greenhouses and conservatories**

| *Year* | *Cash flow* | *Discount factor* | *NPV* |
|---|---|---|---|
| | £'000 | 10% | £'000 |
| 0 | (200) | 1.000 | (200.00) |
| 1 | 50 | 0.909 | 45.45 |
| 2 | 100 | 0.826 | 82.60 |
| 3 | 150 | 0.751 | 112.65 |
| 4 | 150 | 0.683 | 102.45 |
| | | | 143.15 |

**Option C gives the highest net present value and therefore this should be chosen.**

(c) If **funding** is **available** the NPV calculations indicate that all **three options should be undertaken**. (There is no reason, on the face of it why undertaking one option should preclude the undertaking of the others.)

If **funds** are **limited**, it will be necessary to **compare the relative NPVs per £1 invested**.

| | *NPV* | *Investment* | *NPV per £1 invested* | *Ranking* |
|---|---|---|---|---|
| | £'000 | £'000 | £ | |
| Option A | 74.36 | 75 | 0.99 | 1st |
| Option B | 103.39 | 120 | 0.86 | 2nd |
| Option C | 143.15 | 200 | 0.72 | 3rd |

In this case funds should be invested in **option A first**, then in **option B**, then in **option C**, depending upon how much is available.

# 4 Bowland Carpets

(a) An organisation's **distinctive competences**, highlighted in its internal analysis, are those features, skills or processes that differentiates an organisation and is performance/products attractively from its competitors and enable it to obtain a special sphere of influence or a strong competitive position. Competences derive from experience, staff skills and the quality of co-ordination.

**Key or critical success factors**. Organisations need to identify the key success factors, assets and skills needed to compete successfully in a market.

(i) **Strategic necessities** do not necessarily provide an **advantage,** because others have them, but their **absence** will cause a substantial weakness.

(ii) **Strategic strengths** (in which the organisation excels), are superior to those of competitors and provide a base of advantage. The market analysis will also be looking at how these will change in the future and how the assets and skills of competitors can be neutralised by strategies.

Key success factors include good distribution networks, advanced office systems and up-to-date marketing intelligence.

**Mismatches between competences and success factors**

Most organisations doing a SWOT analysis will find a mismatch somewhere. A company may be successful at establishing a strong position during the early stages of market development, only to lose ground later when the key success factors have changed. With consumer products marketing and distribution skills are dominant during the early phases but operations and manufacturing become more crucial as the product moves into the maturity and decline stage.

**Bowland's new strategy**. The management at the US parent company of Bowland Carpets have come up with a new strategy in an attempt to solve the problem of the declining carpet sales in the UK, mainly in the domestic market. The contract and industrial carpet segment will not be affected radically as the distribution network generally uses direct sales.

Bowland UK's competences are the ability to:

(i) Offer a wide range of high quality products at **competitive prices**.
(ii) Sustain **powerful brand names**, presence in different market segments.
(iii) Sustain **good relationships** with distributors.

**Success factors for retailing**

The proposed option of vertical integration into retailing will require a set of key success factors which will include some of these competences. However, there are gaps which are a cause for concern.

The key success factors for vertical integration into retail sales which have been developed in the US will not be totally transferable to the UK and the domestic company has no expertise in this field.

(i) **Distribution**. It is not clear whether the intention is to introduce this strategy as an addition to the current distribution network or instead of it. Both of these options would affect the **relationship with distributors** that has built up over a period and could be very **damaging to sales**. To compensate for this loss, Bowland Carpets would need to have a strong **geographical** presence either in High Street positions or in out-of-town developments. This could be **very costly** in both site selection and development.

(ii) **Expertise** in **retailing** and **distribution**. Staffing and servicing the retail outlets and training the staff in the skills required will be time-consuming and expensive. When customers buy carpets they expect a measuring, fitting and laying service as well as after-sales support. It may be that the UK company can learn from the USA but the culture of marketing household durables is different in both countries.

(iii) The **ability to provide a choice of products and services for the customer**. If there is insufficient choice, Bowland Carpets will have to find competitive manufacturers to fill the gap. This action may defeat the strategy to raise the sales in the **domestic** carpet market.

**Conclusion**. **Bowland's distinctive competences are not appropriate to the key success factors required for retailing**.

# 5 Flexible matrix

(a) **Introduction**

The logic of product portfolio analysis is the same as that applied to share portfolios. Just as financial investors have different investments with varying risks and rates of return, firms should have a portfolio of products (and possibly strategic business units (SBUs)) characterised by different market growth rates and relative market shares. A number of alternative models of portfolio analysis have been developed which include the BCG growth-share matrix, the General Electric multifactor portfolio model and the Shell directional policy matrix.

(b) **BCG Growth-Share Matrix**

The Boston Consulting Group in the mid 1960s developed the BCG matrix as a strategic planning tool with the rationale that relative market share and market growth rates are important for determining appropriate marketing strategies.

| *Market growth rate* | | | |
|---|---|---|---|
| 20%<br>15%<br>10% | **STARS**<br>Moderate<br>+ or –<br>cash flow | **QUESTION MARKS**<br>Large<br>negative<br>cash flow |
| 5%<br>0% | **CASH COWS**<br>Large<br>positive<br>cash flow | **DOGS**<br>Modest<br>+ or –<br>cash flow |

x 10 x 5 x 1 x 0.5 x 0.1

Market share (relative to major competitor)

The logic of the matrix is based on four assumptions.

(i) **Margins and funds generated increase with market share**, as a result of experience and scale effects.

(ii) **Sales growth demands cash** to finance working capital and increases in capacity.

(iii) **Increases in market share need cash** to support share gaining tactics.

(iv) **Market growth slows as the product reaches life cycle maturity**. At this stage, cash surpluses can be generated by high share players to support products still in the growth stages of their life cycle.

BCG stress the need to build a **balanced portfolio** to ensure sufficient **positive net cash flow** to ensure long-term success. This means few or no dogs, and enough cash cows to:

- Turn stars into cash cows as markets mature
- To invest in question marks to build market share, and hence become stars

(c) **Weaknesses of the BCG Approach**

(i) **Oversimplification**. More than two factors that affect cash flow.

(ii) Cash flow as the performance criteria: some argue **return on investment** is more important.

(iii) **Ambiguity in classifications** – it is difficult to separate SBU and product level analysis. In addition, what contributes to a high and low share, or growth rate? These factors make it difficult to plot positions accurately.

(iv) **New products and negative growth** situations are not dealt with.

(v) The strategies suggested by the model tend to be **highly prescriptive** in nature and there are situations where they may be inappropriate. Companies with low market share can still be successful. Cash flow can be large from a small share player, for example when scale and experience effects are small, when a firm has a low cost source of raw material, or if entry barriers are high. PIMS analysis also indicates that **quality** is a partial substitute for market share.

(vi) The questionable **accuracy of data supplied** and/or processing of the data.

(vii) Derivation of 'gospel' figures for a specific business from a **generalist technique** or model.

(d) **General Electric's Multifactor Portfolio Model**

In an attempt to overcome some of the weaknesses of the BCG matrix, General Electric's Multifactor portfolio model takes into account more factors to determine **market attractiveness and competitive position**. Each company needs to determine the factors underlying each dimension in their particular market.

General Electric uses industry attractiveness split into high, medium and low and **business strength** split into strong, medium and weak. The nine cells fall into three distinct strategy and investment recommendations; **invest for growth**, manage selectively for **earnings** and **harvest/withdraw**.

A specific example for the Hydraulic Pumps market (Kotler, 1997) is provided below.

| **Market attractiveness** | Weight | Rating (1–5) | Value |
|---|---|---|---|
| Market size | 0.2 | 4 | 0.8 |
| Market growth rate | 0.2 | 5 | 1.0 |
| Profit margin | 0.15 | 4 | 0.6 |
| Competitive intensity | 0.15 | 2 | 0.3 |
| Technological requirements | 0.15 | 4 | 0.6 |
| Inflationary vulnerability | 0.05 | 3 | 0.15 |
| Energy requirements | 0.05 | 2 | 0.1 |
| Environmental impact | 0.05 | 3 | 0.15 |
| | | | 3.70 |

**Business strength**

| | | | |
|---|---|---|---|
| Market share | 0.1 | 4 | 0.4 |
| Share growth | 0.15 | 2 | 0.3 |
| Product quality | 0.1 | 4 | 0.3 |
| Brand reputation | 0.1 | 5 | 0.5 |
| Distribution network | 0.05 | 4 | 0.2 |
| Promotional effectiveness | 0.05 | 3 | 0.15 |
| Productive capacity | 0.05 | 3 | 0.15 |
| Productive efficiency | 0.05 | 2 | 0.1 |
| Unit costs | 0.15 | 3 | 0.45 |
| Material supplies | 0.05 | 5 | 0.25 |
| R&D performance | 0.1 | 3 | 0.3 |
| Managerial personnel | 0.05 | 4 | 0.2 |
| | | | 3.4 |

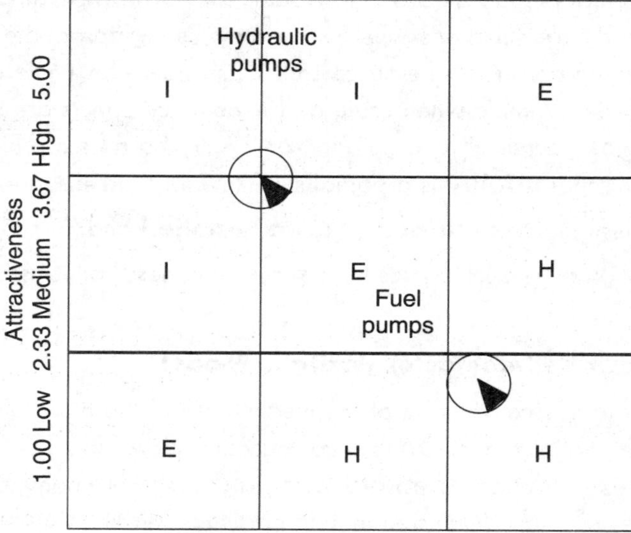


From the portfolio the two BCG factors are subsumed under the two major variables of the GE matrix, and thus the model leads planners to look at more factors in evaluating an actual business or product. In addition, the circle shows the size of the overall market and the company's share within the market plus the direction the business is likely to move in should no change in strategy occur. The hydraulic pumps business is in a fairly attractive part of the matrix whereas fuel pumps are very unattractive. Overall, this portfolio matrix adds greater information into the decision making process.

**Conclusion**

Despite their limitations, portfolio matrices do prove useful in the analysis and ideas generation stage of strategy formulation. As there are a number of matrices to choose from, the strategic planner should consider using more than one and adapt the model to his or her own organisational situation.

# 6 Social change

> **Examiner's comments**. Reasonable answers, with most candidates focusing on demography and new technology – but many ignored the implications for planning and control.

A key stage in the marketing planning and control process is an analysis of the current situation, or **marketing audit**. The audit should consist of an analysis of the wider **macro** environment, the more specific **micro** environment and an **internal analysis** of the organisation. The reason for conducting an audit is to ensure that the strategies, tactics and controls implemented are in line with the current needs, wants, behaviours and contexts of the **target market**. As societies change, so too should the way products and services are marketed. Less than twenty years ago in the UK it was acceptable to market Supersoft shampoo with an image of a rather amused woman being forcibly taken away on the shoulder of a Viking. Equally the idea of a product designer being able to work together with a client hundreds of miles away via an Internet connection was not a possibility.

Societies constantly change. Doyle, in *Marketing Management and Strategy,* offers ten environmental changes which appear to be accelerating:

(a) **Fashionisation**: goods affected by annual model changes, rapid obsolescence and unpredictable demand. New models and new services are becoming the key to enhancing margins.

(b) **Micro-markets**: customers expect customisation of goods to their specific needs. Technology permits ever-finer market segmentation and product range expansion.

(c) **Rising expectations**: brought about by higher quality products and services.

(d) **Technological change**: brought about both product and process improvements together with a society much more receptive to diffusion of technological innovation.

(e) **Competition**: market barriers have fallen with declining tariffs, lower transport costs and speed of information about market opportunities.

(f) **Globalisation**: rising incomes for travel and access to international media have created common demands and opportunities for common suppliers.

(g) **Service**: product advantages are difficult to gain and defend, often competition is based on service augmentation.

(h) **Commoditisation**: today's speciality products are tomorrow's commodities, unless companies can move the goalposts through faster innovation, profit margins decline.

(i) **Erosion of brands**: the fractionisation of previously homogenous markets, together with the growth in own label reliability is reducing the power of the big brands.

(j) **New constraints**: new regulations from the EU in terms of the environment and the raising of ethical standards brings offending companies under increasing scrutiny.

There are a number of ways in which society is changing.

a) An ageing of the population in Europe

b) A growing social divide between relatively prosperous knowledge workers and the rest

c) The fragmentation of traditional consumer life stages (due to fractured career paths, redundancy, self-employment, rising divorce, caring for parents, middle age inheritances and single parent families).

Of all these changes the two which will be selected for further discussion are **demographic change** and **technological change**.

**Demography**

At the beginning of the 1990s people aged over fifty were 17.8m or 31% of the UK population. By 2025 this will rise to 23m, representing a significant increase in the proportion of old to young, non-working to working people in the UK Currently, approximately 30% of the over fifties have no mortgage left to pay, and they represent the inheritance generation (£17bn in 1997). In the UK the over sixty-fives can be divided into three segments:

- 20% well-off
- 30% property rich but cash poor
- 50% state pension

Clearly with the growth in the older consumers and the related reduction in younger people, this brings significant implications for the planning and control for specific product groups. The demand for financial services, medical products, retirement housing and holidays is likely to increase whilst the demand for nightclubs, alcohol, starter homes and jeans is likely to fall. More specifically, the product manager of Thomson Holidays' 'Young at Heart' brand markets to 'JOLLies'; Jet-Setting Oldies with Loads of Loot, or the 20% well-off. At the beginning of the 1990s this represented 60,000 holidays and the market is increasing. When marketing the brand a number of key points emerge.

(a) Good service is vital to repeat purchase.

(b) This segment is responsive to sales promotions which take time to redeem, involve collection and reward rather than competitions, free draws or lotteries.

(c) Media choice is skewed towards the Daily Telegraph and Daily Mail and retirement magazines such as Saga, Yours and Choice.

(d) This group watches a lot of TV. Good audience profiles include 'This Is Your Life' and 'Coronation Street'.

(e) This segment tend to identify with their children rather than with their parents and so think of themselves as 20 years younger.

For those organisations which find themselves in declining markets, they will experience growing competition. Those that remain will need to more closely segment and position their products, consider expanding their product/market focus through market and product development strategies and closely control their cost and profit performance.

**Technology**

Perhaps even more significant than demographic changes is the influence exerted by changing technology on society. The convergence of computing and telecom technologies is significantly changing work, leisure and marketing planning practice. As the cost of IT falls and computer speeds increase, the resultant information revolution is beginning to change how we learn and work. Consumers' acceptance of new technologically based products has also increased; the use of mobile telephones, faxes, home multi media systems, virtual shopping malls and interactive terminals is common. But what are the specific implications for marketing planning and control processes?

(a) **Sales**. The salesperson with a portable PC can run interactive sales demonstrations and automatic order processing.

(b) **Distribution**. The videobooth allows customers to talk directly to staff such as accounts personnel and forms can be signed and transmitted. Electronic data interchange has reduced the costs and speed of the grocery supply chain.

(c) **Product development**. The designer can have video clips of customers' reactions to prototypes from focus groups, designs can be viewed anywhere in the world, amended or approved in minutes rather than days through the post.

(d) **Market research**. Researchers can use software to tailor questions depending on the previous answer. Results can be downloaded for immediate analysis. Real time sales data can be merged, cut and presented in striking visual form and communicating direct to the marketing director.

(e) **Communications**. Companies can produce interactive infomercials such as Sainsburys recipe book and if linked to a home shopping system, purchases can be made. The logistics and costs of advertising are being re-worked due to the ability to send ads. from computer to computer down ISDN phone lines.

(f) **Control**. As the data gathering for the results of product launches moves from months to weeks this feedback is leading to more reactive, time-sensitive, accountable marketing strategies. Retailers can use scanning data to determine which lines should be delisted and which to carry.

Often changes in society are afforded too much significance in relation to the nature and speed of their affects on marketing practice. For example, many writers talked about how consumers would be prepared to pay vast extra amounts for environmentally friendly products. Then we all heard about the caring, sharing, stakeholding nineties. Whilst the ageing population, new technologies, environmentalism and a growing focus on social responsibility are all changes which are taking place, most marketers have kept their balance and not over responded, but adjusted gradually in line with the pace of change. The microwave, like the video recorder, patented just after world war two, was not commercialised until the sixties and took twenty years to achieve wide scale consumer acceptance. That stated, those organisations which practise marketing planning and control successfully will be those which anticipate and respond to changing societal needs.

# 7 Information about competitors

> **Examiner's comments**. The better answers discussed the structure of a competitive information system, the nature of the inputs and how the outputs could then be fed into the strategic marketing process.

A **competitive information system** is an integral element of a marketing information system. The importance of this element is heightened when a company is faced with increasingly competitive market conditions. In this situation, information obtained from the system is invaluable when formulating competitive marketing strategy.

When establishing a competitive information system it is important to consider the operational set-up. The **type of information required** should be specified, and **sources of data** and methods for collection considered. Procedures should then be formulated for **gathering and**

**reporting** the information and responsibility for information gathering assigned. Finally, procedures for **analysing and distributing** the information are needed.

The nature of the inputs to the competitive information system would be as follows.

(a) **Marketing intelligence**

This constitutes information gathered on the marketplace on a day-to-day basis forming continual monitoring to identify trend, change and unexpected event data.

**Sources**

- Trade journals, publications and press articles
- Exhibitions and industry contacts
- Competitor promotional literature and price lists
- Competitors annual reports
- Industry reports eg Mintel, Euromonitor etc
- Trade Associations
- Sales representative reports
- Reports from marketing channels eg distributors and retailers
- Off the peg research data eg AGB Superpanel

(b) **Marketing research**

Where information is needed on an ad-hoc basis to make a specific marketing decision. Information of this type is obtained from two methods.

(i) **Secondary (desk) research**

Where data gathered for another purpose is applied to the problem at hand. A number of sources from the above list would be appropriate in this area eg Industry Reports.

(ii) **Primary (field) research**

Surveys, customer panels and observation research of this type could produce information on issues such as:

- Customer care
- Service/product quality

The **outputs from the system** need to be evaluated, analysed and disseminated to appropriate departments within the company. Information of this type can be used, for example, to build a profile on current and potential market competitors, their market positioning and comparative strengths and weaknesses. Strategically, this information would be invaluable when making decisions in areas such as segmentation and positioning, product and market development as well as building competitor response models. Overall, competitive information systems are invaluable to formulating marketing strategy, particularly in increasing competitive marketplaces.

# 8 Overseas environment

(a) **Environmental factors**

**Political and legal factors**

(i) **Political conditions** in the individual overseas markets (eg overall stability) or sources of supply (eg risk of nationalisation).

(ii) **Relationships between country governments**. If the firm intends to use the plant as a basis for exports to other countries, the country's membership of international trade bodies is important, and political relationships with other states matter.

(iii) In some low wage countries, the **legal framework** is not secure (McDonalds was evicted from a prime leasehold site in Beijing when it was decided to redevelop the property irrespective of the legal agreement).

(iv) **Political connections**. Where the low wage economy has involved state planning, political connections may be more important than legality, and help might be needed to get round a complex and possibly corrupt bureaucracy.

(v) **Local labour** law may be different (redundancies are legally hard to achieve in some countries, eg India).

**Economic factors**

(i) The overall level of **economic activity** and growth.

(ii) The relative levels of **inflation** in the domestic and overseas market.

(iii) **Exchange rate**, its level and volatility. This is relevant if the new plant will source some of its raw materials from overseas.

(iv) **Exchange controls**. Will the firm be allowed to remit profits to its home country?

(v) The relative **prosperity** of individual overseas markets.

(vi) The state of the **labour market**. Cheap labour is often unproductive, because it is untrained and perhaps inefficient. While labour costs may be lower, the apparent saving may be reduced by lower productivity.

**Social and cultural factors**

(i) The **cultures and practices** of customers and consumers in individual markets.

(ii) The **media and distribution** systems in overseas markets.

(iii) The differences in **ways of doing business**.

(iv) The degree to which **national cultural differences** matter for the product concerned. For clothing, the firm might have to consider different sizes, materials (for ideas as to 'formal' or 'leisure wear' and national stylistic preferences (eg bright colours as opposed to sober hues).

**Technological factors**

(i) The degree to which a firm can **imitate** the technology of its competitors.

(ii) A firm's access to domestic and overseas **patents**.

(iii) **Intellectual property** protection varies in different countries.

(iv) **Technology transfer** requirements (some countries regard investments from overseas companies as learning opportunities and require the investing company to share some of its technology).

(v) The relative **cost of technology** compared to labour.

(vi) An appropriate **infrastructure** to enable the technology to be used effectively. Some high-tech plants fail in poor countries because there is no supply of spares or trained engineers. More basically, the firm has to rely on public supplies of electricity and water, and in some countries power cuts are frequent and costly. The firm might have to supply its own generators.

(vii) In some countries **telecommunications** are inefficient and expensive.

Currently, the firm is hoping to exploit low labour costs. How far is this realistic in the long term? If the market is to enjoy overall economic growth, rising prosperity will mean rising incomes and rising wages. If the firm is to make a substantial investment in the local factory, it will have to plan for productivity improvements.

**The overall competitive environment**

(i) This relates to the five forces analysis propounded by Michael Porter.

(1) **Barriers to entry**. Existing firms might have powerful political connections which they can exploit against the competitor from overseas. Customers may prefer the national products and brands. Also the distribution network may be effectively tied up.

(2) **Substitute products**. We are not told what type of clothing is to be made, and who the customers are. In some countries, traditional clothing, made at home, may substitute for factory produced products.

(3) **Bargaining power of customers**. No detail is given of distribution, and how the firm intends to sell its products, but distributors might have high power.

(4) **Bargaining power of suppliers**. Again, we are not told how the factory will be supplied. Local suppliers might welcome the new business.

(5) **Competitive rivalry**. In some countries, local businesses have strong political connections. Whilst overseas investment might be welcome, as official policy, it can all to easily be hindered at local level. Furthermore, in many companies, existing producers are owned by the state, and there may be restrictions on competition. Finally, competitors may have many distribution networks sewn up, and the newcomer may find hurdles greater than expected.

(ii) We can also use Porter's diamond model of **national competitive advantage** to assess the venture.

(1) The **rivalry** between different firms has been discussed above.

(2) **Demand conditions**. The new market might help the firm compete elsewhere, by the demand conditions it possesses, but this seems unlikely.

(3) **Factor conditions**. What is the new market's supply of basic and advanced factors, apart from labour? To what extent is the firm evading other problems by concentrating on low-cost, and low-skill labour, as opposed to improving productivity at home?

(4) **Related and supporting industries**. A country in which there is a cluster of textile and clothing related industries? History often shows that industrialising countries often start off with textiles.

It is also worth mentioning the physical environment. (Shell has received bad publicity about environmental degradation in Ogoniland.)

(b) **Cultural issues and the workforce**

Culture is a shared body of beliefs, values and assumptions, even a way of interpreting the world, which guide the behaviour of individuals. Most organisations have a culture, but this is part of the wider culture of the society in which they exist. The firm will have to deal with the national culture in a number of areas.

(i) **Local education and training**

If low labour costs are a reason for the move, this implies that the processes are fairly labour intensive, as labour costs must be a significant proportion of total costs. The influence of **local education** will make itself felt in a number of areas.

(1) **Basic literacy and numeracy**. Many relatively poor countries, such as Sri Lanka, have high literacy rates in the local language. Sadly, in other poor countries, this is not the case. If this is needed for the factory, the actual supply of labour might be smaller than appears.

(2) **Knowledge of English**. In order to ensure that the factory is properly run, at least some of the local managers and staff need a good working knowledge of business English. In some countries (eg in eastern Europe where Russian was the first foreign language taught) English speakers might be in short supply.

(3) **Technology**. Education and training implications are discussed in (ii) below.

(4) **Attitudes to work**. The firm will have to train its employees, in part to acclimatise them to the corporate culture of the firm. Professor Hofstede contrasted attitudes to work in different countries.

In some countries, disagreeing with the boss is not acceptable behaviour, whereas a boss from the UK may be touting for new ideas.

Continuous improvement programmes require people to show more initiative than a culture based on deference to authority might accept.

Many cultures have a high power-distance, whereas a UK firm might have a low power-distance and a lower group orientation than some Asian countries.

(ii) **Technology**

(1) The firm will have to train its workers how to use the machines and how to maintain them properly, so that their useful life is not shortened through poor management.

(2) If the plant is to develop further and develop new materials, personnel with an appropriate technical knowledge will need to be recruited. Again, some poor countries have quite good universities, so there may be a pool of qualified engineers available for recruitment. It is unlikely, according to Porter, that firms can compete on low labour costs alone, and the firm will invest to enhance the productivity of the labour force.

(3) As is mentioned above, cultural attitudes to technology and the work processes are important. Some labour disciplines regarding machinery need to be enforced, particularly with regard to health and safety.

(4) It is possible that many will welcome the opportunity to raise their skills.

(iii) **Working hours**

Even within Europe, different national cultures suggest different attitudes to time, timekeeping and punctuality. Clearly, the factory has to be operated efficiently, and this might require a greater degree of labour discipline than the people might have expected.

However the firm will be able to offer perhaps better wages than local firms, and will be able to choose employees for which this is not a problem.

Even poor countries have **labour regulations**, and a large factory would be more subject to regulation in this respect than local family businesses or sweatshops. Indeed, there might be legal restrictions on shifts and working hours which have to be respected.

(iv) **Domestic amenities**

In some countries in the past, firms were expected to take a paternalistic approach to employees, and to supply them with **housing**, to ensure **lifetime loyalty**, or other accommodation if the plant is far away from convenient transport. Sometimes such accommodation is restricted to a dormitory arrangement. Few people in wealthier countries would tolerate such an arrangement, but it might be acceptable in poorer countries, especially if transport is expensive or hazardous.

Other amenities can include subsiding the education of workers' children, a good canteen, and health services in the factory. The firm can prove itself a good corporate citizen and earn the respect of the workforce.

# 9 Culture and IM

The extent to which culture lies at the heart of all problems connected with International Marketing depends much on one's definition of culture. There is no universally accepted definition but it is commonly held to centre on the **value systems** used in a particular society. Those value systems apply obviously in areas such as religion and the arts, but if one's definition of culture is wide enough, can also extend into the economic sphere.

It is probably untrue to assert that all the problems connected with International Marketing can be ascribed to cultural differences but certainly they represent a major, and probably the major, influence on International Marketing. The precise extent of the influence depends on the nature of the goods in question. For example, foodstuffs are well known as highly **culturally dependent** whereas building excavators are not! Thus a manager engaged in marketing food would be much more likely to agree with the assertion than one in the construction industry.

The principal impact of culture in International Marketing lies in its influence on the **environment in which the sales/purchase transaction takes place**. It affects the way in which the seller offers his product to the market, the benefits perceived in that offer by the potential customer (and thus the suitability of the goods for their intended purpose) and, particularly, the communications mix by which the seller entices the potential purchaser.

Culture also has a marked influence on **market research and analysis**. The very fact that cultural differences exist requires market research to be much more extensive and thorough than in the domestic market (where the manager's own cultural values will provide a good deal of secondary information). Consequently it also makes market analysis much more expensive and difficult to perform. And since the market research work may itself be culturally bound it is sometimes in itself of questionable validity.

If one confines one's definition of culture to the impact on buyers and sellers as individuals, culture although important is limited to the types of influence noted above and therefore cannot be said to lie at the heart of all international marketing problems.

If the definition of culture is extended to include the influence of individuals' attitudes on the way society as a whole is organised, a whole new range of international marketing problems comes within its ambit. For example the **political and legal structure** of a nation has a major impact on the way any enterprise markets its products within it. This influence extends over the whole marketing mix.

(a) **Product design and quality** is affected by national standards

(b) The **structure of business** is influenced by national norms

(c) The **price** that customers are willing to pay is limited by the benefits perceived in the goods by that culture

(d) The **methods of promotion** may be constrained by a range of political, legal and social constraints and attitudes

All this occurs within the context of any one nation. The culture of a country may even dictate whether a foreign marketer is welcome at all. Mars encountered some hostility in Russia when the population became tired of its relentless promotion of the carefree American life in its advertising. Mars is still a strong force in the country, but marketers had to recognise that local advertising had to be adapted to reflect Russian preoccupations and traditions.

Many countries in fact have **sub-cultures** within them, which multiplies the problems faced by the international marketer. When viewed from the perspective of a multinational enterprise cultural differences become a major factor in the assessment of whether to offer a **standardised** product range or a range **adapted** to meet perceived local needs.

Although there are problems in international marketing that cannot be ascribed to cultural differences (such as the method a business chooses for pricing its products) it is certainly possible to assert confidently that culture lies at the heart of most, if not all, problems in the field.

# 10 Market research in developing countries

Typical problems encountered in conducting **market research** in developing countries are as follows:

(a) Lack of reliable basic demographic and **economic statistics** upon which to develop a workable database.

(b) A general lack of up-to-date **secondary market intelligence** information, including that which is provided by organisations such as the Economist Intelligence Unit.

(c) When data, or information, is found it may be **out-of-date**, **inaccurate** or **irrelevant** for the purpose for which is required.

(d) The **units of measurement** may differ from what is usually expected in the developed world.

(e) Primary data can be difficult to obtain due to **cultural differences**, which in many developing countries do not encourage the disclosure of personal information.

(f) There is a lack of **marketing research agencies** in developing countries.

(g) Lack of telephones, poor transport **infrastructure** and problems of accessibility to respondents all hinder the primary research process.

The absence of reliable and appropriate secondary data presents significant management problems regarding the obtaining of primary data. The problems extend to all aspects of collection, analysis, and interpretation of data, as well as the training and supervision of interviewers.

**Information gaps** may be filled by the following analytical techniques.

(a) Analysis of **international trade statistics** between the developed world and the target developing countries can be used as a **proxy measure** to establish the pattern of trade, and give a first order approximation of market size

(b) Multiple factor indices using **proxy measures**, for example, estimating literacy levels from the number of schools, or government estimates of the number of school age children

(c) **Cross-country comparisons** in which the trade development patterns of an existing developing country are used to estimate the likely development of the target country

(d) **Time series** approaches with estimates of the rate of product (or service) demand growth, based on the stage of development of the target developing country

(e) **Regression analysis** looking for relationships between major variables, for example, examining the relationship between the vehicle population, estimates of GDP per head of population and population of a country to estimate annual demand for cars.

If these analytical techniques do not produce meaningful results then a visit to the target developing countries and gathering information from first hand investigation is the remaining option.

# Further reading

P Doyle, *Value Based Marketing*, Wiley, 2000

J Johansson, *Global Marketing*, Irwin McGraw Hill, 2000

P Doyle, *Marketing Management and Strategy*, Pearson, 2002 3rd ed

C Gilligan & R Wilson, *Strategic Marketing Management*, Butterworth Heinemann, 2003, 3rd ed

G Hooley, J Saunders and N Piercy, *Marketing Strategy and Competitive Positioning*, Prentice Hall, 1998, 2nd ed

I Doole & R Lowe, *International Marketing Strategy*, Thomson Learning, 2002, 3rd ed

O Walker, B Harper, J Mullins and J Larreche, *Marketing Strategy*, McGraw Hill, 2003

D Aaker, *Strategic Marketing Management*, J Wiley & Sons, 2000, 6th ed

S Mathur, *Creating Value*, Butterworth Heinemann, 2001, 2nd ed

H Davidson, *The Committed Enterprise*, Butterworth Heinemann, 2002

P Ahmed & M Rafiq, *Internal Marketing*, Butterworth Heinemann, 2002

H Mintzberg, J Quinn & S Ghoshal, *The Strategy Process*, Pearson, 1999

K Ohmae, *The Mind of the Strategist*, McGraw Hill, 1982

R Stacey, *Strategy Management and Organisational Dynamics*, FT Prentice Hall, 2000

G Hamel & C Prahalad, *Competing for the Future*, HBS Press, 1994

M Porter, *Competitive Advantage*, The Free Press, 1985

T Peters & R Waterman, *In Search of Excellence*, Profile Business, 2004

T Burns & G Stalker, *The Management of Innovation*, OUP, 1994

P Kotler, *Marketing Management*, Prentice Hall, 2002, 11th ed

H Ansoff, *Corporate Strategy*, Pan MacMillan, 1986

G Johnson & K Scholes, *Exploring Corporate Strategy*, Prentice Hall, 1999 5th ed

N Piercy, *Marketing Budgeting*, Croom Helm, 1986

E Gummesson, *Total Relationship Marketing*, Butterworth Heinemann, 1999

D Adcock, *Marketing Strategies for Competitive Advantage*, Wiley, 2000

I Nonaka, *The Knowledge Creating Company*, Oxford Press, 1995

P Senge, *The Fifth Discipline*, Currency, 1994

C Emmanuel, D Otley & K Marchant, *Accounting for Management Control*, Chapman and Hall, 1990

P Drucker, *The Practice of Management*, Longman, 1993

S Dibb, L Simkin, W Pride, O Ferrel, *Marketing: Concepts and Strategies*, Houghton Mifflin, 2000

N Piercy, *Market-led Strategic Change*, Butterworth Heinemann, 2001

C Hofer, D Schendel, *Strategy Formulation*, South Western College Publishing, 1978

H Simon, *Administrative Behaviour*, Simon & Schuster, 1997

W French & C Bell, *Organizational Development*, Prentice Hall, 1995 6th ed

J-P Jeannet, H Hennessey, *Global Marketing Strategies*, Houghton Mifflin, 1995, 3rd ed

# List of key concepts and index

See overleaf for information on other
BPP products and how to order

## CIM Order

To BPP Professional Education, Aldine Place, London W12 8AA
Tel: 020 8740 2211. Fax: 020 8740 1184
email: publishing@bpp.com
online: www.bpp.com

Mr/Mrs/Ms (Full name)

Daytime delivery address

Postcode

Daytime Tel

Date of exam (month/year)

| | 2004 Texts | 2004 Kits | Passcards |
|---|---|---|---|
| **PROFESSIONAL CERTIFICATE IN MARKETING** | | | |
| 1 Marketing Fundamentals | £19.95 ☐ | £9.95 ☐ | £6.95 ☐ |
| 2 Marketing Environment | £19.95 ☐ | £9.95 ☐ | £6.95 ☐ |
| 3 Customer Communications | £19.95 ☐ | £9.95 ☐ | £6.95 ☐ |
| 4 Marketing in Practice | £19.95 ☐ | £9.95 ☐ | £6.95 ☐ |
| **PROFESSIONAL DIPLOMA IN MARKETING** | | | |
| 5 Marketing Research and Information | £19.95 ☐ | £9.95 ☐ | £6.95 ☐ |
| 6 Marketing Planning | £19.95 ☐ | £9.95 ☐ | £6.95 ☐ |
| 7 Marketing Communications | £19.95 ☐ | £9.95 ☐ | £6.95 ☐ |
| 8 Marketing Management in Practice | £19.95 ☐ | £9.95 ☐ | £6.95 ☐ |
| **PROFESSIONAL POST-GRADUATE DIPLOMA IN MARKETING** | | | |
| 9 Analysis and Evaluation | £20.95 ☐ | £9.95 ☐ | £6.95 ☐ |
| 10 Strategic Marketing Decisions | £20.95 ☐ | £9.95 ☐ | £6.95 ☐ |
| 11 Managing Marketing Performance | £20.95 ☐ | £9.95 ☐ | £6.95 ☐ |
| 12 Strategic Marketing in Practice | £26.95 ☐ | N/A | N/A |

**SUBTOTAL** £

**POSTAGE & PACKING**

**Study Texts and Kits**

| | First | Each extra | Online | |
|---|---|---|---|---|
| UK | £5.00 | £2.00 | £2.00 | £ |
| Europe** | £6.00 | £4.00 | £4.00 | £ |
| Rest of world | £20.00 | £10.00 | £10.00 | £ |

**Passcards**

| | First | Each extra | Online | |
|---|---|---|---|---|
| UK | £2.00 | £1.00 | £1.00 | £ |
| Europe** | £3.00 | £2.00 | £2.00 | £ |
| Rest of world | £8.00 | £8.00 | £8.00 | £ |

Reduced postage rates apply if you **order online** at www.bpp.com

**Grand Total** (Cheques to *BPP Professional Education*) I enclose a cheque for (incl. Postage) £

Or charge to Access/Visa/Switch

Card Number

Expiry date Start Date

Issue Number (Switch Only)

Signature

We aim to deliver to all UK addresses inside 5 working days. A signature will be required. Orders to all EU addresses should be delivered within 6 working days.

All other orders to overseas addresses should be delivered within 8 working days.

** Europe includes the Republic of Ireland and the Channel Islands.

## REVIEW FORM & FREE PRIZE DRAW

All original review forms from the entire BPP range, completed with genuine comments, will be entered into one of two draws on 31 January 2005 and 30 July 2005. The names on the first four forms picked out on each occasion will be sent a cheque for £50.

**Name:** ______________________ **Address:** ______________________

______________________________________________

______________________________________________

**How have you used this Text?**
*(Tick one box only)*

- ☐ Self study (book only)
- ☐ On a course: college ______________
- ☐ With BPP Home Study package
- ☐ Other ______________

**Why did you decide to purchase this Text?**
*(Tick one box only)*

- ☐ Have used companion Kit
- ☐ Have used BPP Texts in the past
- ☐ Recommendation by friend/colleague
- ☐ Recommendation by a lecturer at college
- ☐ Saw advertising in journals
- ☐ Saw website
- ☐ Other ______________

**During the past six months do you recall seeing/receiving any of the following?**
*(Tick as many boxes as are relevant)*

- ☐ Our advertisement in *Marketing Success*
- ☐ Our advertisement in *Marketing Business*
- ☐ Our brochure with a letter through the post
- ☐ Our brochure with *Marketing Business*
- ☐ Saw website

**Which (if any) aspects of our advertising do you find useful?**
*(Tick as many boxes as are relevant)*

- ☐ Prices and publication dates of new editions
- ☐ Information on product content
- ☐ Facility to order books off-the-page
- ☐ None of the above

**Have you used the companion Practice & Revision Kit for this subject?** ☐ Yes ☐ No

**Your ratings, comments and suggestions would be appreciated on the following areas.**

| | *Very useful* | *Useful* | *Not useful* |
|---|---|---|---|
| *Introductory section (How to use this text, study checklist, etc)* | ☐ | ☐ | ☐ |
| *Setting the Scene* | ☐ | ☐ | ☐ |
| *Syllabus coverage* | ☐ | ☐ | ☐ |
| *Action Programmes and Marketing at Work examples* | ☐ | ☐ | ☐ |
| *Chapter roundups* | ☐ | ☐ | ☐ |
| *Quick quizzes* | ☐ | ☐ | ☐ |
| *Illustrative questions* | ☐ | ☐ | ☐ |
| *Content of suggested answers* | ☐ | ☐ | ☐ |
| *Index* | ☐ | ☐ | ☐ |
| *Structure and presentation* | ☐ | ☐ | ☐ |

| | *Excellent* | *Good* | *Adequate* | *Poor* |
|---|---|---|---|---|
| *Overall opinion of this Text* | ☐ | ☐ | ☐ | ☐ |

**Do you intend to continue using BPP Study Texts/Kits/Passcards?** ☐ Yes ☐ No

**Please note any further comments and suggestions/errors on the reverse of this page.**

**Please return to: Glenn Haldane, BPP Professional Education, FREEPOST, London, W12 8BR**

## REVIEW FORM & FREE PRIZE DRAW (continued)

**Please note any further comments and suggestions/errors below.**

### FREE PRIZE DRAW RULES

1. Closing date for 31 January 2005 draw is 31 December 2004. Closing date for 31 July 2005 draw is 30 June 2005.
2. Restricted to entries with UK and Eire addresses only. BPP employees, their families and business associates are excluded.
3. No purchase necessary. Entry forms are available upon request from BPP Professional Education. No more than one entry per title, per person. Draw restricted to persons aged 16 and over.
4. Winners will be notified by post and receive their cheques not later than 6 weeks after the relevant draw date. List of winners will be supplied on request.
5. The decision of the promoter in all matters is final and binding. No correspondence will be entered into.